Animal Labour

Animal Labour

A New Frontier of Interspecies Justice?

Edited by
CHARLOTTE E. BLATTNER
KENDRA COULTER
WILL KYMLICKA

Great Clarendon Street, Oxford, OX2 6DP,
United Kingdom

Oxford University Press is a department of the University of Oxford.
It furthers the University's objective of excellence in research, scholarship,
and education by publishing worldwide. Oxford is a registered trade mark of
Oxford University Press in the UK and in certain other countries

© Oxford University Press 2020

The moral rights of the authors have been asserted

First Edition published in 2020

Impression: 1

All rights reserved. No part of this publication may be reproduced, stored in
a retrieval system, or transmitted, in any form or by any means, without the
prior permission in writing of Oxford University Press, or as expressly permitted
by law, by licence or under terms agreed with the appropriate reprographics
rights organization. Enquiries concerning reproduction outside the scope of the
above should be sent to the Rights Department, Oxford University Press, at the
address above

You must not circulate this work in any other form
and you must impose this same condition on any acquirer

Published in the United States of America by Oxford University Press
198 Madison Avenue, New York, NY 10016, United States of America

British Library Cataloguing in Publication Data

Data available

Library of Congress Control Number: 2019941465

ISBN 978-0-19-884619-2

DOI: 10.1093/oso/9780198846192.003.0001

Printed and bound in Great Britain by
Clays Ltd, Elcograf S.p.A.

Links to third party websites are provided by Oxford in good faith and
for information only. Oxford disclaims any responsibility for the materials
contained in any third party website referenced in this work.

Acknowledgements

The initial idea for this project was developed by Charlotte E. Blattner, during her tenure as the Postdoctoral Fellow in Animal Ethics at Queen's University in 2017–18. Earlier versions of the chapters were first presented at a workshop held in May 2018, co-sponsored by the Animals in Philosophy, Politics, Law and Ethics (APPLE) research group at Queen's (directed by Sue Donaldson and Will Kymlicka), and by the Humane Jobs Initiative at Brock University (directed by Kendra Coulter). Special thanks to Sue for her advice and support, and to the rest of the APPLE team, including Alice Hovorka, Agnes Tam, Ryan Wilcox, Omar Bachour, and Frédéric Côté-Boudreau, for their assistance with the workshop. Thanks also to Colette Steer at Grad Chat, to Joanne McArthur and We Animals for permission to use her amazing collection of photographs, to Susanne Cliff-Jungling and Noreen Haun for logistical help, and to the many participants at the workshop for their helpful questions and comments.

Special thanks to Ryan Wilcox for help with the manuscript, and to Dominic Byatt and Olivia Wells at Oxford University Press for their enthusiasm for the project.

Charlotte E. Blattner
Kendra Coulter
Will Kymlicka

Contents

List of Tables	ix
Notes on Contributors	xi

1. Introduction: Animal Labour and the Quest for Interspecies Justice   1
Charlotte E. Blattner, Kendra Coulter, and Will Kymlicka

PART I. THE PROMISE OF GOOD WORK

2. Toward Humane Jobs and Work-Lives for Animals   29
Kendra Coulter

3. Good Work for Animals   48
Alasdair Cochrane

4. Conservation Canines: Exploring Dog Roles, Circumstances, and Welfare Status   65
Renée D'Souza, Alice Hovorka, and Lee Niel

PART II. THE DILEMMAS OF ANIMAL LABOUR

5. Animal Labour: Toward a Prohibition of Forced Labour and a Right to Freely Choose One's Work   91
Charlotte E. Blattner

6. Alienation and Animal Labour   116
Omar Bachour

7. Down on the Farm: Status, Exploitation, and Agricultural Exceptionalism   139
Jessica Eisen

8. The Meaning of Animal Labour   160
Nicolas Delon

9. The Working Day: Animals, Capitalism, and Surplus Time   181
Dinesh J. Wadiwel

10. Animal Labour in a Post-Work Society   207
Sue Donaldson and Will Kymlicka

Index of Authors/People	229
General Index	231

List of Tables

4.1 Behavioural assessment for Alberta dogs	71
4.2 Behavioural assessment for Ontario dogs	75
6.1 Marx on animal production vs. human production	122

Notes on Contributors

Omar Bachour is a PhD candidate in the Philosophy Department at Queen's University. His PhD focuses on the puzzle that while work pervades every aspect of our lives, it is peripheral to contemporary political philosophy. His research explores how a revised conception of alienation in political theory can help diagnose a host of social pathologies missed by current theories of justice, and can inspire postwork imaginaries that challenge the naturalization of work.

Charlotte E. Blattner is a Postdoctoral Fellow at Harvard Law School, where she researches at the intersection of animal and environmental law. From 2017 to 2018, she completed the Postdoctoral Fellowship for Animal Studies at the Department of Philosophy at Queen's University, focusing in particular on issues of animal labour. She earned her PhD in Law from the University of Basel, Switzerland, as part of the doctoral program 'Law and Animals—Ethics at Crossroads', and was a Visiting International Scholar at the Center for Animal Law Studies at Lewis & Clark Law School in 2016. Her book *Protecting Animals Within and Across Borders* (Oxford University Press, 2019) is the first to address the challenges of animal law in an era of globalization.

Alasdair Cochrane is a Senior Lecturer in political theory in the Department of Politics at the University of Sheffield. He is the author of three core texts on animal rights from the perspective of political theory: *An Introduction to Animals and Political Theory* (Palgrave, 2010); *Animal Rights Without Liberation* (Columbia University Press, 2012); and *Sentientist Politics* (Oxford University Press, 2018). He is the co-director of the Sheffield Animal Studies Research Centre (ShARC). He previously taught at the Centre for the Study of Human Rights, London School of Economics.

Kendra Coulter holds the Chancellor's Chair for Research Excellence and is Associate Professor and Chair of the Department of Labour Studies at Brock University in Canada. She is a Fellow of the Oxford Centre for Animal Ethics and a member of the Royal Society of Canada's College of New Scholars, Artists and Scientists. She is an award-winning author who has written widely on many facets of labour involving animals including *Animals, Work, and the Promise of Interspecies Solidarity* (Palgrave Macmillan, 2016).

Nicolas Delon is an Assistant Professor of Philosophy and Environmental Studies at New College of Florida. He earned his PhD in philosophy from University Paris 1 Panthéon-Sorbonne in 2014 and was a Faculty Fellow of Environmental Studies and Animal Studies at New York University from 2014 to 2017 and a Law and Philosophy Fellow at the University of Chicago Law School from 2017 to 2018. He specializes in issues of animal and environmental ethics, with particular interests in moral status, food, captivity, cities, meaning, and social psychology. He has published in journals including the *Journal of Agricultural and Environmental Ethics*, *Philosophical Studies*, and the *Proceedings of the Aristotelian Society*.

xii NOTES ON CONTRIBUTORS

Sue Donaldson is an author and research associate in the Department of Philosophy, Queen's University, Canada. She is the co-author, with Will Kymlicka, of *Zoopolis: A Political Theory of Animal Rights* (Oxford University Press, 2011), and co-convener of the Animals in Philosophy, Politics, Law and Ethics research group (http://animalpolitics.queensu.ca/). Her recent work has been published in *Journal of Political Philosophy*; *Politics and Animals*; *Philosophy Compass*; the *Oxford Handbook of Animal Studies*; the *Oxford Handbook of Citizenship*; and the *Routledge Handbook of the Philosophy of Childhood and Children*.

Renée D'Souza holds a Master of Environmental Studies from Queen's University and a Bachelor of Science from the University of Guelph, majoring in Wildlife Biology and Conservation. Her research interests range from wildlife management and conservation issues to human–animal interactions. Renée's thesis explores the lives of dogs working for conservation in Canada, assessing their welfare and the impacts of their work on the environment.

Jessica Eisen is an Assistant Professor at the University of Alberta Faculty of Law. Her research interests include comparative law, equality law, and human–animal relations. Her scholarship has been published in *The Journal of Law and Equality*, *Animal Law Review*, *The Canadian Journal of Poverty Law*, *International Journal of Constitutional Law* (ICON), *University of Michigan Journal of Law Reform*, *Berkeley Journal of Gender, Law & Justice* and *Transnational Legal Theory*.

Alice Hovorka is Professor and Dean of the Faculty of Environmental Studies at York University. Dr Hovorka leads The Lives of Animals Research Group (http://www.queensu.ca/livesofanimals/) which offers interdisciplinary and action-oriented approaches to studying human–animal relations in Botswana and Canada. She is one of the foremost scholars in the field of animal geographies, including the agenda-setting articles 'Animal Geographies' (I, II, and III) in *Progress in Human Geography*.

Will Kymlicka is the Canada Research Chair in Political Philosophy at Queen's University, where he has taught since 1998. He has published eight books and over two hundred articles, which have been translated into thirty-two languages. His previous books include *Contemporary Political Philosophy* (1990; second edition 2002), *Multicultural Citizenship* (1995), *Multicultural Odysseys* (2007), and *Zoopolis: A Political Theory of Animal Rights* (2011), co-authored with Sue Donaldson.

Lee Niel is an Associate Professor, and the Col K.L. Campbell Chair in Companion Animal Welfare at the Ontario Veterinary College, University of Guelph. Her research examines strategies for directly assessing and improving the welfare of animals in various contexts, as well as understanding the roles that stakeholders play in implementing change. She has published extensively on laboratory and companion animal welfare, and her current research is focused on understanding and preventing fear and aggression in companion cats and dogs.

Dinesh J. Wadiwel is a Senior Lecturer in Human Rights and Socio-Legal Studies in the School of Social and Political Sciences at the University of Sydney. Dinesh's research interests include theories of violence, critical animal studies, and disability rights. He is author of the 2015 monograph *The War against Animals* (Brill) and co-editor (with Matthew Chrulew) of the collection *Foucault and Animals* (Brill). Dinesh is co-convener of the Human Animal Research Network, University of Sydney.

1

Introduction

Animal Labour and the Quest for Interspecies Justice

Charlotte E. Blattner, Kendra Coulter, and Will Kymlicka

Introduction

Most states have a designated public holiday, like Labour Day or May Day, as a day of remembrance for struggles to recognize work, institute labour rights, and to gain a voice for workers (Foner 1986). The labour movement was and continues to be one of the most important social justice movements of our time, within which different forms of exclusion and inclusion are unveiled, contested, and renegotiated. Since its inception in 1887, however, Labour Day has been celebrated without attention to what is arguably the largest, and most exploited, group of workers: non-human animals.

For many people, the idea that animals are workers is incomprehensible, since labour is seen as a distinctly human activity or practice. Karl Marx, a founding father of contemporary labour theories, argued that animals are guided by mere instincts and the necessities of survival, whereas humans can engage in conscious cooperative productive activity.[1] If animals are present in a workplace, it is only as a tool or resource to be used in the labour process of humans, not as co-workers.[2] Similarly, for John Locke, one of the early theorists of contemporary liberalism, humans acquire property rights when they mix their labour with the external world, but animals do not engage in the sort of labour that can generate such claims.[3] For Locke, humans acquire property rights over animals through their labour—for

---

[1] 'We presuppose labour in a form that stamps it as exclusively human. A spider conducts operations that resemble those of a weaver and a bee puts to shame many an architect in the construction of her cells. But what distinguishes the worst architect from the best of bees is this, that the architect raises his structure in imagination before he erects it in reality' (Marx 1967: 177–8).

[2] 'A particular product may be used in one and the same process, both as an instrument of labour and as raw material. Take, for instance, the fattening of cattle, where the animal is the raw material, and at the same time an instrument for the production of manure' (Marx 1990: 288). For further discussion of Marx's views of animals in the labour process, see chapters 6 and 9 of this volume by Bachour and Wadiwel.

[3] According to Locke, it is not 'use' but 'labour' that defines how much of the world each person can appropriate, and only humans labour (Locke 1988: para. 26). For an argument that animals too engage in the sort of labour that generates property rights on Locke's 'labour-mixing' theory, see Milburn 2017.

Charlotte E. Blattner, Kendra Coulter, and Will Kymlicka, *Introduction: Animal Labour and the Quest for Interspecies Justice* In: *Animal Labour: A New Frontier of Interspecies Justice?*.
Edited by: Charlotte Blattner, Kendra Coulter, and Will Kymlicka, Oxford University Press (2020).
© Oxford University Press. DOI: 10.1093/oso/9780198846192.003.0001

example, by capturing, confining, breeding, and training animals—which entitles them to anything produced by these animals. So for both liberal defenders and Marxist critics of capitalism, labour is exclusively performed by humans, while animals figure as mere tools or resources.

Of course, common sayings such as to 'work like a dog' or to be 'a beast of burden' show a popular awareness that animals engage in work-like activities. And indeed, recent research shows that working animals have played a central role in the development of both capitalism and colonialism (Anderson 2004; Skabelund 2011). Yet animals are rarely if ever considered when legal and political debates emerge about workers' rights and labour justice.

Recently, however, as part of a broader 'animal turn' in the humanities and social sciences (Pedersen 2014; Ritvo 2007), a number of scholars have begun to consider whether animals can and should be seen as engaged in work or labour[4] (Beldo 2017; Delon 2017; Hribal 2003, 2012; Johnson 2017; Coulter 2016; Cochrane 2016; Kymlicka 2017; Perlo 2002; Porcher 2017; Wadiwel 2018; Revue Écologie et Politique 2017; Shaw 2018; Lercier 2019; Taylor and Fraser 2019).[5] There have also been some high-profile cases where the idea that animals should be recognized as workers has gained public traction. This seems particularly true in relation to the treatment of military and police dogs, where it is increasingly common to describe them as fellow members of a work team. For example, in 2013, the Nottingham Police decided to award a pension of £500 to all police dogs upon retirement, to help cover costs of food, care, shelter, and medical treatment, in recognition of their service.[6]

These developments have generated a lively literature exploring a range of conceptual, sociological, legal, and normative questions: What do we mean by the concept of labour? Under what social or historical conditions do humans working with animals view them as their co-workers? Do animals themselves have a sense of working or being part of a working relationship, and can this be a source of meaning or well-being for them? And if animals are our co-workers, should this

---

[4] For the purposes of this chapter, we use the terms 'work' and 'labour' interchangeably.

[5] To date, the field of labour studies has been surprisingly resistant to the 'animal turn'—it has proven easier to introduce the labour question to the field of animal studies than to introduce the animal question to the field of labour studies. There is a long-standing literature on the experience of humans who work with animals (e.g. Greene 2009; Hamilton and Taylor 2013), as well as analyses of how animal labour operates as a 'lively commodity' within capitalism (e.g. Barua 2016, 2017; Beldo 2017; Collard and Dempsey 2013). However, it is only recently that scholars have started to focus on the experience and subjectivity of the animals themselves, and on the ethical claims of animal workers as part of interspecies justice.

[6] Upon the inauguration of the pension scheme for police dogs, the Nottingham Police and Crime Commissioner Paddy Tipping said: 'We look after the people who work for us who have been police officers and staff, they get a decent retirement and I think it's important the same is done for the dogs. These animals work hard for the police and they are officers in their own right' (Pleasance 2013). Similar trends can be seen regarding the recognition of military dogs and horses—whether in terms of their labour rights (Kranzler 2013) or broader social recognition and commemoration (Johnston 2012; Kean 2012; McLennan 2018)—as well as for therapy animals (Tumilty et al. 2018).

be legally or politically recognized? Should animals be legally defined as workers, and protected by labour law?

Positioning Animal Labour in the Field of Animal Ethics

Our volume touches on all of these issues, but we are particularly interested in examining how debates on animal labour can open up new perspectives on animal ethics and interspecies justice. Academic and public debates on animal ethics since the 1970s have tended to circle around two competing approaches, often called 'welfarist' and 'abolitionist'.[7] Welfarists believe that it is permissible for humans to use and to harm animals, so long as this done *humanely*, causing animals no suffering beyond what is required for use. Welfarism is therefore also sometimes called the 'humane use' approach. Overall, this approach underpins the legal regulation of the treatment of animals around the world. Animal protection laws permit the imposition of harm and suffering on animals if considered essential to the pursuit of some legitimate human interest. In practice, the most profound harms to animals have been judged 'necessary' to fulfil human preferences regarding cuisine, clothing, and entertainment (Wolfson and Sullivan 2004). As a result, animal protection laws have failed to prevent, and indeed have condoned, the rise of the 'animal industrial complex' (Noske 1997: 22; Twine 2012).

Abolitionists, by contrast, believe that animals have their own lives to lead, and that humans do not have the right to use or harm animals for our benefit.[8] This is a powerful ethical position, but the challenge for abolitionists is to identify what other kinds of relationships between humans and animals would be legitimate and desirable. The answer, for many abolitionists, is that there are no such relationships: abolition requires severing relationships with animals. In the case of domesticated animals, many abolitionists argue for their gradual extinction on the grounds that they have been moulded through selective breeding to serve human purposes, and so can only live in a state of unhealthy and exploitative dependence (Francione and Garner 2010: 103–4).[9] With regard to wild animals, abolitionists argue that justice requires 'letting them be', leaving wild animals to live

---

[7] As we discuss below, this dichotomy ignores other strands in scholarship. These two strands, however, have operated as polarizing magnets in the public and academic debate, generating a sharp divide amongst scholars and activists, inhibiting much-needed progress and diversification of academic inquiry and political strategizing.

[8] The abolitionist view owes much of its key structure to Tom Regan, who argued that animals have inviolable rights, not just preferences or interests, and that respecting animals' rights requires the movement to be 'abolitionist in its aspirations. It seeks not to reform how animals are exploited [...] but to abolish their exploitation' (Regan 2004: xvi–xvii).

[9] For this reason, Donaldson and Kymlicka (2011: 77–8) use the label 'abolitionist/extinctionist' to describe this position.

4 ANIMAL LABOUR

amongst themselves. The resulting abolitionist vision of interspecies justice has been described as 'species apartheid' (Acampora 2005: 221; Milligan 2010: 41 ff.).

The debate between welfarists and abolitionists offers animals two options—rights without relationships (as proposed by abolitionists), and relationships without rights (as proposed by welfarists)—neither of which seems acceptable from a justice perspective (Donaldson and Kymlicka 2017: 50). Recently, however, a growing number of scholars have tried to find a way beyond this impasse, by identifying forms of interspecies social relationships that are not premised on 'humane use'. Theorists have looked for examples of interspecies relations that are based on ideas of shared membership and cooperation, and that are undergirded by rights to protection, provision, and participation (Donaldson and Kymlicka 2011: 53). This has been one impulse behind the much-discussed 'political turn' in animal studies (Ahlhaus and Niesen 2015; Garner and O'Sullivan 2016; Milligan 2015).

It is in this context that the question of animal labour takes on special importance. On the one hand, exploiting animal labour is one of the paradigmatic ways in which humans use animals, and the historical and ongoing treatment of animals as disposable 'beasts of burden' is a perfect illustration of the limits of a welfarist approach. Animal labour has been a site of intense instrumentalization, exploitation, and degradation, and so some animal advocates have concluded that animal liberation requires abolishing all uses of animal labour.

On the other hand, if our goal is to think about possible future relationships that combine robust rights with ideas of membership and cooperation, then relationships of work are a compelling site for further analysis. There may be certain activities that animals enjoy doing, whose social, legal, and political recognition as 'work' could have transformative effects. From this perspective, animal labour, properly recognized and regulated, could serve as a potentially valuable site of social membership, personal meaning, and material security, and an exemplary case of how to secure both rights and relationships with animals.

After all, as we noted at the start of this chapter, this is one of the roles that labour has played in struggles for social justice. In the human case, there is a long and ongoing history of struggle, not to abolish all work, but to secure the dignity of work, through improved working conditions and labour rights, and through prohibiting degrading or forced labour. Good work is widely seen as a fundamental human value, both for its intrinsic properties (such as learning and skill development) and for the way it can foster other positive goods, such as belonging and social membership (Yeoman 2014; Gheaus and Herzog 2016). It is for this reason that excluding various groups from paid work—such as women, immigrants or migrants, or people with disabilities—amounts to a form of unjust discrimination, and is a violation of their right to work as a path to freedom, autonomy, contribution, and membership. For many in the labour movement, a good society is one that seeks to provide opportunities for dignified work to all its members, and that provides appropriate recognition for the work its members do.

If so, then we can ask whether interspecies justice might include room for animal labour. This might involve recognizing the work animals already do, and pushing for the sorts of conditions that could make work valuable to animals. Access to the social role of 'worker', and to the rights that go with this status, could play a transformative role in shifting from our current relations of instrumentalization and exploitation to relations of shared membership and cooperation. Following Jessica Eisen (chapter 7), we might call this the 'labour-recognition-transformation thesis'. Our aim in this volume is to carefully and critically assess this prospect, and to identify both the possibilities and pitfalls of looking to work as a site for interspecies justice.

Animal Labour and the Animal Turn

While our immediate motivation for the volume is to explore how animal labour fits into debates in animal ethics about interspecies justice, we are drawing upon (and hope to contribute to) a much richer set of literatures in the humanities, social sciences, and life sciences that make up the growing field of 'animal studies'. Labour studies is not the only field that has been built on the assumption of human exceptionalism. On the contrary, we might say that all of the humanities and social sciences have been premised on anthropocentrism. As Noske notes, the social sciences 'present themselves pre-eminently as the sciences of discontinuity between humans and animals' (1997: 66). Animals have been considered incapable of being members of our society, or of participating in social life, because they are (allegedly) driven solely by biological instincts, in contrast to humans who are social actors who learn social norms and cultural conventions. Animals have thus been relegated to 'nature', whereas the humanities and social sciences focus on what are seen as uniquely human processes of social interaction tied to culture, language, and reason. The exclusion of animals from the category of 'labour' is a manifestation of this wider human exceptionalism. Animals might engage in instinctual activities, but 'labour' is said to require uniquely human capacities of norm-governed and language-based social interaction.

The idea that there is a radical discontinuity between humans and animals has now been challenged in multiple ways, across disciplines. It would be impossible to summarize all the relevant developments in the humanities and social sciences, but we would highlight four key innovations that are particularly germane to the question of animal labour.

First is the expansion and diversification of our understanding of *animals' minds, emotions, social relations, and cultures*. The specific terms used vary depending on the individual scholar and/or the discipline in question, and here we are referring to a larger cross-section of scholarship on how animals think, feel, and act. One high-profile development was the 2012 Cambridge Declaration on

6 ANIMAL LABOUR

animal consciousness, confirming the scientific consensus that a wide range of animals are indeed sentient and experience their world consciously.[10] For the purposes of this volume, however, what is important is not just the science of sentience, but also the growing scientific evidence about the nature of animals' *social lives*. Pioneers in what has become the field of cognitive ethology have expanded (or unsettled) scientific conventions regarding the study of animal behaviour and cognition by recognizing animals' active negotiation of social dynamics (e.g. Bekoff 2004). Such scholars have enlisted concepts like play, morality, and empathy to paint a nuanced and complex picture of animals as individuals and to illuminate their intra- and interspecies communities. In place of older reductionist views of animals as blind followers of their instincts, this research has helped contribute to a more holistic understanding of animals as both biological and social beings.

Much of the early work in cognitive ethology focused on wild animals, such as wolves or apes, and how social norms of fair play and cooperation are taught and learned within their communities (what Bekoff famously called 'wild justice' (2009)). But the research has also extended to study domesticated animals, and to how they, too, comply with and negotiate social norms. Crucially for our purposes, researchers are increasingly documenting that these social norms can take an interspecies form. Social norms do not just apply to interactions amongst animals from the same species, but also to interactions across species, for example, amongst dogs and cats (Feuerstein and Terkel 2008), or between cows and humans (Porcher and Schmitt 2012). Many social scientists who work on human–animal relations have long noticed this remarkable level of interspecies sociability (e.g. Laurier, Maze, and Lundin 2006), but cognitive ethology and complementary empirical fields like evolutionary cognition (e.g. De Waal and Ferrari 2010) have now provided firm 'scientific' authenticity and valuable data to bolster the existence of cooperative norm-governed social relationships across species lines.[11]

These scientific findings help prepare the ground for thinking about animal labour as a site of interspecies justice, highlighting the scope for social cooperation between animals and humans. But it naturally raises the question: if humans and animals can engage in cooperative activities based on social norms, who sets those norms? And this leads to a second important area of innovation in animal studies: namely, the focus on animal *agency*. In the past, animal advocates have often portrayed animals as passive victims of human domination. This emphasis on passive victimhood may have unintentionally reproduced the perception that

---

[10] http://fcmconference.org/img/CambridgeDeclarationOnConsciousness.pdf.

[11] For a helpful overview, see Lorini 2018. There is also important knowledge exchange and cross-fertilization in the other direction, as research in the humanities and social sciences is influencing scientific research in areas such as ethnoprimatology (Fuentes 2012; Malone et al. 2014) and feminist primatology, led by researchers like Barbara Smuts (e.g. 2001) and Linda Fedigan (e.g. 1992).

animals are unable to exercise meaningful choice or agency, and that it is always humans who must determine the terms of relationships with animals.

Increasingly, however, animal studies scholars are interested in exploring the ways in which animals are intentional and competent actors who actively pursue their own interests and shape social relations. How and why people think critically, act, and affect their own life and the lives of others (within constrained conditions and contexts), individually and collectively, are questions that have long been of interest to critical human-focused analysts. The same principles are increasingly being applied to animals by various scholars interested in how animals shape and co-constitute relationships in diverse contexts, and in moving beyond seeing animals simply as victims (Corman 2017; Hathaway 2015).[12] This scholarship does not deny that animals are harmed by many human actions, or that people and other species are differently positioned within relations of power, but it does recognize that animals have voices and subjectivities. Social actors act, they are not merely acted upon.[13]

Scholars have different ways of conceptualizing animal agency. Some have conceptualized animals' agency as manifesting primarily in acts of defiance and perceived resistance against conditions of domination (e.g. Hribal 2007; Wadiwel 2016, 2018), while other critical scholars have focused on how animals' agency is manifested, even within the larger context of oppression, in a multiplicity of ways including how they influence, contest, cope, negotiate, and/or care (e.g. Birke and Thompson 2017; Carter and Charles 2013; Coulter 2014; Gillespie forthcoming; McFarland and Hediger 2009; Nance 2013; Pearson 2015).

These bodies of literature seek not only to acknowledge the active presence of animals' minds, but also to understand how they use their minds across contexts in a sociological sense. In relation to the sociopolitical and ethical dimensions of labour, this recognition means seeing animals as agents and, relatedly, as subjects, who 'can shape elements of their lives, share their views, and make certain choices, albeit not under conditions of their choosing' (Coulter 2018b, 67). A central question for this volume is whether and how animals can exercise voice at work, and how work could be reorganized so that animals can exercise greater agency regarding the nature and terms of the work relationship.

---

[12] We can even see some movement in this direction in the field of animal welfare science. This field has traditionally operated with a reductive conception of animal welfare as biological health or bodily functioning, but some animal welfare science researchers are adopting a more robust commitment to broader questions about animals' own sense of value and agency (e.g. Fraser 1999; Mellor 2016; Mendl and Paul 2004). Indeed, Palmer and Sandoe (2018) say that incorporating agency is the key challenge facing animal welfare science.

[13] Dale Jamieson notes that 'agency' remains an exception to the general trend to question human exceptionalism. People increasingly accept continuities between humans and animals in relation to 'intelligence, emotion, tool use, social learning, mind-reading, mirror recognition, deception, altruism and cooperation...Agency, however, is one area in which the retreat from human uniqueness is halting' (Jamieson 2018).

8   ANIMAL LABOUR

If animals are indeed agents capable of expressing their preferences about their relationships with us, then this raises questions about whether and how humans are responsive to these preferences. If animals have voices, is anyone listening to them? And this leads to a third important area of development in animal studies: namely, a new focus on the nature and ethics of interspecies communication (Meijer 2013). We noted earlier that debates on animal rights are often reduced to a 'welfarist-versus-abolitionist' dichotomy. In fact, however, there has been a long-standing feminist approach to animal ethics that highlights values of care, relationship, and, above all, responsiveness. Ecofeminists like Josephine Donovan and Carol J. Adams (2007), Greta Gaard (2011), Marti Kheel (2007), and Val Plumwood (2005) have analysed the interlinked oppression of women and animals, arguing for a political and ethical project rooted in reciprocity, an ethics of care (Donovan and Adams 2007), and concepts like entangled empathy (Gruen 2015) or 'intersubjective attunement' and 'call and response ethics' (Willett 2014). The focus here is not just on animals' capacity for agency and voice, but on (mutual) capacities to listen and be responsive, as the core of an ethical relationship.[14] In relation to work, this raises questions about whether the workplace instantiates an ethic of responsiveness, and whether this sort of responsiveness should be seen as inherent to care work. Care work in this sense is done both by humans and animals (e.g. in animal-assisted therapy), yet rarely receives social recognition, due in large part to gendered perceptions of what constitutes 'real work'. There is a rich tradition in feminist political economy of theorizing the gendered nature of paid and unpaid care work, including through the concept of social reproduction (e.g. Bezanson 2006; Luxton and Bezanson 2006), and these frameworks can be helpfully applied to think about animals' labour (Coulter 2016b).

These three developments—ideas of sociability, agency, and communication—all help to explain why animal labour has become more visible and interesting for scholars working on human–animal relations, including those working on ideas of interspecies justice and what Coulter (2016) has called interspecies solidarity. These insights unsettle the inherited dichotomy between 'human society' and 'animal nature', and enable us to think of work as a potential site of social interaction between humans and animals, where the terms of that relationship would be mutually negotiated, drawing on an ethics of responsiveness that is attuned to animals' voices and subjectivities.

Of course, we are very far from such a world, in part because decisions about labour take place within a larger political context from which animals are excluded. Animals have no representation when governments pass laws governing

---

[14] Against the view that there is a radical epistemic abyss separating humans from non-human animals, such that other humans are transparent to us whereas other animals are opaque to us, Andrews argues that the challenges of understanding other human and animal minds are continuous (Andrews 2011).

labour and the workplace, and animals (or their advocates) have no legal or political standing to challenge these laws once passed, or to challenge the decisions of employers. Animals are intensely governed in modern societies, yet there are no existing political mechanisms to solicit their preferences about how they are governed, or to ensure that decisions affecting them are responsive to those preferences (Smith 2012; Donaldson and Kymlicka 2016).

This has led to the fourth development we want to highlight: the political turn in animal studies. We earlier described the political turn as motivated by a desire to reconcile 'rights' and 'relationships', but more specifically, it insists that any such reconciliation requires attending to fundamentally political questions about the representation and participation of animals in our collective decision-making. This political turn draws on ideas about interspecies sociability, agency, and communication, but seeks to scale them up and embed them within the broader framework of democratic politics, on a macro-level, if you will. We need not only an interspecies ethics of intersubjective attunement, but also an interspecies politics. And this too is an issue taken up in our volume: how can we institutionalize the participation and representation of animals in collective decisions about work?

In short, our exploration of animal labour is heavily indebted to and informed by a number of broader developments in the fields of animal studies. We hope that our volume will contribute to these broader debates. Indeed, we would argue that animal labour is an excellent test case for many of these ideas. After all, we are very far from having an adequate understanding of animal subjectivities and voices, or of the scope for interspecies cooperation and communication, yet these issues are being negotiated on a daily basis in countless workplaces around the world. We hope to show that animal studies has much to learn by a careful and cautious exploration of animal labour, and of animals' experiences of it.

The Dangers of Animal Labour

While a range of developments in animal studies have opened up space for thinking about non-exploitative work relationships with animals, other developments might lead us to be sceptical of this possibility. As we noted earlier, work has often been a site of the most intense instrumentalization of animals. If we come to see animals as workers or co-workers, would this challenge their instrumentalization? Not necessarily. A quick look at existing practices would suggest that recognizing animals as workers can coexist quite comfortably with their instrumentalization.

In fact, there is a long history of factory farms, labs, and circuses describing animals as willing partners and workers. The vivisection industry in particular is known for these kinds of euphemisms (Birke et al. 2007). Even when scientists withdrew food, water, and social interaction for extended periods of time in order

10 ANIMAL LABOUR

to get animals to 'cooperate', these strategies of 'positive reinforcement' (Huston et al. 2013: 2062) are described as 'allow[ing] the animals to cooperate voluntarily with husbandry and/or research procedures' (Schapiro et al. 2003: 167). The language of work has also been used by some in industrial agriculture, as in a flyer entitled 'Benefit Package of a Dairy Cow':

> To start with, the cows receive full-time pay for part-time work. The work (of being milked) takes about 20–30 minutes per day. The employer provides paid medical coverage, with a doctor (veterinarian) on call 24/7, 365 days per year. Meals are prepared by a nutritionist, with room service and clean up every time. There is a full-time housekeeper who even cleans the bathrooms. A paid team of experts is always available for these bovine beauties; hair dresser, pedicurist and spa facilities are provided. There is 24-hour surveillance. No need for online dating [...] there is mate selection provided through a directory of selective traits, and could be a different mate each year. All transportation is provided free of charge for a lifetime.   (quoted in Adams 2017: 25)

As Adams points out, there is a lot wrong with this description.[15] In the modern dairy industry, cows do not choose to produce milk for human consumption. Cows are not 'dating'; they are forcibly impregnated by artificial insemination; and they are not part-time workers with lots of free time on their hands—rather, they are held in continuous confinement. We would not speak of prisoners and hostages as having leisure time; or of raped women as not having to worry about finding a mate; or force-fed people as having a nutritionist; or being prematurely killed as having a 'lifetime'. Yet some people talk about farmed animals this way, in part because the corporate interests that market dairy products want to project the idea that animals *want* to be made pregnant, *want* to give their milk, *want* to feed us, *want* to be consumed (Adams 2017: 34).

Any realistic approach to animal labour needs to recognize this danger. Humans have a vested interest in legitimizing the use of animals, and simply introducing the language of 'animal labour' is unlikely by itself to overcome the limits of the 'humane use' model of animal exploitation. The idea of animal labour risks being used as further justification for industries that objectify animals, rather than prompting changes that would treat animals as subjects who have their own experiences, desires, and relationships, and a right to live according to them.

Given these dangers, abolitionists unsurprisingly argue that the safest strategy is simply to abolish all forms of animal labour. But while it is important not to ignore

---

[15] As Adams notes, the flyer—circulated to shoppers at a grocery store—is clearly tongue-in-cheek, and does not represent standard industry narratives. But the very fact that consumers are supposed to find this description humorous, rather than offensive, is evidence that the industry relies on (and seeks to reproduce) public indifference to animals' (un)freedom.

the danger of 'labour washing', nor should we ignore the potential for institutionalized labour rights and safeguards to improve the treatment of animals in the short term, or for labour to help cultivate more just multispecies social relations in the future.[16] This raises difficult questions about sequencing and transitions. Conceptualizing animals as workers could have a meaningful effect on people's attitudes towards animals. But perhaps these transformative effects are only possible if we have already moved beyond the humane use framework, and embraced strong legal safeguards of animal rights. Can recognizing animals as workers help us move to a society of interspecies justice, or is talk of animal labour only safe once we have already transcended existing exploitive relations?

These are difficult questions, and our contributors offer a range of answers, as we discuss in the next section. However, we would note that similar questions arise with virtually all social justice movements, including the history of human labour struggles.[17] Drawing on these experiences, we would suggest that 'labour' is partly descriptive but also partly normative. Descriptively, we can recognize that there are awful forms of harmful, exploitative, degrading, and/or forced labour, but normatively, we can say that 'labour' contains within it ideas (or ideals) of cooperation, consent, recognition, and dignity. These two sides represent points on a wider continuum that can range from exploitation to justice (Skrivankova 2010).[18]

Our working hypothesis for this volume is that animal labour cannot and should not be reduced to its purely descriptive content in a way that locks animals into their current status as exploited beasts of burdens. Rather, its value as a new scholarly and political paradigm rests on its normative content, and its potential to help create, augment, and deepen human–animal relationships rooted in respect, rights, justice, solidarity, and mutual flourishing.

This may seem utopian, but as we noted earlier, there are already glimpses of such a transformation, if only in a few very specific sectors. How to move along the continuum toward mutual flourishing and justice is the central question of this volume. With both the pitfalls and promises in mind, we believe that questions of animal labour provide a crucial test case for broader questions about interspecies justice, and allow us to draw important lessons about the possibility of good and caring forms of interspecies social relationships.

---

[16] It should be noted that industry tropes of farmed or lab animals as 'workers' are never accompanied by any acceptance that the animals should be *legally* defined as workers. On the contrary, agricultural and research industries have resisted any and all efforts to secure workplace rights for those animals (such as rights to a safe working environment; right to a retirement, etc.). For legal purposes, they still want animals to be defined as property or equipment, not as co-workers or personnel (Kymlicka 2017: 149).

[17] For an interesting attempt to draw lessons for animal advocacy from the history of labour struggles, see Anderson 2011.

[18] For a related discussion of the continuum of animal labour, see Coulter's chapter 2 in this volume.

Overview of the Volume

With these questions in mind, we have recruited an international and interdisciplinary group of scholars to explore the prospects and challenges of animal labour as a site of interspecies justice. Our contributors draw on multiple disciplines and methodologies, including labour studies, critical animal studies, political theory, geography, law, ethics, Marxist theory, and feminist political economy. Unsurprisingly, they articulate different views about the appropriate place of animal labour, just as indeed they differ about the nature and value of human labour. For example, some authors argue that wherever work is commodified—as in a capitalist economy—there will be exploitation and alienation of both humans and animals. If so, then including animals into the social status of 'worker' will be a Pyrrhic victory, replacing one form of instrumentalization for another. For others, however, where labour is properly regulated, with provisions for fair wages, workplace safety, rest and leisure, retirement pensions, and rights to workplace participation, then it can serve as a genuine source of flourishing, for both humans and animals.

As we will see, debates about animal work cannot be divorced from these long-standing debates about the meaning and value of human labour. However, our aim in this volume is not to recapitulate those older debates, but to highlight the distinctive promise of labour *for animals*. Our starting place is that animals deserve a place in this world, and that just relationships between humans and animals require asking what kinds of relationships (if any) animals want to have with us, including what kinds of working relationships. What kinds of work would animals choose to engage in? What kinds of work would be meaningful for animals, and when would they experience it as a source of flourishing? What background principles and procedures must be in place so that animal labour becomes a viable route to interspecies justice?

To that end, we have organized the volume into two main sections: the first on 'The Promise of Good Work', and the second on 'The Dilemmas of Animal Labour'.

The Promise of Good Work

We begin in chapter 2 with **Kendra Coulter**, whose 2016 book on *Animals, Work, and the Promise of Interspecies Solidarity* helped initiate this field of scholarship. In this chapter, Coulter develops and refines her account of 'humane jobs'. Humane jobs are those jobs that are good for people and animals, and which promise to deliver on interspecies solidarity. Coulter builds on feminist theories, particularly feminist political economy and care ethics, as well as the on-the-ground efforts of people who work with animals regularly, to identify the key preconditions of humane jobs, including respect, reciprocity, labour protections, autonomy, suitability, and interest. This framework suggests that animal labour as such is neither good nor bad. It needs to be assessed in a nuanced, contextualized case-by-case way, and on this basis, harmful jobs can be eliminated, humane jobs can be quantitatively expanded and qualitatively improved, and new alternatives can be developed. While there are no universal prescriptions about how to promote humane jobs, Coulter does emphasize two challenges that need to be overcome. The first is to broaden our conception of work beyond the narrow focus on paid work. The sort of work that is likely to be good for animals and for humans is often devalued in our society, such as various forms of service, caring, and subsistence work. Second, we need to expand the focus from 'work' to 'work-lives'. Even when animals are engaged in 'good work' that is meaningful and satisfying—as perhaps with certain kinds of therapy work or conservation work—they may be subject to deprivation in their non-work-lives, whether in terms of harsh training before they enter work, or social isolation in their after-work hours, or inadequate care in their post-work retirement. Coulter argues that humane jobs are not sufficient on their own, but rather we ought to be emphasizing animals' work-lives in a full sense.

In chapter 3, **Alasdair Cochrane** offers a complementary account of 'good work' for animals. Cochrane notes that while we can often agree about what jobs are bad for animals, less is known about the conditions under which animals flourish at work, hence what constitutes *good* work for animals. In the human case, we not only strive to protect human workers from harm, but we also seek to create decent work. Many states have adopted policies to help individuals lead meaningful, autonomous, and fulfilling working lives, ranging from the public provision of education and training, giving career advice, and providing investment in sectors of the economy to maintain or boost the availability of good jobs. These policies rest on the idea that work is an important source of human well-being, self-respect and self-identity, mental health, and so on. But is decent work similarly important to animals' well-being? Cochrane argues that it can be. Some forms of work may in fact be crucial for some animals' well-being, insofar as they (i) provide pleasure, including through affording opportunities to use and develop skills; (ii) allow for the exercise of animals' agency; and (iii) provide a context in which animals can be esteemed as valuable workers who are recognized as members of the communities in which they labour. Cochrane, as with many other authors of this volume, is under no illusion that the sort of work currently assigned to animals meets these conditions of good work. This does not, however, release us from the duty to provide opportunities for animals to flourish at work. As Cochrane clarifies, the right to decent work is what we owe animals on grounds of justice.

In chapter 4, **Renée D'Souza, Alice Hovorka, and Lee Niel** offer a detailed case analysis of one possible kind of 'good work' for animals—namely, conservation work by dogs. Drawing on fieldwork with two teams in Alberta and Ontario,

14 ANIMAL LABOUR

Canada, the authors explore whether conservation canines' jobs—assisting biologists and conservationists with environmental protection and wildlife research—are examples of humane jobs. In recent years, the contributions that dogs can make to environmental work has been documented. However, whether this environmental work is good for the dogs themselves has rarely been studied. D'Souza, Hovorka, and Niel use an interdisciplinary approach combining animal welfare science and qualitative social science to assess a range of factors that affect the quality of animals' work experience: what tasks dogs currently perform for conservation; the selection, breeding, and training procedures for these jobs; and their welfare and quality of life as a result of this work. Their conclusions are mixed. There is strong evidence that this sort of work engages the interests and inclinations of the animals, and hence that it could be an example of good work. On the other hand, there are many features of their work—and their broader work-lives—which animals have little or no say over, and which reflect and perpetuate their subordinate status. This contextualized approach enables the authors to point to how the lived reality of conservation canines can be changed and improved to live up to the goals of humane jobs and work-lives.

The Dilemmas of Animal Labour

With these visions of good work in place, the volume then turns to a series of complications and challenges to the promise of animal labour, focusing in particular on issues of consent, alienation, death, reproduction, and time.

As we noted earlier, some critical scholars are hesitant to endorse the emancipatory potential of animal labour, particularly when fundamental rights of animals are not yet recognized. The prohibition on forced labour and the right to freely choose one's work are two such rights. In chapter 5, **Charlotte Blattner** explores why these rights are essential to animals, and how they could be implemented. As she notes, several authors have argued that animals should have a right to remuneration, safe working conditions, retirement, and medical care as workers. However, fewer authors have argued that working animals have a right to self- or co-determination. Even in 'good' jobs with relatively high welfare standards, animals are typically denied a right to enter, exit, or shape labour relations on their own terms. This, as Blattner notes, stands in stark contrast to what we consider the bare minimum rights of human workers, where forced labour is categorically prohibited. It also stands in stark contrast to the growing evidence in cognitive ethology and animal welfare science about the importance of choice and agency for animals. In the first part of the chapter, she makes the case, based on empirical evidence and moral arguments, that animals require robust rights of self-determination, including the right to enter and exit work relationships, and the prohibition of forced labour. In the second part, Blattner draws on recent advances in bioethics to explore how different models of dissent, assent, and consent can guarantee animals' self-determination at work. She argues that we must secure the initial and periodic consent of animals, provide them with a wide range of employment options, and a right to exit. She also defends robust rights to co-determination about conditions at work, management, and oversight. Only under these conditions can animals have sufficient voice to ensure that labour is indeed good for them, and an expression of how they want to lead their lives.

The concept of 'consent' is just one of many concepts within labour studies that needs to be rethought for an interspecies context. Another such concept is that of alienation. As a young Hegelian, Marx famously formulated a theory of alienation to describe how deeply the conditions of capitalism affect the well-being of humans as workers, their social structures, and their physical and mental states. Various scholars have attempted to show that animals, too, are alienated from their products, the act of production, their species-life, and fellow beings. But, as **Omar Bachour** points out in chapter 6, attempts to apply Marx's theory of alienation to animal labour have not fully addressed the ways that Marx's account rests on a specific kind of 'humanism'. For Marx, to live a truly unalienated human life means precisely that we differentiate ourselves from the animals, and from our animal nature within. Overcoming alienation is fundamentally a matter of asserting species distinction and species hierarchy. Bachour argues that this humanist model is multiply flawed on its terms, but also—and importantly for our purposes—has little emancipatory potential for animals. Drawing on the work of Rahel Jaeggi (2014), he proposes an alternative 'appropriative model' of alienation, and argues that it offers a more promising starting point for assessing animal labour. On this model, animals are not 'fixed in their life activity', as Marx contends, but rather they actively transform and assimilate their environment, altering both what is appropriated and the appropriator. This has radical implications for our understanding of animal labour, how it is alienated under capitalism, and how this alienation may be overcome. The appropriative model, as Bachour envisions it, would offer both a richer account of the value of labour, while also avoiding the familiar speciesist, gendered, and productivist biases of traditional accounts of labour.

One of the central dilemmas of the literature on animal labour is the distance between ideal and realities. The more we think through the requirements of consent, for example, or alienation, the greater the distance between our ideal of 'good work' and the realities of animals' lives in our society, even under the best conditions. And this raises difficult questions about whether the labour-recognition-transformation thesis might not, in the end, be irrelevant, or even counterproductive, to the actual needs of most animals. This is the worry motivating **Jessica Eisen** in chapter 7. As she notes, the literature on animal labour is disproportionately focused on work done by a relatively small number of animals, particularly companion, service, and rescue animals. There is much less attention

16   ANIMAL LABOUR

paid to the vast majority (98 per cent) of domesticated animals in our society—namely, farmed animals. What, if anything, does a labour lens contribute to thinking about justice for the nameless individuals bred, kept, and killed by the billions for human convenience? Does a labour perspective help us better identify what is wrong with our treatment of farmed animals, or help us identify better remedies? Eisen is sceptical on both counts. For one thing, scholars of labour law have already identified the farm as a 'site of exception', exempted from having to comply with many standard labour rights, leaving agricultural workers amongst the most vulnerable and least protected workers in the global north. Advocates might hope to extend and strengthen the application of labour law to the farm context, to better protect both human and animal workers. But as Eisen notes, the exceptional status of agriculture is deep and enduring, stretching from labour law to environmental law to animal protection. The prospects for securing justice through recognition as an agricultural worker are remote. A labour lens also risks occluding the conditions of routine confinement, and forced reproduction and death, which define the conditions of modern animal agriculture, including its allegedly 'humane' versions. Eisen concludes by suggesting that if we want to find alternative ways of relating to animals that combine rights and relationships, we should look not to work, but to relations of family and friendship, which provide models of membership and cooperation without the risk of legitimizing exploitation.

Eisen's worry that a labour lens could be used to legitimize animal agriculture is an important one, as we discussed above. Indeed, this position has been defended by one of the main theorists of animal labour, Jocelyne Porcher (2017). In chapter 8, **Nicolas Delon** carefully analyses Porcher's account to identify how she seeks to reconcile the idea that farmed animals are our co-workers with the belief that we can kill and eat our co-workers. In *The Ethics of Animal Labour: A Collaborative Utopia*, Porcher sets out to 'reinvent' our relationship to animals through labour in order to better 'live with' them. She argues that maintaining meaningful relationships with animals is itself valuable, and that work is the key to maintaining this 'link' between humans and domesticated animals. She acknowledges that industrialized animal farming does not qualify as a meaningful form of working together, yet insists that traditional husbandry practices are forms of good work for both humans and animals. Traditional animal husbandry is the only alternative, she claims, to either industrialized factory farming or the extinction of domesticated animals, and so helps maintain the link between humans and animals. Delon identifies several flaws in this argument. In order to defend the killing of animals as a part of 'good work', he suggests, Porcher ends up with a distorted account of both the value of work and the harm of death. Moreover, Porcher fails to see that there other alternatives between extinction and exploitation that maintain the link without requiring (or permitting) killing as a 'necessary evil'. Delon's chapter then considers relationships between humans and domesticated animals that do not centre around killing or even work for food production purposes. He envisions alternative interspecies relationships that could be meaningful for both humans and non-humans, including forms of work, but which preclude the forms of exploitation that Porcher's view entails.

Dinesh Wadiwel, in chapter 9, explores struggles over work-life, and in particular struggles over time. In the chapter in *Capital* on 'The Working Day', Marx describes the historic contestation between capital and labour over the length of the working day, which would remain a pivotal issue for the labour movement in its struggle for the eight-hour working day. Wadiwel suggests that thinking about the 'working day' offers a useful angle to assess the prospects for animal labour. He argues that while the concept of a 'working day' may be applicable to some animal labourers, the reality is that the working day never stops for most forms of labour done by animals under capitalism, particularly in intensive forms of agriculture, such as fish farming. In the first part of his chapter, Wadiwel explores how time can operate as a productive focus for thinking about animal labour, particularly as it applies to farmed animals. He argues that demands made by other social movements—such as the environmental justice movement—to 'slow down capitalism' through reduced work, reduced production, and reduced consumption, resonate with the goals of animal advocates to de-intensify animal production, deliberate over consumption practices, and reduce systematic violence against animals. In the second part, Wadiwel develops strategies for change, by exploring the opportunities and constraints that might accompany strategic alliances with other social movements over the politics of time. In particular, he notes that animal labour opens the door to questioning and negotiating, on a political level, what constitutes 'necessary labour' in our society.

Like Wadiwel, **Sue Donaldson and Will Kymlicka** argue in chapter 10 that the goal for animal advocates should not just be to improve the quality of animal work, but also to reduce it, or at any rate to decentre work as the basis for meaning and membership. Labour has been seen historically as the key to achieving several core values, including individual security and self-sufficiency, self-development and freedom, social standing and recognition, fairness in contribution to and distribution of goods, and source of life purpose and meaning. Insofar as these values are also relevant to animals, this suggests that we should seek to include animals into the world of labour—to recognize that animals, as well as humans, are workers, and deserve access to the security, self-development, status, community, and purpose wrapped up in the role of being a worker. But as Donaldson and Kymlicka note, the reality is that the sort of work available in the contemporary labour market fails to deliver many of these goods, much of the time, for many humans, and there are good reasons to believe that work would not deliver these goods for many animals either. Moreover, thanks to technological development, there is no necessity for everyone to engage in a lifetime of full-time work (or to be socialized and trained for such a life of work). Indeed, the cultural expectation that

18 ANIMAL LABOUR

everyone should be 'productive' has become culturally pernicious and environmentally unsustainable. These developments have generated a growing academic and public discussion of the idea of a 'post-work' society, but this literature has not yet explored whether or how animals fit into such a society. Donaldson and Kymlicka argue that animals would not only benefit from the shift to a post-work society, but can in fact exemplify it, engaging in socially beneficial activities that do not fit standard models of wage labour and economic production, including caring, serving, teaching/learning, creating, etc. Instead of bringing animals into our current work society and upholding values traditionally tied to 'productive' work, Donaldson and Kymlicka suggest that animals might help us imagine a post-work world—bringing to the fore new conceptions of community, and a richer and more inclusive ethos of citizenship.

Future Directions

These contributions are just a slice of the vast array of questions and challenges raised by animal labour. We are still at the very early stages of the debate, and much work remains to be done, at multiple levels, in terms of identifying relevant social practices of animal labour, clarifying the appropriate moral standards for evaluating these practices, improving our understanding of animals' experiences of work, and formulating legal and institutional structures that would both be effective in soliciting animals' preferences while also providing secure and reliable rights protections. The chapters in this volume open up important new perspectives, but in the process, they often lead to even more complicated questions, many of which are still not answered in the case of human labour. In this final section, we want to take the opportunity to identify a few of the questions that we think should guide future research.

Many of our contributions have focused on domesticated animals, since these are the animals whom we have historically made to work for us. For centuries if not millennia, we have forced them to labour for us, often under horrendous conditions (Hribal 2003, 2012). We need to condemn unjust labour practices, but we cannot remedy these injustices by denying animals a place in the world or relegating them to confinement and boredom. Many animals are avid learners and enjoy solving problems, taking on social roles, and caring for their relevant community. If animal labour can help domesticated animals achieve these goals, shouldn't we explore that possibility?

But what about wild or liminal animals? Is it helpful to think about them as engaged in labour, and if so, what legal or political implications follow? Many wild animals avoid human settlements and clearly indicate that they do not wish to be associated or spend time with us, which seems to rule out cooperative work with humans. But animal labour should not be exclusively defined by human involvement, and we might instead recognize animal labour wherever animals make meaningful contributions to caring for others and engaging in ecosocial reproduction (Coulter 2016b, 2018). What kinds of legal safeguards would help ensure that wild animals are able to engage in such subsistence and reproductive labour, and to enjoy the fruits of their labour? Could ideas of (wild) animal labour help to support claims to habitat and environmental protection, and thereby bridge animal ethics and environmental ethics?

Related to this point, we might ask how animal labour can help to develop a more intersectional form of animal ethics. Several of our authors discuss how perceptions of labour—whether human or animal—are deeply gendered, in terms of what is recognized as work, what work secures which rights, and who is expected to do what kinds of work. This is one example of a more general trend in animal studies to explore intersectional forms of oppression and liberation, including the relationships between disability, race, and species (e.g. Deckha 2012; Kim 2015; jones 2016; Taylor 2017). As Donaldson and Kymlicka note (chapter 10, this volume), labour has been a central basis, not only for distinguishing humans from animals, but also for categorizing and ranking human in-groups and out-groups. We hope and expect that the further development of a labour lens within animal studies will shed light on these linkages.

And this in turn raises important strategic questions about whether or how animal activists can deploy the labour lens in their social movements and political mobilization. Does the idea of animals as workers have potential resonance in the larger public, and can it help put the animal question 'on the map'? Can it help form coalitions between human and animal labour struggles, rather than pitting one against the other? Can concepts like interspecies solidarity and humane jobs help emphasize human–animal interconnectedness?

In the long list of tasks that lie ahead, we would also want to more explicitly expand the animal labour lens beyond the global north, to consider how it is understood in the mental and physical space of non-western and Indigenous individuals and communities. And we need to develop new methodologies for studying animals' experience of labour: methods that allow us to move beyond humanist understandings of worthiness, inclusion, and participation without compromising legal and institutional safeguards for animals (Coulter 2018b; Hamilton and Taylor 2017; Hamilton and Mitchell 2018; Johnson 2017). Some developments in critical animal geography and certain approaches to multispecies ethnography are offering new avenues for exploring meaningful relations as perceived by non-human animals, including in sanctuary settings (Abrell 2016; Gillespie 2018), and these may help us explore postcolonial and posthumanist visions of peaceful coexistence (Pacini-Ketchabaw, Taylor, and Blaise 2016). As we noted earlier, the broader field of animal studies is rapidly evolving, and we believe that the study of animal labour can benefit from, and in turn can enrich, this exciting field.

20 ANIMAL LABOUR

References

Abrell, Elan. 2016. *Saving Animals: Everyday Practices of Care and Rescue in the US Animal Sanctuary Movement*. Doctoral dissertation, City University of New York.

Acampora, Ralph. 2005. 'Oikos and Domus: On Constructive Co-habitation with Other Creatures'. *Philosophy and Geography* 7(2): 219–35.

Adams, Carol. 2017. 'Feminized Protein: Meaning, Representations, and Implications'. In *Making Milk: The Past, Present and Future of our Primary Food*, edited by Mathilde Cohen and Yoriko Otomo, 19–40. London: Bloomsbury.

Ahlhaus, Svenja, and Peter Niesen. 2015. 'What is Animal Politics? Outline of a New Research Agenda'. *Historical Social Research* 40(4): 7–31.

Anderson, Jerry. 2011. 'Protection for the Powerless: Political Economy History Lessons for the Animal Welfare Movement'. *Stanford Journal of Animal Law and Policy* 4: 1–63.

Anderson, Virginia. 2004. *Creatures of Empire: How Domestic Animals Transformed Early America*. Oxford: Oxford University Press.

Andrews, Kristin. 2011. 'Beyond Anthropomorphism: Attributing Psychological Properties to Animals'. In *The Oxford Handbook of Animal Ethics*, edited by Tom Beauchamp and R.G. Frey, 469–94. Oxford: Oxford University Press.

Barua, Maan. 2016. 'Lively Commodities and Encounter Value'. *Environment and Planning D: Society and Space* 34(4): 725–44.

Barua, Maan. 2017. 'Nonhuman Labour, Encounter Value, Spectacular Accumulation: The Geographies of a Lively Commodity'. *Transactions of the Institute of British Geographers* 42: 274–88.

Bekoff, Marc. 2004. 'Wild Justice and Fair Play: Cooperation, Forgiveness, and Morality in Animals'. *Biology and Philosophy* 19(4): 489–520.

Bekoff, Marc. 2009. *Wild Justice: The Moral Lives of Animals*. Chicago: Chicago University Press.

Beldo, Les. 2017. 'Metabolic Labor: Broiler Chickens and the Exploitation of Vitality'. *Environmental Humanities* 9(1): 108–28.

Bezanson, Kate. 2006. *Gender, the State, and Social Reproduction: Household Insecurity in Modern Times*. Toronto: University of Toronto Press.

Birke, Lynda, Arnold Arluke, and Mike Michael. 2007. *The Sacrifice: How Scientific Experiments Transform Animals and People*. West Lafayette, IN: Purdue University Press.

Birke, Lynda, and Kirrilly Thompson. 2017. *(Un) Stable Relations: Horses, Humans and Social Agency*. London: Routledge.

Carter, Bob, and Nickie Charles. 2013. 'Animals, Agency and Resistance'. *Journal for the Theory of Social Behaviour* 43(3): 322–40.

Cochrane, Alasdair. 2016. 'Labour Rights for Animals'. In *The Political Turn in Animal Ethics*, edited by Robert Garner and Siobhan O'Sullivan, 15–32. London: Rowman and Littlefield.

Collard, Rosemary-Claire, and Jessica Dempsey. 2013. 'Life for Sale? The Politics of Lively Commodities'. *Environment and Planning A* 45: 2682–99.

Corman, Lauren. 2017. 'Ideological Monkey Wrenching: Nonhuman Animal Politics Beyond Suffering'. In *Animal Oppression and Capitalism. Volume 2: The Oppressive and Destructive Role of Capitalism*, edited by David Nibert, 252–69. Santa Barbara: Praeger Press.

Coulter, Kendra. 2014. 'Herds and Hierarchies: Class, Nature, and the Social Construction of Horses in Equestrian Culture'. *Society and Animals* 22(2): 135–52.

Coulter, Kendra. 2016. *Animals, Work, and the Promise of Interspecies Solidarity*. Basingstoke: Palgrave.

Coulter, Kendra. 2016b. 'Beyond Human to Humane: A Multispecies Analysis of Care Work, Its Repression, and Its Potential'. *Studies in Social Justice* 5(2): 199–219.

Coulter, Kendra. 2018. 'How the Hard Work of Wild Animals Benefits Us Too'. *The Conversation*. https://theconversation.com/how-the-hard-work-of-wild-animals-benefits-us-too-96084 [Accessed 2 July 2019].

Coulter, Kendra. 2018b. 'Challenging Subjects: Towards Ethnographic Analyses of Animals'. *Journal for the Anthropology of North America* 21(2): 58–71.

Deckha, Maneesha. 2012. 'Toward a Postcolonial, Posthumanist Feminist Theory: Centralizing Race and Culture in Feminist Work on Nonhuman Animals'. *Hypatia* 27(3): 527–45.

Delon, Nicolas. 2017. 'L'animal Compagnon de Travail: L'éthique des Fables Alimentaires'. *Revue Française d'Ethique Appliquée* 4: 61–75.

De Waal, Frans, and Pier Ferrari. 2010. 'Towards a Bottom-Up Perspective on Animal and Human Cognition'. *Trends in Cognitive Sciences* 14(5): 201–7.

Donaldson, Sue, and Will Kymlicka. 2011. *Zoopolis: A Political Theory of Animal Rights*. Oxford: Oxford University Press.

Donaldson, Sue, and Will Kymlicka. 2016. 'Rethinking Membership and Participation in an Inclusive Democracy: Cognitive Disability, Children, Animals'. In *Disability and Political Theory*, edited by Barbara Arneil and Nancy Hirschmann, 168–97. Cambridge: Cambridge University Press.

Donaldson, Sue, and Will Kymlicka. 2017. 'Animals in Political Theory'. In *The Oxford Handbook of Animal Studies*, edited by Linda Kalof, 43–65. Oxford: Oxford University Press.

Donovan, Josephine, and Carol Adams, eds. 2007. *The Feminist Care Tradition in Animal Ethics: A Reader*. New York: Columbia University Press.

Fedigan, Linda. 1992. *Primate Paradigms: Sex Roles and Social Bonds*. Chicago: University of Chicago Press.

Feuerstein, N. and Joseph Terkel. 2008. 'Interrelationship of Dogs (*canis familiaris*) and Cats (*felis catus L.*) Living Under the Same Roof'. *Applied Animal Behaviour Science* 113: 150–65.

Foner, Philip. 1986. *May Day: A Short History of the International Workers' Holiday, 1886–1986*. New York: International Publishers.

Francione, Gary, and Robert Garner. 2010. *The Animal Rights Debate: Abolition or Regulation?* New York: Columbia University Press.

Fraser, David. 1999. 'Animal Ethics and Animal Welfare Science: Bridging the Two Cultures'. *Applied Animal Behaviour Science* 65(3): 171–89.

Fuentes, Agustin. 2012. 'Ethnoprimatology and the Anthropology of the Human-Primate Interface'. *Annual Review of Anthropology* 41: 101–17.

Gaard, Greta. 2011. 'Ecofeminism Revisited: Rejecting Essentialism and Re-Placing Species in a Material Feminist Environmentalism'. *Feminist Formations* 23(2): 26–53.

Garner, Robert, and Siobhan O'Sullivan, eds. 2016. *The Political Turn in Animal Ethics*. London: Rowman & Littlefield.

Gheaus, Anca, and Lisa Herzog. 2016. 'The Goods of Work (Other Than Money!)'. *Journal of Social Philosophy* 47(1): 70–89.

Gillespie, Kathryn. 2018. *The Cow with Ear Tag #1389*. Chicago: University of Chicago Press.

Gillespie, Kathryn. forthcoming. *Doing Multispecies Ethnography: Reflections on a Feminist Geographic Approach to Pedagogy*.

Greene, Ann. 2009. *Horses at Work: Harnessing Power in Industrial America*. Cambridge: Harvard University Press.

Gruen, Lori. 2015. *Entangled Empathy: An Alternative Ethic for our Relationships With Animals*. Brooklyn: Lantern Books.

Hamilton, Lindsay, and Laura Mitchell. 2018. 'Knocking on the Door of Human-Animal Studies: Valuing Work Across Disciplinary and Species Borderlines'. *Society & Animals* 26: 1–20.

Hamilton, Lindsay, and Nik Taylor. 2013. *Animals at Work: Identity, Politics and Culture in Work with Animals*. Leiden: Brill.

Hamilton, Lindsay, and Nik Taylor. 2017. *Ethnography After Humanism: Power, Politics and Method in Multi-Species Research*. London: Palgrave.

Hathaway, Michael. 2015. 'Wild Elephants as Actors in the Anthropocene: The Role of Non-Humans in Shaping Animal Welfare Movements'. In *Animals in the Anthropocene: Critical Perspectives on Non-human Futures*, edited by the Human Animal Research Network Editorial Collective, 221–42. Sydney: Sydney University Press.

Hribal, Jason. 2003. '"Animals are Part of the Working Class": A Challenge to Labour History'. *Labour History* 44(4): 435–53.

Hribal, Jason. 2007. 'Animals, Agency, and Class: Writing the History of Animals from Below'. *Human Ecology Review* 14(1): 101–12.

Hribal, Jason. 2012. 'Animals are Part of the Working Class Reviewed'. *Borderlands* 9: 1–37.

Huston, Joseph, Maria de Souza Silva, Mara Komorowski, Daniela Schulz, and Bianca Topic. 2013. 'Animal Models of Extinction-Induced Depression: Loss of Reward and its Consequences'. *Neuroscience & Biobehavioral Reviews* 37(9): 2059–70.

Jaeggi, Rahel. 2014. *Alienation*. Trans. F. Neuhouser and A. Smith. New York: Columbia University Press.

Jamieson, Dale. 2018. 'Animal Agency'. *Harvard Review of Philosophy* 25: 111–26.

Johnson, Elizabeth. 2017. 'At the Limits of Species Being: Sensing the Anthropocene'. *South Atlantic Quarterly* 116: 275–92.

Johnston, Steven. 2012. 'Animals in War: Commemoration, Patriotism, Death'. *Political Research Quarterly* 65(2): 359–71.

Jones, pattrice. 2016. *Intersectionality and Animals*. https://www.nlg.org/wp-content/uploads/2016/09/intersectionality-and-animals.pdf [Accessed 7 Dec. 2018].

Kean, Hilda. 2012. 'Animals and War Memorials: Different Approaches to Commemorating the Human-Animal Relationship'. In *Animals and War*, edited by Ryan Hediger. Brill.

Kheel, Marti. 2007. *Nature Ethics: An Ecofeminist Perspective*. Lanham: Rowman & Littlefield.

Kim, Claire Jean. 2015. *Dangerous Crossings: Race, Species, and Nature in a Multicultural Age*. Cambridge: Cambridge University Press.

Kranzler, Michael. 2013. 'Don't Let Slip the Dogs of War: An Argument for Reclassifying Military Working Dogs as "Canine Members of the Armed Forces"'. *University of Miami National Security & Armed Conflict Law Review* 4: 268–94.

Kymlicka, Will. 2017. 'Social Membership: Animal Law Beyond the Property/Personhood Impasse'. *Dalhousie Law Journal* 40(1): 123–55.

Laurier, Eric, Ramia Maze, and Johan Lundin. 2006. 'Putting the Dog Back in the Park: Animal and Human Mind-in-Action'. *Mind, Culture, and Activity* 13: 2–24.

Lercier, Marine. 2019. 'Welfare protection of the animal-athlete in the sports company in light of the evolution of the legal regime for animals', *Derecho Animal* 10/1: 59–75.

Locke, John. 1988. *Two Treatises of Government: Treatise II*, edited by Peter Laslett. Cambridge: Cambridge University Press.

Lorini, Giuseppe. 2018. 'Animal Norms: An Investigation of Normativity in the Non-Human Social World.' *Law, Culture and the Humanities*.

Luxton, Meg, and Kate Bezanson, eds., 2006. *Social Reproduction: Feminist Political Economy Challenges Neo-Liberalism*. Kingston: McGill-Queen's University Press.

Malone, Nicholas, Alison Wade, Agustin Fuentes, Erin Riley, Melissa Remis, and Carolyn Robinson. 2014. 'Ethnoprimatology: Critical Interdisciplinarity and Multispecies Approaches in Anthropology'. *Critique of Anthropology* 34(1): 8–29.

Marx, Karl. 1967. *Capital: A Critique of Political Economy*. New York: International Publishers.

Marx, Karl. 1990. *Capital Vol. I: A Critique of Political Economy*. London: Penguin.

McFarland, Sarah, and Ryan Hediger, eds. 2009. *Animals and Agency: An Interdisciplinary Exploration*. Leiden: Brill.

McLennan, Matthew. 2018. 'Norms for the Public Remembrance of Nonhuman Animals'. *Ethics, Politics & Society* 1: 63–81.

24 ANIMAL LABOUR

Meijer, Eva. 2013. 'Political Communication with Animals'. *Humanimalia* 5(1): 28–51.

Mellor, David. 2016. 'Updating Animal Welfare Thinking: Moving Beyond the "Five Freedoms" Towards "A Life Worth Living"'. *Animals* 6(3): 1–21.

Mendl, Michael, and E.S. Paul. 2004. 'Consciousness, Emotion and Animal Welfare: Insights from Cognitive Science'. *Animal Welfare* 13(1): 17–25.

Milburn, Josh. 2017. 'Nonhuman Animals as Property Holders: An Exploration of the Lockean Labour-Mixing Account'. *Environmental Values* 26(5): 629–48.

Milligan, Tony. 2010. *Beyond Animal Rights: Food, Pets, and Ethics.* London: Continuum.

Milligan, Tony. 2015. 'The Political Turn in Animal Rights'. *Politics and Animals* 1(1): 6–15.

Nance, Susan 2013. *Entertaining Elephants: Animal Agency and the Business of the American Circus.* Baltimore: Johns Hopkins University Press.

Noske, Barbara. 1997. *Beyond Boundaries: Humans and Animals.* Montreal: Black Rose.

Pacini-Ketchabaw, Veronica, Affrica Taylor, and Mindy Blaise. 2016. 'Decentering the Human in Multispecies Ethnographies'. In *Posthuman Research Practices*, edited by Carol Taylor and Christina Hughes, 149–67. Basingstoke: Palgrave.

Palmer, Clare, and Peter Sandøe. 2018. 'Welfare'. In *Critical Terms for Animal Studies*, edited by Lori Gruen. Chicago: University of Chicago Press.

Pearson, Chris. 2015. 'Beyond "Resistance": Rethinking Nonhuman Agency for a "More-Than-Human" World'. *European Review of History* 22(5): 709–25.

Pedersen, Helena. 2014. 'Knowledge Production in the "Animal Turn": Multiplying the Image of Thought, Empathy, and Justice'. In *Exploring the Animal Turn: Human-Animal Relations in Science, Society and Culture*, edited by Erika Andersson Cederholm, Amelie Björck, Kristina Jennbert, and Ann-Sofie Lönngren, 13–19. Lund: Pufendorfinstitutet.

Perlo, Katherine. 2002. 'Marxism and the Underdog'. *Society & Animals* 10(3): 303–18.

Pleasance, Chris. 2013. 'Police Dogs to get a Pension Plan'. *The Daily Mail*, 4 November 2013. https://www.dailymail.co.uk/news/article-2487540/Police-dogs-pension-plan-Animals-given-1-500-help-pay-medical-bills-retire-service.html [Accessed 2 July 2019].

Plumwood, Val. 2005. *Environmental Culture: The Ecological Crisis of Reason.* Milton Park: Routledge.

Porcher, Jocelyne, and Tiphaine Schmitt. 2012. 'Dairy cows: workers in the shadows?' *Society & Animals* 20(1): 39–60.

Porcher, Jocelyne. 2017. *The Ethics of Animal Labor: A Collaborative Utopia.* Basingstoke: Palgrave.

Regan, Tom. 2004. *The Case for Animal Rights*, 2nd ed. Berkeley: University of California Press.

Ritvo, Harriet. 2007. 'On the Animal Turn'. *Daedalus* 136(4): 118–22.

Schapiro, Steven J., Mollie A. Bloomsmith, and Gail E. Laule. 2003. 'Positive Reinforcement Training as a Technique to Alter Nonhuman Primate Behavior: Quantitative Assessments of Effectiveness'. *Journal of Applied Animal Welfare Science* 6(3): 175–87.

Shaw, Rosemary. 2018. 'A Case for Recognizing the Rights of Animals as Workers'. *Journal of Animal Ethics* 8(2): 182–98.

Skabelund, Aaron. 2011. *Empire of Dogs: Canines, Japan, and the Making of the Modern Imperial World*. Ithaca: Cornell University Press.

Skrivankova, Klara. 2010. *Between Decent Work and Forced Labour: Examining the Continuum of Exploitation*. Joseph Rowntree Foundation.

Smith, Kimberly. 2012. *Governing Animals: Animal Welfare and the Liberal State*. Oxford: Oxford University Press.

Smuts, Barbara. 2001. 'Encounters with Animal Minds'. *Journal of consciousness studies* 8(5–6): 293–309.

Revue Écologie et Politique. 2017. Special Issue on 'Travail Animal, L'autre Champ du Social'. *Revue Écologie et Politique* 54: 5–121.

Taylor Nik, and Heather Fraser. 2019. 'The Work of Significant Other/s: Companion Animal Relationships in the Future'. In *Companion Animals and Domestic Violence*, 185–217. Cham, Palgrave Macmillan.

Taylor, Sunaura. 2017. *Beasts of Burden: Animals and Disability Liberation*. New York: New Press.

Tumilty, Emma, Catherine Smith, Peter Walker, and Gareth Treharne. 2018. 'Ethics Unleashed: Developing Responsive Ethical Practice and Review for the Inclusion of Non-Human Animal Participants in Qualitative Research'. In *The SAGE Handbook of Qualitative Research Ethics*, edited by Ron Iphofen and Martin Tolich. London: Sage.

Twine, Richard. 2012. 'Revealing the Animal-Industrial Complex: A Concept and Method for Critical Animal Studies'. *Journal for Critical Animal Studies* 10(1): 12–39.

Wadiwel, Dinesh. 2016. 'Do Fish Resist?'. *Cultural Studies Review* 22(1): 196–242.

Wadiwel, Dinesh. 2018. 'Chicken Harvesting Machine: Animal Labour, Resistance and the Time of Production'. *South Atlantic Quarterly* 117(3): 525–48.

Willett, Cynthia. 2014. *Interspecies Ethics*. Columbia University Press.

Wolfson, David, and Mariann Sullivan. 2004. 'Foxes in the Hen House: Animals, Agribusiness, and the Law: A Modern American Fable'. In *Animal Rights: Current Debates and New Directions*, edited by Cass Sunstein and Martha Nussbaum, 205–33. Oxford: Oxford University Press.

Yeoman, Ruth. 2014. 'Conceptualising Meaningful Work as a Fundamental Human Need'. *Journal of Business Ethics* 125(2): 235–51.

PART I
THE PROMISE OF GOOD WORK

2

Toward Humane Jobs and Work-Lives for Animals

Kendra Coulter

Homo Sapiens' approaches to labour and political economics are causing serious physical, psychological, emotional, and intergenerational harm to animals. Moreover, the industries that are most damaging to animals also fuel pollution, climate change, and ecological devastation, endanger public health, and primarily provide lousy and dangerous work for people. These facts make it clear that in addition to critique, alternatives are sorely needed. Therefore, I have proposed the concept of humane jobs as a way to conceptualize and foster work that is good for both people and animals. The idea of humane jobs is inspired by the promise of interspecies solidarity, and by the need to reconcile and transcend both perceived and real divisions between labour and animal advocacy to help forge more just political economic futures. The challenges demand changes in our daily practices, workplace cultures, politics, and economics. I chose the specific wording *humane jobs* building from the existing vocabulary of 'good jobs' and 'green jobs', and as an accessible, pithy term which is easily understandable to a broad range of people. The concept is designed to be politically actionable.

Because so much institutionalized violence against animals results from human actions, there is a particular need to create workforce alternatives for people. This includes a) the creation of more humane jobs numerically in order to expand positive areas of work and replace those that are harmful; and b) the improvement of some existing areas of work through better working conditions in order to make them more humane. When envisioning a future of humane jobs in more ethical and sustainable societies, most often what is needed is the replacement of destructive industries and the creation of humane job alternatives for people. In these cases, animals benefit from the promotion of humane jobs through either the elimination of harm (their use, exploitation, intensive confinement, and death), or from the expansion and improvement of human labour which is focused on caring for and protecting other species.

Yet the premise of humane jobs is also an opportunity to think more carefully about a third dimension: animals' potential participation in certain kinds of work,

---

Kendra Coulter, *Toward Humane Jobs and Work-Lives for Animals* In: *Animal Labour: A New Frontier of Interspecies Justice?*. Edited by: Charlotte Blattner, Kendra Coulter, and Will Kymlicka, Oxford University Press (2020).
© Oxford University Press. DOI: 10.1093/oso/9780198846192.003.0002

30   ANIMAL LABOUR

and, specifically, whether there could be humane jobs for animals.[1] I have suggested the following:

> At this point, my view is that it is not unreasonable for some domesticated animals to be engaged in certain kinds of work, if both the jobs and the labor relationships are characterized by respect and reciprocity, and if animals are afforded protections and positive entitlements underscored by interspecies solidarity, particularly if buttressed by formal political frameworks. Animals can enjoy and even benefit from certain kinds of work and labor relationships as members of multispecies workplaces and societies.   (Coulter 2016c: 73)

This supposition shares commonalities with Sue Donaldson and Will Kymlicka's theorizing about multispecies futures and zoopolitics, particular their insistence on both protections and positive entitlements[2] (defence from and rights to), and their emphasis on complementary and corresponding political and legal structures (2011: see especially chapter 5). They posit that if we wish to recognize and build more ethical multispecies societies, animals could be included in the 'give and take of social life' (2011: 137; see also Kymlicka 2017) which could include certain kinds of work and gain social membership from doing so. I, too, have suggested that if we are going to recognize domesticated animals as members of our societies, it might not be unreasonable for some to contribute through certain engagements in labour. Thus, like Alasdair Cochrane (2016), I have suggested that key labour protections which are afforded to some (albeit not enough) human workers hold lessons for thinking about animals' engagements in work and what rights they should have, including 'safety standards, breaks, days off, vacation, the right to refuse work on a daily or permanent basis, and life after work' (Coulter 2016a: 160).

Notably, I have also argued that what some or likely many animals are owed is the right *not* to work for people at all; much labour being required of animals is not ethically defensible, regardless of the benefit humans may garner from it. Particularly for farmed animals, there is a strong case to be made that 'what we should redistribute...is autonomy over their own bodies and lives, and the right to engage in their own social reproductive and caregiving labours' (Coulter 2016b: 214). Undoubtedly, a homogenizing approach to animal labour is not appropriate

---

[1] I use the term animals (and not non-human animals) to refer to species other than *Homo Sapiens* for linguistic efficiency and to avoid continually referring to other animals by but one of the species to which they do not belong. As Frans de Waal (2016) puts it, we could just as easily refer to them as non-penguin animals, for example.

[2] This dual emphasis is reflected in much scholarship on animal law, and also increasingly used by animal welfare scientists. See, for example, Mellor (2016).

or helpful. Animal labour is not singular or monolithic, and cannot be universally condemned or condoned.

Accordingly, there is now a need for more robust analysis and proposals, and this volume offers diverse perspectives on the challenges and possibilities. This chapter contributes to the discussion by further interrogating the idea of humane jobs for animals. After demarcating key facets of the intellectual terrain and my theoretical roots and sociopolitical scope, I outline some basic principles and elucidate vocabulary which can be used for both better understanding and improving animals' experiences of work.

As a labour scholar, I know all-too-well that work can be oppressive, miserable, and detrimental; a source of meaning, pride, and fulfilment; or something more complex. Moreover, how we conceptualize work matters, and is not simply an intellectual exercise. For some, the idea of work is always negative and imbued with unpleasant connotations. Such a perception is inevitability going to lead to opposition to all forms of animal labour. If work is recognized as not one but rather many different processes, experiences, and potentialities, then we can think more thoroughly and precisely. The world of work is better understood as akin to a 3D mosaic, with elements of commonality and overlap, vastly different colours, and sections that are many textures and tones simultaneously. From there we can begin to more fully see and interrogate the possibilities for humane jobs for animals. I also suggest that humane *jobs* are a start but that we ought to be emphasizing humane *work-lives*. I conclude by identifying a few potential frameworks that could be enlisted, expanded, and potentially combined in order to more fully assess and potentially foster humane jobs for animals.

For this exploratory discussion, I build from the theoretical and political roots outlined, and from research on human–animal workplaces and relations, particularly those with dogs and horses. Methodologically this research includes fieldwork, direct observation (of animals and people), and interviews, among other data-collection techniques. I thus learn from the practical, on-the-ground efforts of people who work with animals regularly, as well as from animals' engagements in work and their multifaceted expressions of agency and subjectivity.

It is tempting to outline a utopian vision or one-size-fits-all answer. I reject the appropriateness of the latter for many reasons. I see value in the former, without question, but also a pressing need for ambitious but usable ideas. Indeed, how 'ambitious' is perceived will vary a great deal among differently positioned academics, and in the eyes of those on the front lines working with and for animals on a daily basis. This chapter is thus both inductive and generative, and it offers areas of potential and of possible applicability, rather than tidy solutions or a single prescription. It is intended to inspire a larger and more careful, collaborative, and reflexive conversation, one attuned to ethical aspirations, dynamics of social change, pragmatic realities, and different groups of people and animals.

32   ANIMAL LABOUR

The Intellectual and Sociopolitical Terrain

I propose that we augment, expand, and/or modify existing anthropocentric vocabularies in order to better understand animals, but see the conventional and dominant ways of thinking about labour as insufficient for encouraging more holistic and multidimensional understanding of the breadth and depth of animals' engagements in work, and for developing new approaches to it. This is, in large part, because existing framings are both *androcentric* and Eurocentric. Marx's emphases continue to shape scholarship on labour in significant ways and 'work' is still often or first associated with wage labour, and, in many cases, specific kinds of work like manual labour. This is despite decades of feminist and cross-cultural research that has highlighted many kinds of unpaid labour, including domestic work, as well as the diversity of subsistence and other livelihood strategies that people have used and continue to employ. This gendered academic pattern is not unique to the social sciences or scholarship on work, as has been made clear by feminist analyses of science and especially primatology (see, for example, Hager 1997; Haraway 1989). Who does scholarship and what they prioritize affect what is seen, not seen, and emphasized. Similarly, political structures and economic systems continue to frame 'work' in particular ways and, as countless feminist political economists have highlighted, the unpaid, domestic, and reproductive labour which subsidizes every economic system continues to be discounted (see, for example, Luxton 1980; Luxton and Bezanson 2006; Waring 1999).

This simultaneously andro- and anthropocentric context has had a significant impact on how animals' labour is approached. It has often meant an emphasis on animals' physical and manual labour, and on the most obvious examples of labour they do with people (pulling carts, assisting police, serving as guide dogs). These aspects are, of course, relevant, but are only one part of a more complex picture, one which not includes animals' bodily strength in a narrow sense, but also involves multidimensional embodied affective, relational, and interactive processes through which they engage their thoughts, emotions, abilities to understand, assess, and communicate, as well as their agency (Coulter 2019). A more multifaceted and nuanced approach to animals' labour is needed not only to better understand it, but to think carefully about what is really involved and what could be ethically appropriate.

Some elements of Marxian thought can be usefully enlisted for analysing certain elements of animal labour and some animals (see Wadiwel, chapter 9 of this volume). Noske's (1989, 1997) adaptation of the Marxian concept of alienation is also a helpful framework for interrogating animals' experiences of industrial agriculture and comparable sites, in my view (see also Stuart, Shewe, and Gunderson 2013). More recent Marxian-rooted approaches like labour process theory, and particularly its gendered strands, also offer some helpful concepts and diagnostic tools, such as emotional labour, emotion work, and body work, which can be used to facilitate a more multifaceted view of animals' labour. I see underutilized and noteworthy potential in feminist approaches to labour for more thoroughly understanding animals' labour—and, in particular, for developing ethically and politically engaged approaches to it.

Feminist analyses of labour often have a number of intellectual roots, one of which is Marxian analysis. But what is distinct and particularly helpful about feminist political economy and similar bodies of scholarship is that proponents are more interested in the intricacies, experiences, and social processes of different kinds of work and workers, and they pay more attention to interactive, service, caring, and unpaid work, and how these are located in particular contexts. If we are interested in what animals actually *do* when they are working (in contrast to macro-level or structural analysis, for example), these lenses are valuable. Animals are, of course, not directly paid wages for their work in a conventional sense. Feminist scholars emphasize unpaid work and offer theoretical frameworks for fostering deeper understanding of and appreciation for it—and for those who do it. Labour and value are differently conceptualized by feminists than by traditional Marxian scholars. As a result, mining feminist scholarship when seeking to (analytically) understand and (politically) improve the labour of animals makes sense.

In that spirit, it is imperative to note that wild animals engage in their own self-controlled individual and collective forms of subsistence and care work, which together constitute social reproductive labour and what I call *ecosocial* reproduction (Coulter 2016a, especially chapter 2; 2016b). Similarly, I recognize forms of informal or voluntary labour, including the care and protective work companion animals' may choose to do for people with whom they share their lives (Coulter 2016b; see Fitzgerald 2007; Lem et al. 2013; Irvine 2013a, 2013b for empirical studies of such dynamics). As part of expanding our analytical lenses beyond not only the anthropocentric but also the androcentric and Eurocentric conceptualizations of work which dominate so much scholarship on labour, recognizing the myriad ways animals of all kinds engage in work of different kinds is important. Women have long fought to have the full range of their *labours* recognized as such and properly valued, including by labour organizations and researchers. A key lesson from feminist scholarship is the need, as Nancy Fraser (1997) puts it, to *recognize* different kinds of work and social groups whose members are often marginalized and devalued.[3] This insight is highly relevant to animal studies.

Because this discussion focuses on humane *jobs*, here I focus on formal work and occupations which humans could or do assign to animals. I use the terms work, labour, and jobs and occupation, and there are some differences among these terms. Work and labour can refer to larger and whole processes, or to specifics types of tasks or processes such as care work, emotional labour, or

---

[3] See Coulter 2016b for a longer discussion of the potential applicability of Fraser's ideas of recognition and redistribution for animals.

emotion work. Work and labour can be formal or informal (providing care in a job is formal, while the provisioning of care for your family still involves work but is done informally). Jobs or occupations tend to highlight an employment title or classification, such as therapy animal or service dog, and are more often formal and assigned. The term humane jobs (and work-lives) may encompass all of these dimensions and reflect the fact that the work animals are assigned may meet anthropocentric classifications of part- or full-time, or, more likely, something more complex. As noted, my focus here is on work and jobs that people assign to animals.

The terms we use to describe the verbs of working are also of interest. At different times I refer to engagements (in work), participation, performance/performing, and to work or jobs being mandated, assigned, or given. I endeavour to use these terms with precision (participation is decidedly different from something being mandated), as they have distinct meanings with different connotations. However, I also see that they may be inadequate or at least incomplete.

Notably, I am cognizant that different cultural and historical processes have produced and reproduced many kinds of gendered, classed, ethnoracial, and colonial inequities and privileges among humans, and that these are entangled with human–animal relations and multispecies work contexts in complex and uneven ways. These intra- and international dynamics and their implications cannot be properly synthesized here; what is most crucial is to establish the scope and limitations of this discussion of humane jobs. As this is an early attempt develop a vocabulary and ideas for possible evaluative criteria for assessing humane jobs, I focus on the global north, and on colonial/settler labour interactions with/uses of animals.

This does not mean that animals who are used for work in the global south or in indigenous communities rooted in the global north suffer any less when they are harmed or that they do not deserve better lives. Rather, a different approach is needed given the history and ongoing effects of colonialism, imperialism, and neoliberal globalization which have significantly affected global socioeconomic realities, impoverished many places, displaced and disrupted traditional interspecies relations, created frequent extinctions and species endangerment, and profoundly altered the environment. It is not appropriate to apply the exact same standards which can and should be achievable in highly industrialized (and, in some cases, deindustrializing) contexts to poor communities, or to posit a monolithic blueprint for the entire planet. At the same time, certain ideas that are fundamental to my vision of humane jobs, such as interspecies solidarity, extend from Eurocentric patterns of thought and political action, but also share key facets with a number of indigenous worldviews. Colonial societies/descendants of colonizers have much to learn about multispecies dynamics from a number of indigenous peoples. These are important lines of inquiry and exchange which are increasingly being taken seriously by indigenous and non-indigenous scholars alike. In this chapter, for the reasons outlined above, here I concentrate on the labours given to animals by non-indigenous people in the global north.

Towards Humane Jobs for Animals: Some Basics

To start, I differentiate between potential engagements in work, and death. Discussions of farmed animals' labour are included in this volume, and I have considered them in more detail elsewhere. The killing of animals and the use of farmed animals' bodies and bodily labours to produce commodities for human consumption have no potential to offer humane jobs for animals.[4] At the most basic level, a humane job must be 'good' for animals. Being killed prematurely for the production of commodities cannot be justified as beneficial to those being killed. Farmed animals could potentially be employed in humane jobs in other ways, but commodity production is not one of them. Ending an animal's life in as pain-free a way as possible as an act of mercy is different. So, to be clear, asking someone to work and guaranteeing their premature death are very different.

I also argue that a foundational requirement of potential humane jobs for animals is that only already domesticated species and individual animals are ethically appropriate for consideration. I begin from the position that wild and/ or captive animals should not be working for people.[5] Those currently put to work in circuses and similar sites should be afforded retirement in sanctuaries or other suitable spaces. That is the least we should do for these animals. They should be entitled to retirement, dignity, and a great deal of autonomy.[6]

Consequently, the animals potentially having humane jobs are predominantly dogs and probably some horses and small domesticated companion animals, but what are currently called farmed animals could also participate in care work on care farms or in animal-assisted therapy. These are animals who are highly social,

---

[4] One possible exception concerns the not-for-profit gathering and consumption of eggs from small flocks of chickens who will live out their lives in full and are afforded substantial freedom of movement (which stands in stark contrast to the large majority of modern 'egg production'). The production of the eggs by hens' bodies is a naturally occurring process, while still an example of a kind of body work. Eggs will be continually produced by hens, whether humans gather them or not. By contrast, given the availability of plant-based milks and the complete lack of a biological need to consume other animals' milk, particularly as adults, I am not convinced that even the most ethically sensitive killing-free dairy farms—of which there are only a handful—are sustainable in the medium or longer term. See Milburn (2018) and Fischer and Milburn (2019) for a more extensive discussion of these dynamics.

[5] A noteworthy example from the global south is the employment of some formerly wild rats to locate landmines and detect tuberculosis. As I have noted (Coulter 2016a), the introduction of work can contribute to changes in how animals previously viewed as pests or parasitic are understood, which can positively benefit the animals doing the work, and those who remain wild. This is a case that warrants more analysis, but, as noted, this chapter focuses on the global north.

[6] What specific rights animals ought to have on/in sanctuaries or in future interspecies communities is the subject of a growing body of scholarship. See, for example, the work of Elan Abrell (2016) and Sue Donaldson and Will Kymlicka (2015).

including across species lines, and who have shown willingness or even enthusiasm for working with and for us. However, 'this does not automatically mean everything we currently ask (or require) these animals to do is defensible. Similarly, simply because many animals of a particular species are willing to do work for us, that does not mean every individual wants to work, or to do so every day' (Coulter 2017: 175). In other words, I would suggest that humane jobs for dogs are possible, for example, but that does mean that all types of canine labour are appropriate, or that every dog is suitable for any occupation. Service, therapy, and facility dogs require particular temperaments, personalities, and attitudes. The same applies to equine-assisted or other farm-based therapy work. Both the *emotional labour* (the outwardly performative dimensions) and the linked *emotion work* demands (the internal management of feelings) of these kinds of jobs are significant. Not all individuals are able to or want to perform emotional labour or engage in emotion work in these ways. High-energy dogs, for example, are better suited for other tasks, and will be more likely to prefer more physically rigorous work, such as detection/scenting (search and rescue, endangered species or poacher detecting, etc.).[7] Here animals' breeds play a role, but genetic reductionism is not useful. Domesticated animals are both biological and social beings, and are therefore affected by their physical make-up *and* their life histories and experiences (Coulter 2018).

These dynamics also segue with the question of consent and the right to choose whether to work or not. Such dynamics are bound up with much larger questions about animals' legal status, the details of which are significant, substantive, and beyond the scope of this discussion (see Kymlicka 2017 for a synthesis). Nevertheless, I would suggest that an essential element of humane jobs for animals is that the animal be both *suitable for and interested in* the job, regardless of their legal status. Animals should not be asked to do things which do not smoothly extend from their physical and psychological abilities, and which they do not want to do. This does not mean animals cannot be challenged in certain ways that are ethically defensible (see Cochrane's chapter 3 in this volume), but rather that dramatic distortions of their abilities and *demands* are inappropriate.

Animals' acts of resistance have long interested abolitionists, but as noted in this volume's introduction, animals' agency is now recognized as manifesting in a broader range of actions including disobedience as well as positive/protective defiance, collaboration, initiative, care, among others. Most animals, even those who are socioculturally and economically privileged in human terms, still have their lives largely organized by humans to suit human purposes. Yet on-the-ground, in a number of human–animal contexts, the dynamics of consent are somewhat more complex, and processes of negotiation occur on a daily basis as

---

[7] See chapter 4 by D'Souza, Hovorka, and Niel in this volume.

animals make their views known. Assertions that all human–animal work relationships are about domination and coercion are inaccurate and are not often rooted in direct or long-term observation or proper understanding of such spaces.

For example, even though horses may not be able to choose where they live or with whom they work, many people are increasingly striving to be attuned to what specifically the horses want to do, for how long, and why. In a growing number of equine cultures and contexts, antiquated training practices like 'breaking' horses have been replaced with interactive strategies premised on collaboration, a commitment to understanding, and tools of communication, not coercion. Once horses are actively participating in different activities with people, communicative negotiations often continue. Birke and Thompson (2018: 125) call these 'applications to withdraw' and identify them as active processes driven by awareness of horses' sentience and agency (see also Coulter 2014; Dashper 2017). Harmful practices have not been completely eradicated by any means, and humans who rely on animals for income are undoubtedly affected by this financial relationship. But dialogic processes and ethically informed approaches are more common in many horse–human contexts than critics who do not study such cultures directly allege.

Similarly, among the service dog users and the social workers facilitating animal-assisted therapy that I have studied, such dynamics are equally if not more salient. Therapy animals normally work part-time and either travel to sites or are visited. Service animals (guide, personal support, emotional support, PTS [post-traumatic stress], and other formal titles) more often labour for and live with one specific person, and may be 'on-call' around the clock, although specific times for leisure are normally also provided. For social workers, counsellors, and others engaged in animal-assisted therapy, an ethic of care is driving the work in a full sense, so it is not particularly surprising that those in the field are demonstrating a strong commitment to caring as an active process (see, for example, Evans and Gray 2011; Ryan 2014). In my preliminary research with equine-assisted therapists in Canada, 76 per cent of them identify the horses as healers, 66 per cent see them as co-therapists, and 45 per cent as co-workers. Notably 'worker' is not normally a term therapists ascribe to themselves (see Carlsson 2017) because the term still evokes the image of a blue-collar, manual, male labourer in many cultures and is linked with narrowly Marxian-rooted conceptualizations of labour. But the horses' active participation in the formal context of therapy and as *provisioning* care work is being explicitly recognized in a growing number of cases.

More significantly, many practitioners have established guidelines that they employ in their own practice to respect and protect the animals. These can reflect and outline guiding or foundational ethical principles, and/or practical logistics such as the length of sessions, the frequency of sessions, and the right for animals to remove themselves while working. This third dimension is commonly

38 ANIMAL LABOUR

highlighted, and again is framed as an ongoing *process*, one involving the practitioners' continuous attentiveness to the animals. Many of the people who work with therapy animals are adamant about removing the animals whenever they show signs of discomfort or fatigue, and/or changing the expectations or sites altogether, based on feedback from the animals. Some assert that their first responsibility is to the animals.

For young women in particular who employ service and guide dogs, both the physical and emotional well-being of the animals is a high priority. This has translated into the creation of interspecies languages through which the dogs can indicate their discomfort and desire to be removed or released; positive opportunities for the dog to engage in different activities; and ways for the dog to communicate what they want to do (through responses to specific collars/vests, for example). I do not know the degree to which these approaches are generalizable, and as someone who believes strongly in data, I am reluctant to make a broad claim. I do note that in the scholarly arena, there is a shortage of empirical studies of animals' labour in both service and therapy but that a number of research projects focusing on such dynamics are underway. There are also scholarly critiques of practices in service and therapy that make broad statements about how animals are treated therein, yet these are not rooted in extensive, or, in some cases, *any* fieldwork. There is a clear need for more research.

Such developments do not solve the challenge of consent by any means, but add important nuance to the conversation and suggest areas for further inquiry.[8] Admittedly, most of my discussion has focused on interactive and localized expressions of agency, what Sue Donaldson and Will Kymlicka (2016a) deem micro-agency. Here I have also focused on animals' desire to withdraw from work or workplace activities, rather than exploring their potential ability to choose to do specific work for others, something I have considered more elsewhere and referred to as informal voluntary labour (Coulter 2016a: ch. 2). Blattner's chapter 5 in this volume also delves more deeply into questions of consent. I am not certain that animals are cognitively able to comprehend the high standard of assent or the full implications of consenting to an occupation. They may only be able to indicate interest or a lack thereof in specific tasks or labour processes, not the very process of work itself (see also Cochrane 2014). Nevertheless, if an animal continually rejects the requisite tasks, it would certainly be reasonable to translate that into a rejection of the job. These are not simple issues and there is a need to think beyond the everyday and interactive, to the organizational, policy, and larger political level, and about what our responsibilities are to animals, whether they can fully understand or not. Here I have proposed a very basic set of standards that I see as the most basic fundamentals in order to encourage further discussion. We ought

---

[8] See Coulter 2016a especially pp. 78–9 and pp. 142–3 for longer albeit still insufficient discussions of the complexities of free/unfree labour for humans and other species alike.

to aim higher and for a more robust approach to animals' potential engagements in humane jobs.

Toward Humane Jobs *and* Work-Lives for Animals: Experiences in Context

A more holistic, contextualized, and multidimensional approach to animals and their working lives is integral to analysis of the potential for them to engage in humane jobs. I have proposed the continuum of suffering and enjoyment as a tool which can be applied to all contexts where animals are being asked (or required) to engage in labour. The concept is designed to challenge humans to determine where animals' work fits thereon and why. The continuum is thus intended, first and foremost, to emphasize animals' experiences which can be positive, negative, or something more complicated. It also encourages us to recognize commonalities/patterns and context-specific differences, as well as fluidity and changes which can occur quite quickly or acutely, or over a longer period of time.

Where animals' experiences of labour will be located on the continuum will be affected by a range of factors including:

- the species;
- the individual animal's own preferences, personality, and agency;
- animals' bodies and physical well-being;
- animals' minds, emotions, and psychological well-being;
- animals' social interactions and relationships with people and other animals; this includes employers and/or co-workers, and interactional dynamics which are 'away' from formal work;
- the environment(s), the objects therein (or absent), and animals' interactions with both;
- the occupation;
- the tasks or labours required or involved;
- the equipment used and how it is employed;
- the time of year and/or weather.

Animals will communicate about their physical and psychological state in deliberate and unintentional ways, and humans have an ethical responsibility to not only be attuned to animals' modes of communication, but to take what they are saying seriously. This requires being attentive to body language, gestures, sounds, facial and eye expressions, levels of energy, degrees of (inter)activity, overall comportment, and so forth, and awareness of both species-level patterns identified by ethologists and comparable researchers, as well as individual specificities. For example, all horses indicate anger and a desire for someone to step away

40 ANIMAL LABOUR

by pinning their ears back. This is how they communicate such a desire in 'horse'.[9] This gesture is decidedly different than the simple act of them turning their ears backwards which can be about listening or a reflection of boredom. In the interest of fostering correct interpretation, knowledge of animals as both biological beings and social actors—collectively and individually—is essential for properly determining where they fit on the continuum. This also reaffirms the value and importance of building from the knowledge of front-line workers, particularly those who are conscientious and committed to knowing the animals with/for whom they work. The continuum is intended to complement and build from the growing bodies of cognitive ethology and animal welfare science, and offer a more 'sociological' framing which is understandable and usable by researchers and workers alike.

Indeed, in some cases, the job assigned to an animal may fit somewhere in between the two poles of the continuum, and it might be possible to move the job over to the enjoyment side through specific changes to the tasks and/or their duration, some specifics of the work, the animal's opportunities outside of work, and so forth. At the same time, it is important to recognize that an animal's experiences may have previously been positioned on the enjoyment side but can shift into more negative terrain for a number of reasons including because of an atypical isolated event or development, or because the animal is ageing, a friend was taken away, the job is repetitive and more monotonous, etc. The continuum is thus a useful analytical starting place which can be enlisted to begin to determine whether the employment might be considered humane for the animals, whether certain changes could help and are thus needed, or if there is little to no potential to remedy the situation and therefore an alternative should be found (often retirement but in certain cases a more substantive change in occupation could be appropriate).

The multifaceted set of factors influencing animals' experiences outlined above also make clear that labour is a process, and a highly social process. Animals' formal engagements in work affect their experiences, relationships, and lives 'away' from work—and vice versa. Without question, what happens 'outside' of work affects their minds and bodies, and therefore their work. As a result, we ought to consider the formal work/jobs, but not in isolation. A more thorough approach recognizes not only animals' work but also their *work-lives*. As is the case for humans, there is no rigid separation of their embodied existence and experiences. Strained familial relationships affect moods, levels of energy, degrees of focus, and so on, when 'at work', for example. Similarly, experiences of disrespect, conflict, and demands on the job bleed into and influence 'home life'. The number and type of connections are extensive.

---

[9] Here the labour process concept of communication work can be helpful for understanding the creation of interspecies languages at work (see especially Coulter 2016a).

Feminist scholars have long critiqued dichotomous conceptualizations of the public and private spheres for these (and other) reasons. Cognizance of such inextricability and fluidity has, in some cases, translated into tangible changes in how labour organizations—and certain employers—operate. Compensation for or the providing of childcare during 'after hours' meetings is one example. Discussions of 'work–life balance' have sought to mitigate employment pressures and how they affect workers' lives more broadly. Some labour unions have explicitly sought to recognize and create spaces for organizing around the challenges workers face in their homes, communities, and 'everyday lives' (Kenny 2011). Jane McAlevey (2016) has highlighted the practical importance of these connections and of seeing 'whole workers'.

The concept of work-lives extends from this and similar bodies of scholarship, and from recognition of the realities of human and animal lives. Studying or caring only about 'work' results in an incomplete and partial picture of labour and reflects an androcentric and 'Western' post-enlightenment pattern of binary creation. In contrast, through the concept of work-lives, we see workers in their actual contexts. This involves taking their physical, intellectual, and emotional well-being before and after formal work seriously. It therefore involves thinking about their lives both a) before and after work on a daily basis, and b) before and after their formal careers over the course of their lives. For humans we do the latter to some degree, and thus have developed childcare and early childhood education, as well as pensions, elder care, and the very idea of retirement. I argue that we need to do something similar for animals. The concept of work-lives encourages a holistic approach that re-places animals into their own lives twenty-four hours a day, each year of their lives. In keeping with the breadth of considerations outlined alongside the continuum of suffering and enjoyment, it means taking seriously animals' social desires and needs, their relationships, the structure of their days, their housing, among other interrelated factors. It involves seeing them not only as 'whole workers' but also as whole beings. They have interests, relationships, and desires that are connected to and affected by, yet also separate from their formal work—and vice versa.

Toward Humane Jobs: Next Steps?

In the anthropocentric literatures and political debates about job quality, terms like good work, decent work, and meaningful work are used, and enlisted differently. Notably, some such conceptualizations prioritize both material conditions (pay, hours, benefits, etc.) and experiential dimensions (feelings of respect, dignity, having opportunities to express one's knowledge and creativity, and/or for upward mobility). These elements inform my thinking about humane jobs for animals, despite not being tidily applicable. As noted earlier, I have developed

42 ANIMAL LABOUR

multiple facets under the humane jobs umbrella, most of which focus on replacing harmful human labour in order to move the economy and workforce away from damaging industries and practices, and to create humane jobs to both replace those eliminated, and to proactively foster more caring and sustainable societies. This seems to be the top priority for those interested in animal well-being and multispecies labour issues given the number of animals affected and the severity of their suffering.

So when grappling with the prospects for humane jobs *for* animals, is the goal simply for animals who work for us to tolerate their jobs and not be harmed by them—is that a high enough bar? Conversely, do particular kinds of labour pursued under the appropriate conditions offer enjoyment and other benefits to animals who participate? Or would humane jobs be something in the middle? These are also questions without easy answers. Alasdair Cochrane's contribution to this volume explores them in more detail, and our chapters should be read as complementary, with his offering a more philosophical and aspirational emphasis. In a similar vein, a small collection of scholarship is beginning to interrogate what rights animals could or ought to have if they are seen as community members or, potentially, citizens (see, for example, Donaldson and Kymlicka 2011). What are the implications if we ask tough questions like what kind of lives animals would like to live? This is particularly crucial if we take seriously the *lives* aspects of potential humane work-lives for animals, and seek to ensure them their species-equivalent of bread and roses—not only what they need, but what they desire and can relish. Humane jobs are not only an opportunity to eliminate suffering, but also an invitation to generate and cultivate progressive new ideals, relationships, and multispecies cultures.

Overall, I am hesitant to take a prescriptive approach which seeks to define in more detail what exactly humane jobs for animals are and are not, and I am particularly reluctant to do so without more data. That said, I see particular potential for humane jobs for animals to engage in the provisioning of care work, an arena of great interest to feminists. I have no qualms about arguing that jobs that engage animals in caring for others are promising areas of potential for achieving a high benchmark of humane-ness. Other fields, including conservation, also offer possibilities, as do cross-field tasks like scent-detection. Yet more empirically rooted and context-specific analysis is needed and should be ongoing, as made clear by D'Souza, Hovorka, and Niel's chapter 4 in this volume.

Indeed, the challenges of developing more robust and specific approaches to defining humane jobs for animals are about both the what and the how. What are the principles, rights, protections, and/or benefits that should be afforded to animals? And how are these principles, rights, protections, and/or benefits a) assessed, and b) promoted and enforced? There is no single answer to any of these questions, and I would posit that the specifics are best determined in collaborative and context-specific ways shaped by the particulars of the place, time, employment sector/sub-sector, and individuals involved. Both animal-focused practice and/or scholarship, and anthropocentric labour praxis will offer ideas.

Possibilities may rest in frameworks such as Nussbaum's (2000) 'capability' theory, which highlights central capabilities: life, bodily health, bodily integrity, senses, imagination, and thought, emotions, practical reason, affiliation, other [or own] species, play, control over one's environment,[10] and in the other frameworks elucidated in this volume's introduction. At the same time—or alternatively— existing anthropocentric frameworks used to promote job quality may also have utility, in addition to having the pragmatic utility of being a familiar approach to worker well-being which could be more easily 'taken up' by humans accustomed to such tools and strategies. For example, a core set of labour rights could be created, akin to those Cochrane (2016) and I have proposed. These could include the right to refuse work, the right to healthy and safe conditions, and the right to leisure time and autonomy, and additional, context-specific dimensions reflective of the particulars of the individual animals involved and the type of work in which they are engaged. Such fundamentals could form the foundation, and then workplace, sector-specific, or even individualized, animal-specific principles could be developed to reflect additional needs, rights, details, and benefits.

The related matters of assessment and enforcement or regulation are salient, and there may be roles for labour unions, public policy, and legislation. How the organizations which most commonly and widely advocate for such protections for human workers—labour unions—will or will not be involved is an open question. My research has not identified any contemporary collective agreements which conceptualize animals as honourary members or beings worthy of the union's protection specifically, and unions'/unionized workers' efforts more often either focus on human concerns, or argue that animals benefit when people are better treated/have greater protections, smaller workloads, etc. (which can be correct in some instances).[11] Sweden's public sector union, Kommunal, stands out as the exception which has begun to lead discussions about the animals with whom their human members work in animal-assisted therapy and other care workplaces. Indeed, human-focused care workers and those already working with animals in the care sector are likely to have insights of value. Unions' efforts could extend to collective bargaining and/or social unionist strategies such as coalition formation. Unions representing workers in animal-harming industries will likely defend their existing members therein, however, they may ultimately realize that 'a just and caring society cannot condone the exploitation and oppression of others, and cannot be built atop a mass, unmarked animal graveyard' (Coulter 2016b: 213).

---

[10] See Lerner and Silfverberg 2019 for an analysis of the potential applicability of this list to horses in equine-assisted therapy.

[11] There are occasional historical examples of unionized workers who used their bargaining power to try to obtain more for animals (see McShane and Tarr 2007, especially chapter 2).

44 ANIMAL LABOUR

There are few if any labour laws governing animals' work, and protective practices, when present in certain therapeutic and similar sites, remain voluntary and largely individualized. More reflection and research are needed about what public policy or legislation governing animals' conditions would be helpful. As part of this process, key insights could be gleaned from the guidelines developed and being implemented by practitioners on their own, and from generating new ideas.

I also see potential in developing an interspecies equivalent to gender-based analysis, a conceptual and analytical approach which seeks to determine how different actions, policies, and programmes affect women and men similarly and differently. Intersectionality-based policy analysis has gone further and argued for examination of how different groups of women and men are similarly and differently positioned, and affected by a range of social factors such as class, ethnoracial identity, citizenship status, ability, sexuality, and so on. Species could be added to the mix as another axis of inequality. Alternatively, the idea of intersectionality, or internal heterogeneity (or something less academic and more accessible), could be applied to examine how different animals are themselves infused with socially constructed and biologically rooted factors that shape their position within multi-species workplaces. In contexts where animals and humans are working side by side, such multispecies analytical tools, along with the continuum of suffering and enjoyment, could be employed to assess how specific practices and changes would affect both human and animal workers, and as part of developing the most ethical paths forward. Both ethological and ethical frameworks will be helpful when observing, interpreting, assessing, and making recommendations.

In this chapter I have sought to begin a more comprehensive discussion about humane jobs and work-lives for animals, and how to think about the prospects for certain animals to have both. Yet in many ways, I have raised more questions than I have answered. Indeed, in the small but growing body of scholarship on human–animal labour, the emphasis is often on what animals do for us. Although this is important, it is not sufficient. We ought to be thinking more carefully about this question: what can and should we do for animals? There is much more work for us to do.

References

Abrell, Elan L. 2016. *Saving Animals: Everyday Practices of Care and Rescue in the US Animal Sanctuary Movement.* Doctoral dissertation, City University of New York.

Birke, Lynda, and Kirrilly Thompson. 2018. *(Un)Stable Relations: Horses, Humans and Social Agency.* London: Routledge.

Carlsson, Catharina. 2017. 'Triads in Equine-Assisted Social Work Enhance Therapeutic Relationships with Self-Harming Adolescents'. *Clinical Social Work Journal* 45(4): 320–31.

Cochrane, Alasdair. 2014. *Animal Rights Without Liberation: Applied Ethics and Human Obligations*. New York: Columbia University Press.

Cochrane, Alasdair. 2016. 'Labour Rights for Animals'. In *The Political Turn in Animal Ethics*, edited by Robert Garner and Siobhan O'Sullivan, 15–32. London: Rowman & Littlefield.

Coulter, Kendra. 2014. 'Herds and Hierarchies: Class, Nature, and the Social Construction of Horses in Equestrian Culture'. *Society & Animals* 22(2): 135–152.

Coulter, Kendra. 2016a. *Animals, Work, and the Promise of Interspecies Solidarity*. New York: Palgrave Macmillan.

Coulter, Kendra. 2016b. 'Beyond Human to Humane: A Multispecies Analysis of Care Work, its Repression, and its Potential'. *Studies in Social Justice* 10(2): 199–219.

Coulter, Kendra. 2016c. 'Humane Jobs: A Political Economic Vision for Interspecies Solidarity and Human–Animal Wellbeing'. *Politics and Animals* 2(1): 67–77.

Coulter, Kendra. 2017. 'Towards Humane Jobs: Recognizing Gendered and Multi-species Intersections and Possibilities'. In *Gender, Work, and Climate Change in the Global North: Work, Public Policy and Action*, edited by Marjorie Griffin Cohen, 167–82. Milton Park: Routledge.

Coulter, Kendra. 2018. 'Challenging Subjects: Towards Ethnographic Analyses of Animals'. *Journal for the Anthropology of North America* 21(2): 58–71.

Coulter, Kendra. 2019. 'Horses' Labour and Work-Lives: New Intellectual and Ethical Directions'. In *Equine Cultures in Transition: Ethical Questions*, edited by Jonna Bornemark, Petra Andersson, and Ulla Ekström von Essen, 17–31. Milton Park: Routledge.

Dashper, Katherine. 2017. 'Listening to Horses: Developing Attentive Interspecies Relationships Through Sport and Leisure'. *Society & Animals* 25(3): 207–24.

De Waal, Frans. 2016. *Are We Smart Enough to Know How Smart Animals Are?* New York: WW Norton.

Donaldson, Sue, and Will Kymlicka. 2011. *Zoopolis: A Political Theory of Animal Rights*. Oxford: Oxford University Press.

Donaldson, Sue, and Will Kymlicka. 2015. 'Farmed Animal Sanctuaries: The Heart of the Movement?' *Politics and Animals* 1(1): 50–74.

Donaldson, Sue, and Will Kymlicka. 2016a. 'Rethinking Membership and Participation in an Inclusive Democracy: Cognitive Disability, Children, Animals'. In *Disability and Political Theory*, edited by Barbara Arneil and Nancy Hirschmann, 168–97. Cambridge: Cambridge University Press.

Evans, Nikki, and Claire Gray. 2011. 'The Practice and Ethics of Animal-Assisted Therapy with Children and Young People: Is It Enough that We Don't Eat Our Co-Workers?' *British Journal of Social Work* 42(4): 1–18.

Fischer, Bob, and Josh Milburn. 2019. 'In Defence of Backyard Chickens'. *Journal of Applied Philosophy* 36(1): 108–23.

Fitzgerald, Amy J. 2007. '"They Gave Me a Reason to Live": The Protective Effects of Companion Animals on the Suicidality of Abused Women'. *Humanity & Society* 31(4): 355–78.

46 ANIMAL LABOUR

Fraser, Nancy. 1997. *Justice Interruptus: Critical Reflections on the 'Postsocialist' Condition*. New York: Routledge.

Kenny, Bridget. 2011. 'Reconstructing the Political? Mall Committees and South African Precarious Retail Workers'. *Labour, Capital and Society/Travail, capital et société* 44(1): 44–69.

Kymlicka, Will. 2017. 'Social Membership: Animal Law Beyond the Property/Personhood Impasse'. *Dalhousie Law Journal* 40(1): 123–55.

Hager, Lori D. (ed.). 1997. *Women in Human Evolution*. New York: Routledge.

Haraway, Donna J. 1989. *Primate Visions: Gender, Race, and Nature in the World of Modern Science*. New York: Routledge.

Irvine, Leslie. 2013a. *My Dog Always Eats First: Homeless People and Their Animals*. Boulder, CO: Lynne Rienner Publishers.

Irvine, Leslie. 2013b. 'Animals as Lifechangers and Lifesavers: Pets in the Redemption Narratives of Homeless People'. *Journal of Contemporary Ethnography* 42(1): 3–30.

Lem, Michelle, Jason B. Coe, Derek B. Haley, Elizabeth Stone, and William O'Grady. 2013. 'Effects of Companion Animal Ownership Among Canadian Street-Involved Youth: A Qualitative Analysis'. *Journal of Sociology & Social Welfare* 40(4): 285–304.

Lerner, Henrik, and Gunilla Silfverberg. 2019. 'Martha Nussbaum's Capability Approach and Equine Assisted Therapy'. In *Equine Cultures in Transition: Ethical Questions*, edited by Jonna Bornemark, Petra Andersson, and Ulla Ekström von Essen, 57–68. Milton Park: Routledge.

Luxton, Meg. 1980. *More Than a Labour of Love: Three Generations of Women's Work in the Home*. Toronto: Canadian Scholars' Press.

Luxton, Meg, and Kate Bezanson (eds.). 2006. *Social Reproduction: Feminist Political Economy Challenges Neo-Liberalism*. Kingston: McGill-Queen's University Press.

McAlevey, Jane F. 2016. *No Shortcuts: Organizing for Power in the New Gilded Age*. Oxford: Oxford University Press.

McShane, Clay, and Joel Tarr. 2007. *The Horse in the City: Living Machines in the Nineteenth Century*. Baltimore: John Hopkins University Press.

Mellor, David J. 2016. 'Updating Animal Welfare Thinking: Moving Beyond The "Five Freedoms" Towards "A Life Worth Living"'. *Animals* 6(3): 1–20.

Milburn, Josh. 2018. 'Death-Free Dairy? The Ethics of Clean Milk'. *Journal of Agricultural and Environmental Ethics* 31(2): 261–79.

Noske, Barbara. 1989. *Humans and Other Animals: Beyond the Boundaries of Anthropology*. London: Pluto Press.

Noske, Barbara. 1997. *Beyond Boundaries: Humans and Animals*. Montréal: Black Rose Books.

Ryan, Thomas (ed.). 2014. *Animals in Social Work: Why and How They Matter*. New York: Palgrave Macmillan.

Stuart, Diana, Rebecca L. Schewe, and Ryan Gunderson. 2013. 'Extending Social Theory to Farm Animals: Addressing Alienation in the Dairy Sector'. *Sociologia Ruralis* 53(2): 201–22.

Waring, Marilyn. 1999. *Counting For Nothing: What Men Value and What Women Are Worth*. Toronto: University of Toronto Press.

3

Good Work for Animals

Alasdair Cochrane

The idea that animals enjoy work is a familiar one. Indeed, one handler was recently quoted in a news story in the UK saying: 'Sam lives for the joy of working, praise from me—and the occasional doughnut' (Burchell 2013). Sam is a 'rothound': a golden Labrador whose job is to detect dry rot in Britain's stately homes. Rothounds are of huge value to those charged with conserving historical buildings because of their ability to sniff out the fungus that causes the rot at source. This allows the rot to be treated much more accurately and effectively than if it were left to humans alone. Peter Monaghan, Sam's handler and trainer, came across Sam in a rescue centre in Cumbria in the North of England, after his previous family had found him too boisterous to live with. As he makes clear in the quotation, Mr Monaghan is convinced that Sam is leading a flourishing life, and that this is down to his work.

Such sentiments about working animals are commonplace. It is normal to hear people who work alongside animals saying that the animals *enjoy* their work, *thrive* in their work, and even *need* to work (see chapter 4 of this volume by D'Souza, Hovorka, and Niel). And such descriptions are given for a wide range of animals working in a variety of different forms of employment—whether it be dogs herding sheep, horses being ridden for human therapy, geese acting as guards, cats preying on pests, and so on.

But are these claims valid? Are some forms of work good for certain animals? Or are these claims nefarious attempts to justify the human use and exploitation of animals? This chapter seeks to explore whether work can be good for certain animals, and if so, what such work might look like.

To be clear, the chapter is not focused on identifying the ways in which work is *bad* for animals. Other scholars have successfully exposed and condemned the brutal and exploitative practices carried out against them in the name of work (Noske 1997). Indeed, the extent of the harms perpetrated against working animals—on farms, in laboratories, in puppy mills, in combat training, and so on—has led many to conclude that such suffering is a *necessary* feature of animal work, and thus to call for its abolition (Francione 2008). In more recent years, however, there has been a trend within animal studies scholarship to imagine how more just interspecies relations might be brought about (Donaldson and

---

Alasdair Cochrane, *Good Work for Animals* In: *Animal Labour: A New Frontier of Interspecies Justice?*. Edited by: Charlotte Blattner, Kendra Coulter, and Will Kymlicka, Oxford University Press (2020).
© Oxford University Press. DOI: 10.1093/oso/9780198846192.003.0003

Kymlicka 2011). As part of this, I have conducted research (Cochrane 2016) into whether particular forms of work for some animals might be rendered *harmless* if reformed and regulated by recognition of working animals' *labour rights*. This chapter seeks to go beyond the question of harmless work, and contribute to the question of what Kendra Coulter (2017) has called 'humane work'; that is, work which is positively *good for* animals. After all, when it comes to the work done by human beings, few of us believe that jobs should merely be harmless. Many of us believe instead that we ought to organize societies so that they provide opportunities for 'decent', 'meaningful', or what I will call 'good work': that is, work which actively contributes to individuals' well-being and flourishing. For this reason, many states at least aim to instigate policies that do not just protect human workers from harm, but also help individuals to lead meaningful, autonomous, and fulfilling working lives. Such policies range from the public provision of education and training, giving career advice, and providing investment in industry and other sectors to boost or maintain employment.

So can work also promote the well-being of non-human animals? This chapter will argue that in some circumstances good work for animals is possible. In so doing, it will survey four of the most common proposed elements of good work for humans—self-realization, pleasure, autonomy, and self-respect—to see if and how they might apply to animals. It will conclude by arguing that good work for animals has a three-fold basis: it provides pleasure, including through affording opportunities to use and develop skills; it allows for the exercise of animals' agency; and it provides a context in which animals can be esteemed as valuable workers and members of the communities in which they labour.

Before starting in earnest, it is important to be clear about the type of animal work with which this chapter is primarily concerned. The focus of the chapter will be on that work conducted by domesticated animals and assigned by humans within mixed human–animal societies; what Coulter (2016: 61) has labelled 'formal work'. So I borrow from Samuel Clark (2017: 62), to take work to refer to those familiar things that are done in 'fields, factories, offices, schools, shops, building sites, call centres, homes, and so on, to make a life and living'. However, this is not to deny that domesticated animals do not perform other forms of labour, as for example companion animals do when they protect and care for others in homes all around the world. And nor is it to deny that wild animals also work, whether that be in providing subsistence for themselves, or certain vital services for human beings and other species (Coulter 2016: 60–1). I focus on formal work in particular because I am primarily interested in understanding if work can be good for animals when it is assigned and directed by humans. Whether the chapter's conclusions have relevance for the other forms of work which animals carry out is left for future consideration and research.

50 ANIMAL LABOUR

Self-Realization

According to Jon Elster (1986), at the centre of Marxism is a specific conception of the good life—*self-realization*—which is facilitated by free, creative, and skilful productive activity (see also Attfield 1984: 147–8). This understanding of human well-being is perfectionist in nature, whereby individual flourishing is tied to the exercise of the essential capacities of one's species (Attfield 1984: 145; Clark 2017: 63). On this Marxist view, the essential capacity of humans—their 'species-being'—is to intentionally labour on and transform the world. The claim is not merely that certain types of work can promote particular humans' interests in some circumstances. Rather, the claim is much stronger: that the good life consists in self-realization, which consists in good work.

So what must our work look like in order for it to be self-realizing? According to Elster (1986: 100), self-realizing work must be active, skilful, and driven towards a goal. It can thus be contrasted with consumption (which is passive), drudgery (which lacks skill), and spontaneous interaction (which is not goal-driven). Most clearly, then, good and self-realizing work can be contrasted with the highly stratified division of labour in industrial societies, in which persons specialize in very specific and often repetitive tasks to standards and speeds set by others. In contrast to the dominant view in the history of Western political thought, whereby humans must be free from work in order to develop the highest parts of their nature (Kandiyali 2014: 117), this position sees free, conscious, and creative productive labour *as* the highest parts of our nature.

So might good work for *animals* be that which is self-realizing? Initially, there are reasons to be doubtful. After all, Marx famously excluded animals from his account of productive labour. For him, the work of humans and animals is qualitatively different: humans produce beyond physical need, but animals do not; humans can produce as a species, while animals can only produce as individuals; and humans labour according to a range of standards, but animals only produce according to fixed standards for their species (Marx 1994: 64). Marx would thus reject the idea that free and conscious labour is even possible for non-human animals, let alone necessary for their self-realization and flourishing.

And yet, there are good reasons to reject the qualitative distinctions that Marx draws between human and non-human work. We can certainly find examples of non-human animals working in ways which Marx assumes to be the sole preserve of humans: predator animals, for instance, often kill beyond their physical needs (Cochrane 2010: 100). And we can find examples of humans who fail to live up to these standards: young infants, for example, cannot meaningfully be said to labour at all, let alone as part of 'a species'. For these reasons, the differences in the work of humans and animals seem to be of degree rather than kind (Clark 2014).

Furthermore, self-realization does appear to be a concept which can straight-forwardly be applied to animals. After all, self-realization is achieved through the exercise of one's species' essential capacities—and certain forms of animal work seem to facilitate this. Sam the rothound, for example, is quite obviously developing and utilizing his advanced capacities of smelling and tracking. And other examples are easy to think of: training and using pigeons to carry messages can be considered to be developing their remarkable navigation skills; pigs used to search woodlands for truffles are exercising their capacities of smelling and rooting in the earth; geese used to guard property are utilizing their skills of sight, defence, and intimidation; and so on. In all these cases, then, the work might be considered to be 'good' insofar as it contributes to the animals' self-realization.

In my view, however, there are three reasons to be sceptical of seeing good work for animals as that which is self-realizing. The first relates to the very connection between well-being (whether human or animal) and self-realization. Put simply, we ought to doubt this perfectionist understanding of the good life. For the idea that there is a single determinate standard of individual flourishing for each species which is objectively correct seems extremely dubious (Arneson 1987: 520). For example, it is far from obvious why a human who freely chooses a passive and highly pleasurable life of consumption ought to be judged as having low levels of well-being. Indeed, given our different personalities, histories, and desires, it at least seems likely that there are a variety of ways in which individuals can flourish. So while we might recognize that creative and skilful productive activity is enormously valuable for many humans, and perhaps even to be encouraged, it seems wrong to claim that this is the *only* means to lead a life that is good for the individual whose life it is.

Secondly, even if we do accept that self-realization is constitutive of the good life, that still does not show that *work* is necessary to secure it. For example, in the human case, activities that are skilful, creative, and goal-driven can be enacted outside of work. In fact, with shorter hours and higher pay, individuals might be able to achieve even more excellence in their leisure time (Arneson 1987: 525). And the same argument holds true for animals. For example, homing pigeons might be able to better exercise and develop their skills of navigation outside of a working environment—indeed, they are now often commonly trained and used simply for fun.

The final reason to reject identifying good work for animals with self-realization is that it might actually be inimical to animal well-being. In fact, there is always good reason to be wary of applying perfectionist understandings of flourishing to non-human animals, in part because it can often lead to animals' self-realization being equated with self-sacrifice and 'realization-for-others'. For example, perfectionist understandings of well-being can lead to the problematic idea that what is natural for an animal is also deemed to be good for that animal. But such a conclusion cannot meaningfully be drawn in relation to, say, a prey animal being eaten alive (Cripps 2010). Moreover, some applications of perfectionist arguments to domesticated working animals are just as worrying. Indeed,

52 ANIMAL LABOUR

the exploitation of working animals is often justified by claims such as 'they were born to do such work', and 'this is what they are for' (Emery 2013). To an extent, these claims are right: domesticated animals have been selectively bred over centuries in order to possess traits and perform tasks that serve human ends. In this way, these traits and tasks are in some way 'essential' to these animals. However, that does not mean that the use and development of these traits and tasks are good for the animals themselves. Such a line of argument would lead us to some odd conclusions. For example, the so-called Beltsville pigs were injected as embryos with a human growth hormone gene so that they grew bigger, leaner, and quicker than other agricultural pigs (Christiansen and Sandøe 2000). So it makes some sense to say that these animals were self-realizing, excelling as they did in their capacity for carrying meat. However, since these animals suffered from severe organ and joint damage, as well as from a range of other pathologies, it would be absurd to say that they led lives that were good for them.

Skills and Pleasure

While I think that that it is wrong to identify good work with self-realization, there remains something plausible in the idea that good work should entail the opportunity to use and develop one's skills. After all, there is no doubt that using and developing skills can be an important source of *pleasure* in individuals' lives. This is certainly true for humans. For example, in Samuel Clark's (2017) account of good work, a central role is given to the pleasure received from the development of our skills. He argues (67) that the movement between immediate involvement in a task and critical self-evaluation of what one is doing provides a crucial source of satisfaction (see also Attfield 1984: 143). Elster (1986: 104) concurs, arguing that while the 'start-up costs' of skill development might make it unattractive initially, these quickly diminish to be overwhelmed by the enormous gratification that individuals receive from their achievements. In this way, Clark (66) differentiates the skill-developing activity of learning a musical instrument from spot-welding on a production line. The former demands critical self-attention and the conditions for pleasurable skill development; while the latter demands repetitive, non-consciously directed work which is planned and evaluated by someone else.

There are several advantages to understanding work which develops capacities and skills as good insofar as it is a source of pleasure, as opposed to good insofar as it represents the essence of the human species. In the first place, it allows us to eschew the perfectionist view that conducting skill-enhancing productive labour *is* the good life. For example, we can acknowledge that while work which utilizes and enhances skills promotes well-being, it is not the *only* source of human well-being. We can thus recognize the important role of leisure, rest, consumption, and idleness as components of human well-being (Russell 1935). Furthermore, it also allows us to acknowledge that pleasurable skill development can take place outside of work, as Clark's example of learning a musical instrument illustrates. Finally, we can also recognize that there are pleasurable forms of work other than that which are skilful. Indeed, many of us would concur that routine labour can provide its own enjoyments—whether that be because it can provide a holiday from thought (Attfield 1984: 143), because of the satisfaction gained from producing the necessities of life, or because of the enjoyment afforded by social engagement. However, while the pleasures that can be derived from routine and unskilled work must be acknowledged, it is unlikely that humans get much satisfaction if they are *only* pursuing narrow and routine tasks which never provide any opportunity to use and develop their skills. As such, the *opportunity* to derive pleasure from the exercise of skill seems like a necessary condition of good work for humans.

But can the same be said for non-human animals? Do some animals also enjoy developing and using their skills? And do they thus take satisfaction from forms of labour which allow them to do so? There is good reason to believe that many do. Intuitively, at least, it seems perfectly reasonable to suppose that animals do not just suffer from being denied the ability to exercise their natural capacities, but in fact take enjoyment from using them. As William Morris (1886: 21) writes: 'I think that to all living things there is a pleasure in the exercise of their energies, and that even beasts rejoice in being lithe and swift and strong.' And from an evolutionary perspective, it makes sense for animals to take pleasure from the successful use and development of the skills that will help them to flourish (McGowan et al. 2014: 577). Furthermore, there are a number of behavioural studies which have confirmed these assumptions and demonstrated that some animals take real satisfaction from their accomplishments, in much the same way as Elster has described for humans. For example, Hagen and Broom (2004) designed a study with cattle to see if they responded emotionally to their own achievements in an operant learning task. One group of heifers was trained to press a panel to receive a food reward, while a control group was not. The study found that the cattle who mastered the task in order to receive a food reward demonstrated a greater emotional response than the cattle who received the reward without performing the task. A similar study to test the 'eureka effect' in dogs also found that animals achieved a more positive affective state when reacting to their own problem-solving achievements (McGowan et al. 2014).

Now, the conclusion to be drawn from this is not that each and every type of work which allows animals to experience such 'eureka effects' can be considered good. After all, if work entails fleeting moments of pleasure, but in overall terms is experienced as painful, monotonous, frustrating, and so on, then it cannot plausibly be considered as conducive to well-being. Rather, then, the claim is that a necessary (but not sufficient) condition of good work for animals, like for humans, is that it involves the opportunity to take pleasure from the development and use

54   ANIMAL LABOUR

of skills. Once again, this is not to say that such pleasures cannot be found outside of work, or that routine work cannot bring its own enjoyments. But given that all sentient animals possess a variety of physical and mental skills, it seems right that a necessary condition of good work for animals is the opportunity to employ them.

How might such opportunities be provided? What kinds of work will allow animals to take pleasure in developing their skills? While much will depend on the work, skills, and animal in question, there is no doubt of the importance of *variety* in the work (see Morris 1886: 32). This is in part because all animals have numerous skills and capacities. Current forms of employment often allow animals to excel in one particular capacity—sniffing, carrying, hunting, fetching, watching, and so on—to the neglect of all others. But a dog has far more skills than the ability to smell, for example. As such, if a dog such as Sam the rothound is employed primarily to 'sniff', for his work to be good, it must also provide opportunities for him to take enjoyment from using and developing his athletic, social, problem-solving, and other capacities. So the argument here is *not* that good work rules out specialization. It is rather that good specialist jobs must be constructed so as to allow for a range of skills to be employed. Relatedly, without any variety in the work undertaken, it will be very hard for skills to be honed and developed. It is through being confronted with new challenges that individuals come to grow and develop their capacities, and this is as true for animals as it is for humans. For these reasons, then, we can say that good work for animals must have variety in the tasks that are performed; variety to both use and develop the different skills they possess.

But work can also provide sources of pleasure which are not solely attached to the development of skills and capacities—and this is true for both humans and animals. Again, which kinds of work will foster pleasure obviously depends on the species and personality of the individual in question. Nonetheless, I think that it is reasonable to propose that pleasant surroundings and appropriate relations with others are vital (Morris 1886: 34). Starting with pleasant surroundings, then, it is obvious that the majority of contemporary animal workers labour in conditions that are extremely dangerous to their health and vital interests. For work to be harmless for animals it must eradicate these dangers; but for it to be *good*, it must also provide surroundings in which animals can experience stimulation, fun, and joy. The kinds of working environments which help animals to experience pleasure will of course vary. One factor will be how far those environments enable animals to exercise their natural capacities, but others will involve fostering simple pleasures like the ability to feel the warmth of the sun, the cool of the wind, and the comfort of shade. Securing such conditions is clearly easier for some forms of work than for others. For example, it seems relatively straightforward to provide a pleasurable working environment for those pigs who are used to locate and extract truffles; after all, this work necessarily takes place outside in large, open, stimulating woodland. On the other hand, while it might be relatively easy to secure harmless conditions for assistance dogs, creating environments which facilitate joy and pleasure might be tougher. This is simply because most of their working lives are spent in human houses and urban settings. Nonetheless, this should not mean that creating joy-inducing conditions is impossible; with sufficient thought and imagination, for example with plenty of outdoor access and activity, perhaps they too can enjoy their working environments.

Of course, it is not just the physical environment in which they work that can help promote pleasure in the lives of working animals. Social relations can be an important source of joy too. On the one hand, working with others can be important for skill development, in order that individuals can learn, be trained, and hone their particular capacities. But good social relations can be an independent source of pleasure at work. Work should not be regarded simply as a productive activity; for it can also be a tremendous source of joy, laughter, companionship, and fun. In most instances, the reason why work fosters such feelings is because it fosters good social relations. It is important to note that those pleasurable social relations can take place within and between species. Indeed, Jocelyne Porcher (2014) takes the argument one step further to argue that the primary rationale for humans to work with animals is to live and socialize them with.

But what then of solitary work? It is clear that some humans get considerable pleasure from conducting creative, skilful, intensive work all on their own. The lone author or artist working on their magnum opus offers a vivid example of this. But the pleasure some receive from solitary work does not undermine the wider claim that *appropriate* social relations are important for good work. Furthermore, few enjoy working alone all of the time, suggesting that good work must therefore provide the *opportunity* to engage with others. In addition, it is worth remembering that even solitary work relies on important forms of social support (Clark 2017: 69); for no work is or can be conducted entirely independently. Finally, it is likely that fewer animals enjoy solitary work compared to humans. After all, domesticated animals have been bred in part because of their social natures and ability to thrive in mixed human–animal societies. As such, the appropriate social relations for working animals are very likely to be those which entail considerable engagement with others.

In summary, then, we can say that good work for animals is work from which they can take pleasure through having the opportunity to use and develop their various capacities, in pleasant surroundings, and with appropriate social relations. Are these conditions sufficient for good work? The next section argues that they are not.

Autonomy and Agency

Several scholars have argued that good work is not just that which is pleasurable, but also that which is *autonomous*. Autonomy usually refers to the ability to make

56 ANIMAL LABOUR

fundamental choices about the direction of one's life. Autonomous agents can frame, revise, and pursue their own conceptions of the good (Rawls 1993: 72), and it is usually regarded as essential to autonomous agents' well-being to be able to make choices in pursuit of that good (Raz 1988). It is for this reason that Adina Schwartz (1982) argues that it is seriously problematic that so many contemporary workers are employed in jobs where the ends, pace, and standards of the work are set by others than themselves. And more positively, Andreas Eshete (1974: 42) argues that, 'A central feature of meaningful work is that it is autonomous ... Other things being equal, we take pride in work which displays our part in its making.'

For work to be autonomous, then, it clearly needs to be freely chosen. According to the literature, this would seem to require three things of work conducted by humans. First, and most obviously, individual workers should be free to take up and leave particular forms of employment. Slavery and forced labour evidently violate autonomy and are thus the antithesis of good work for humans. Second, when individuals freely choose to work for a corporation or other organization, they should also be able to help direct the goals and strategy of that entity through forms of workplace democracy. And finally, according to Schwartz (1982: 641) respect for autonomy also demands that there must be a sharing of supervisory and routine tasks so that there is no permanent distinction between those who decide and those who execute decisions.

Some might object that all of this is too demanding. For it might be claimed that the importance of autonomy to human well-being relates to their whole lives, meaning that sacrificing some autonomy while in work is fine, so long as humans' lives are autonomous overall. In response, however, Schwartz persuasively argues that autonomy is a matter of integrating one's plans across all areas of one's life (1982: 638), including work, which is certainly a fundamental aspect of our lives. And secondly, she points to evidence which suggests that engaging in non-autonomous work directed by others can lead to a lack of invention and agency outside of work (1982: 637).

But while we might accept autonomy as a necessary component of good work for humans, is the same true in the case of animals? At first blush, there are reasons to be doubtful. For one, autonomy is not as central to the well-being of the vast majority of animals as it is for humans. This is quite simply because most animals are unable to frame, revise, and pursue their own conceptions of the good (Cochrane 2009). While all sentient animals certainly have agency and possess desires which they act upon, they do not have the capacity to reflect on those desires and integrate them into a life plan or set of goals. For this reason, interfering in the lives of animals and making fundamental choices about their lives on their behalf is not necessarily problematic as it is for most humans. While we would rightly regard raising, training, and keeping a human to go and hunt for dry rot or for truffles as a gross affront on human autonomy, doing the same to a dog or a pig is not as obviously problematic. Indeed, it is animals' lack of autonomous agency which makes employing them in work that they have not chosen *not* morally equivalent to human slavery or forced labour.

So does this mean that autonomy is unimportant or irrelevant for good work for animals? Not exactly. For as stated, while animals might not have the capacity to possess or reflect on a 'conception of the good', and thus have no interest in making choices which relate to that good, they do very much have desires and an interest in acting upon those desires. In other words, sentient animals have *agency*. Given that being able to exercise this agency is very often important to the well-being of animals, it is a very plausible criterion of good work for animals.

What would agency-respecting good work for animals look like? In my view, there are at least three aspects to work which respects and promotes animals' agency. In the first place, animals' agency must be respected when animals are chosen for work, and when work is chosen for them. Non-human animals cannot fully consent to being employed in the same way that humans can: they can neither fully understand the purposes for which they are being employed, nor the terms under which they will labour. It is thus plausible to see all forms of animal work as in some sense 'forced' (Cochrane 2016: note 7). Nonetheless, animals can still express desires about whether they want to work, and in what roles. Indeed, current practice in the selection of dogs to work as service or assistance animals often entails choosing individuals with not only the right skills and traits, but also the right *personalities*. Harmless work would thus seem to require *not* selecting for work those animals who resist human company and who refuse to comply with tasks set by others. And in terms of good work, while we cannot select animals who actively desire to sniff out cancers, act as guards, and so on, we can select those who not only seek human company, but also desire the stimulation of being set tasks and problems to solve.

Of course, once animals are selected for work, they will usually also need to be trained in the tasks to be performed. Since animals cannot be fully aware of what precisely they are being trained for, and since they are unlikely to actively desire the precise activities that the training involves, it might seem that training *necessarily* compromises their agency. Nonetheless, I believe that animals' agency can still be respected when they are trained for work. Obviously, for this training to be harmless, many traditional and existing practices, which often involve the use of painful restraints and punishments, must come to an end. Instead, good work must involve forms of training with activities which are desirable because they are enjoyable for the animals involved. For example, Sam's training involved hunting for toys which had been scented appropriately—tasks which his trainer claimed Sam, as a boisterous and lively dog, enjoyed enormously. Of course, this is not to say that training cannot be challenging and even at times frustrating. As previously noted, the development of new skills and capacities often requires effort which can be discomforting. But for such exertions to be considered elements of good work, it must be part of an overall programme that is ultimately desirable for the animals involved.

58 ANIMAL LABOUR

Finally, good work for animals must also permit animals to exercise their agency within the work itself. First of all, in order to be harmless and not engender frustration on the part of animals, animals should have some say over the tasks that they perform. This will again require *variety* in the work: animals should have the opportunity to select from a range of different tasks in their work. But, in my view, good and not merely harmless work requires more than this. For good agency-respecting work also requires animals to have their desires respected in *the planning and strategies* of the organizations for whom they work. In other words, good work requires animals to be included within schemes of *workplace democracy* (Blattner 2019). This is important not only to ensure that these organizations do not enact plans which might be inimical to animal workers, but also to put policies on the table which will enhance the joy and satisfaction that animals receive from their work. In other words, workplace democracy is an important means by which to instigate the kinds of pleasurable and agency-respecting conditions outlined so far.

But how can animal workers participate in workplace democracy? While it is true that animals cannot reflect on and vote for their preferred plans and policies, their interests can still be represented in decision-making. Dedicated representatives of animal workers—like the union representatives of human workers—can speak up for their interests to ensure that their voices help to shape its future direction. It is of course true that the representatives of animals cannot be held to account via periodic election in the same way as the representatives of humans. Nonetheless, other means of ensuring that these representatives act upon the desires of animal workers are available. For one, we can ensure that these representatives are trained in what Andrew Dobson (2014: 175) has called the art of 'good listening'. While animals cannot directly voice their desires, representatives can still listen for and hear them through being attentive to body language, eye movement, facial expression, habit, and so on (Donovan 2006: 321; Meijer 2013). Furthermore, while animals may not be able to choose and select their preferred candidates, a human proxy electorate could certainly do so on their behalf, making accountability through elections a clear possibility (see Dobson 1996; Ekeli 2005).

In sum, then, good work for animals is that which promotes both pleasure and agency. Are pleasure and agency the sufficient conditions of good work for animals? The next section examines a possible further criterion—one which has been proposed as an important element of good work for humans: self-respect.

Self-Respect and Esteem

Jocelyne Porcher (2014: 4) argues, in keeping with many other scholars outlining the conditions for good work, that, 'Work is central to the construction of identity and to the construction of social relations.' And there is surely no doubt that for the majority of humans, an individual's work is an important aspect of that person's identity. Put simply, feeling good about the work that one conducts is an important source of self-respect. It is worth noting that this type of satisfaction is independent of the other pleasures individuals might find in their work. So, for example, a singer might take certain fleeting pleasures from working on the stage, such as when taking the applause of the audience. However, it would be odd to regard such work as good for that individual if the singer saw no value in singing, and was ashamed to make a living out of public performance. Work confers self-respect, then, when it relates to one's autonomous plan of life (Attfield 1984: 144). If the work an individual does conflicts with the aims and ideals that they care about, then it will not confer self-respect and could not plausibly be regarded as 'good'.

As we have already seen, most non-human animals lack the autonomous capacities to frame, revise, and pursue their own conceptions of the good. On this basis, it is hard to see how self-respect can be a necessary element of good work for animals. For example, it is difficult to imagine that an animal who performs on stage could get the same kind of existential angst as a human singer. If an animal wants to perform and takes pleasure from so doing, then it seems initially plausible that such work ought to be considered good for the animal.

However, in the human case, self-respect is not always thought of as something that is derived *solely* from one's own values and judgements. *Other people's* judgements matter just as much, if not more. For this reason, many argue that self-respect is dependent on the *esteem* of others (Atffield 1984: 145). Indeed, John Elster (1986: 106) even goes so far as to argue that esteem is, 'The most important value for human beings', and that, 'Self-esteem derives largely from the esteem accorded one by other people.' Whether or not we agree that esteem is of ultimate value in this way, we surely concur that if others recognize one's work as worthy and valuable, this acts as an important source of self-respect and well-being. And esteem is not and should not be conferred only on those who undertake jobs that are highly paid or which takes years of training. As Elster (106) rightly states, even drudgery can be a source of esteem if it produces things that others want and need.

But does the esteem of others matter for the work which animals conduct? At first glance, it might seem that it does not. After all, it is unlikely that animals will actually *know* whether or not they are held in esteem by others. This is not to say that animals cannot feel shame or embarrassment, and perhaps even pride. But coming to a more fine-grained judgement about whether the work they do is respected and valued by the wider community seems far less likely. Animals generally have little understanding of the ultimate purposes of their work, nor of how that work is regarded by others. It might seem, then, that neither self-respect nor the esteem of others is a necessary component of good work for animals.

60   ANIMAL LABOUR

In my view, however, such a judgement is too hasty, and there is reason to believe that the esteem of society makes a significant contribution to the work of animals too. In the first place, we can be reasonably confident that *not* being held in esteem can lead to harmful treatment in the workplace. If working animals are not respected as workers, but instead despised, disrespected, or commodified, then there is ample evidence that this leads to abuse. The most obvious example of this is the cruel acts which are perpetrated against animals in slaughterhouses (Pachirat 2011; Smithers 2017). Given this, we can reasonably assume that if animals *are* held in esteem by the communities in which they labour, they are more likely to receive better treatment, and not be regarded as mere tools or instruments for human ends. As Coulter (2016: 155) points out, one cannot condone killing someone with whom you feel solidarity.

But while esteem might be important for ensuring that animals' work is harmless, can it also make it *good*? Might societal esteem contribute to the flourishing of individual animals? I believe that it has an indirect role here too. For if a society esteems animals as valuable workers, it seems that it must also get close to recognizing them as active and contributing *fellow members* of that community (Kymlicka 2017: 147). And as several scholars (Donaldson and Kymlicka 2011) have pointed out, animals require recognition as members of our societies in order to live well, and to enjoy the rights that come along with that status—rights to residency, healthcare, retirement provision, political representation, and more.

By way of illustration, consider the case of those animals who work in the police or military. Some of these animals already possess a kind of 'quasi-membership status' in certain communities. For example, these are the few animals to whom some societies have variously awarded retirement pensions (Pleasance 2013), medals of bravery (Baynes 2017), and memorials commemorating those who have died in service (Kean 2014; Johnston 2012). And such acknowledgement is in large part because of the *work* that they conduct. These animals perform tasks that are so familiar to us as work, and which so obviously contribute to the functioning of society, it is little wonder they are widely considered as both workers, and also *quasi-members* of our communities.

To be clear, my point is not that police and military animals are treated perfectly. Obviously, they are not, and are often asked to perform tasks that unjustifiably expose them to incredible risk. Nor is my point that the work which police and military animals conduct is especially worthy of esteem, while other work is not. Just as my aim is not to support the existing ways in which animals are used for work (cf. Eisen 2019), nor is it to support the existing ways on which their work is esteemed. Rather my goal is to point to some *possibilities* of what esteem can and could do for working animals. If animals' work were esteemed as it should be, it would make it more likely that they would be recognized as fellow members of our society, and hence more likely that they would enjoy the entitlements such status affords.

But is societal esteem of animals' work *necessary* for their flourishing? Some might think not. After all, societies could simply recognize the membership of animals directly through granting them full membership status. Indeed, this is the route to membership for human non-workers, and it would presumably have to be the path for animal non-workers too. As such, why can't societies just assign membership to working (and other) animals, irrespective of how that work is viewed by wider society? While societies should of course recognize membership in this way, there is some reason to believe that in order to both *establish and secure* the status of working animals as members, the social esteem of their work is a necessary condition. For there is certainly no doubt that in the absence of a sufficient basis of mutual recognition and support within a community, the formal legal standing of individuals can start to erode in practice (see Doppelt 1984: 72). And in contemporary societies, as the experience of so-called 'welfare ghettoes' demonstrates, one of the most important bases of such support is that which comes through recognizing and valuing each others' work. Put simply, and as the examples of police and military dogs show, valuing the work of animals may be a crucial step in both establishing and securing the status of animals as members of our societies.

In sum, then, I believe that a necessary condition of good work for animals is that it is esteemed by society. This is on the basis that without esteem, the social standing of working animals is in jeopardy. For example, even if Sam the rot-hound takes immense pleasure from his work, without wide recognition that his work is a valuable contribution to society, his status within that society will always be uncertain. Just as it is hard to kill those with whom we have solidarity, it is hard to deny the political status of those whose work we esteem. That is why some have granted pensions to police dogs, and why many are horrified when military service animals are abandoned in conflict zones (Hediger 2013). Good work is that which enhances animals' well-being; and the social esteem of others can facilitate that by establishing and securing their membership in our societies.

Conclusion

This chapter has defended the view that work can not only be harmless but also *good* for certain animals. In so doing, it has argued that good work for animals has a three-fold basis: it is work which provides pleasure, including through affording opportunities to use and develop skills; which allows for the exercise of animals' agency; and which provides a context in which animals can be esteemed as valuable workers who are recognized as members of the communities in which they labour. If an animal conducts work of this kind, then we can feel confident that this work is helping that animal lead a flourishing life.

There is clearly no doubt that very few animals currently employed in human societies enjoy harmless, let alone good work. This should obviously be a source of regret. Moreover, it would also seem to provide a *pro tanto* case to transform our societies so that they provide opportunities for such forms of work; and for employers to strive to create such conditions for the human and animal workers under their charge.

Does this then mean that states *must* provide opportunities for good animal work as a matter of *justice*? It might be the case, for instance, that justice only demands that work is harmless, not that it is also beneficial (see Arneson 1987). However, if esteem is as crucial to the establishment of animals' proper social standing as has been suggested, then justice would also seem to demand good work for animals. After all, without good work, the very basis for establishing and securing membership for working animals will be blocked. The ultimate conclusion of this chapter, then, is that our duties with respect to working animals lie not only in eradicating the serious harms that are currently perpetrated against them, but also in making efforts to get societies to recognize, value, and esteem the work which animals undertake.

References

Arneson, Richard. 1987. 'Meaningful Work and Market Socialism'. *Ethics* 97: 517–45.

Attfield, Robin. 1984. 'Work and the Human Essence'. *Journal of Applied Philosophy* 1: 141–50.

Baynes, Chris. 2017. 'Army Dog Who Helped Save British Troops During Taliban Attack in Afghanistan Awarded Bravery Medal', *The Independent*, 17 November 2017. https://www.independent.co.uk/news/uk/home-news/army-dog-mali-awarded-animal-victoria-cross-dickin-medal-bravery-afghanisan-taliban-attacks-save-a8060606.html

Blattner, Charlotte. 2019. 'Animal Labour: Toward a Prohibition of Forced Labour and a Right to Freely Choose One's Work'. In *Animal Labour: A New Frontier of Interspecies Justice?*, edited by Charlotte Blattner, Kendra Coulter, and Will Kymlicka, 91–115. Oxford: Oxford University Press.

Burchell, Helen. 2013. 'The Sniffer Dog With a Nose for Historic Homes' Dry Rot'. *BBC News*, 28 September. http://www.bbc.co.uk/news/uk-england-23956871

Christiansen, S. B., and Peter Sandøe. 2000. 'Bioethics: Limits to the Interference with Life'. *Animal Reproduction Science* 60–1: 15–29.

Clark, Jonathan L. 2014. 'Labourers or Lab Tools?: Rethinking the Role of Lab Animals in Clinical Trials'. In *The Rise of Critical Animal Studies: From the Margins to the Centre*, edited by Nik Taylor and Richard Twine, 139–64. Abingdon: Routledge.

Clark, Samuel. 2017. 'Good Work'. *Journal of Applied Philosophy* 34: 61–73.

Cochrane, Alasdair. 2009. 'Do Animals Have an Interest in Liberty?'. *Political Studies* 57: 660–79.

Cochrane, Alasdair. 2010. *An Introduction to Animals and Political Theory*. Basingstoke: Palgrave.

Cochrane, Alasdair. 2016. 'Labour Rights for Animals'. In *The Political Turn in Animal Ethics*, edited by Robert Garner and Siobhan O'Sullivan, 15–32. London: Rowman & Littlefield.

Coulter, Kendra. 2016. *Animals, Work and the Promise of Interspecies Solidarity*. Basingstoke: Palgrave.

Coulter, Kendra. 2017. 'Humane Jobs: A Political Economic Vision for Interspecies Solidarity and Human-Animal Well-Being'. *Politics and Animals* 3: 31–41.

Cripps, Elizabeth. 2010. 'Saving the Polar Bear, Saving the World: Can the Capabilities Approach Do Justice to Humans, Animals and Ecosystems?'. *Res Publica* 16: 1–22.

Dobson, Andrew. 1996. 'Representative Democracy and the Environment'. In *Democracy and the Environment: Problems and Prospects*, edited by William M. Lafferty and James Meadowcroft, 124–39. Cheltenham: Edward Elgar.

Dobson, Andrew. 2014. *Listening for Democracy*. Oxford: Oxford University Press.

Donaldson, Sue and Will Kymlicka. 2011. *Zoopolis: A Political Theory of Animal Rights*. Oxford: Oxford University Press.

Donovan, Josephine. 2006. 'Feminism and the Treatment of Animals: From Care to Dialogue'. *Signs* 31(2): 305–29.

Doppelt, Gerald. 1984. 'Conflicting Social Paradigms of Human Freedom and the Problem of Justification'. *Inquiry* 27: 51–86.

Eisen, Jessica. 2019. 'Down on the Farm: Status, Exploitation and Agricultural Exceptionalism'. In *Animal Labour: A New Frontier of Interspecies Justice?*, edited by Charlotte Blattner, Kendra Coulter, and Will Kymlicka, 139–59. Oxford: Oxford University Press.

Ekeli, Kristian Skagen. 2005. 'Giving a Voice to Posterity—Deliberative Democracy and Representation of Future People'. *Journal of Agricultural and Environmental Ethics* 18: 429–50.

Elster, Jon. 1986. 'Self-Realization in Work and Politics: The Marxist Conception of the Good Life'. *Social Philosophy and Policy* 3: 97–126.

Emery, Noemie. 2013. 'Born to Run'. *The New Atlantis* 38, Winter/Spring: 71–80.

Eshete, Andreas. 1974. 'Contractarianism and the Scope of Justice'. *Ethics* 85: 38–49.

Francione, Gary L. 2008. *Animals as Persons: Essays on the Abolition of Animal Exploitation* New York: Columbia University Press.

Hagen, Kristen and Donald Broom. 2004. 'Emotional Reactions to Learning in Cattle'. *Applied Animal Behaviour Science* 85: 203–13.

Hediger, Ryan. 2013. 'Dogs of War: The Biopolitics of Loving and Leaving the U.S. Canine Forces in Vietnam'. *Animal Studies Journal* 2: 55–73.

Johnston, Steven. 2012. 'Animals in War: Commemoration, Patriotism, Death'. *Political Research Quarterly* 65: 359–71.

64 ANIMAL LABOUR

Kandiyali, Jan. 2014. 'Freedom and Necessity in Marx's Account of Communism'. *British Journal for the History of Philosophy* 22: 104–23.

Kean, Hilda. 2014. 'Animals and War Memorials: Different Approaches to Commemorating the Human-Animal Relationship'. In *Animals and War: Studies of Europe and North America*, edited by Ryan Hediger, 237–62. Leiden: Brill.

Kymlicka, Will. 2017. 'Social Membership: Animal Law beyond the Property/Personhood Impasse'. *Dalhousie Law Journal* 40: 123–55.

Marx, Karl. 1994. 'Economic and Philosophic Manuscripts' (selections). In *Karl Marx: Selected Writings*, edited by Lawrence H. Simon, 54–81. Indianapolis, IN: Hackett.

McGowan, Ragen T.S., Therese Rehn, Yezica Norling and Linda J. Keeling. 2014. 'Positive Affect and Learning: Exploring the "Eureka Effect" in Dogs'. *Animal Cognition* 17: 577–87.

Meijer, Eva. 2013. 'Political Communication with Animals'. *Humanimalia* 5 (2013): 28–51.

Morris, William. 1886. 'Useful Work versus Useless Toil'. *The Socialist Platform* 2: 19–39.

Noske, Barbara. 1997. *Beyond Boundaries: Humans and Animals*. Montreal: Black Rose Books.

Pachirat, Timothy. 2011. *Every Twelve Seconds: Industrialized Slaughter and the Politics of Sight*. New Haven: Yale University Press.

Pleasance, Chris. 2013. 'Police Dogs to Get a Pension Plan'. *The Daily Mail*, 5 November.

Porcher, Jocelyne. 2014. 'The Work of Animals: A Challenge for Social Sciences'. *Humanimalia: a Journal of Human/Animal Interface Studies* 6: 1–9.

Rawls, John. 1993. *Political Liberalism*. New York: Columbia University Press.

Raz, Joseph. 1988. *The Morality of Freedom*. Oxford: Clarendon Press.

Russell, Bertrand. 1935. *In Praise of Idleness: and Other Essays*. London: Allen and Unwin.

Schwartz, Adina. 1982. 'Meaningful Work'. *Ethics* 92: 634–46.

Smithers, Rebecca. 2017. 'All Slaughterhouses in England to Have Compulsory CCTV'. *The Guardian*, 11 August. https://www.theguardian.com/environment/2017/aug/11/all-slaughterhouses-in-england-to-have-compulsory-cctv

4

Conservation Canines

Exploring Dog Roles, Circumstances, and Welfare Status

Renée D'Souza, Alice Hovorka, and Lee Niel

Introduction

Dogs are involved in all kinds of work. This work is often mandated by humans and includes providing joy, comfort, and compassion, offering assistance with physical mobility or transport, and assisting search and rescue operations. The work that dogs do can range in circumstances of enabling to exploitative, and range in experiences from enjoyment to suffering. With so many dogs working on behalf of, for, and with people, how might we begin to assess what work is enjoyable, beneficial, and even empowering for the dogs themselves?

Kendra Coulter (2016) posits the idea of 'humane jobs' that are good not only for the people but also for the animals involved. According to Coulter, animals clearly benefit when their use, exploitation, confinement, or death are eliminated from jobs and labour processes, and when there exists increased human attention to caring for and protecting other species. She also argues that it is 'not unreasonable for some domesticated animals to be engaged in certain kinds of work' if founded upon respect, reciprocity, and protection of rights; indeed, animals may enjoy or benefit from 'work and labour relations as members of multispecies workplaces and societies' (Coulter 2016: 73). Building on this conceptual frame of interspecies solidarity, our aim is to engage assessment tools from animal welfare science and qualitative social sciences to document and analyse dog welfare in the conservation sector. Specifically, we explore the roles, circumstances, and welfare status of conservation canines in Canada to assess the extent to which their jobs might be considered 'humane'. To do so, we explore tangible and moral issues related to dog enjoyment of and suffering within conservation work; we highlight the complexity of dogs' work-lives related to issues of freedom and consent.

The organizational structure of our chapter is as follows. First, we offer a contextual overview of dogs working in the conservation sector, including a summary of existing scholarship exploring dog roles, circumstances, and welfare.

Renée D'Souza, Alice Hovorka, and Lee Niel, *Conservation Canines: Exploring Dog Roles, Circumstances, and Welfare Status* In: *Animal Labour: A New Frontier of Interspecies Justice?*. Edited by: Charlotte Blattner, Kendra Coulter, and Will Kymlicka, Oxford University Press (2020). © Oxford University Press.
DOI: 10.1093/oso/9780198846192.003.0004

66   ANIMAL LABOUR

Second, we detail our interdisciplinary methodological approach as grounded in an ethogram of dog behaviour from animal welfare science, as well as semi-structured interviews and participant observation from social sciences. Third, we present our findings from conservation canine teams in Alberta and Ontario, Canada. Fourth, we discuss how our findings might inform assessment of 'humane' jobs—or indeed work-lives offering enjoyment, control, agency, respect, and recognition—for dogs in this sector, for animal labourers more broadly, and for possibilities of further fostering interspecies solidarity.

Conservation Canines

Conservation canines are detection dogs trained to assist biologists and conservationists with environmental protection and wildlife research (AEP 2016b; CC 2018a; WD4C 2015b). Humans have employed dogs for conservation work for more than a century (Reed et al. 2011; Zwickel 1980) and today dogs can be found working for conservation all over the world. Given their scent detection abilities, dogs are employed to locate various animals and plants (Akenson et al. 2004; Arnett 2006; Cablk and Heaton 2006; Goodwin et al. 2010; Gsell et al. 2010; Homan et al. 2001; Mathews et al. 2013; Paula et al. 2011; Savidge et al. 2010; Reindl-Thompson et al. 2006; Robertson and Fraser 2009). Dogs are also employed to locate the scat of various animals to assist with population size and range estimates (Arandjelovic et al. 2015; Beckmann et al. 2015; Brook et al. 2012; Chambers et al. 2015; Cristescu et al. 2015; Davidson et al. 2014; Fukuhara et al. 2010; Harrison 2006; Kerley 2010; Long et al. 2007; Oliveira et al. 2012; Rolland et al. 2006; Smith et al. 2003; Wasser et al. 2004).

Existing scholarship assesses the efficacy of using conservation canines. Studies, for example, identify environmental variables most affecting dogs' ability to detect scat such as precipitation and wind speed/variability (Reed et al. 2011) or highlight preferred physical, psychological, and social dog traits such as tactile nerve strength given variable search environments or high play/food drive (Beebe et al. 2016; Hurt and Smith 2009). Studies also compare dog detection rates with those of humans or conservation equipment/techniques. Dogs detect four times as many scats (Smith et al. 2001) and 29 per cent more faecal samples compared to humans (Oliveira et al. 2012). Dogs are also as effective compared to genetic scat analyses (DeMatteo et al. 2014), surveys by automatic cameras, hair-snares, and scent stations (Harrison 2006; Long et al. 2007), and live-trapping species (Duggan et al. 2011). Finally, studies (Beebe et al. 2016; Miller et al. 1996; Shubert 2012) and conservation organizations (CC 2018b; WD4C 2015a) purport that conservation work gives 'unwanted' shelter dogs a purpose at the same time as nature is conserved (Beebe et al. 2016; Miller et al. 1996; Shubert 2012).

Notably, one in 200–300 shelter dogs exhibits the degree of play drive required for conservation work, and 40 per cent of this limited pool complete training successfully (Hurt and Smith 2009).

The Canadian conservation canine landscape is diverse, with dogs performing a variety of jobs; in Canada, environmental programmes such as conservation canines fall under provincial (rather than federal) jurisdiction and are managed by particular provincial ministries and departments. In Alberta, dogs assist the provincial government with invasive species detection (primarily mussels on watercrafts) and a Karelian bear dog assists a Fish and Wildlife Officer with bear aversion in neighbourhoods and parks. In Ontario, Manitoba, and Saskatchewan, dogs work alongside provincial conservation officers as multispecies enforcement units; they detect gunpowder odour to assist with evidence recovery for crimes such as poaching. In British Columbia, dogs track and protect against cougars who threaten or attack livestock or local communities; recently the Ministry of Environment added a canine team to assist with invasive mussel detection at inspection stations, while an enforcement dog is also available to serve in court cases for evidence recovery. In other provinces, dogs work on specific short-term projects, such as in Quebec where dogs assisted biologists with wood turtle population estimates through nest detection during 2015, or do conservation work as a secondary task (e.g. poaching), such as in New Brunswick where dogs are trained to Royal Canadian Mounted Police standards and work alongside police officers. Alberta and Ontario conservation canine teams were chosen as case studies for this study given their teams' willingness to participate, variety of dog work performed, and proximity to researchers. These two provinces also have the largest canine teams and arguably the most developed and sustained dog-focused conservation programmes. Thus, while offering unique and comparative provincial insights, these case studies together offer a cross-section of conservation canine work in Canada.

Methodology

Our study explores the roles, circumstances, and welfare status of conservation canines in Canada to assess the extent to which their jobs might be considered humane. To do so we employ an interdisciplinary approach combining animal welfare science, specifically behavioural observations of dogs and environmental assessments, and qualitative social science, specifically interviews and participant observation. While the former offers insights into dogs' emotional states during work, the latter provides narrative, relational, and contextual information on dog–handler encounters and dog circumstances in a particular situation or locale. This research was approved by the Queen's University General Research Ethics Board

68   ANIMAL LABOUR

and the University Animal Care Committee; no research permits were required. This chapter is based on D'Souza's Master's thesis work as supervised by Hovorka (D'Souza 2018).

Field research took place between May and September 2017. Data collection included dog behaviour assessments conducted for eight dogs (Alberta n=3, Ontario n=5) during work tasks (n=300 total assessments). Behavioural assessments began when a handler commanded their dog to search for a target and finished when the dog alerted to a target. An ethogram was used to document common and reliable input-based dog welfare criteria (i.e. indicative of the state of the animal) and relational dynamics (i.e. dog–handler interactions). Dog behaviours previously shown to be indicative of dog stress were recorded (e.g., Beerda et al. 1999; Stellato et al. 2017), including posture (e.g. ears, body, tail position), avoidance (e.g. dog looks/moves away), paw-lifting, yawning, panting, and nose- or lip-licking; tail-wagging was also recorded as a potential measure of positive affect. Relational dynamics reflect whether handlers were using reward-based or aversive training and communication methods; criteria included physical contact (e.g. abrupt and firm leash tugs), yelling or praising, and offering rewards (e.g. toys or treats). Supplementary notes were recorded on outcome-based welfare criteria (i.e. details about the dog's environment), such as weather conditions, work environment, and equipment used (e.g. electronic shock collars/e-collars). Systematic all-occurrence observational trials were established for recording data continuously (Altmann 1974; Lehner 1992) except for posture, which was recorded at the beginning and end of each trial, and at five-minute intervals if applicable. Data were analysed using descriptive statistics to explain patterns present (Marshall and Jonker 2010; Shi and McLarty 2009). For each occurrence of a criterion, the percentage of trials in which the dog or handler performed the behaviour was calculated for each dog, as well as for all dogs involved in the study; then, the average percentage of trials in which the action occurred across all dogs was calculated (see Tables 4.1 and 4.2).

Data collection also included in-depth interviews with dog handlers (Alberta n=3, Ontario n=7) thus aligning with and building upon other studies documenting dog welfare based on human perceptions and insights (e.g. Burrows et al. 2008; Lane et al. 1998; Lefebvre et al. 2007; Piva et al. 2008; Yamamoto et al. 2015). Semi-structured interviews focused primarily on dog personality, behaviours while working and resting, interaction with other dogs or people, daily exercise and activities, work schedule, and working/living conditions. Other questions focused on handlers' career trajectories, training and skills acquisition, and job satisfaction. Interviews were recorded, transcribed, and analysed using qualitative content analysis to illicit key themes (Kvale 2011). Additionally, secondary documents such as annual programme reports and media coverage provided valuable information about conservation canine programmes.

Findings

This section presents our findings on the roles, circumstances, and welfare status of conservation canines in Alberta and Ontario, Canada, as well as vignettes to reflect the daily lives of dogs and handlers working in the conservation realm.[1]

Alberta Case Study

Rocky's ears perk up when he hears a rumble. His nostrils flare as he sniffs intently in the direction of the noise. He gets up quickly when he sees it pull into the lot—the first watercraft of the day. He's excited, but well behaved, so he sits patiently while his handler, Lisa, comes to get him out of his kennel. 'Good boy, Rock!' she exclaims while putting his booties on his two front feet, which ensure he does not scratch any boats. He can't wait to get out and search.

Rocky trains all year on zebra mussel detection. He doesn't know why he's looking for them but when he finds one, he gets to play with his ball. Rocky loves the occasions when he does get to play with his ball, so he jumps up to search every time a new boat comes by. Some people get out of their cars to take pictures and videos and talk to Lisa about him. He doesn't know what the big fuss is about.

After searching a few boats, Lisa realizes that Rocky has become discouraged, so she plants an old mussel on the boat to remind him what he's looking for and how much fun his job can be. When he finds it, he sits down, indicating that one of his target odours is present. Lisa checks to confirm the presence of the mussel and then throws him his ball. Rocky jumps three feet off the ground and catches it, squeaking it with joy. He walks up to the other staff at the inspection station and squeaks his ball at them with pride. Lisa throws it in the air a couple more times, allowing him to enjoy his reward to the fullest, before returning him to his kennel. He lays down patiently awaiting the next watercraft.

The Alberta conservation canine team is operated by the Environment and Parks ministry of the Government of Alberta through the Aquatic Invasive Species unit. The team consists of three dog–handler pairs who work at watercraft inspection stations, searching all passing vessels (typically before a provincial border) for zebra and quagga mussels. If a mussel or still water is detected, the vessel must be

---

[1] The names of all dogs and handlers/participants involved have been replaced with pseudonyms.

70 ANIMAL LABOUR

thoroughly flushed with hot water and air dried before proceeding. This programme is mandated by the Fisheries (Alberta) Amendment Act 2015 and the Ministerial Order as per Section 32 (14) of the Fisheries (Alberta) Act (AEP 2016b). Alberta is currently free of zebra mussels—something they hope to sustain given that this invasive species would cost over CAD 75 million per year to manage (AEP 2017; AP 2017; AEP 2016a). The Alberta conservation canine team was initiated via partnership with Working Dogs for Conservation (WD4C), an organization that trains dogs for conservation work worldwide. The Alberta dogs were acquired by WD4C who obtains 'unwanted' dogs from shelters to offer dogs, in part, a second chance at a good life (WD4C 2015a). Dogs are selected at various ages and work until eight or ten years old. WD4C also conducts most of the training of the Alberta dogs—once a handler is paired with a dog they train together. Training activities involve scent recognition of a target object (often via positive reinforcement with a toy) and obedience practice (often via positive punishment using a physical or verbal reprimand, including electronic shock collars).

Dogs on the Alberta team are provincial government property with handlers caring for them twenty-four hours per day, seven days per week. Dogs live inside their handlers' homes where they can roam freely. They work 7.25-hour-long shifts with breaks as deemed necessary by handlers (dependent upon dogs' behaviours) and with two days off per week. During summer months, dogs accompany their handlers to the inspection stations where they either sit outside together or stay in a kennel in the work vehicle so that they do not get distracted. On hotter days, handlers keep dogs inside the air-conditioned office while they wait for vessels so that they do not overheat. Dogs are housed in crates in the work vehicle, parked in the shade, with water readily available; dogs might spend several hours in the work vehicle at a time. When travelling, dogs are housed inside the handler's hotel room with them. During off-season, handlers bring their dogs to the government office where they sit beside their desk, and in some cases are allowed to roam freely. During their downtime, some handlers would take their dogs on walks and hikes in the local neighbourhoods. Most of the Alberta dogs have few interactions with other dogs or people besides the handler. Handlers can adopt a dog upon the dog's retirement, although it is uncertain what might happen if the handler retires earlier than their dog.

Behavioural assessments suggest that dogs exhibited signs of both positive emotional states and stress at different times on the Alberta conservation canine team (Table 4.1). Dogs appeared to be motivated to perform their work, often exhibiting high energy. They also wagged their tails in 80 per cent of trials, which suggests a positive emotional state during trials; tail-wagging also occurs during periods of conflict or stress, and should therefore be interpreted with caution. Dogs showed signs of stress in 33 per cent of trials, demonstrating lowered posture, avoidance (looking/turning away), yawning, or lip/nose licking. Alberta

EXPLORING DOG ROLES, CIRCUMSTANCES, AND WELFARE STATUS   71

Table 4.1 Behavioural assessment for Alberta dogs

Behavioural Indicator	AB Dogs	Min	Max	All Dogs
dog showed lowered body posture	4.6%	3.2%	7.3%	6.2%
dog showed avoidance	14.4%	2.4%	21.1%	10.2%
dog lifted paw	0.0%	0%	0%	0.0%
dog yawned	3.4%	2.1%	4.9%	2.2%
dog panted lightly or heavily	52.0%	26.8%	75.4%	76.4%
dog panted heavily	12.1%	0%	31.2%	25.5%
dog licked lips/nose	27.3%	8.4%	39.3%	24.0%
dog showed any signs of stress	58.0%	39.0%	77.1%	79.0%
dog showed signs of stress excluding panting	33.2%	29.5%	36.1%	30.7%
dog wagged tail	80.3%	62.1%	100%	81.1%
handler made aversive contact with dog	2.0%	0%	4.9%	8.7%
handler yelled at dog	1.2%	0%	2.5%	0.5%
handler praised dog	92.8%	80%	100%	96.9%

Note: Percentages were calculated for each dog across all trials and in terms of maximum and minimum percentages across dogs. Each shade corresponds with a specific dog (light grey indicates that two or more dogs had the same result); shading is displayed to show patterns and variability within dogs. Total number of trials for Alberta dogs n = 197, three dogs; and for all dogs n = 298, seven dogs. All Dogs category reflects combined Alberta and Ontario datasets.

dogs were praised by their handlers in 93 per cent of trials (thus offered food, toys, or verbal/physical praise) and were punished (e.g. leash pops) in 3 per cent of trials. Alberta handlers were sensitive to their dog's stress, noting when they showed avoidance or anxiety, and responded by offering them a break and a walk in a different locale (i.e. inside if they were outside or vice versa). It was uncommon for handlers to use aversive verbal (max = 2.5 per cent) or physical (max = 4.9 per cent) cues towards the dogs.

Notably, Alberta dogs varied considerably in their behavioural responses during trials, as illustrated by the minimum and maximum values provided in the shaded cells in Table 4.1. Based on general trends, these responses did not appear to be directly related to the types of interactions that occurred between the dog and handler. For example, the dog (coded as the darkest grey) that most frequently showed signs of stress was also the dog whose handler used the fewest aversive verbal and physical cues towards them. This behavioural variation suggests that individual dogs manifest stress in different ways (Beerda et al. 2000; Malmkvist et al. 2003; Mason and Mendl 1993; Rooney et al. 2007). Further, signs of stress may or may not be related to work per se and instead related to the dog's personality (i.e. genetics) and early experiences (Horwitz and Mills 2009; Saetre et al. 2006; Storengen et al. 2014; Zapata et al. 2016).

72 ANIMAL LABOUR

Interviews with handlers reveals their perceptions of their dog's welfare, as well as their insights on dog–handler relations in the conservation realm. First, handlers expressed genuine connection to their dogs and concern for their well-being:

We really believe in the handler bond with the dogs, so we live full-time with our dogs and our dogs are fully integrated into our families and our lives at home. We find that really important for trust because if I ask the dog to do something, he needs to be able to trust me that I want him to look there or do that. And you know something, if he's trying to tell me something I need to know what he's trying to tell me out in the field.

We live together, work together, train together, and recreate together. I always add that in because people are like 'what do you do on your days off?' and like I said, [my dog] comes with me. We go to the river, we go canoeing—him and I went fly fishing last summer . . . So it's that aspect that we are partners together.

I think the best part is just being able to work as a team with him, and seeing him—I don't know, just how independent he is, and kind of contributing to that, and learning about him. And seeing the different responses he has to things. Yeah, I guess just seeing his success and being able to be a partner with him.

I would never turn my back on that dog . . . That dog's going with me forever.

Second, handlers discussed their dog's behaviour largely in terms of stress and associated mitigation strategies:

[My dog] . . . has separation anxiety. So, you know, realizing that wherever I go, he comes with me. Or I have to figure out a solution. He kind of struggles with his social skills sometimes, so then I've kind of been struggling with how to work with him on that. And it's not always kind of clear what to do or what's gonna work. I'm working on it at home and that's a location that is comfortable, it's known, he knows it. And so I can slowly build up to things at home [by gradually leaving him alone for longer periods of time] . . . It was either because he was a rescue—there could've been something that happened in that first year and a half and that's why he was surrendered. Or, because he was surrendered, and he didn't have anybody to attach to when he got attached to me . . .

One of the things [my dog's] quite afraid of different surfaces, or stairways . . . like those concrete stairs, or any stairway that you can see through. He's not cool with that. So the way I deal with that is, usually I'll just kind of like encourage him to investigate it . . . I'll just walk up to the beginning of it and take a few steps on it. He'll usually be interested but concerned, and so then I'll just stand there, and he'll just kind of check it out. So I wouldn't drag him onto it . . . I try to be kind of

EXPLORING DOG ROLES, CIRCUMSTANCES, AND WELFARE STATUS 73

supportive but, you know, 'this isn't a big deal, it's okay.' Sometimes I'll use food to kind of encourage him, so like with [a] dock, like maybe toss it a little bit farther than what he can reach and let him go get it. So he'll figure out that like, 'I went there, it wasn't that bad.'

Third, handlers claimed that, despite various stressors, their dog is happy and loves their work:

They love [conservation work]; it's the most fun thing in their lives.

I think he really—he's proud of what he does. In the sense that when he finds [the target], he knows it's something special.

And then the other part is seeing how [my dog] gets excited, right. And not just in the training, but in working and showing off to people, and you know, he'll go up to a total stranger and squeak his ball. You know, he's happy and in the moment, and I think that makes me feel happy, too.

Fourth, handlers claimed that the lives of their dogs have improved through their work:

Two out of three of our dogs were in shelters. So, I mean now they have a job that they love, they get to be with their human every day, to go to work every day, and you know, their health and safety is our utmost concern. So if the dog is panting and tired, time to go in the air conditioning, you know, take a nap.

That whole network of other dogs and people and everything else, you can tell that he's living a much happier life than he was before.

He gets a lot of exercise, he gets a lot of attention. And then I think it's really great because he has this job, and so he doesn't get left at home for long periods of time...So I think he's kind of, health-wise, he's taken care of.

Fifth, handlers see their dog as an effective contributor to environmental protection and education:

I compared the accuracy and the efficiency of the trained watercraft inspectors versus the canines that Working Dogs for Conservation had trained to do this. And it probably won't surprise you to hear the results: the dogs outperformed the humans in both categories—they were much quicker, and they were able to detect 100 per cent of the fouled watercraft in that trial; the humans came in at about 75 per cent.

Partially because of the fact that I love educating kids and the public in general. I love to see how [my dog] is a tool to see the education. Sometimes you can't educate somebody, and then they see a dog, and then all of a sudden, they're a dog person, so they're gonna be more open to what you're trying to say.

[The dogs] are also just amazing ambassadors, and I honestly think that's one of the greatest values we're finding, is the PR potential with them. You know, when you have people by law having to stop at a watercraft inspection station now, and they've already been in traffic for eight hours and construction for two of it in the hot summer, it really helps when they see a dog at the watercraft inspection station... it's really helping to educate people who might otherwise not be as interested.

Ontario Case Study

Bruno starts barking excitedly when he sees Aaron, his handler, pouring his morning coffee. His outdoor pen overlooks the side of Aaron's house, and the open window offers a view to the living room where he can see his handler getting ready to take him out. It's only 7a.m. but Bruno can't wait to get up and start training.

Bruno is new to the canine team so he's still learning the ropes. He has a strong hunting drive, which is the reason he was chosen for their field team working to protect the province's natural resources. Dogs like Bruno assist the conservation officers by searching for shell casings and other evidence of poaching, as well as a variety of other target odours.

The sun is beaming but Bruno has a full day ahead of him of practising to search for and detect target odours, track a human being, and run an agility course. It's hard work but he has so much energy and he loves playing with his ball or receiving a treat once he has done something good.

The Ontario conservation canine team is operated by the Ministry of Natural Resources and Forestry division of the Government of Ontario. The team consists of a supervisor and six canine-handler pairs across the province who work to protect natural resources by assisting field conservation officers to resolve crimes, like poaching or fishing over legal limits, by locating evidence such as shell casings or hidden animal parts/fish. This programme does not mandate canines as part of enforcement teams; rather, dogs have been employed as an additional tool. The Ontario dogs were initially sourced from shelters; today the team prefers to purchase dogs from brokers that breed dogs for specific physical and personality traits that are desirable for this work. Dogs are selected at one or two years old and work until eight to ten years of age.

Dogs on the Ontario team are provincial government property. Handlers care for them day and night with dogs residing in outdoor kennels on their personal property. Kennels include an insulated portion for dogs during winter months; some handlers allow their dogs inside their garage or house when temperatures are deemed excessively cold or hot, or when there are too many pests. Dog–handler pairs work throughout the year with fall busy with hunting season and summer busy with fishing season. Work schedules may be as long as twelve hours, with much of this spent in transit. Work vehicles are fully equipped with dog kennels and constant access to water. When handlers are away from the vehicle, they tend to leave it running with dogs inside the truck kennel to ensure an appropriate temperature conditions (e.g. heat in the wintertime, air conditioning in the summer). Work vehicles have intricate alarm systems in case of emergency. Dogs do not spend much time with other people or dogs; handlers want to ensure their dog does not listen to commands for others and does not get distracted by other nearby dogs.

Similar to the Alberta case, behavioural assessments suggest that dogs exhibited signs of both positive emotional states and stress at different times on the Ontario conservation canine team (Table 4.2). Dogs wagged their tails in 82 per cent of trials on average, which suggests positive emotional states during work, but again, needs to be interpreted with caution. Furthermore, dogs often exhibited high energy when it came time to complete work tasks, suggesting they were motivated

Table 4.2 Behavioural assessment for Ontario dogs

Behavioural Indicator	ON Dogs	Min	Max	All Dogs
dog showed lowered body posture	7.3%	0%	15.8%	6.2%
dog showed avoidance	7.1%	0%	10.5%	10.2%
dog lifted paw	0%	0%	0%	0%
dog yawned	1.3%	0%	5.1%	2.2%
dog panted lightly or heavily	94.8%	89.5%	100%	76.4%
dog panted heavily	35.5%	18.0%	56.7%	25.5%
dog licked lips/nose	21.5%	7.7%	36.7%	24.0%
dog showed any signs of stress	94.8%	89.5%	100%	79.0%
dog showed signs of stress excluding panting	28.9%	7.7%	42.1%	30.7%
dog wagged tail	81.7%	71.8%	96.7%	81.1%
handler made aversive contact with dog	13.8%	0%	26.7%	8.7%
handler yelled at dog	0%	0%	0%	0.5%
handler praised dog	100.0%	100%	100%	96.9%

Note: Percentages were calculated for each dog across all trials and in terms of maximum and minimum percentages across dogs. Each shade corresponds with a specific dog (light grey indicates that two or more dogs had the same result); shades are displayed to show patterns and variability within dogs. Total number of trials for Ontario dogs n = 101, four dogs; and for all dogs n = 298, seven dogs. All Dogs category reflects combined Alberta and Ontario datasets.

76   ANIMAL LABOUR

to participate. Dogs exhibited stress in 29 per cent of trials, demonstrating lowered posture, avoidance, yawning, or lip/nose-licking. Ontario dogs were praised by their handlers in 100 per cent of trials (thus offered food, toys, or verbal/physical praise) and were punished (with physical contact) in 14 per cent of trials. Ontario handlers responded to their dog's stress by encouraging or commanding them to continue with the task at hand, ultimately offering rewards when the dog completed the original request satisfactorily. Handlers often used aversive physical cues (max=26.7 per cent) towards the dogs. Notably, Ontario dogs varied considerably in their behavioural responses during trials, as illustrated by the shaded cells in Table 4.2. For example, one dog (darkest grey) displayed high levels of stress-related behaviour while another dog (second-darkest grey) displayed fewer signs. This suggests, as per the Alberta case, that individual dogs manifest stress in different ways and that stress may relate to personality or early experiences more so than work tasks per se.

Interviews with handlers reveal their[2] perceptions of their dog's welfare, as well as their insights on dog–handler relations in the conservation realm. First, handlers expressed genuine connection to their dog[3] and concern for their well-being:

[My dog] is bonded with one person so he doesn't have a whole community or family of people that he has to learn to read and understand. He's got really one set of expectations that he knows well, from me, because being a professional dog trainer and handler... he gets the benefits of consistent training and reasonable expectations. So I think that's, you know, these are all the reasons why I think his overall well-being is better than that of just about any dog, in my opinion. He gets to come to work, he gets to travel with me wherever I go. So the person that he's bonded with, we're rarely separated.

I know if I was a dog I'd want his position. Overall like I said, 90 per cent of the time we're doing something involving him... If he had lived his life [as a] pet, would it have been as good as what he has now? I would say probably not. Because every day we do something for him. At the end of the day... my position revolves around him. So whether he's in the truck all day [like] today, I made sure the truck's on, the air conditioning's on, he's comfortable. You know, I go out and check on him, usually every 2–3 hours I'll go out and make sure everything's okay, let him out for the bathroom. So he's constantly getting that attention.

These dogs have the best lives in the world... [My dog] gets the best medication, the best vaccines, he gets fantastic food. I basically get paid to take care of him. So even small things like brushing his teeth, keeping his nails clipped, keeping him groomed.

---

[2] The pronoun 'their' is used to refer to all handlers on the Ontario team to protect identities.

[3] Masculine pronouns are used to refer to all dogs on the Ontario team to protect identities. Masculine pronouns were selected rather than feminine as five out of six dogs on the Ontario team are male.

EXPLORING DOG ROLES, CIRCUMSTANCES, AND WELFARE STATUS 77

That's all stuff that I get paid to do. So he's well taken care of. He gets good food, he gets water all the time. He's consistently being kept active... The length of how long I get to work him is [dependent upon] how good I take care of him. And the better that I take care of him, the longer we're gonna be able to work as a team.

Working dogs, it's just so interesting and every single day is different... It's crazy, you have to do stuff with them every single day, and it's like climbing a mountain. It's so challenging, and it's so rewarding, and I love watching the dog progress, and it's great. Sorry, I could go on and on about it forever.

Second, handlers discussed their dog's behaviours by noting occasional stressors and mitigation strategies. More often, handlers expressed frustration with their dog's tendencies while also noting (albeit separately) their dog's ability to express 'natural' behaviours:

If he shows signs of fear or apprehension, I'll work him to show that he can have success in a spot even where he has some fears... So when you go [to a place the dog is afraid of], he shows some hesitation—the tail goes down, he slows his pace, and he's looking around a little bit more. So what I do is I'll put a shell casing out there, and I'll continue to motivate the dog or get him to work, which he does, he doesn't stop. And then he finds that casing and I reward the dog. So in my mind I'm teaching the dog that even though he has fear in these locations, he can still have a success, and he can still have fun... And then we play with the ball for half an hour, you know and walk out of there, the dog's tail is up, his head is up, he's got the ball, he's happy and successful. That's how I deal with neurotic behaviour from a dog.

The most frustrating experiences are when you want to work and the dog doesn't. On the canine [training] course I had a period there where it just became too much for the dog and we had to take some time off. Where you're building and I want to keep building but the dog's telling you, 'I've had enough.' So you've gotta listen to the dog and stop, take it easy when you have to take it easy even though you want to continue to work, if your dog doesn't you've got to change things up.

The frustration is they are so eager, so energetic that it's physically hard on us. This dog that I have now anyway, there is no slow button for him, there is no off button. It's 100 per cent all the time, or he's sleeping—one of the two... When I'm tired of dragging my butt through the clear-cut, he's still dragging me: 'Come on, let's go let's go!' And it's hard to keep up to a dog sometimes.

If you don't have control of a dog, you don't have a dog you can use. So you have to have a dog that is obedient... Meaning that I have to be able to let the dog in the bush, and command him back and forth through the bush... No matter what happens, whether a rabbit takes off or a deer takes off, we have to be able to command the dogs to search an area, not chase animals, not go for a swim... They

78   ANIMAL LABOUR

*have all these desires—they want to run, they want to play—so we have to make
sure that we can focus those drives into something that's useful for us.*

*It's their nose and their hunting drive—they're doing something they want to do.
So [members of our team] all use hunting-type breeds, right, and their genetics
drives them to search for stuff and hunt for stuff. So . . . instead of hunting for
rabbits, they're hunting for a shotgun shell.*

Third, handlers claimed that their dog is happy and loves their work:

*When you open the door, the dogs cannot wait to get in the truck [to go to work].
It's like they're rocking towards the truck, it's like 'all right, let's go.' The dogs live
for this; it's the best thing that's ever happened to them. Whether they're getting on
a quad, or they're getting on a snowmobile. They just—life is good.*

*He seems to have a lot of fun when he's out searching. He loves to be off-lead, he
loves to be in the bush, he loves to run. He has a lot of fun—it seems to me like he
has a lot of fun when we're working.*

*I know that [he enjoys the work] because when I come out in the morning in my
pyjamas to let the dog out, he's slower to get about his business, he goes and does
his business, comes back to the kennel and waits for his kibble. If I go outside in my
uniform, his energy is greater, he goes to the truck and I have to kind of remind
him that he's gotta go take a leak before he gets in the truck, but he's really wound
up to get in that truck and get going.*

Fourth, handlers claimed that the lives of their dogs have improved through their
work:

*Being a service dog—which I think these dogs are, or a police dog—you couldn't
ask for a better job for a dog or a better life for a dog. Because he gets to spend his
entire life with the handler, in the vehicle, driving, searching for stuff, you know,
hunting every day. It couldn't be better.*

*I think he's better working than [being] a pet dog. Especially with him, his drives are
very high, so as a pet he would be very tough to handle in a house, in that type of setting.*

*He has no clue what his future looked like for him potentially eight years ago, being
at the dog pound two or three times in his young life. Right, he has no clue that
maybe you know, the next time you might get put down.*

Fifth, handlers see their dog as an effective contributor to environmental protection and education:

*It's sort of an incredibly amazing feeling of accomplishment when you take your
dog out and there's some ecologist saying they had an animal shot three days ago,*

EXPLORING DOG ROLES, CIRCUMSTANCES, AND WELFARE STATUS   79

and 'we've recovered the animal but we want to find the bullet that was shot,' because if we get that we can make an arrest of the guy that poached this animal. And they're always amazed at how well the dogs do.

I believe a lot of what we contribute to natural resource law enforcement is the deterrent factor we provide. There's the perception and knowledge from the public that dogs, they know that if they are trying to sneak stuff through by officers there's a good chance that if there's a dog team on site, or if the dog catches up with them, that they'll be revealed. So I think there's a high deterrent factor in that respect. We are highly visible in the communities. People know we have the dogs, so I think that's the other neat thing they provide. Not only that but they're good to gap any kind of relationships with the public, a lot of people can relate to dogs, and they're a good educational tool that way.

People knowing that we have canine units, it definitely has a positive impact. They will double think or triple think their thoughts of, 'I'm gonna poach today,' just knowing that we're out there.

People love knowing that the dogs are doing [work with us], and especially since in the past most of our dogs were rescued dogs to start with, people were really appreciative of the fact that we would take those dogs and teach them how to do something and go and do it with them.

Discussion

Do dogs enjoy or suffer on account of their conservation jobs? Our findings suggest that conservation canines have opportunities for enjoyment, with some aspects of their training and work likely having a negative impact on their welfare. Dogs in Alberta and Ontario perform detection work that requires manoeuvring tight crevices, running through dirt and mud, mouth-breathing to ensure full scent capture, communicating with and obeying handlers, and resisting urges to chase non-target objects, interact with other dogs or persons, or take a break. Indeed, a number of stress-related behaviours were exhibited while dogs were working. However, in the majority of work trials observed, dogs also exhibited behaviours that suggest positive emotional states, and handlers interacted with dogs more often with positive than aversive techniques. Further, handlers spoke with enthusiasm, pride, and enjoyment regarding their dogs and conservation work more broadly; they viewed dogs' work as vital to public education and environmental protection. Based on these data, conservation canine jobs have the potential to be humane for dogs, as well as for humans and for the environment more broadly.

Yet our research raises questions as to what is meant by 'jobs' or 'work' and how to assess holistically the lives of working dogs. Indeed, dog circumstances and experiences within the conservation realm involve much more than identifying

80   ANIMAL LABOUR

invasive species or deterring poachers. While these specific work tasks are part of a dog's work day (be it 7.25 hrs or 12 hrs for Alberta and Ontario teams respectively), so too is enduring extensive transport from one locale to another or sitting in a vehicle for hours on end until needed. Further, dog–handler interactions extend well beyond communicating during work tasks given that dogs are fully dependent on their handlers for food, shelter, and overall well-being throughout the day and night. Work/non-work boundaries are blurred such that dogs are always-already labourers that are meant to be ready to work. Thus we join Coulter (chapter 2, this volume) in arguing that we must strive for—and assess—humane *work-lives* that consider holistically the lives of working animals. We must acknowledge that animals, even dogs who are socially and economically privileged, have their *whole lives* largely organized to suit human purposes.

Our interdisciplinary assessment of conservation canine welfare offers preliminary insights into dog work-lives and raises key concerns that must be considered as part of a 'humane' context. Specifically, the extent to which dogs are offered and ensured, throughout their work-lives, the five freedoms of animal welfare, namely freedom from hunger or thirst, from discomfort, from pain, injury or disease, from fear and distress, as well as freedom to express normal behaviour (FAWC 2009). While these freedoms were met in some instances of Alberta and Ontario conservation canine work, rest, transport, leisure, etc., they were not in others—notably occurring in places and moments connecting work and non-work. For example, some dogs received limited sustenance during mealtimes to motivate them during work tasks rewarded with food; dogs endured inhospitable climatic conditions while performing work tasks (e.g. searching during extreme heat and rewarded with air-conditioned hotel accommodation) or during non-work hours (e.g. residing in a minimally insulated outdoor kennel during extreme cold so as to endure effectively these conditions during work tasks); and dogs were discouraged from socializing with other dogs and people during non-work hours to again ensure focus during work tasks. Further, some handlers used e-collars to shock dogs as part of their obedience regimen. This technique is deemed unnecessary and unethical, and resulting in long-term welfare concerns (BSAVA 2003; Beerda et al. 1998; Hiby et al. 2004; Overall 2007; Schalke et al. 2007; Schilder and van der Borg 2004).

Our interdisciplinary assessment of conservation canine welfare also offers preliminary insights into conservation canine guidelines and regulations. Oversight of welfare throughout dog work-lives is left to individual handlers who are entrusted to provide sufficient care and appropriate working/living environments. We observed that Alberta and Ontario handlers have a variety of opinions on, knowledge of, and approaches to work- and non-work based interactions, and specifically for provision of meals, accommodation, socialization, and reward-based incentives. While our findings suggest similar welfare outcomes despite these differences, handler interviews and participant observations clearly reflect the context-specificity of conservation canine work-lives. This raises questions

EXPLORING DOG ROLES, CIRCUMSTANCES, AND WELFARE STATUS   81

regarding the need and possibilities for standardized and regulated implementation of freedoms of animal welfare in this and other animal labour realms. That no national, provincial, or institutional guidelines exist for the care and use of working dogs is a notable shortcoming. As Coulter (2016: 156) states, animal 'needs and desires must be taken seriously through changes in perceptions and practices, and through regulation and enforcement.' To this end, we recommend clear welfare guidelines specifically on food provisioning, climatic conditions, socializing opportunities, and aversive techniques to ensure humane work-lives for conservation canines. We also recommend systematic, rigorous, and regular welfare assessments of individual dogs on canine teams that engage animal welfare science and social science methods to gauge dog enjoyment and/or suffering as experienced within their entire work-lives.

Pushing further, we wish to recast our animal welfare-based discussion along the lines of an interspecies solidarity perspective that more fully attends to dogs' choice and agency as part of their work-lives. During and beyond work trials, we observed numerous instances of handlers allowing dogs freedom-of-choice or dogs influencing a particular situation. For example, when a dog began to avoid a subject or target, their handler reacted by giving the dog a break or ending their shift early. Dogs thus have opportunities to opt out of specific work tasks throughout the day. Yet we also observed instances where dogs were urged to continue and re-focus on the work task at hand through positive coaxing or aversive measures. Such scenarios were context-specific in terms of individual dogs and individual handlers. Ultimately, it was difficult to discern choice and agency possessed by dogs and handlers in these daily scenarios; decisions regarding duration of work, types of work tasks, etc. were varied, as well as continually and relationally negotiated. Questions remain, then, as to the extent to which Alberta and Ontario dogs' work-lives are rigorously prescribed and controlled by handlers, and the implications of this on dogs themselves.

More broadly, questions arise as to the choice dogs have to join the conservation labour force in the first place and/or leave it when they feel motivated to do so. In terms of the former, handlers select dogs largely based on biological rationales given dog olfactory capabilities, agility, and a 'natural drive' for running or hunting. Handlers claimed that conservation work 'saves' dogs that might otherwise remain in shelters or be euthanized given their unsuitability for adoption as pets on account of their high energy levels. Handlers further argued that dogs serve as environmental ambassadors, encouraging public participation in conservation and deterring degradation and crime. In terms of the latter, a dog's ability to leave their conservation job is largely premised on its 'failure' in training or work tasks; few details are available regarding dogs' fate beyond their work-lives.

Ultimately, and not surprisingly, dogs' work-lives in the conservation realm are substantively shaped and controlled by humans. While dogs appear to enjoy many of the work tasks involved, issues of control, respect, reciprocity, and protection of

82 ANIMAL LABOUR

rights for dogs must be addressed if these dogs are to fully enjoy or benefit from this work as members of a multispecies workforce. Specifically, dogs must be acknowledged as co-workers with freedom of choice and agency rather than as efficient instruments of conservation. While handlers spoke of the comradery experienced as part of the canine team, more often than not their commentaries reproduced assumptions that conservation work allows dogs to 'do what they are meant to do' (e.g. biologically driven or bred for hunting purposes) or that their lives are an 'improvement over the alternative' (e.g. shelter lives or euthanasia). Hence conservation canine work reinforces ideas that dogs cannot possibly lead alternative lives free from human imagination and domination. The fact that dogs 'seem happy' doing conservation work means that welfare measures of enjoyment and suffering may reproduce the use of dogs as conservation labourers.

And although it might be difficult to assess animal welfare and ethics-based criteria of control, membership, and solidarity as benchmarks for 'humane' jobs and work-lives, it is important that we do so to build further upon the tools provided by interdisciplinary animal welfare assessments.

In conclusion, we have explored the roles, circumstances, and welfare of dogs working for conservation in Alberta and Ontario in order to assess the extent to which conservation canine work may be considered 'humane'. Our research highlights a holistic methodology bridging animal welfare science and qualitative social sciences, and also considers ethical and moral issues related to animal work. By doing so it illuminates the need to consider animals' work-lives rather than simply the work tasks involved. It also illuminates the complexity and nuance of specific contexts and the individuals (human and non-human) involved. Finally, it urges us to consider the underling motivations and assumptions wrapped up with animal labour—often (re)producing instrumentalist and utilitarian views—and to recast animal labour as progressive and promoting interspecies solidarity. This requires attention to animals' enjoyment of work, their ability to express choice and agency, and their recognition and respect as co-workers. Ultimately, we hope that our research serves as a springboard for other scholars to investigate holistically animal–human labour relations and contexts. We hope that other researchers and professionals may build upon this research so as to make informed changes in animal labour industries and to offer humane jobs for the benefit animals, humans, and the environment.

References

Akenson, James, Mark Henjum, Tara Wertz, and Ted Craddock. 2004. 'Use of Dogs and Mark-Recapture Techniques to Estimate American Black Bear Density in Northeastern Oregon'. *Ursus 12*: 203–10.

Alberta Environment and Parks (AEP). 2016a. 'Alberta Aquatic Invasive Species Program 2015 Annual Report—Alberta Environment and Parks'. Retrieved from:

http://aep.alberta.ca/fish-wildlife/invasive-species/aquatic-invasive-species/documents/AquaticInvasiveSpecies-2016AnnualRpt-July2017.pdf via http://aep.alberta.ca/fish-wildlife/invasive-species/aquatic-invasive-species/default.aspx [Accessed 13 April 2018].

Alberta Environment and Parks (AEP). 2016b. 'AIS Conservation K-9 program'. Retrieved from: http://aep.alberta.ca/recreation-public-use/boating/watercraft-inspections/ais-conservation-k-9-program.aspx [Accessed 13 April 2018].

Alberta Environment and Parks (AEP). 2017. 'Aquatic Invasive Species'. Retrieved from: http://aep.alberta.ca/fish-wildlife/invasive-species/aquatic-invasive-species/default.aspx [Accessed 27 March 2018].

Alberta Parks (AP). 2017. 'Aquatic Invasive Species'. Retrieved from: https://www.albertaparks.ca/albertaparksca/science-research/aquatic-invasive-species/ [Accessed 12 April 2018].

Altmann, Jeanne. 1974. 'Observational Study of Animal Behavior: Sampling Methods'. *Behavior* 49(3): 227–66.

Arandjelovic, Mimi, Richard Bergl, Romanus Ikfuingei, Christopher Jameson, Megan Parker, and Linda Vigilant. 2015. 'Detection Dog Efficacy For Collecting Faecal Samples From the Critically Endangered Cross River Gorilla (*Gorilla gorilla diehli*) for Genetic Censusing'. *Royal Society Open Science* 2(2): 140423.

Arnett, Edward. 2006. 'A Preliminary Analysis on the Use of Dogs to Recover Bat Fatalities at Wind Energy Facilities. *Wildlife Society Bulletin* 34: 1440–5.

Beckmann, Jon, Lisette Waits, Aimee Hurt, Alice Whitelaw, and Scott Bergen. 2015. 'Using Detection Dogs and RSPF Models to Assess Habitat Suitability for Bears in Greater Yellowstone'. *Western North American Naturalist* 75(4): 396–405.

Beebe, Sarah, Tiffani Howell, and Pauleen Bennett. 2016. 'Using Scent Detection Dogs in Conservation Settings: A Review of Scientific Literature Regarding Their Selection'. *Frontiers in Veterinary Science* 3(96): 1–13.

Beerda, Bonne, Matthijs Schilder, Jan A.R.A.M. van Hoof, Hans de Vries, and Jan Mol. 1998. 'Behavioural, Saliva Cortisol and Heart Rate Responses to Difference Types of Stimuli in Dogs. *Applied Animal Behaviour Science* 58: 365–81.

Beerda, Bonne, Matthijs Schilder, Jan A.R.A.M. van Hoof, Hans de Vries, and Jan Mol. 1999. 'Chronic Stress in Dogs Subjected to Social and Spatial Restriction. I. Behavioural Responses'. *Physiology & Behaviour* 66(2): 234–54.

Beerda, Bonne, Matthijs B.H. Schilder, Jan A.R.A.M. van Hoof, Hans W. de Vries, and Jan Mol. 2000. Behavioural and Hormonal Indicators of Enduring Environmental Stress in Dogs. *Animal Welfare* 9: 49–62.

Brook, S.M., P. van Coeverden de Groot C. Scott, P. Boag, B. Long, R.E. Ley, G.H. Reischer, A.C. Williams, S.P. Mahood, Tran Minh Hien, G. Polet, N. Cox, and Bach Thanh Hai. 2012. 'Integrated and Novel Survey Methods for Rhinoceros Populations Confirm the Extinction of *Rhinoceros sondaicus annamiticus* from Vietnam'. *Biological Conservation* 155: 59–67.

British Small Animal Veterinary Association (BSAVA). 2003. 'Position Statement: Electronic Training Devices: A Behavioural Perspective'. *Journal of Small Animal Practice* 44: 95–96.

84 ANIMAL LABOUR

Burrows, Kristen, Cindy Adams, and Suzanne Millman. 2008. 'Factors Affecting Behaviour and Welfare of Service Dogs for Children With Autism Spectrum Disorder'. *Journal of Applied Animal Welfare Science* 11: 42–62.

Cablk, Mary, and Jill Heaton. 2006. 'Accuracy and Reliability of Dogs in Surveying for Desert Tortoises (*Gopherus agassizii*)'. *Ecological Applications* 16: 1926–35.

Chambers, Carol, Christina Vojta, Elisabeth Mering, and Barbara Davenport. 2015. 'Efficacy of Scent-Detection Dogs for Locating Bat Roosts in Trees and Snags'. *Wildlife Society Bulletin* 39(4): 780–7.

Conservation Canines (CC). 2018a. 'Sniffing Out Solutions'. https://conservationcanines.org/ [Accessed 27 March 2018].

Conservation Canines (CC). 2018b. 'We Find Dogs Who Are Out of Options'. https://conservationcanines.org/meet-the-dogs/ [Accessed 27 March 2018].

Coulter, Kendra. 2016. *Animals, Work, and the Promise of Interspecies Solidarity*. New York: Palgrave.

Cristescu, Romane, Emily Foley, Anna Markula, Gary Jackson, Darryl Jones, and Céline Frère. 2015. 'Accuracy and Efficiency of Detection Dogs: A Powerful New Tool for Koala Conservation and Management. *Scientific Reports* 5: 8349.

D'Souza, Renée. 2018. *Conservation Canines: Exploring Dog Roles, Circumstances & Welfare Status*. Masters of Environmental Studies Thesis. Kingston Canada: Queen's University.

Davidson, Gregory, Darren Clark, Bruce Johnson, Lisette Waits, and Jennifer Adams. 2014. 'Estimating Cougar Densities in Northeast Oregon Using Conservation Detection Dogs'. *The Journal of Wildlife Management* 78(6): 1104–14.

DeMatteo, Karen, Miguel Rinas, Carina Arguelles, Bernardo Holman, Mario Di Bitetti, Barbara Davenport, Patricia Parker, and Lori Eggert. 2014. 'Using Detection Dogs and Genetic Analyses of Scat to Expand Knowledge and Assist Felid Conservation in Misiones, Argentina'. *Integrative Zoology* 9: 623–39.

Duggan, Jennifer, Edward Heske, Robert Schooley, Aimee Hurt, and Alice Whitelaw. 2011. 'Comparing Detection Dog and Livetrapping Surveys for a Cryptic Rodent'. *The Journal of Wildlife Management* 75(5): 1209–17.

Farm Animal Welfare Council (FAWC). 2009. 'The Origins of the Five Freedoms'. Retrieved from: webarchive.nationalarchives.gov.uk/20121010012427/http://www.fawc.org.uk/freedoms.htm [Accessed 13 April 2018].

Fukuhara, Ryoji, Takako Yamaguchi, Hiromi Ukuta, Sugot Roy, Junichi Tanaka, and Go Ogura. 2010. 'Development and Introduction of Detection Dogs in Surveying for Scats of Small Indian Mongoose as Invasive Alien Species'. *Journal of Veterinary Behavior* 5: 101–11.

Goodwin, Kim, Rick Engel, and David Weaver. 2010. 'Trained Dogs Outperform Human Surveyors in the Detection of Rare Spotted Knapweed (*Centaurea stoebe*)'. *Invasive Plant Science and Management* 3: 113–21.

Gsell, Anna, John Innes, Pim de Monchy, and Dianne Brunton. 2010. 'The Success of Trained Dogs to Locate Sparse Rodents in Pest-Free Sanctuaries'. *Wildlife Research* 37: 39–46.

Harrison, Robert. 2006. 'A Comparison of Survey Methods for Detecting Bobcats. *Wildlife Society Bulletin* 34(2): 548–552.

Hiby, Elly, Nicola Rooney, and J.W.S. Bradshaw. 2004. 'Dog Training Methods: Their Use, Effectiveness and Interaction with Behaviour and Welfare. *Animal Welfare* 13(1): 63–69.

Homan, Jeffrey, George Linz, and Brian Peer. 2001. 'Dogs Increase Recovery of Passerine Carcasses in Dense Vegetation'. *Wildlife Society Bulletin* 29: 292–6.

Horwitz, Debra, and Daniel Mills. 2009. 'Separation-Related Problems in Dogs and Cats'. In *BSAVA Manual of Canine and Feline Behavioural Medicine*, edited by Debra Horowitz and Daniel Mills. 2nd ed. Gloucester: British Small Animal Veterinary Association.

Hurt, A., and D.A. Smith. 2009. 'Conservation Dogs'. In *Canine Ergonomics: The Science of Working Dogs*, edited by William Helton, 175–94. Boca Raton, FL: CRC Press.

Kerley, Linda. 2010. 'Using Dogs for Tiger Conservation and Research'. *Integrative Zoology* 5: 390–5.

Kvale, Steinar. 2011. *Doing Interviews*. London: Sage.

Lane, D.R., J. McNicholas, and Glyn Collis. 1998. 'Dogs for the Disabled: Benefits to Recipients and Welfare of the Dog. *Applied Animal Behaviour Science* 59: 49–60.

Lefebvre, Diane, Claire Diederich, Madeleine Delcourt, and Jean-Marie Giffory. 2007. 'The Quality of the Relation Between Handler and Military Dogs Influences Efficiency and Welfare of Dogs. *Applied Animal Behaviour Science* 104: 49–60.

Lehner, Philip. 1992. 'Sampling Methods in Behavior Research. *Poultry Science* 71(4): 643–9.

Long, Robert, Therese Donovan, Paula Mackay, William Zielinski, and Jeffrey Buzas. 2007. 'Comparing Scat Detection Dogs, Cameras, and Hair Snares for Surveying Carnivores'. *Journal of Wildlife Management* 71(6): 2018–25.

Malmkvist, Jens, Steffen Hansen, and Birthe Damgaard. 2003. 'Effect of the Serotonin Agonist Buspirone on Behaviour and Hypothalamic-Pituitary-Adrenal Axis in Confident and Fearful Mink'. *Physiology & Behavior* 78: 229–40.

Marshall, Gill, and Leon Jonker. 2010. 'An Introduction to Descriptive Statistics: A Review and Practical Guide. *Radiography* 16(4): e1–e7.

Mason, G., and M. Mendl. 1993. 'Why is There No Simple Way of Measuring Animal Welfare?' *Animal Welfare* 2(4): 301–19.

Mathews, Fiona, Michael Swindells, Rhys Goodhead, Thomas August, Philippa Hardman, Daniella Linton, and David Hosken. 2013. 'Effectiveness of Search Dogs Compared with Human Observers in Locating Bat Carcasses at Wind-Turbine Sites: A Blinded Randomized Trial. *Wildlife Society Bulletin* 37(1): 34–40.

86   ANIMAL LABOUR

Miller, D.D., S.R. Staats, C. Partlo, and K. Rada. 1996. 'Factor Associated with the Decision to Surrender a Pet to an Animal Shelter. *Journal of the American Veterinary Medical Association* 209: 738–42.

Oliveira, Márcio, Darren Norris, José Ramirez, Pedro H. de F. Peres, Mauro Galetti, and José Duarte. 2012. 'Dogs Can Detect Scat More Efficiently Than Humans: An Experiment in a Continuous Atlantic Forest Remnant'. *Zoologia* 29(2): 183–6.

Overall, Karen. 2007. 'Why Electric Shock is Not Behaviour Modification'. *Journal of Veterinary Behaviour: Clinical Applications and Research* 2: 1–4.

Paula, João, Miguel Costa Leal, Maria João Silva, Ramiro Mascarenhas, Hugo Costa, and Miguel Mascarenhas. 2011. 'Dogs as a Tool to Improve Bird-Strike Mortality Estimates at Wind Farms. *Journal for Nature Conservation* 19: 202–8.

Piva, Elisabetta, Valentina Liverani, Pier Attilio Accorsi, Giuseppe Sarli, and Gualtiero Gandini. 2008. 'Welfare in a Shelter Dog Rehomed with Alzheimer Patients. *Journal of Veterinary Behavior* 3: 87–94.

Reed, Sarah, Allison Bidlack, Aimee Hurt, and Wayne Getz. 2011. 'Detection Distance and Environmental Factors in Conservation Detection Dog Surveys'. *Journal of Wildlife Management* 75(1): 243–51.

Reindl-Thompson, Sara, John Shivik, Alice Whitelaw, Aimee Hurt, and Kenneth Higgins. 2006. 'Efficacy of Scent Dogs in Detecting Black-Footed Ferrets at a Reintroduction Site in North Dakota'. *Wildlife Society Bulletin* 34: 1435–9.

Robertson, Hugh, and James Fraser. 2009. 'Use of Trained Dogs to Determine the Age Structure and Conservation Status of Kiwi *Apteryx* spp. Populations'. *Bird Conservation International* 19: 121–9.

Rolland, Rosalind, P.K. Hamilton, Scott Kraus, B. Davenport, Roxanne Gillett, and Samuel Wasser. 2006. 'Faecal Sampling Using Detection Dogs to Study Reproduction and Health in North Atlantic Right Whales (*Eubalaena glacialis*)'. *Journal of Cetacean Research and Management* 8(2): 121–5.

Rooney, Nicola, Samantha Gaines, and John Bradshaw. 2007. 'Behavioural and Glucocorticoid Responses of Dogs (*Canis familiaris*) to Kennelling: Investigating Mitigation of Stress by Prior Habituation'. *Physiology & Behavior* 92: 847–54.

Saetre, P., E. Strandberg, P.-E. Sundgren, U. Pettersson, E. Jazin, and T.F. Bergström, and T.F. 2006. 'The Genetic Contribution to Canine Personality'. *Genes, Brain and Behavior* 5: 240–8.

Savidge, Julie, James Stanford, Robert Reed, Ginger Haddock, and Amy Yackel Adams. 2010. 'Canine Detection of Free-Ranging Brown Treesnakes on Guam'. *New Zealand Journal of Ecology* 35(2): 174–81.

Schalke, Esther, James Stichnoth, Stefen Ott, and R. Jones-Baade. 2007. 'Clinical Signs Caused by the Use of Electric Training Collars on Dogs in Everyday Life Situation'. *Applied Animal Behaviour Science* 105: 369–80.

Schilder, Matthijs, and Joanne van der Borg. 2004. 'Training Dogs with Help of the Shock Collar: Short and Long Term Behavioural Effects'. *Applied Animal Behaviour Science* 85: 319–34.

Shi, Runhua, and Jerry McLarty. 2009. 'Descriptive Statistics'. *Annals of Allergy, Asthma & Immunology* 103: S9–S14.

Shubert, Jan. 2012. 'Dogs and Human Health/Mental Health: From the Pleasure of their Company to the Benefits of their Assistance' *U.S. Army Medical Department Journal* 21(04/2012): 21–9.

Smith, Deborah, Katherine Ralls, Barbara Davenport, Brice Adams, and Jesus Maldonado. 2001. 'Canine Assistants for Conservation' *Science* 291(5003): 435.

Smith, Deborah, Katherine Ralls, Aimee Hurt, Brice Adams, Megan Parker, Barbara Davenport, M.C. Smith, and Jesus Maldonado. 2003. 'Detection and Accuracy Rates of Dogs Trained to Find Scats of San Joaquin Kit Foxes (*Vulpes macrotis mutica*)'. *Animal Conservation* 6: 339–46.

Stellato, Anastasia, Hannah Flint, Tina Widowski, James Serpell, and Lee Niel. 2017. 'Assessment of Fear-Related Behaviours Displayed by Companion Dogs (Canis familiaris) in Response to Social and Non-Social Stimuli'. *Applied Animal Behaviour Science* 188: 84–90.

Storengen, Linn Mari, Silje Christine Kallestad Boge, Solveig Johanne Strøm, Gry Løberg, and Frode Lingaas. 2014. 'A Descriptive Study of 2015 Dogs Diagnosed With Separation Anxiety'. *Applied Animal Behaviour Science* 159: 82–9.

Wasser, Samuel, Barbara Davenport, Elizabeth Ramage, Kathleen Hunt, Margaret Parker, Christine Clarke, and Gordon Stenhouse. 2004. 'Scat Detection in Wildlife Research and Management: Application to Grizzly and Black Bears in the Yellowhead Ecosystem, Alberta, Canada'. *Canadian Journal of Zoology* 82: 475–92.

Working Dogs for Conservation (WD4C). 2015a. 'Rescues2TheRescue: This Program Will Save Thousands of Shelter Dogs by Putting Them to Work for Dog Organizations Around the World'. http://wd4c.org/workingdogidrescue.html [Accessed 27 March 2018].

Working Dogs for Conservation (WD4C). 2015b. 'What We Do'. https://wd4c.org/ [Accessed 27 March 2018].

Yamamoto, Mariko, Marissa Yamamoto, and Lynette Hart. 2015. 'Physical Activity and Welfare of Guide Dogs and Walking Activity of their Partners. *Anthrozoos* 28(2): 277–89.

Zapata, Isain, James Serpell, and Carlos Alvarez. 2016. 'Genetic Mapping of Canine Fear and Aggression'. *BMC Genomics* 17: 572.

Zwickel, F.C. 1980. 'Use of Dogs in Wildlife Biology'. In *Wildlife Management Techniques Manual*, edited by D. Schemnitz, 531–6. 4th edition. Bethesda, Maryland: The Wildlife Society.

PART II

THE DILEMMAS OF ANIMAL LABOUR

5

Animal Labour

Toward a Prohibition of Forced Labour and a Right to Freely Choose One's Work

Charlotte E. Blattner

It's a universal fantasy, isn't it?—the animals learn to speak, and at last we learn what they're thinking, our cats and dogs and horses: a new era in cross-species understanding. But nothing ever works out quite as we imagine. When the Change happened it affected all the mammals we have shaped to meet our own needs. They all could talk a little, and they all could frame their thoughts well enough to talk. Cattle, horses, goats, llamas; rats, too. Pigs. Minks. And dogs and cats. And we found that, really, we prefer our slaves mute.

(Johnson 2009)

Recognizing Exploitation and Unfolding Agency

What does a just world look like for animals? No one asks animals this question. Instead, researchers meticulously search for the answer in scholarly writings *about* animals. For decades, the literature in animal studies has fractured along the rights vs. welfarism binary. The impasse has stalled debate, but an emerging strand of scholarship offers us a new path. Scholars have begun to argue that animal labour can offer a way out, and operate as a basis for their recognition, rights, and membership (Kymlicka 2017).

Many animal advocates hesitate to define animals as 'workers', given the magnitude of their exploitation. According to Weisberg, rather than being workers, animals are more appropriately described as worked-on objects, and '[t]o call them anything else is to gloss over the brutal reality of the total denial of their ability to act in any meaningful way—namely, as self-determining *subjects*' (Weisberg 2009: 36). In response, Jason Hribal acknowledges the importance of

---

Charlotte E. Blattner, *Animal Labour: Toward a Prohibition of Forced Labour and a Right to Freely Choose One's Work* In: *Animal Labour: A New Frontier of Interspecies Justice?*. Edited by: Charlotte Blattner, Kendra Coulter, and Will Kymlicka, Oxford University Press (2020). © Oxford University Press.
DOI: 10.1093/oso/9780198846192.003.0005

92 ANIMAL LABOUR

critical scholarship that exposes the objectification and commodification of animals,[1] but says that he finds these arguments

> both bewildering and frustrating. They are bewildering because the circuits of capitalism are exposed. The issue at hand—animals as products or commodities—is made clear. Pronouncements are made: 'we need to stop thinking of animals in this way'. But then we are told that animals are super-exploited living commodities. They are frustrating because this is the acceptance of defeat. It is denial of alternatives. It is the rejection of agency. Commodities, like capital, are dead. (Hribal 2012: 22)

Analyses of how animals are worked-upon objects in our society throw into stark relief how badly they are treated, but they so deeply 'bury animals under the verbiage and power of capital that they disappear from view' (Hribal 2012: 22). These descriptive accounts of animal commodification offer no path to a more just world in which animals figure as agents with a voice.

Hribal suggests that a labour lens offers a way forward: indeed, it is 'the labor of other animals that injects [animals] with their value that is living. It is the struggle of other animals against that labor that is vibrant' (2012: 22). He argues that the normative value of the labour lens is obscured when we theorize about animals solely in commodity terms. This normative value consists in recognizing that animals are treated unjustly precisely because they are subjects. Recognizing animals as workers does not mean endorsing their exploitation or stripping them of rights to refuse work. Rather, we should recognize animals as exploited workers—or, as Torres would say, members of the 'superexploited' class (Torres 2007: 37)—and establish the sorts of legal rights, institutions, and practices that protect animal workers from degradation and oppression, and that allow them to flourish.

For scholars who specialize in animal labour, those rights and institutions include the right to remuneration, safe working conditions, retirement, medical care, and collective bargaining (Cochrane 2016). These rights flow quite naturally from the concept of animal labour, and help us envision more just working relations with animals. But are they sufficient to ensure that work is a place of happiness and meaning for animals? In the case of human workers, a crucial protection against exploitation is their right to freely choose their work, and the concomitant prohibition of forced labour. Should this right to self-determination[2] form part of the emancipatory project of 'animal labour', too? Should animals be

---

[1] Hribal refers in particular to Noske 1997; Pachirat 2011.

[2] Scholars use various terms to describe a sphere or rights to self-governance, self-rule, autonomy, liberty, freedom, participation, and the like. I speak of 'self-determination' because many of these other terms are easily conflated with unrealistic and undesirable forms of unlimited freedom, or resonate with a particularly individualistic and overly rational conception of autonomy.

able to decide whether they want to work or not, or what type of work they want to do? These questions are the focus of the first part of this chapter. In the second part, I explain how animals' right to self-determination could be secured at work, examining different models of dissent, assent, and consent and the best way to design these to secure animals' agency, both in theory and practice.

Free Labour for Humans, Forced Labour for Animals?

Few scholars who specialize in animal labour pay any attention to the question of self-determination. For example, Porcher's *The Ethics of Animal Labor*, in the chapter *Work and Freedom*, acknowledges that the worker's subjectivity is an essential component of work (Porcher 2017: 25), but she explores the subjectivity only of French farmers threatened by EU-level decision-making (Porcher 2017: 52). Even Clark, in his gripping analysis of 'lab animals' as labourers, gives animals voice only through their acts of resistance (Clark 2014: 159).[3] Neither articulates an account of self-determination as a basic right of animal workers. This may reflect a wider trend in the animal ethics literature to diminish or deny animals' capacities or interests in making choices. It is not uncommon, even for animal rights theorists, to say that animals 'cannot vocalize their own interests', are 'of course unable to consent' and 'obviously unable to directly participate' in decision-making (Linzey and Linzey 2018: 12; Parry 2016: 146). On such views, it would seem that rights of self-determination could not apply to animal workers.

This is indeed the position that Cochrane defends. He famously argues that animals have no intrinsic interest in liberty, and hence need not be granted rights to liberty, autonomous decision-making, self-determination, and the like when engaged in work. Cochrane grants animals non-intrinsic interests in liberty but argues these can be achieved by enacting laws that ensure animals do not suffer (Cochrane 2016: 20–1) or experience harm (Cochrane 2012).

It is worth exploring Cochrane's argument in depth.[4] Schmidt summarizes Cochrane's line of argument this way (Schmidt 2015: 94–5):

P1: To have a moral right to freedom, one needs to have a sufficient intrinsic interest in freedom.

P2: To have a sufficient and intrinsic interest in freedom implies that freedom by itself contributes to a person's wellbeing.

P3: Only in case of autonomous persons does freedom contribute by itself to their wellbeing (because only for autonomous persons does unfreedom

---

[3] On the resistance of animals, see also Hribal (2003, 2007, 2010) and Wadiwel (2018).
[4] There are many other schools of thought that do not accord rights to autonomy to animals, but Cochrane's is exemplary in its explicit argumentation.

94 ANIMAL LABOUR

undermine the ability to 'frame and pursue their own conception of the good' (Cochrane 2009: 666)).

P4: Non-human animals are not autonomous persons.

C1: Therefore, freedom does not by itself contribute to the wellbeing of non-human animals.

C2: Therefore, non-human animals do not have an intrinsic interest in freedom.

C3: Therefore, non-human animals do not have a moral right to freedom.

Cochrane later applied this line of argumentation specifically to labour, so we can add:

> C4: 'Therefore, animals are not harmed when they are interfered with, used for particular purposes, or even have their desires shaped and moulded by others, granted doing so does not harm their wellbeing.' (Cochrane 2012: 73)
>
> C5: '[S]ubjecting an external will on them, say through directing them to the performance of certain kinds of labour, is not intrinsically problematic in the way that it is for persons'. (Cochrane 2016: 20)

C4 and C5 deny to animals what is widely considered the bare minimum for human workers. According to the International Labour Organization's (ILO) Declaration on Fundamental Principles and Rights at Work,[5] one of the four fundamental principles and rights at work is the prohibition of forced and compulsory labour (article 2b). The prohibition of forced labour and the concomitant right to freely choose one's work are also guaranteed by the UN's International Covenant on Civil and Political Rights (1996, article 8(3)), the International Covenant on Economic, Social and Cultural Rights (1996, article 6(1)), the Convention on the Elimination of All Forms of Discrimination against Women (1981, article 11), the Convention on the Rights of Persons with Disabilities (2008, article 27(1)), and the Convention on the Rights of the Child (1990, article 32 in connection with article 12). Given the axiomatic role of the prohibition of forced labour and the concomitant right to freely choose one's work for virtually all forms of human labour, can we dismiss these rights for animal workers as easily as Cochrane does?

Animals' Broad and Intrinsic Interests in Self-Determination

Cochrane argues that interests in autonomy, on the one hand, and well-being, on the other, belong to different categories of interests, but that autonomy and

---

[5] ILO 1998. This is widely considered a quasi-constitutional document of labour law (Fudge 2007: 30).

well-being overlap when lack of autonomy results in harm or suffering (Cochrane 2012: 73; 2016: 24). In the context of animal labour, Cochrane defines harm or suffering as arising from practices such as holding animals in unsuitable environments or close confinement, requiring animals to perform dangerous tasks (work at war, or for the police), or the use of violence against animal workers (Cochrane 2009: 669; 2016: 24). He does not, however, believe that animals have an interest in the free choice of work, or that they suffer from the denial of this freedom (Cochrane 2012: 76). This is in stark contrast to any 'fully-abled' human, who Cochrane says suffers not just from work that causes pain or lacks pleasure, but also from the absence of an opportunity to choose her work and pursue the life she considers good (Cochrane 2012: 76).

This distinction between autonomy and well-being may initially seem reasonable, but there is growing evidence that the harm and suffering caused by depriving animals of liberty has a much greater diameter than Cochrane imagined. Inherited views on animal liberty constantly underestimate the degree to which autonomous decision-making is conducive, indeed integral, to animals' well-being. In an experiment in the 1960s, Seligman and Maier subjected two groups of dogs to the same uncontrolled stressors: electric shocks. Only one group could press a panel to end the shocks for both groups. On Cochrane's analysis, having the right not to be subjected to electric shocks would be sufficient to remedy the problematic aspects of the experiment, so it should not matter which group was able to press the panel. But Seligman and Maier showed that the dogs in the group that could control the stressors recovered quickly, while the dogs without control exhibited signs of learned helplessness (Seligman and Maier 1967). This finding suggests there is something special about self-determined action for animals. More recently, researchers showed that marmosets were calmer if they could turn the light in their cages on or off (Buchanan-Smith and Badihi 2012). Self-determination seems to yield short- and long-term benefits for animals, whereas lack of autonomous decision-making and control creates short- and long-term harm and suffering.[6] Animals, in other words, often need to make or 'own' a decision in order to flourish and experience work as a meaningful activity.

One could argue that real choice is unnecessary, and that animals need only to believe they have made their own decisions. In a work environment, animals—if nudged in the desired direction and given controlled choices—might be encouraged to believe that they 'own' the decision to work, but they do not need fully-fledged rights to self-determination because unlike human workers, they 'cannot reflect and pursue their own conception of good work' (Cochrane 2016: 20; see also Garner 2016: 462). To stick with Seligman and Maier's dogs, sceptics could argue that creating the perception of self-determination suffices to ensure their

---

[6] The fact that we fail to explain most processes to animals may exacerbate these negative effects (Schmidt 2015: 103).

96 ANIMAL LABOUR

well-being, because dogs do not think about the good life outside the lab, and thus do not require a full set of choices.

But empirical evidence shows that individual preferences of animals cannot be predicted by their 'species-typical behaviour'. Animals have their very own individual preferences for, e.g., specific foods, locations, social partners, activities, and objects (Slocombe and Zuberbühler 2006) and they invest considerably into getting what they like (Hopper et al. 2015). A sceptic could object that this demonstrates only that animals' instrumental interest in autonomy is broader than is generally acknowledged, and that we could still satisfy those individual preferences if we passed laws to guarantee suitable work environments. These limited interests in satisfying individual preferences and in 'owning' a decision or type of work would still not suffice to grant animals a stand-alone right to self-determination at work. Consider an animal with ten feasible job options, including becoming a caretaker, a rescuer, a mine-tracker, a food inspector at the airport, or a yoga assistant.[7] Another animal, in contrast, is denied choice and is trained from the start as a yoga assistant. Let us imagine that both prefer assisting in yoga lessons to any other option. If autonomy has intrinsic value, the first set of options is more valuable than the second set of options, even if both animals would choose to become yoga assistants. For Cochrane, however, if we can predict that the animals' preferences are consistent with being a yoga assistant, there is no need to provide other options.

Recent research throws these assumptions into serious doubt. Having choices has a considerable positive effect on animals. Giant pandas (Owen et al. 2005), polar bears (Ross 2006), goats and sheep (Anderson et al. 2002), and many other animals were less stressed and made positive behavioural changes when provided with, e.g., more space, access to different rooms, or a choice about where to spend time. Rhesus monkeys preferred completing a series of cognitive tasks in a self-chosen order rather than an assigned order (Perdue et al. 2014). Research with giant pandas and polar bears (Owen et al. 2005; Ross 2006) showed that animals preferred choices even when they did not take advantage of them. Chimpanzees and gorillas responded positively to having the choice to go outside (demonstrating positive social behaviour like grooming, lower cortisol levels, a steep drop in signs of anxiety and restlessness), even if they chose to stay inside (Kurtycz et al. 2014). These findings, which have only recently received broader attention (Kurtycz 2015), have far-reaching consequences for our ethical evaluation of animal autonomy. They suggest that animals have broad, solid, and, most importantly, intrinsic interests in self-determination. To return to the example of the yoga assistant, because the first set of options is more valuable to animals, they should be given a broad and meaningful range of options, whether or not their

---

[7] I am adapting here an example from Carter 1999: 42.

choice can usually be predicted. This argument for choice trickles down to virtually all aspects of work, including the type of work, work processes, who to work with, how often to work, how long to work, how variable or repetitive work is, the work environment and atmosphere, the form, type, and frequency of remuneration, and play at work.

Towards an Inclusive Account of Self-Determination

There is growing evidence, therefore, that Cochrane's account fails to take into account animals' interests in self-determination. There is also growing evidence that his account fails to capture *humans'* interests in self-determination. For Cochrane, as we've seen, the interest of 'fully-abled' humans in self-determination derives from the fact that humans rationally 'form and pursue their own conception of the good'. Recent literature on human neurobiology and psychology reveals that we are all far less rational than philosophers suppose. The claim that humans are rational subjects is looking more and more like a fantasy.[8] Of course, Cochrane might respond that this just means that most of us are not entitled to rights to self-determination. But this would turn autonomy into an elitist club for the super-privileged, and would almost certainly operate to reproduce hidden sexist, ableist, racist, and classist agendas.[9] Moreover, it simply misidentifies our interest in self-determination. We value our freedom to choose even when our choices are impulsive, unconscious, or in other ways not rationally scrutinized. And if so, we have no reason to deny that animals too have an interest in their freedom to choose (Côté-Boudreau 2016; Pedersen 2011: 68). When we argue that animals lack autonomy based on standards we humans cannot meet, we uphold a deeply unjust system that reinforces our speciesist biases. We should instead err on the side of caution when we make assumptions about animals' interests and capacities, and we should expect animals to have strong and intrinsic interests in self-determination—whether they rationally reflect on their ends or not.

---

[8] This research decentres the glorification of (i) human will (ii), rationality and (iii), consciousness. Re (i), biological and neurocognitive sciences suggest that our mental states are epiphenomena of brain states, undermining the traditional notion of 'will'. Libet and Wegner's experiments show that brain activity precedes the agent's conscious decision to take action by a few hundred milliseconds (Libet 2005; Wegner 2002), so our brain makes the decision before we are conscious of it. Re (ii), far from rationally assessing the possible outcomes of our actions, most of us engage in a number of irrational biases. For example, we accept treatment that promises a 60 per cent survival rate, but reject treatment that claims 40 per cent of those treated will die (Załuski 2016: 42). We also tend to inaccurately assess probabilities because we use mental shortcuts (heuristics) to reach a decision (Tversky and Kahnemann 1974). Re (iii), much of the activities of the human mind are automatic and unconscious (Wilson 2002).

[9] Aristotle, Augustine, Thomas Aquinas, David Hume, Immanuel Kant, Georg Wilhelm Friedrich Hegel, Arthur Schopenhauer, and Friedrich Nietzsche all publicly maintained that women had no autonomy rights, because they were 'naturally less capable of rational thought and action, and thus incapable of genuine moral agency' (Warren 1997: 7).

98   ANIMAL LABOUR

Extending rights to self-determination beyond the rational 'fully-abled human' may seem like a tall order, but in fact we have already moved in this direction. The *lex lata* shows that in practice, rationality has little bearing on who gets to self-determine labour relationships, or on who can be forced to work. Although the ILO provides for some exceptions to the principle that labour may not be forced,[10] these exceptions to do not centre around rational autonomy or its lack. The prohibition of forced labour is accepted as fundamental for all persons, including those considered 'non-autonomous' on Cochrane's definition. ILO members have bound themselves by the Convention against Forced Labour (1932) not to use any form of forced or compulsory labour 'as a means of racial, social, national or religious discrimination' (article 1e). In my view, we should expand this list to include discrimination based on species membership, and clarify that forced labour cannot be used to reinforce speciesist biases. The case of animal workers makes plain that workers can have interests in liberty regardless of their capacities for rational reflection (Giroux 2016: 33). We must therefore change our under-standing of self-determination, by recognizing common ground and diversity among those who flourish as active participants in labour relationships. At minimum, this requires that we begin to take seriously all those capable of expressing their interests in determining for themselves if, what, how, and with whom they want to work.

The Prohibition of Forced Labour and the Right to Enter and Exit Work

The right to enter and exit work relationships on one's own terms is the logical counterpart to the prohibition of forced or compulsory labour. Forced or com-pulsory labour is defined in the ILO Convention against Forced Labour as 'all work or service which is exacted from any person under the menace of any penalty and for which the said person has not offered himself voluntarily' (1932, art. 2). For Marxists, every form of labour in the capitalist wage system amounts to forced labour, because the threat of economic ruin is always hanging over the worker's head like the sword of Damocles. The liberal democratic take is less critical. In its 2005 report *A Global Alliance Against Forced Labour*, the ILO clarified that forced labour goes beyond 'situations of pure economic necessity, as when a worker feels unable to leave a job because of the real or perceived absence of employment alternatives' (ILO 2005: 5). Forced labour must not be so narrowly read as to rely only on penal sanctions; it can also refer to economic penalties, the threat of

---

[10] As in the case of military service, prison labour, work done in emergencies, or minor communal services (Convention against Forced Labour, ILO, 1932, art. 2a–e).

dismissal, the threat of losing rights and privileges, the threat of violence, or psychological menace (ILO 2005: 5–6). The ILO recognizes that workers often enter labour contracts out of their own choice only to find that they are not free to withdraw their labour (ILO 2009: 6). Consent to work must thus be both *initially* and *periodically* secured—in the absence of force, coercion, compulsion, menace, or threat of loss of privileges—and all workers must have the freedom to revoke or withdraw their consent at any point.

If animals do have broad interests in self-determination, then the basic principle that workers cannot be forced to work, and are free to enter and exit work, must also apply to them. This does not however mean that we simply expand the existing requirements of consent—the standard test in employment law—to animal workers. That proposal seems 'fantastic' to most scholars (Nussbaum 2006: 333). How then can we operationalize this right to choose work? I will explore three different models—dissent, assent, and consent—and evaluate which model might best secure the right of animals to enter and exit work.

The Right to Dissent

Dissent is the standard model used for research with young children or people with severe mental disabilities. Of all models, it sets the lowest threshold for someone to be regarded as a self-determining agent. Rather than having to understand and rationally assess risks and benefits, an individual needs to be able to experience suffering, pain, or distress, and to show that said suffering, pain, or distress is unwanted. Standard research procedures do not yet grant animals a right to dissent, but scholars increasingly argue that animals are capable of dissent and already dissent persistently, and that their dissent should be accorded normative weight (Botero 2017; Fenton 2014; Kantin and Wendler 2015).

In *Fear of the Animal Planet* (2010), Hribal uncovers stories of elephants who broke free of their chains and sought revenge against those who maltreated them with bullhooks; tigers who leapt out of their enclosures in the San Francisco Zoo in 2006 and tracked down visitors who tormented them; and whales who targeted trainers that confined them and separated them from their offspring. More and more newspapers have reported on sheep escaping from the slaughterhouse, pigs jumping off transport trucks, and cows preferring to swim into the open sea rather than enduring heart-wrenching conditions aboard transport ships. At work, animals feign ignorance, reject commands, slow down work processes, refuse to work in heat or without adequate food, take breaks without permission, reject overtime, complain vocally, engage in open pilfering, break equipment, rebuff new tasks, escape, and initiate confrontations (Hribal 2007: 103).

The many ways in which animals protest, complain about, and resist forced work or inadequate working conditions do not go unheard. When he examined

100   ANIMAL LABOUR

the lives of animal workers from the seventeenth to the nineteenth century, Hribal noted: 'Most owners, managers, or observers of laboring animals—whether through their written word or through their counteractions—fully admitted to the presence of such resistance' (Hribal 2003: 449). But this scope for resistance is being deliberately silenced. The current trend in industrial production is to counter animals' resistance with technological and organizational automatization like chicken-harvesting machines, aquaculture design, and the like (Wadiwel 2018: 526). By foreclosing any possibility to encounter animals' resistance, we lose one of the most valuable checks on the right-or wrongfulness of our actions. Institutionalizing the dissent model for animal work would ensure that animal workers are heard, and this would help secure animals' welfare and respect their agency (Fenton 2014: 135; Kantin and Wendler 2015: 463). Dissent thus seems an excellent model to secure just relationships with animals, including relationships at the workplace.

However, the dissent model does have limits. First, and most notably, it is only an opt-out system. It does not require us to ensure animals *want* to work; only that they do *not disagree* to work. Some might consider these two sides of the same coin, but an opt-out system often is structurally biased in favour of humans profiting from animal labour, while an opt-in system would give animal workers the benefit of the doubt, by erring on the side of caution. Second, the dissent model disregards the structural, institutional, and interpersonal biases against animals that render their environment largely unresponsive to their concerns and reduce their ability to meaningfully resist (Meijer 2016: 66). Animals whose resistance goes unheard will often develop learned helplessness, which renders them inarticulate—as Despret suggests in her description of Harlow's rhesus monkeys (Despret 2004: 124). A system that blindly treats the absence of dissent as evidence of voluntary acceptance is likely to legitimate and reiterate existing forms of oppression. Third, claims that animals are only capable of dissent reduce them to mere reactants, passive beings to whom things happen. It ignores the manifold ways in which animals shape and change the world around them, and initiate and foster relationships. This criticism does not mean that we should completely reject dissent as a standard, but we must consider other options that can help better secure animals' interests.

The Right to Assent

The next step beyond dissent is assent. Assent is an agreement obtained from those deemed incapable of 'informed consent'—e.g., those who are 'not able to enter into a legal contract' (Ford et al. 2007: 20)—but whose preferences and desires cannot simply be brushed aside when making decisions that concern them. In the context of work, assent requires a subject's explicit, affirmative agreement to

TOWARD A PROHIBITION OF FORCED LABOUR   101

work, and their understanding of the nature of work.[11] It is therefore an opt-in provision. The assent model for animal workers would be part of a participatory rights agenda (Dockett and Perry 2011: 233), since it recognizes them as able to participate in important social and institutional structures, and fosters a communicative relationship with them.

There are relatively few discussions of whether or how the assent standard can be applied to animals. On its own, it seems unable to prevent harms caused to animals (e.g., Kantin and Wendler 2015: 470). But in fact, the assent model is typically combined with some account of guardianship, and in that sense, can be seen as a form of 'mediated consent'. On a mediated consent model, we need both an animal's assent *and* the consent of their (legal) guardian (Mancini 2017: 227).

This introduction of a guardian complicates the link between assent and self-determination. In most versions of an assent model, the guardian plays two distinct roles. First, they interpret the animal's communicated subjective will (to assess whether they indeed 'assent'); and, second, they are authorized to override that subjective will if they judge it to be in the animal's own best interest from an 'objective' or 'informed' standpoint. The guardian is thus both an *interpreter* of the animal's subjective will and a *protector* of the animal's best interest.

This may seem like an ideal solution because it ensures responsiveness to animals' preferences in a human-dominated world while protecting them— where necessary—from making overly risky decisions. What it ignores, however, is the dangers of the over-paternalistic power of guardians. If the subjective will of the animal to participate comes into conflict with the guardian's assessment of risks and benefits, the decision-making power of the guardian will trump that of the animal. Experts in child research call this a 'Catch-22', where assenting subjects are considered competent if they agree with their guardian but incompetent if they fail to take the guardian's advice (Neill 2005: 49; Shield and Baum 1994).

Paternalistic patterns are deeply entrenched in human–animal relationships, even in contexts that are allegedly governed by love rather than instrumental profit. Companion cats are routinely held indoors because 'they don't know about the dangers that await them outside the safe home'; domestic dogs are permanently leashed outdoors because 'they wouldn't be able to handle traffic'; etc. If we endorse the assent model without providing guidance for cases when judgements conflict, we risk trivializing animals' intrinsic interest in autonomy and their role as co-citizens and full members of our common society. Animals should have the opportunity to choose their own path, which includes making 'mistakes'. As Parsons et al. succinctly put it, 'Never go along with assent because it's missing a huge opportunity' (Parsons et al. 2016: 136).

---

[11] For an application to this model in the case of young children, see Dockett and Perry 2011.

102 ANIMAL LABOUR

The Right to Consent

This naturally raises the question whether we can allow animals to make their own choices without these choices being filtered and mediated by guardians. In the field of human bioethics, the right to give such unmediated consent is typically tied to the idea of 'informed consent'. Individuals are authorized to give their own consent to an activity (such as work), without needing the approval of a guardian, if they know the risks and benefits of work and its alternatives, know that one can withdraw anytime, have the capacity to make a choice, and can communicate their choice (Wellesley and Jenkins 2015: 632).

This idea of informed consent is widely seen as the ethical gold standard. Like the assent model, it is an opt-in rather than opt-out system, which is particularly desirable when past injustices are long-standing and deep-rooted. It also puts a legal and moral onus on officials to ensure that individuals understand what they are agreeing to, and prohibits attempts to manipulate individuals into consenting through fear or inducements. It therefore is intended to protect subjects from physical and psychological harm, and to ensure that decision-makers understand what they consent to and are not overburdened by a decision (De Lourdes Levy et al. 2003: 629).

Most scholars assume that animals 'obviously' cannot give consent in this form: they cannot sign written contracts and, even if they could, they would not understand the terms and conditions of the contract. To pretend that animals can consent, when they clearly do not understand the risks involved, would be politically dangerous. Indeed, as noted in the Introduction to this volume, animal exploitation industries often claim that animals consent to participate in research, agriculture, or entertainment. The pretence of consent becomes a weapon to defend animal exploitation, not an effective protection against it.

This would seem to imply that in the case of animals, we must rest content with dissent and assent, and not reach for the higher standard of consent. However, there is growing sense amongst many commentators that we need to rethink the standard of consent, even in the human case. History shows that the informed consent model, rather than protecting vulnerable individuals from being overburdened by a decision, often excludes them from the group of decision-makers and reinforces their marginalization through its strong focus on language and rationality (Greenhough and Roe 2011: 48). Even for able-bodied, adult humans, the 'paper-based' standard of consent can fail to capture what is at stake. People are asked to sign contracts and agree to terms and conditions they have a hard time understanding, and may end up being bound by decisions that do not feel authentically their own (Parsons et al. 2016: 138).

The Havasupai case illustrates this problem. In the early 1990s, Arizona State University recruited members of the Havasupai Tribe to participate in a research project on Type II diabetes, a common disease among members living in remote parts of the Grand Canyon region. Tribal members were asked to supply blood samples and gave researchers blanket consent 'to study the causes of behavioural/ medical disorders'. The blood samples were used for other research projects unrelated to Type II Diabetes, in particular, to study the origin of the tribe and inbreeding among members. The Havasupai Tribe challenged the contract they had signed, arguing that it was so broadly formulated as to be virtually meaning-less, and that it had been written in English, the second language of most Havasupai members. The Arizona court rejected these arguments and determined that the degree of information and the consent given on this basis were sufficient for the contract to remain valid under the law.[12] In this case, and many others, the legal test of informed consent offers no guarantee of an ethical relationship, and no guarantee that the relationship will develop in ways that are responsive to the interests of all parties.

To address these defects of informed consent, some authors have been thinking about new models of consent that are not atomistic, rationalist, and exclusionary. Greenhough and Roe (2011), for example, argue that in biomedical science and health geography, the body, which is relational, situated, and affectual, plays a key role in shaping relations. The relationships that matter most to people, and in which they are best at expressing their preferences, are constituted by 'more-than-verbal forms of communication' (Greenhough and Roe 2011: 49). On this model, meaningful or authentic consent is not determined by signing forms that with-stand judicial scrutiny; rather, authentic consent is a practice—an 'embodied skill'. An ethically defensible approach to consent would not just attend to legal signatures, but would be responsive in an ongoing way to embodied expressions of fear, anxiety, confusion, hesitation, mistrust, and other manifestations of the withdrawal of authentic consent.

As Greenhough and Roe note, this idea of embodied consent may have important potential for thinking about animals' rights to self-determination. Just as the body plays a vital role in shaping human relationships, it is a central means of communication among animals. Animals readily use their bodies, their facial expressions, and their chemical, olfactory, and other senses, to communi-cate willingness to embark on or to reject a project. As experts in somatic sensibility, animals have a tremendous repertoire of communicative skills. These are the forms of embodied behaviour and expressions that we must understand if we want to learn about animals' preferences. When we approach the question of consent from this perspective, we shift the question from 'Can animals sign and understand contracts?' to 'Under what conditions do animals consent in lived relationships with one another, and can we develop a similar model for human–animal relationships?' Once we accept that animals are

---

[12] *Tilousi v. Arizona State Univ. Bd. of Regents*, No. 04-CV-1290, 2005 WL 6199562 (D. Ariz., Mar. 3, 2005) (U.S.).

104   ANIMAL LABOUR

experts on their own lives (Greenhough and Roe 2011: 60), our focus shifts from trying to fit animals into our world to developing background conditions that help animals maximally secure their interests on their own terms and under their own conditions. In paediatric ethics, there is a general presumption that participation must be secured 'to the greatest extent possible in the decision-making process' (Tri-Council 2014: art. 3.9a), and I would argue the same principle requires that we empower animals, in this sense, to make their own decisions through embodied consent.

How exactly would this differ from the assent model? Embodied consent, as I envision it, would not rely on a legal guardian in the same way. Like the assent model, the embodied consent model requires both *interpretation* (what is the animals' subjective will?) and *protection* (would allowing the animal to act upon her subjective will threaten her basic objective interests?). As we saw earlier, in the case of the assent model, these dual tasks are assigned to a single human: the legal guardian. By contrast, an embodied consent model would separate those tasks, and moreover would not leave either to the sole discretion of a single individual. Rather, embodied consent would operate through public discussion (as the basis for *interpretation*) and public standard-setting (as the basis for decisions about *protection*). Let me explain these two processes.

Interpretation: Embodied consent is inherently relational rather than atomistic; it relies on a host of verbal and non-verbal signals of communication and is developed through direct social and personal experience.[13] Interpretation does not lie with one single legal guardian, but shifts to the social environment of animals, which varies depending on where the animals are and what work they do. At first sight, this might appear to open up the opportunity for individuals to evade responsibility, leading to a version of the 'tragedy of the commons'. But if carefully designed, embodied consent expands the network of people responsible for correctly interpreting animals' preferences. We can avoid making animals dependent on a single interpreter,[14] and multiply their chances of contesting paternalistic routines and structures by involving multiple parties, with different views and experiences. If we demand that the community attends and carefully listens to animals, and takes their desires and preferences seriously, citizens will

---

[13] Embodied consent can only be secured from animals in a safe, responsive, and trusting environment (Noble-Carr 2006). Animals must have enough time to make considered decisions, and consent must be obtained on an ongoing basis, rather than as a one-off (Dockett and Parry 2011: 234).

[14] Donaldson and Kymlicka have argued that even well-intentioned farmed animal sanctuaries risk becoming 'total institutions'—operating on a paternalist model that limits animals' participation in key decisions affecting their lives and that can diminish animals' well-being and ultimately infringe their rights (2015: 56–7). Having only one guardian-interpreter, without formal rules that guide or limit the interpreter's actions, can similarly create a total environment for animal workers that thwarts their rights. See also Gheaus' argument that vulnerable individuals should not be subject to 'monopolies of care' (Gheaus 2018).

gradually become experienced and skilled interpreters for animals, just as they become more experienced in listening to and understanding other people. Rather than perpetuating the common view that animals need a guardian to protect them, community interpretation would move us toward normalizing, empowering, and including animals as decision-makers.

Protection: Like the assent model, embodied consent would ascribe certain objective interests to animals—interests considered so vital they could justify overriding an animals' expressed subjective will. However, these interests would be understood differently from the assent model. Determining the limits of an animal's subjective will is not assigned to the judgement of an individual guardian, but would be secured primarily through the collective elaboration of legal rules against particular kinds of harms or risks or force. As with human labourers in liberal democracies, there would be procedural and substantive limits to animals' ability to consent in the workplace. On the procedural side, consent must be secured absent of force, fraud or deceit, duress, or any 'ulterior form of constraint or coercion' (Nuremberg Code 1949: art. 1). On the substantive side, individuals would not be permitted to consent to death (or killing, more precisely), or to severe violations of their bodily and mental integrity.

These limits illuminate another crucial difference. Whereas the assent model positively determines the conditions under which an animal's volition is valid, the embodied consent model delineates the 'outer limits' of animals' ability to consent by negatively determining when their consent is invalid. This means the test is far less pervasive, and more likely to avoid paternalism, domination, and instrumentalization. It provides a learning laboratory so animals learn from their own mistakes and secures broad rights to self-determination that enable animals to develop their own modes of being and living.

Not every animal will necessarily profit from suddenly having this much self-determination, particularly if they are abused survivors or have suffered from overly paternalistic relationships that have generated learned helplessness. Donaldson and Kymlicka draw on the literature on citizenship for children to argue for 'scaffolding' meaningful choice for animals (2016b). Scaffolding emerges from a social constructivist theory that suggests we foster animals' ability to make decisions by reasonable measures like structured interaction, learning, and training. We could begin to empower animals to make use of their right to dissent, and gradually move towards the assent model. We would not stop there, however, because if we maintained the assent standard as the default for animals, we would fail to envision a society legitimated and governed by processes accessible to all members. Once animals acquire the necessary expertise to make self-determined decisions as embodied consenters, some of the scaffolds (i.e., the legal guardian) can be removed.

So the embodied consent model is, I believe, genuinely distinct from, and preferable to, both the dissent and assent models. However, it also differs from the original standard of informed consent. We can distinguish embodied consent from informed consent along two lines. First, embodied consent does not rely on the sovereign will of isolated individuals, but involves a more 'distributed' account of freedom, recognizing how we rely on others to make our will effective. Second, the mode of communication is not based on legalistic forms of communication (e.g., signature) that risk concealing important information. Embodied consent relies on a more holistic approach by interpreting body language and intersubjective somatic communication.

Embodied and informed consent are, however, *alike* in key respects, including the importance of information. Even on an embodied conception of consent, animals cannot be asked for their consent unless they have access to all information necessary to make an informed decision. Animals may not understand human language well enough to determine the possible risks and benefits of an offer, but this does not absolve humans of our responsibility to inform animals. We must learn more about how animals collect and share information. We know that when animals make decisions, they can communicate them directly to other animals. In large groups, for example, many communicate locally with spatial neighbours to express their viewpoint via body posture, ritualized movement, specific vocalization, chemical trails, or other cues (Conradt and Roper 2005: 454). Decision-making among animals may sometimes be spontaneous and animals may instinctively make certain decisions, just as we do. But they often make decisions after engaging in complex and elaborate informative and deliberative processes. New research reveals that many animals spend considerable time collecting data and assessing it before making their decision (Cronin and Stumpe 2014: 7; King and Sueur 2011: 1251; Möglich and Hölldobler 1974). These insights should prompt us to be more creative in developing ethical and political standards of human–animal relationships, so *we* can better inform animals of their options.

Like informed consent, embodied consent also requires that the addressees of information understand the information they receive. Some animals who were previously bereft of choice (e.g., due to confinement or paternalism) might not be experienced enough to understand certain information and gauge the risks and benefits of a particular decision. For these animals, the appropriate test may be mediated assent. But, as I argued above, as animals expand their expertise through experience, mediated assent should slowly be replaced by the more capacious standard of embodied consent.

In short, embodied consent is a feasible and compelling standard to use in work contexts as it maximally secures animals' agency. Where appropriate procedural limits (against force, fraud or deceit, duress) and substantive limits (against death and severe violation of one's mental and bodily integrity) are in place, and where appropriate practices for scaffolding animals' choices have been adopted, an animal's subjective will should generally be authoritative. We may still want and need the traditional 'informed consent' standard for certain high-stakes medical and legal decisions, but embodied consent is arguably a more realistic test for many day-to-day decisions, for both animals and humans.

If this argument is correct, then securing animals' right to free work is both possible and necessary. It will involve all three of the standards we have discussed: dissent, assent, and (embodied) consent. Dissent should be available to animals at all times to immediately halt work that makes them uncomfortable or that they do not want to do. Embodied assent mediated by individual guardians can be used to assess whether, what type, with whom, and how long animals want to work, but this model on its own is not sufficiently capacious to secure animal interests. Embodied consent mediated with collective safeguards fills the gap, charting a path to taking animals seriously as self-determining agents, and pushing us to learn, as a society, to pay attention and respond to the manifold ways in which animals communicate. A system that adopts embodied consent sends a clear message to animals that they are in a safe environment where their preferences are respected.

Putting the Test into Practice

To gauge the usefulness of these propositions, it might help to look at a concrete example like the canine conservation programmes that D'Souza, Hovorka, and Niel examine in chapter 4 of this volume. How do these programmes fare in terms of securing the dogs' right to freely chose work? It seems that the two canine conservation teams they explore—in Alberta and Ontario—do not meet the test of consent to work when recruiting dogs. It's true that the main focus of both teams is to recruit dogs with high energy and strong play drives, and one might think that these traits are a proxy for consent since they ensure 'that the dogs are consistently motivated to work' (D'Souza 2018: 16). But this method sidesteps, rather than secures, the animals' right to enter and exit work. Dogs are not given the time necessary to assess the situation, probe their potential future work place, get to know their co-workers, or make informed decisions. Instead, employers look for dogs who 'jump' at the job without thinking twice about it. There are good reasons to believe that some breeding dogs have a single drive, and when employed to serve that drive, animals are ultimately deprived of conscious and self-determined choice and simply 'made to consent' to the purposes *we want them* to serve. Giving animals a range of options would require a very different recruitment process. As one of the managers of the canine teams stated, in explaining why they have moved to recruiting animals from dedicated breeders:

108　ANIMAL LABOUR

'it takes a lot more time and effort to find a dog from a shelter with the right traits for their work' (D'Souza 2018: 70).

There are similar gaps with respect to animals' *ongoing* consent to work. The provincial governments of Alberta and Ontario do not seem to have formal practices in place that secure and give effect to the dogs' dissent. Only if a dog's dissatisfaction with their work manifests as unfitness to work can a dog refuse to work on a given day or exit the programme. The departments may therefore continue to employ dogs who are unhappy at work, who would have chosen a different task, or who may want to switch peers or trainers.[15]

In fact, the case of conservation canines can be seen as an example of the Catch-22 discussed earlier in systems of mediated assent based on a single guardian. Trainers can be considered as government-appointed legal guardians for the dogs, and certainly many trainers express a commitment to this sort of guardianship.[16] They are often deeply connected to the dogs they work with, and are in a good position to gauge their many embodied forms of communication, and there is every reason to believe that they prioritize and protect the safety of the animals. However, as Balcombe argued, 'a safer life is by no means a better life' (Balcombe 2009: 2014; Donaldson and Kymlicka 2016b: 188), and the canine conservation programme seems to discount any intrinsic interest in autonomy. When the dogs live, work, train, and recreate with a single trainer, and that one person has a monopoly on interpreting the dog's assent (D'Souza 2018: 79–80), there is clear risk of bias and paternalism. Responsibility is unnecessarily concentrated in one person, who may easily misunderstand, misinterpret, or read their own preferences into a dog's behaviour, and there are no safeguards in place to prevent this. If we used embodied consent, we would instead opt to create multiple layers of responsibility for interpretation, and have more accessible and transparent rules on protection to govern the limits of the dogs' decision-making authority.

A Broader Quest for Animal Workplace Democracy

Over the centuries, humans have come to rely on and expect the benefits that they reap from the work of animals. Most societies still view animals as mere input

---

[15] That the teams have difficulty giving full effect to the dogs' resistance is implied in the following passage: 'The most frustrating experiences are when you want to work and the dog doesn't. On the canine [training] course I had a period there where it just became too much for the dog and we had to take some time off. Where you're building and I want to keep building but the dog's telling you, "I've had enough." So you've gotta listen to the dog and stop, take it easy when you have to take it easy even though you want to continue to work, if your dog doesn't you've got to change things up' (D'Souza 2018: 80).

[16] As D'Souza et al. note, in reality, the conservation canines are legally defined as property, and hence do not benefit from any legally recognized form of guardianship, but it seems that many of the human handlers think of themselves in guardian-like terms.

TOWARD A PROHIBITION OF FORCED LABOUR 109

factors, tools, or resources to deploy for human ends. These views and expectations have long been affirmed, legitimated, and protected by law. The growing recognition of animal labour is part of a countermovement to this history. It posits animals as beings with agency, who invest their subjectivity in work (Porcher 2017). Acknowledging animal labour need not gloss over our exploitation of animals. As Hamilton says, 'to define work as work does not preclude the recognition of exploitation' (2016: 125). Based on the idea that work is a continuum that can range from exploitation to justice (Skrivanvoka 2010; Coulter 2019), scholars are demanding robust rights for working animals, including the right to retirement, safe working conditions, and collective bargaining (Cochrane 2016).

In this chapter, I have argued that for labour to become a site of interspecies justice, animals must also have the right to enter and exit the labour relationship, to freely choose their work, and not be subject to forced labour. Animals are harmed by unfreedoms to a far greater extent than we currently acknowledge. Even when choice and control do not deliver specific instrumental benefits, they considerably increase animals' well-being, which demonstrates that animals have intrinsic interests in self-determination and require rights to secure the fulfilment of those interests.

Formulating effective standards of self-determination will not be easy, and we need to constantly remember that work environments can easily be manipulated to manufacture animal consent. Some argue, for example, that cows have a meaningful range of options if they can choose between being milked inside or being milked in a meadow by a mobile robot (Driessen 2014). But can we reasonably speak of self-determination when cows are forced to dwell in a certain place, fenced in by railings they did not erect, are impregnated by force, and are separated from their newborns against their will? If we take seriously an animal's right to choose to enter and exit work relationships, we must provide them with a much wider range of choices about possible lives (Donaldson and Kymlicka 2016a: 237).

In that sense, we need to embed our account of freedom at work within a larger account of interspecies justice that attends to the deeper power relations that structure employment. What is not in a contract, what is considered nonnegotiable for an individual animal worker, is just as important as what is in the contract (Coulter 2017: 74). While I have focused in this chapter on the self-determination rights of individual animals to enter and leave work, a fuller account of interspecies justice would require attending to issues of collective self-determination as well, including co-determination rights about conditions at work, management, and oversight. We need, in short, to incorporate animals into our conception of 'workplace democracy' (Gomez and Gomez 2016: 4), and of democracy more generally (Donaldson and Kymlicka 2011). Only when animals have the right to self-determination *and* co-determination at work, does labour have a reasonable chance of becoming a site of interspecies justice.

110 ANIMAL LABOUR

Because rights to self- and co-determination at work are process-oriented (Fudge 2007: 59; Langille 2005: 431), and do not predetermine the outcomes, we should be ready for animals' voices to radically change the concept of labour as we know it today. Rights to self- and co-determination ensure that we do not straightjacket animals into our preconceived ideas of labour. I began with Johnson's quote, and in conclusion would like to return to it. Conferring rights to self-determination on animal workers requires we answer the following questions: Will we continue to silence and exploit animal workers? Or are we prepared to listen and attend to their interests, desires, and preferences, incorporate their visions of a workplace community, and radically change our own views about interspecies justice?[17]

References

Anderson, Ursala, Marcie Benne, Mollie Bloomsmith, and Terry Maple. 2002. 'Retreat Space and Human Visitor Density Moderate Undesirable Behavior in Petting Zoo Animals'. *Journal of Applied Animal Welfare Science* 5(2): 125–37.

Balcombe, Jonathan. 2009. 'Animal Pleasure and its Moral Significance'. *Applied Animal Behaviour Science* 188(3/4): 208–16.

Botero, Maria. 2017. 'From What Kind of Research Can They Dissent? Distinguishing between Biomedical and Behavioral Research in Granting Dissent and Assent to Chimpanzees Used in Experimentation'. *Cambridge Quarterly of Healthcare Ethics* 26: 288–91.

Buchanan-Smith, Hannah, and Inbal Badihi. 2012. 'The Psychology of Control: Effects of Control over Supplementary Light on Welfare of Marmosets'. *Applied Animal Behaviour Science* 137(3): 166–74.

Carter, Ian. 1999. *A Measure of Freedom*. Oxford: Oxford University Press.

Clark, Jonathan L. 2014. 'Labourers or Lab Tools? Rethinking the Role of Lab Animals in Clinical Trials'. In *The Rise of Critical Animal Studies: From the Margins to the Centre*, edited by Nik Taylor and Richard Twine, 139–65. Oxon: Routledge.

Cochrane, Alasdair. 2009. 'Do Animals Have an Interest in Liberty?'. *Political Studies* 57: 660–79.

Cochrane, Alasdair. 2012. *Animal Rights without Liberation: Applied Ethics and Human Obligations*. New York: Columbia University Press.

Cochrane, Alasdair. 2016. 'Labour Rights for Animals'. In *The Political Turn in Animal Ethics*, edited by Robert Garner and Siobhan O'Sullivan, 15–32. London: Rowman and Littlefield.

---

[17] I would like to thank all of the participants in the workshop 'Animal Labour: Ethical, Legal and Political Perspectives on Recognizing Animals' Work' at Queen's University for their feedback on an early draft of this paper. Special thanks to Will Kymlicka and Kendra Coulter for their detailed comments, suggestions, and interest in the topic.

Conradt, Larissa, and Timothy J. Roper. 2005. 'Consensus Decision Making in Animals'. *TRENDS in Ecology and Evolution* 20(8): 449–56.

Côté-Boudreau, Frédéric. 2016. *Inclusive Autonomy: A Theory of Freedom for Everyone.* PhD. Thesis, Queen's University, Kingston.

Coulter, Kendra. 2019. 'Toward Humane Jobs and Work-Lives for Animals'. In *Animal Labour: A New Frontier of Interspecies Justice?*, edited by Charlotte Blattner, Kendra Coulter, and Will Kymlicka, 29–47. Oxford: Oxford University Press.

Coulter, Kendra. 2017. 'Humane Jobs: A Political Economic Vision for Interspecies Solidarity and Human–Animal Wellbeing'. *Politics and Animals* 2(1): 67–77.

Cronin, Adam, and Martin Stumpe. 2014. 'Ants Work Harder During Consensus Decision-Making in Small Groups'. *Journal of the Royal Society Interface* 11: 1–8.

De Lourdes Levy, Maria, Victor Larcher, and Ronald Kurz. 2003. 'Informed Consent/Assent in Children: Statement of the Ethics Working Group of the Confederation of European Specialists in Paediatrics (CESP)'. *European Journal of Pediatrics* 162: 629–33.

D'Souza, Renée. 2018. *Conservation Canines in Canada: Roles, Welfare & Environmental Impacts.* Thesis for the Degree of Master of Environmental Studies. Queen's University, Kingston, ON.

D'Souza, Renée, Alice Hovorka, and Lee Niel. 2019. 'Conservation Canines: Exploring Dog Roles, Circumstances, Welfare Status'. In *Animal Labour: A New Frontier of Interspecies Justice?*, edited by Charlotte Blattner, Kendra Coulter, and Will Kymlicka, 65–87. Oxford: Oxford University Press.

Despret, Vinciane. 2004. 'The Body We Care for: Figures of Anthropo-zoo-genesis'. *Body and Society* 10(2/3): 111–34.

Dockett, Sue, and Bob Perry. 2011. 'Researching with Young Children: Seeking Assent'. *Child Indicators Research* 4: 231–47.

Donaldson, Sue, and Will Kymlicka. 2011. *Zoopolis: A Political Theory of Animal Rights.* Oxford: Oxford University Press.

Donaldson, Sue, and Will Kymlicka. 2015. 'Farmed Animal Sanctuaries: The Heart of the Movement? A Socio-Political Perspective'. *Politics and Animals* 1(1): 50–74.

Donaldson, Sue, and Will Kymlicka. 2016a. 'Between Wilderness and Domestication: Rethinking Categories and Boundaries in Response to Animal Agency'. In *Animal Ethics in the Age of Humans*, edited by Bernice Bovenkerk and Jozef Keulartz, 225–42. Cham: Springer.

Donaldson, Sue, and Will Kymlicka. 2016b. 'Rethinking Membership and Participation in an Inclusive Democracy: Cognitive Disability, Children, Animals'. In *Disability and Political Theory*, edited by Barbara Arneil and Nancy Hirschmann, 168–97. Cambridge: Cambridge University Press.

Driessen, Clemens. 2014. 'Animal Deliberation'. In *Political Animals and Animal Politics*, edited by Marcel Wissenburg and David Schlosberg, 90–106. London: Palgrave.

Fenton, Andrew. 2014. 'Can a Chimp Say "No"? Reenvisioning Chimpanzee Dissent in Harmful Research'. *Cambridge Quarterly of Healthcare Ethics* 23: 130–9.

112   ANIMAL LABOUR

Ford, Karen, Judy Sankey, and Jackie Crisp. 2007. 'Development of Children's Assent Documents Using a Child-centred Approach'. *Journal of Child Health Care* 11(1): 19–28.

Fudge, Judy. 2007. 'The New Discourse of Labor Rights: From Social to Fundamental Rights'. *Comparative Labor Law & Policy* 29(1): 29–66.

Garner, Robert. 2016. 'Animals and Democratic Theory: Beyond an Anthropocentric Account'. *Contemporary Political Theory* 16(4): 459–77.

Gheaus, Anca. 2018. 'Children's Vulnerability and Legitimate Authority over Children'. *Journal of Applied Philosophy* 35: 60–75.

Giroux, Valéry. 2016. 'Animals Do Have an Interest in Liberty'. *Journal of Animal Ethics* 6(1): 20–43.

Gomez, Rafael, and Juan Gomez. 2016. *Workplace Democracy for the 21st Century: Towards an Agenda for Employee Voice and Representation in Canada.* Toronto: Broadbent Institute.

Greenhough, Beth, and Emma Roe. 2011. 'Ethics, Space, and Somatic Sensibilities: Comparing Relationships between Scientific Researchers and their Human and Animal Subjects'. *Environment and Planning D: Society and Space* 29: 47–66.

Hamilton, Carrie. 2016. 'Sex, Work, Meat: The Feminist Politics of Veganism'. *Feminist Review* 114: 112–29.

Hopper, Lydia, Laura Kurtycz, Stephen Ross, and Kristin Bonnie. 2015. 'Captive Chimpanzee Foraging in Social Setting: A Test of Problem Solving, Flexibility, and Spatial Discounting'. *PeerJ* 3: e833.

Hribal, Jason. 2003. '"Animals are Part of the Working Class": A Challenge to Labor History'. *Labor History* 44(4): 435–53.

Hribal, Jason. 2007. 'Animals, Agency, and Class: Writing the History of Animals from Below'. *Human Ecology Forum* 14(1): 101–12.

Hribal, Jason. 2010. *Fear of the Animal Planet: The Hidden Story of Animal Resistance.* Petrolia: CounterPunch.

Hribal, Jason. 2012. 'Animals Are Part of the Working Class Reviewed'. *Borderlands* 11: 1–37.

International Labour Organization. 1998. *Declaration on Fundamental Principles and Rights at Work.* Adopted at its 86th Sess. Geneva, June 1998.

International Labour Organization. 2005. *A Global Alliance Against Forced Labour.* [online] http://www.ilo.org/public/english/standards/relm/ilc/ilc93/pdf/rep-i-b.pdf.

International Labour Organization. 2009. *The Costs of Coercion: Global Report under the Follow-up to the ILO Declaration on Fundamental Principles and Rights at Work.* International Labour Conference, 98th Sess., 2009, Report I(B).

Johnson, Kij. 2009. *The Evolution of Trickster Stories among the Dogs of North Park after the Change.* [online] http://podcastle.org/2009/07/09/pc060-the-evolution-of-trickster-stories-among-the-dogs-of-north-park-after-the-change/.

Kantin, Holly, and David Wendler. 2015. 'Is There a Role for Assent or Dissent in Animal Research?' *Cambridge Quarterly of Healthcare Ethics* 24: 459–72.

King, Andrew, and Cédric Sueur. 2011. 'Where Next? Group Coordination and Collective Decision Making by Primates'. *International Journal of Primatology* 32: 1245–67.

Kurtycz, Laura. 2015. 'Choice and Control for Animals in Captivity'. *The Psychologist* 28(11): 892–94.

Kurtycz, Laura, Katherine Wagner, and Stephen Ross. 2014. 'The Choice to Access Outdoor Areas Affects the Behavior of Great Apes'. *Journal of Applied Animal Welfare Science* 17(3): 185–97.

Kymlicka, Will. 2017. 'Social Membership: Animal Law beyond the Property/Personhood Impasse'. *Dalhousie Law Journal* 40: 123–55.

Langille, Brian. 2005. 'Core Labour Rights—The True Story (Reply to Alston)'. *European Journal of International Law* 16(3): 409–37.

Libet, Benjamin. 2005. *Mind Time: The Temporal Factor in Consciousness*. Cambridge: Harvard University Press.

Linzey, Andrew, and Clair Linzey. 2018. 'Introduction: The Challenge of Animal Ethics'. In *Palgrave Handbook of Practical Animal Ethics*, edited by Andrew Linzey and Clair Linzey, 1–24. London: Palgrave.

Mancini, Clara. 2017. 'Towards an Animal-centred Ethics for Animal–Computer Interaction'. *International Journal of Human-Computer Studies* 98: 221–33.

Meijer, Eva. 2016. 'Interspecies Democracies'. In *Animal Ethics in the Age of Humans*, edited by Bernice Bovenkerk and Jozef Keulartz, 53–72. Cham: Springer.

Möglich, Michael, and Berthold Hölldobler. 1974. 'Social Carrying Behavior and Division of Labor During Next Moving in Ants'. *Psyche* 81: 219–36.

Neill, Sarah. 2005. 'Research With Children: A Critical Review of Guidelines'. *Journal of Child Health Care* 9(1): 46–58.

Noble-Carr, Debbie. 2006. 'Engaging Children in Research on Sensitive Issues'. *Institute of Child Protection Studies, Australian Catholic University and ACT Department of Disability, Housing and Community Services*. [online] http://www.acu.edu.au/icps.

Noske, Barbara. 1997. *Beyond Boundaries: Humans and Animals*. Montreal: Black Rose Books.

Nussbaum, Martha. 2006. *Frontiers of Justice: Disability, Nationality, Species Membership*. Cambridge: Harvard University Press.

Owen, Megan, Ronald Swaisgood, Nancy Czekala, and Donald Lindburg. 2005. 'Enclosure Choice and Well-being in Giant Pandas: Is It all about Control?'. *Zoo Biology* 24(5): 475–81.

Pachirat, Timothy. 2011. *Every Twelve Seconds: Industrialized Slaughter and the Politics of Sight*. New Haven: Yale University Press.

Parry, Lucy. 2016. 'Deliberative Democracy and Animals: Not So Strange Bedfellows'. In *The Political Turn in Animal Ethics*, edited by Robert Garner and Siobhan O'Sullivan, 137–53. London: Rowman and Littlefield.

114 ANIMAL LABOUR

Parsons, Sarah, Gina Sherwood, and Chris Abbott. 2016. 'Informed Consent with Children and Young People in Social Research: Is There Scope for Innovation?' *Children & Society* 30: 132–45.

Pederson, Helena. 2011. 'Release the Moths: Critical Animal Studies and the Posthumanist Critique'. *Culture, Theory and Critique* 51(1): 65–81.

Perdue, Bonnie, Theodore Evans, David Washburn, Duane Bumbaugh, and Michael Beran. 2014. 'Do Monkeys Choose to Choose?' *Learning & Behavior* 42(2): 164–175.

Porcher, Jocelyne. 2017. *The Ethics of Animal Labor: A Collaborative Utopia*. Cham: Palgrave.

Ross, Stephen. 2006. 'Issues of Choice and Control in the Behaviour of a Pair of Polar Bears'. *Behavioural Processes* 73(1): 117–20.

Sandøe, Peter, and Clare Palmer. 2014. 'For Their Own Good'. In *The Ethics of Captivity*, edited by Lori Gruen, 135–54. Oxford: Oxford University Press.

Schmidt, Andreas. 2015. 'Why Animals have an Interest in Liberty'. *Historical Social Research* 40(4): 92–109.

Seligman, Martin, and Steven Maier. 1967. 'Failure to Escape Traumatic Shock'. *Journal of Experimental Psychology* 74(1): 1–9.

Shield, J.P.H., and J.D. Baum. 1994. 'Children's Consent to Treatment'. *British Medical Journal* 308: 1182–3.

Skrivankova, Klara. 2010. 'Between Decent Work and Forced Labour: Examining the Continuum of Exploitation'. *JRF Programme Paper: Forced Labour*. Joseph Rowntree Foundation.

Slocombe, Katie, and Klaus Zuberbühler. 2006. 'Food-associated Calls in Chimpanzees'. *Animal Behaviour* 72(5): 989–99.

Torres, Bob. 2007. *Making a Killing: A Political Economy of Animal Rights*. Oakland: AK Press.

Tri-Council, Canadian Institutes of Health Research, Natural Sciences and Engineering Research Council of Canada, and Social Sciences and Humanities Research Council of Canada (2014). *Tri-Council Policy Statement: Ethical Conduct for Research Involving Humans*. [online] Ottawa: Secretariat on Responsible Conduct of Research. http://www.pre.ethics.gc.ca/eng/policy-politique/initiatives/tcps2-eptc2/Default/.

Trials of War Criminals before the Nuremberg Military Tribunals under Control Council Law, 1949. 10(2), pp. 181–2. Washington, D.C.: US Government Printing Office. [online] http://www.dartmouth.edu/%7Ecphs/docs/nuremberg-code.doc.

Tversky, Amos, and Daniel Kahneman. 1974. 'Judgment under Uncertainty: Heuristics and Biases'. *Science* 185: 1124–31.

Wadiwel, Dinesh. 2018. 'Chicken Harvesting Machine: Animal Labour, Resistance and the Time of Production'. *South Atlantic Quarterly* 117(3): 525–48.

Warren, Mary Anne. 1997. *Moral Status: Obligations to Persons and Other Living Things*. Oxford: Oxford University Press.

Wegner, Daniel. 2002. *The Illusion of Conscious Will*. Cambridge: MIT Press.

Weisberg, Zipporah. 2009. The Broken Promises of Monsters: Haraway, Animals and the Humanist Legacy. *Journal for Critical Animal Studies* 7(2): 21–61.

Wellesley, Hugo, and Ian Jenkins. 2015. 'Consent in Children'. *Anaesthesia and Intensive Care Medicine* 16(12): 632–4.

Wilson, Timothy. 2002. *Strangers to Ourselves: Discovering the Adaptive Unconscious*. Cambridge: Harvard University Press.

Załuski, Wojciech. 2016. 'The Concept of Person in the Light of Evolutionary Theory and Neuroscience'. In *New Approaches to the Personhood in Law: Essays in Legal Philosophy,* edited by Tomasz Pietrzykowski and Brunello Stancioli, 35–46. Frankfurt a.M.: Peter Lang.

6

Alienation and Animal Labour

Omar Bachour

Introduction

In the 1971 *Chomsky-Foucault Debate*, Foucault registers a misgiving about the attempt to define human nature 'in terms borrowed from our society, from our civilization, from our culture' (Chomsky and Foucault 2006: 43). To illustrate his point, Foucault offers the following example:

> The socialism of a certain period, at the end of the nineteenth century and the beginning of the twentieth century, admitted in effect that in capitalist societies man hadn't realized the full potential for his development and self-realization; that human nature was effectively alienated in the capitalist system. And it dreamed of an ultimately liberated human nature. What model did it use to conceive, project and eventually realize this human nature? It was in fact the bourgeois model.   (Chomsky and Foucault 2006: 43)

The universalization of the bourgeois model, for Foucault, meant that an unalienated society was one that transposed a sexuality of the bourgeois type, a family of the bourgeois type, an aesthetic of the bourgeois type, etc., on to its conception of a 'liberated' human nature (Chomsky and Foucault 2006: 43–4). A similar problem has attended the application of the alienation critique to animals, with the unintended consequence of reproducing the 'fantastic species-narcissism' it aims to counter (Benton 1993: 32).

On the one hand, an analysis of alienated animal labour has much to contribute to our understanding of the systems of animal oppression under capitalism. On the other hand, the humanist model of alienated labour, drawn from Marx's early works, which dominates the current literature, is predicated on a concept of 'species-being' that presupposes an untenable dichotomy between humans and animals, leaves no room for animal agency or flourishing, and severely limits the application, scope, and emancipatory potential of the alienation critique. Ted Benton sums up the dilemma as follows:

> In short a good deal of the content of Marx's contrast between a fulfilled or emancipated human life, and a dehumanized, estranged existence can also be

Omar Bachour, *Alienation and Animal Labour* In: *Animal Labour: A New Frontier of Interspecies Justice?*.
Edited by: Charlotte Blattner, Kendra Coulter, and Will Kymlicka, Oxford University Press (2020).
© Oxford University Press. DOI: 10.1093/oso/9780198846192.003.0006

applied in the analysis of the conditions imposed by intensive rearing regimes in the case of non-human animals. But the 'humanist' philosophical framing of Marx's concept of estrangement renders the extension of that analysis beyond the human case literally unthinkable. This form of 'humanism' conceptualizes the needs of animals as instinctual and fixed in a way that leaves no room for a morally significant difference to emerge between mere existence and thriving, or living well. (Benton 1993: 59)

This chapter attempts to chart a way out of this dilemma by putting forward an 'appropriative' rather than 'humanist' model of alienated animal labour that allows us to avail ourselves of the rich social and political dimensions of the alienation critique while avoiding the difficulties that attend it. The first section begins with a general definition of alienation before surveying Marx's account of alienated labour as well as various attempts to apply his account to animals. The second section focuses in particular on the notion of species-being, which underpins Marx's entire theory of alienated labour, and argues that its humanist presuppositions preclude any coherent application to animals. The final section puts forward an appropriative model of alienated animal labour and makes the case that this account overcomes the difficulties outlined in the previous section, giving way to an emancipatory conception of unalienated animal labour.

The Alienation Critique and the 'Animal Question'

At its most general, the concept of 'alienation' [*Entfremdung*] refers to 'a *deficient relation one has to oneself, to the world, and to others*' (Jaeggi 2014: 5).[1] While this '*relation of relationlessness*' (Jaeggi 2014: 1–2, 25) is often described in terms of its psychological components—powerlessness, meaninglessness, normlessness, social estrangement, and self-estrangement (Seeman 1959, 1972; Schacht 1970: ch. 5, 1994; TenHouten 2017)[2]—Marx was the first to utilize the concept as a diagnostic social and political tool in his critique of capitalism. Supplementing the critique of exploitation,[3] the 'alienation critique' refers to the way in which the nature and purpose of labour is distorted under capitalism. Although the concept did not originate with Hegel and Marx (Schacht 1970: ch. 1), it 'became from the

---

[1] Here, and throughout the chapter, all italics in quotations are in the original.

[2] For the purposes of this chapter, the two psychological components of alienation that interest us are 'powerlessness' understood as the inability to experience oneself as effective in the world and 'homelessness' understood as the inability to make oneself at home in the world. Any credible theory of alienation must offer an account of this dual loss.

[3] The relationship between Marx's concept of exploitation and his concept of alienation remains contentious. While many commentators who focus on the former have little to say about the latter, I believe that the concept of alienation provides the *content* for Marx's critique of exploitation, but I will not address this here.

118 ANIMAL LABOUR

eighteenth century onward, a cipher used to communicate the "uncertainty, fragmentation, and internal division" in humans' relations to themselves and to the world that accompanied the growth of industrialization' (Jaeggi 2014: 6).

The concept of alienation is useful not only in showing how the social processes and relations under capitalism have been ruthlessly channeled into the service of production, whether through the commodification of animal and human life, the increasing division of labour, the production of exchange-values over use-values, or the unrelenting domination, fragmentation, and instrumentalization of human–animal lifeworlds (Benton 1993; Dickens 1996; Noske 1997; Torres 2007; Gunderson 2011; Nibert 2017), but more fundamentally it is valuable in showing how the labour process is vitiated and transformed from a means for animals and humans to experience themselves as agents and make themselves at home in the world into a pathological mode of existence that brutalizes them.

Marx applied the alienation critique only to human workers, but various attempts have been made to extend it to animal workers. The majority of these attempts rely on Marx's account of alienated labour in the *Economic and Philo-sophic Manuscripts of 1844*. Marx's theory of alienation in the *1844 Manuscripts* is often celebrated as adding an ethical dimension to his thought. As we shall see, however, this ethical dimension rests on a decidedly 'humanist' foundation, tied to the idea of a distinctly human 'essence' or species-life that individuals are alien-ated from.

Marx's 1844 account identifies four distinct forms of alienation in labour:

- Firstly, in alienated labour, the *product of labour* stands opposed to the worker as an alien object: the more she produces, the poorer she becomes. The sensuous world of objects appears foreign and hostile (Marx 1994b: 59–62).
- Secondly, in alienated labour, the *process of production* is a torment for the worker. Her work 'is not voluntary, but coerced, forced labor'. She 'feels miserable and unhappy', at ease only outside work. Moreover, the activity of production belongs not to her, but to another (Marx 1994b: 61–2).
- Thirdly, in alienated labour, the worker is alienated from *other human beings*, who confront her as hostile workmasters, competitors or mere instruments for the satisfaction of her immediate needs (Marx 1994b: 64–8). This gives rise to a 'mutual alienation'. 'No one is gratified by the production of another.' Production is a 'battle and the one with more insight, energy, power and cleverness is the winner' (Marx 1994a: 50–1).
- Fourthly, in alienated labour, the worker's *species-life*, the capacities and powers of the species, is subordinated to individual life, making her essential nature a means for her physical existence. The worker is alienated from her 'spiritual nature', her *'human essence'*, her 'own body' and 'nature outside [herself]' (Marx 1994b: 61–3).

We can sum up Marx's account as follows: in alienated labour, the worker is alienated from (i) the products of her labour, (ii) the process of production, (iii) other human beings, and (iv) her species-life.

Can this framework be applied to animals' labour? One of the earliest attempts to do so can be found in Barbara Noske's 'de-animalization' theory. Noske argues that animals under conditions of capitalist production are alienated from their bodies and offspring; from their bodily functions; from their own societies, potential human–animal relations and surrounding nature; and, finally, from their species-life (Noske 1997: 18–21).[4]

Perhaps the most thorough attempt to apply this model to animals is Diana Stuart et al.'s critique of the dairy sector, according to which dairy cows suffer from:

Product Alienation. In commercial milk production, the dairy cow's milk is turned into an alien force that dominates her. Forced to produce as much milk as possible, the dairy cow is subject to specialized grain feeding, bovine growth hormone shots, intense cycles of artificial insemination, impregnation, hyperlactation, and mechanized milking machines (Stuart et al. 2012: 210), lasting up to four or five years at most (out of their natural twenty-year life spans), after which the cow's existence is deemed no longer profitable and she is sent to slaughter. Her calves are taken from her at birth (in order not to interfere with milk production), causing great distress to the calves and to their mother, 'who often makes her feelings plain by constant calling and bellowing for days after the infant is taken' (Singer 1975: 136). Female calves are reared on milk *substitutes* (which are cheaper) until they are ready to produce milk around their second year of life, while male calves are sold off to veal producers. Not only is the product of the dairy cow expropriated from her; it is turned *against* her, transforming her into 'a fine-tuned milk machine' who, 'at peak production ... [b]ecause her capacity to produce surpasses her ability to metabolize her feed ... begins to break down and use her own body tissues; she begins "milking off her own back"' (Singer 1975: 137).

Labour-Process Alienation. The dairy cow's short existence centres on milk production and the creation of offspring to ensure continued lactation as well as a steady line of milk producers after her body fails and she is sold for slaughter. All other activities—socialization (including kinship and play), travel, foraging, mating, and rearing calves—take a back seat to lactation: her genetic make-up, body, movements, diet, environment and sleep cycles are all geared towards a process of ceaseless production (Stuart et al. 2012: 210–11). Not only is the dairy cow's activity restricted to lactation to the exclusion of all others, but the production

---

[4] For other discussions of animal alienation in the literature, see Benton 1993; Dickens 1996: 52–70; Torres 2007: 39–40; Gunderson 2011: 265–6; Murray 2011: 98–100; Stuart et al. 2012; Coulter 2016: 87–91.

120 ANIMAL LABOUR

process is not voluntary, but coerced, forced labour (Stuart et al. 2012: 210). To maximize milk output, dairy cows are fed 'high-energy concentrates such as soybeans, fish meal, brewing by-products and even poultry manure' that their digestive systems cannot adequately process. The daily bovine growth hormone injections cause them constant soreness, routine infections, and chronic mastitis, often to the benefit of large pharmaceutical companies (Singer 1975: 138).

Community Alienation. Industrial dairy cows are alienated from their calves, from bulls, from other dairy cows, and from their relationship with human beings (Stuart et al. 2012: 211–12). As we saw above, their offspring are taken from them at birth: some female calves are kept in order to become replacement dairy cows, others to be reared as beef, while male calves are sold to veal producers or, if their upkeep proves costlier than their market price, killed directly (Singer 1975: 136–7). Reproductive technologies, such as artificial insemination, ensure that the relationship between dairy cows and bulls in factory farms is non-existent. Despite having a deep need for kinship, dairy cows are also estranged from other cows, and display signs of aggression due to the high levels of stress stemming from the demands of production, cramped housing conditions, and the sheer scale of concentrated animal feeding operations (CAFOs) (Stuart et al. 2012: 211–12).

Based on this analysis, Stuart et al. conclude that Marx's theory of alienation is well-suited for analysing aspects of animal production under capitalism. It shows how animals are central to issues of 'capital accumulation, exchange value, labour, private property, [and] praxis', how the labour process in capitalist societies 'inhibits the unfolding of latent potentialities', including the slumbering powers and capacities of animal workers; and it brings to light the material interest that humans and animals share in meeting the needs of living beings rather than those of the economy and profit maximization (Stuart et al. 2012: 203).

These efforts to apply the alienation critique of animal labour are, at first glance, plausible and illuminating. But it is worth noting that these efforts only in fact apply the first three dimensions of Marx's account. Stuart et al. struggle to apply Marx's final dimension, namely, alienation from 'species-life'. As we will see, this exposes deeper problems with the very foundations of Marx's 1844 account.

Difficulties with the Humanist Model:
The Trouble with Species-Being

Marx's concept of species-life has always vexed animal scholars, even when they have sought to extend the alienation critique to animals. Noske, for example, has no difficulty applying the first three aspects of the humanist model to animals— alienation from the products of labour; alienation from the process of labour, and alienation from fellow creatures—but when it comes to species-life, she essentially treats it, not as a separate dimension, but as a recapitulation of the first three dimensions, 'encompass[ing] everything: product, productive activity and the animal's relation to nature and to its own society' (Noske 1997: 20). Others also struggle to extend Marx's account of alienation from species-life to animals. Ryan Gunderson, for example, while defending the value of the alienation critique, maintains that 'Marx's theory of human alienation presupposes that humanity's "essence" is to create and perfect social life through free, reflective, and creative labor...I do not think this assumption can be carried over into the nonhuman animal realm without significant theoretical and practical problems' (Gunderson 2011: 266). Stuart et al. make a very similar acknowledgement that Marx's account of species-life as cannot be 'directly applied to nonhuman animals without fundamental theoretical and practical problems' (Stuart et al.: 2012: 207).

While acknowledging these 'fundamental theoretical and practical problems' with applying Marx's account of species-life to animals, these authors do not believe they preclude applying the rest of his 1844 account of alienation to animal labour. I will argue, however, that these problems are in fact fatal to the project, and require us to develop an entirely different model of alienation.

The crux of the problem, as I see it, is that Marx's 1844 account is 'humanist', in a very specific sense. The problem is not that he focuses exclusively on human workers while ignoring animals. On the contrary, animals play a central role in his story. The problem is that he defines unalienated humanity precisely *in opposition to animality*. At every step of the argument, his vision of unalienated human production is defined precisely as transcending or escaping animality. Table 6.1 documents this constant tendency to define human work in opposition to animal work.

In short, the humanist model defines species-life in direct opposition to the life activity of the animals. And as a result, the vision of unalienated labour it endorses is also defined in contrast to animal life. In Rinehart's words, unalienated labour 'brings out and reflects distinctly human attributes, that is, those that differentiate humans from all other forms of life' (Rinehart 2006: 12).

The implications of the argument, I believe, are fatal to any attempt to extend the humanist model of alienated labour to animals. It is important to emphasize again that the reason Marx did not apply his account of alienated labour to animals was not oversight, as if he simply forgot to consider the possibility that animals work. On the contrary, Marx acknowledges that animals work—he only denies that they are capable of producing self-consciously, universally, freely and in a socially coordinated manner: 'To be sure animals also produce. They build themselves nests, dwelling places, like the bees, beavers, ants, etc. But the animal produces only what is necessary for itself or for its young. It produces in a one-sided way' (Marx 1994b: 64). As the author of one recent textbook on work and the labour process puts it,

122   ANIMAL LABOUR

Table 6.1 Marx on animal production vs. human production

Animals	Human Beings
'The animal is immediately one with its life activity, not distinct from it. The animal is *its life activity*.'	'Man makes his life activity itself into the object of will and consciousness. He has conscious life activity. It is not a determination with which he immediately identifies. Conscious life activity distinguishes man immediately from the life activity of the animal. Only thereby is he a species-being.'
'The animal produces only what is immediately necessary for itself and its young. It produces in a one-sided way...'	'...man produces universally'.
'The animal produces under the domination of immediate physical need...'	'...man produces free of physical need and only genuinely so in freedom from the whole of nature.'
'The animal only produces itself...'	'...man reproduces the whole of nature.'
'The animal's product belongs immediately to its physical body...'	'...man is free when he confronts his product.'
'The animal builds only according to the standard and need of the species to which it belongs...'	'...man knows how to produce according to the standard of any species and at all times knows how to apply an intrinsic standard to the object. Thus man creates also according to the laws of beauty.' (Marx 1994b: 63–4)
'[The] beginning is as animal as social life itself at this stage. It is merely herd-consciousness, and at this point man is only distinguished from sheep by the fact that with him consciousness takes the form of instinct or that his instinct is a conscious one.'	'Men can be distinguished from animals by consciousness, by religion or anything else you like. They themselves begin to distinguish themselves from animals as soon as they begin to *produce* their means of subsistence...By producing their means of subsistence men are indirectly producing their actual material life.' (Marx 1978c: 150, 158)
'...the animal does not enter into "*relations*" with anything, it does not enter into any relation at all. For the animal, its relation to others does not exist as a relation.'	'Language *is* practical consciousness...language, like consciousness, only arises from the need, the necessity, of intercourse with other men. Where there exists a relationship, it exists for me...' (Marx 1978c: 158)
'It does not happen elsewhere—that elephants produce for tigers, or animals for other animals. For example. A hive of bees comprises at bottom only one bee, and they all produce the same thing.'	'The fact that...need on the part of one can be satisfied by the product of another, and vice versa...proves that each [individual] reaches beyond his own particular need...and that they relate to one another as human beings; that their common species-being [*Gattungswesen*] is acknowledged by all.' (Marx 1973: 243)
'A spider conducts operations that resemble those of a weaver, and a bee puts to shame many an architect in the construction of her cells...'	'...but what distinguishes the worst architect from the best of bees is this, that the architect raises his structure in his imagination before he erects it in reality.' (Marx 1978a: 344)

Other species also work, but in contrast to our conscious and goal-directed labour, that of nonhuman species is largely unlearned, automatic and instinctive. Unlike, for example, spiders whose web-spinning essentially is transmitted genetically and unlearned, human labour involves planning and conscious objectives. In short, humans have the distinct capacity to both conceptualize and execute work, and through this unity of mental and manual labour to develop ourselves and our communities.   (Rinehart 2006: 12–13)

It is worth distinguishing two different ways in which this human/animal distinction underpins Marx's account of alienation: first, there is a direct opposition between the productive powers of humans and animals, and second, there is a more indirect opposition within persons between 'natural powers' (understood as animal-like) and 'species powers' (understood as distinctly human). Both undermine the possibility of extending the alienation critique to animals.

The direct opposition between humans and animals derives from Marx's commitment to the idea of a *differentia specifica*: the doctrine that what distinguishes humans from other species determines what is most essential to us. This doctrine requires investing whatever is unique or distinctive to humans with supreme value, and discounting whatever is seen as shared with animals. Jon Elster sums up Marx's *differentia specifica* as follows: 'Marx distinguishes men from other animals on the basis of (i) self-consciousness, (ii) intentionality, (iii) language, (iv) tool-using, (v) tool-making and (vi) cooperation' (Elster 1985: 62). Marx is often criticized for overstating these differences, but it is important to recognize that the differentia *requires* denying that animals can share in any of the valuable features of work. If valuable work is to be included in the human essence—if it is to be part of our species-being—then it must be something that is unique or distinctive to humans. If our powers of production were continuous with those of animals, then labour could no longer be a site in which we develop our 'distinctly human' capacities or express our unique species 'essence'. The differentia doctrine requires establishing radical discontinuities between human and animal production.

If we are to extend the alienation critique to animals, we need to jettison the differentia, and argue directly for the value of different forms and dimensions of labour, regardless of how distinctive or unique they are to us as humans. As Will Kymlicka points out,

[Marx] argued that freely cooperative production [i.e., species-life] is our distinctive human excellence because this is what differentiates us from other species—it is what defines us *as humans*. But this 'differentia' argument is a non sequitur...Whether or not other animals have the same capacity for productive labour as humans has no bearing on the question of the value of that capacity in our lives. There is no reason to think that our most important capacities are those that are most different from other animals.   (Kymlicka 2002: 193)

124   ANIMAL LABOUR

David Leopold agrees: '[The] connection between the *differentia specifica* of the species and the importance of any particular aspect of human flourishing appears mistaken' (Leopold 2009: 225).

Leopold suggests that abandoning Marx's *differentia specifica* does not require abandoning his vision of unalienated labour since 'whatever he may himself have thought, that account is neither dependant on, nor supported by [it]' (Leopold 2009: 226). He argues, for example, that if we discover an extraterrestrial species who engage systematically in productive activity 'it is hard to see why the importance to humankind of fulfilling work...would be by diminished by [such] a discovery' (Leopold 2009: 225–6). On Leopold's view, talk about what is 'distinctively human' is simply a rhetorical flourish that can be dropped without changing the substantive of Marx's account of unalienated labour.

But the reality is that the opposition between humans and animals plays a 'foundational, structuring role' in the humanist model (Benton 1993: 33). And we can see this most clearly if we shift to the second role that the human–animal distinction plays in Marx's account, as a distinction *within the individual*.

Underlying the distinction between the species-life of humans and the fixed life activity of animals is the distinction between 'species powers' and 'natural powers', which Marx also speaks of in terms of 'senses' (Ollman 1976: 82–4). We can summarize Marx's account of natural powers as follows: for sustenance ('eating, drinking'); for warmth and shelter ('heat, clothing, housing'); for sexual activity ('procreation', 'the *relationship* of *man* to *woman* as a *natural* species-relationship') (Marx 1994b: 62–3, 70); for basic hygiene ('the simplest *animal* cleanliness'); for movement (to 'roam', 'physical *exercise*'); and for an environment conducive to health ('fresh air', 'a dwelling in the *light*') (Marx 1988: 117–18). By contrast, species powers include aesthetic pleasure ('a musical ear, an eye for the beauty of form'); artistic expression (to 'sing, paint'); culture (to 'go to the theatre', to 'travel'); emotional and moral fulfilment (to 'will, love'); intellectual activity (to 'read books', to 'theorize', 'learning'); and recreation (to 'drink', to 'fence', to 'go to the dance hall') (Marx 1988: 108–9, 118–19).

Marx conceives of species powers in terms of the formation and refinement of the five senses through a humanized nature. Subordinated to 'crude, practical needs', however, the senses exist only in a restricted form: 'For the starving man food does not exist in its human form but only in its abstract character as food. It could be available in its crudest form and one could not say wherein the starving man's eating differs from that of *animals*' (Marx 1994b: 75).

Therefore, alienation, according to Marx, entails an inversion of the order of needs such that the worker 'feels that he is acting freely only in his animal functions—eating, drinking, and procreating, or at most in his shelter and finery—while in his human functions he feels only like an animal. The animalistic becomes the human and the human the animalistic' (Marx 1994b: 62).

It follows that overcoming alienation, under the humanist account, involves the transformation of animal functions into human functions, i.e., the transformation of natural powers into species powers. Although Marx acknowledges that 'eating, drinking, and procreation are genuine human functions', he maintains that 'separated from the remaining sphere of human activities [i.e., from individuals' species-life] and turned into final and sole ends, they are animal functions' (Marx 1994b: 62). According to Bertell Ollman,

> The distinction between natural and species powers stands out clearly if we try to conceive of one without the other. This is easy to do for natural powers—we see them every day in all animals. Natural powers are the processes of life devoid of human attributes. It is inconceivable, however, how species powers could exist without natural powers, without the qualities man shares with all living things... Man without any relations to nature is a relationless void; without any specifically human relations to nature, he is an animal... If natural powers can be viewed as establishing the framework in which life itself goes on, then species powers express the kind of life which man, as distinct from all other beings, carries on inside this framework. (Ollman 1976: 83)

In short, while the humanist account acknowledges that humans share natural powers with animals, this recognition is not used to cast doubt on the stark opposition between animal and human functions. Rather, the relationship between natural and species powers is deployed precisely to *underscore* the difference between animals and humans.

This distinction between natural powers and species powers within each individual, and the imperative to transform animal functions into human functions, generates a further imperative to transform our natural environment into a 'humanized' environment. Species-life for Marx is not simply a matter of species membership, but a result of our historical and practical engagement with nature. Marx's account of human flourishing involves 'transforming the process of satisfying basic needs into an affirmation of the richness inherent in human faculties... by developing drives into new realms of sophistication and subtlety' (Mulhall 1998: 20). But this all-around development of capacities and drives can only take place within a communal matrix in which the social structures and cultural sphere of society have been humanized. Stephen Mulhall gives the following examples: 'wine connoisseurship requires cultivation of the vine, aesthetic appreciation requires humanly-shaped objects, and modern production processes require machines. In the absence of such appropriately cultivated objects, the exercise of distinctively human drives is impossible' (Mulhall 1998: 21).

Marx holds that the 'complete emancipation of all human senses and aptitudes' rests on the fact that 'these senses and aptitudes have become *human* both

126 ANIMAL LABOUR

subjectively and objectively' (Marx 1994b: 74). This explains his startling assertion that 'the *development* of the five senses is a labor of the whole previous history of the world' (Marx 1994b: 75). The humanization of nature is also a condition for the development of human nature in a second way. It is necessary not only for the exercise and refinement of human capacities, but also for their *formation*. In the face of starvation and want, the social capacities have 'only a *narrow* meaning', if any at all. It follows from this that 'the *senses* of social man *differ* from those of the unsocial. Only through the objectively unfolded wealth of human nature is the wealth of subjective *human* sensibility either cultivated or created' (Marx 1994b: 75). In short, both the creation and deployment of human capacities requires a socially humanized nature as well as mediating communal structures and modes of association.

Even if individuals do not directly contribute to the preservation and development of social structures, 'a significant portion of their activity results in the production of things which are needed by other human beings in their society, and which thereby preserve the existence of that society' (Mulhall 1998: 24). Not only is individual production directed at the needs and wants of society as a whole, but the producers, as we saw, also rely on a matrix of goods and services provided by others. Therefore, the wealth of resources available to, and *produced by*, individuals is always *social* in nature: the process of individual production (re)produces society as a whole. Thus, industry, for Marx, is 'the *open* book of man's *essential powers*' (Marx 1994b: 76). Benton sums up the implications of this historical humanization of nature as follows:

> [T]his historical-developmental process, peculiar to the human species, consists in an augmentation of our transformative powers *vis-à-vis* nature, amounting to a residueless 'humanization' of nature; an associated augmentation of our knowledge both of ourselves and of nature (towards a synthesis of the two); a transformation of our sensory powers, equivalent to the 'humanization of the senses'; and a transformation in the structure of need.   (Benton 1993: 32)

We can see here that the human/animal distinction takes three forms within this historical development of species-being: (i) the animal is associated with an embryonic stage of historical development; (ii) the earlier one is on the historical continuum, the more animal-like one is; and (iii) the animal lacks the capacity for historical transcendence, which characterizes the full actualization of species-life. Given this, it is difficult to see how the humanist model could be extended to animals at all, since the historical species potential that constitutes its account of flourishing is built not only in direct opposition to the animal but on the *negation* of animality.

This suggests, contra Leopold, that the differentia is not simply a rhetorical flourish to Marx's account of alienation, but is in fact its core. As Jaeggi puts it, 'labor—unalienated labor—counts for Marx as the human being's essential characteristic. What makes someone into a human is that, in distinction to the animal, she is capable of consciously forming herself and her world through social cooperation' (Jaeggi 2014: 14). Without this appeal to differentiating ourselves from the animal, and its associated distinction between natural powers and species powers, the humanist account of alienation is left hanging suspended in mid-air. As we will see below, if we drop the differentia, and evaluate various forms and dimensions of work on their own terms, unfiltered by claims to species differentiation, we are likely to end up with a very different account of alienation, which (following Jaeggi) I will call the 'appropriative' model.

Before turning to this alternative, however, I would like to note two further implications of the humanist model which undermine its potential as a framework for thinking about animal labour. First, having contrasted the ahistorical natural production of animals with the historical social production of humans, Marx essentially precludes the possibility that animals are part of our social life and social progress. Society, for Marx, is an exclusively human product and achievement. When Marx says that as a species-being an individual 'makes his own species' (Marx 1994b: 62), he emphasizes that this depends on what he calls '*social organs*'—i.e., social structures or species endowments, which includes the entire history of cooperative labour activity that individuals utilize in deploying and refining their human powers and capacities (Marx 1994b: 74). These social organs are seen as the practical embodiment of our *differentia specifica*. But just as the differentia is untenable theoretically, so too these 'social organs' and species endowments are not—and have never been—purely the product of human activity alone. As Kendra Coulter points out in her discussion of animal labour, 'the global portrait of human evolution includes great diversity . . . but the universal involvement of animals is noteworthy. Animals were central to the formation of every human society and mode of production on the planet' (Coulter 2016: 5). Not only have animals always worked alongside humans in order to produce, transform, and shape their environment, but they have also been 'central to society's basic schemes of social cooperation: to our economy, our modes of leisure, our forms of education and science' (Kymlicka and Donaldson 2016: 695).[5]

Thinking of social organs as the product of interspecies historical and social processes makes clear the imperative to extend the alienation critique to animals. The invisible labour extracted from animals not only goes unrecognized, but is used to reproduce hostile 'social organs', such as factory farms and other systems

---

[5] Not all Marxists have been blind to the contributions of animals to the history of labour. For example, the Turkish communist poet, Nazim Hikmet, ends his poem 'On Ibrahim Balaban's Painting "Spring"' with the following image: 'Here is plowed earth, / here is man: / lord of the rocks and mountains, the birds and the beasts. / Here are his sandals, here the patches on his breeches. / Here is the plow, / and here are the oxen, their rumps sadly covered with horrible / sores' (Hikmet 2002: 128).

128   ANIMAL LABOUR

of animal exploitation, that are turned brutally against them. Marx himself seems to hint at this conclusion when he argues that

> The 'essence' of the freshwater fish is the water of the river. But this ceases to be the 'essence' of the fish and is no longer a suitable medium for its existence as soon as the river is made to serve industry, as soon as it is polluted by dyes and other waste products and navigated by steamboats, when its water is diverted into canals and this fish is deprived of its medium of existence by simple drainage.   (Marx 1994: 128)

Unfortunately, the human/animal distinction at the heart of the humanist model rules out any attempt to theorize alienation within interspecies social relations.

A second implication of the humanist model is its unrelenting 'productivism' (Sayers 2011: 33). As we have seen, work for Marx is defined primarily in terms of material production. This narrow conception of labour leaves little room for conceptualizing the multifarious forms of animal work identified by Coulter, from subsistence labour to care work (Coulter 2016). This is of course a familiar feminist critique of Marx's model of labour, as overly focused on traditionally male forms of material production while ignoring or denigrating traditionally female forms of social reproduction. This critique applies even more strongly to animals.

In short, the humanist model fails on multiple grounds. It is built around a human–animal distinction that (i) requires drawing sharp discontinuities between the productive activities of humans and animals; (ii) evaluates work precisely in terms of its distancing from animality (whether animals without or the animal powers within); (iii) fails to capture the breadth of work done by animals in our society, and their role in producing our 'social organs'; and (iv) fails to provide an emancipatory conception of unalienated animal labour. I will argue that the 'appropriative' model of alienation, described in the next section, offers a remedy to these problems.

If this analysis is correct, however, it raises a puzzle: why have so many theorists thought that Marx's account can be applied to animals? After all, as we saw earlier, various authors readily acknowledge the 'theoretical and practical problems' in applying Marx's account to animals (Gunderson 2011: 266), so why do they cling to it? Part of the answer, perhaps, is simply that there have been few alternative accounts of alienation to draw upon. But theorists have also hoped that Marx's idea of species-being can be reinterpreted and recuperated.

One possible remedy suggested by Gunderson, and adopted by a number of animal scholars, is to 'take into account the natural behaviors of the species...in comparison to its behaviors in a human-mediated conditions' as the content of an animal's species-life (Gunderson 2011: 266). This is also the solution adopted by Benton (1993) in his nuanced attempt to defend a nonreductive naturalism, as well as Dickens (1996), and Stuart et al. (2012) in their analysis of the alienation of dairy cows from their species-being.

Benton argues that each species has its own characteristic species-life, a mode of life in which organisms confirm or manifest their essential powers beyond mere organic survival. According to Benton, these 'flourishing conditions' will vary from species to species and are determined in large part empirically by the sciences of ethology and ecology (Benton 1993: 47). Under regimes of private property, these conditions are either distorted or denied altogether, resulting in pathological modes of life.

According to Dickens, animals 'can be seen as having a species or natural being, internal structures and powers which will persist and affect their growth and development during their lifetimes' (Dickens 1996: 62). In the specialized division of labour under capitalism, animals' species-being and natural-being are 'treated as disaggregate wholes' with horrendous results (Dickens 1996: 63).

Finally, Stuart et al. use the term species-being 'to describe the unique nature of dairy cows without anthropogenic constraint, or more simply, to describe the nature of cows when they are free from human exploitation'. While they acknowledge that this is not in line with the classical Marxist definition of species-being, 'which signifies what is distinctly human', they agree with Benton and Dickens that 'it is suitable to recognise the species-specific capacities and needs of nonhuman animals and how an animal's life-activity ("species character") is distorted and stunted under capitalist conditions' (Stuart et al. 2012: 207).

We can think of this strategy, in effect, as responding to Marx's claim about the human *differentia specifica* by arguing that each animal species has its own differentia. If there is a distinctly human way to produce, from which humans can be alienated, so too there is a distinctly pig or chicken way to produce, from which they can be alienated. The main problem with this proposal, however, is its tendency to reify some allegedly species-specific essence that exists independent of 'human-mediated conditions'. This approach simply is not useful for domesticated animals who have been bred for generations to live and work alongside humans, or indeed for many liminal animals who have adapted over generations to human conditions. For these animals, their good may lie in developing powers and capacities quite different from the species-specific powers and capacities of their wild counterparts, including powers for interspecies cooperative work. In its own way, this appeal to animals' *differentia specifica* simply repeats Marx's problem of exaggerating the discontinuities between humans and animals and ignoring the fact that our 'social organs' have been constructed through interspecies relations.

Appeal to species-typical natural behaviours is also dangerous in its inattention to the way that the good of individual animals may diverge from species-typical standards. Individual animals may wish to develop new productive powers, including perhaps novel forms of interspecies cooperation. The fact that such

130 ANIMAL LABOUR

novel activities are not 'natural' is not in itself determinative of its value. As Alasdair Cochrane points out, the approach 'rests on an implausibly perfectionist understanding of animal well-being, in which an animal's own good is assessed against some ideal "natural" standard'. Moreover, there are many conditions which may be considered natural to a species—e.g., injury, starvation, disease—that cannot be said to improve the welfare of the animal and, conversely, many interventions that may improve the animal's welfare which cannot be considered natural (Cochrane 2016: 21).

Given its problematic nature, some commentators are inclined to simply drop, rather than attempt to recuperate, the notion of species-being, and to limit the alienation critique to the other three aspects. But as I suggested earlier, any attempt to discard the notion of species-being leaves the alienation critique unmotivated. After all, why should the separation of the labourer from the products of her labour matter to begin with? The notion of species-being furnishes the proponent of the humanist model with a clear answer: these estrangements matter because they thwart our distinctly human powers and capacities to freely and self-consciously create ourselves and our humanized world. Without the concept of species-being, the humanist model cannot explain why the first three aspects of alienated labour matter, nor can it provide a satisfactory account of flourishing in the form of unalienated labour. The concept of species-being plays an essential, but ultimately untenable, role in the humanist model. What then is the alternative? We turn to this next.

The Appropriative Model of Alienated Animal Labour

Following Hegel, Marx defines labour as 'a process in which both man and Nature participate, and in which man...opposes himself to nature as one of her own forces, setting in motion...the natural forces of his body, in order to appropriate Nature's productions in a form adapted to his own wants' (Marx 1978a: 344). Thus, we can define labour or work broadly as 'an intentional activity designed to produce a change in the world' (Sayers 2011: 33).

For both Hegel and Marx, the labour process is conceived of as the externalization and objectification of essential powers and capacities. This has a material and social aspect. By objectifying ourselves through our products, we come to recognize our will, goals, and capacities as real and objective, since they are made material through our labour. At the same time, by transforming the natural world we come to feel at home in it, relating not only to the products of our labour and to the world, but also to those in it. For Hegel, the labourer 'humanizes his environment, by showing how it is capable of satisfying him and how it cannot preserve any power of independence against him. Only by means of this effectual activity is he no longer merely general, but...actually aware of himself and at home in his environment' (Hegel 1975: 256). 'By acting on the external world and changing it, [the labourer] at the same time changes his own nature' (Marx 1978a: 344). This is done 'in order, as a free subject, to strip the external world of its inflexible foreignness and to enjoy in the shape of things only an external realization of himself' (Hegel 1975: 31).

Rahel Jaeggi describes the appropriative model as follows:

> The human being produces *herself* and her *world* in a single act. In producing her world, the human being produces herself and vice versa. And, insofar as this process is successful, she makes the both the objective world and herself her own. That is, she recognizes *herself* (her will and capacities) in her own activities and products and finds herself through this relation to her own products; she realizes herself, therefore, in her appropriative relation to the world as the product of her activities.   (Jaeggi 2014: 14)

The concept of appropriation is a form of praxis in which something is not merely passively taken up, but actively transformed and assimilated, altering both what its appropriated and the appropriator. Thus 'appropriation refers to a way of establishing relations to oneself and the world, a way of dealing with oneself and the world' (Jaeggi 2014: 36). Overcoming alienation, then, cannot be understood essentialistically as the recovery of a lost nature (human or otherwise); nor as the realization of a true essence or species-specific capacity; nor teleologically as a completable historical process—but as a successful or unimpeded act of appropriation.

The shift from the *content* of appropriation ('what' is willed) to the *form* of appropriation ('how' it is willed) should appeal directly to animal scholars, since it is concerned not with willing something in particular, but rather with the capacity to will and appropriate one's self and the world in a free and self-determined manner. On this view, an unalienated life

> is not one in which specific substantial values are realized but one that is lived in a specific—unalienated—manner. The belief that everyone should be able to live her own life no longer stands in opposition... to the project of [the] alienation critique. Rather, the absence of alienating impediments and the possibility of appropriating self and world without such impediments is a condition of freedom and self-determination.   (Jaeggi 2014: 36)

Abstracting from the content of appropriation, the charges of anthropocentricism, essentialism, and perfectionism that afflicted the humanist model are neutralized. The central question becomes: what material conditions, socio-economic structures, ideological regimes, etc., prevent animals from successfully appropriating their environments? Modes of life are pathological in so far as animal acts of appropriation are impeded or foreclosed altogether.

132   ANIMAL LABOUR

Of course, the same human/animal distinction is still operative in the Hegelian–Marxist formulations of the appropriative model. For example, after Marx describes the act of appropriation as one in which the labourer 'develops his slumbering powers and compels them to act [on nature] in obedience to his sway', the sentence is immediately followed by the claim that '[w]e are not now dealing with those primitive instinctive forms of labour that remind us of the mere animal...We pre-suppose labour in a form that stamps it as exclusively human' (Marx 1978a: 344). But now we are in a position to bring the disciplines of ecology, ethology, labour studies, paleo-anthropology, and sociobiology, among others, to bear on the question of animal labour, the putative distinction between humans and animals, and the nature of needs (Ingold 1983; Elster 1985: 62–8; Benton 1993: 34–69; Noske 1997: 80–170; Wilde 2000; Hribal 2003, 2010; Coulter 2016), without the risk of undermining the alienation critique in the process. In the case of the humanist model, to reject the human/animal distinction was to topple the concept of species-being, and with it, the primary motivation for an account of alienated labour.

By contrast, the appropriative model is concerned only with the form of appropriation. Once it is shown that animals also appropriate their external environments, the account is indifferent to the content of what is appropriated. Explorations of animal agency, desires, needs, wants, and the various ways in which animals appropriate their environments become central, since unsuccessful or impeded acts of appropriation (frustrating these desires, needs, and wants) will estrange animals from themselves, the world, and others. The rejection of the human/animal distinction in no way undermines the alienation critique so conceived; it only makes such explorations more salient.

What the appropriative model does rule out, however, is the view of animals as mere instances of their species, appropriating the world partially by its rigid standards, fixed in their life activity and animal functions, and relegated ahistorically, and without remainder, to the domain of nature.

The appropriative model also succeeds in overcoming the limitations of the humanist model in another way. As we saw earlier, the humanist model suffers from a narrow conception of labour, issuing in charges of 'productivism', since it 'regards work which creates a material product as the paradigm for all work' (Sayers 2011: 33). Given the breadth of work done by animals, the application of the humanist model fails to capture these myriad forms of labour. By contrast, the appropriative model, following Hegel,

> treats all these different sorts of work as form-giving activities in the sense that they are all ways of imparting form to matter. 'Productivist' types of works that create material products, such as craft and manufacture, figure as particular kinds of labour, but it is quite clear that Hegel is not trying to assimilate all work to this

ALIENATION AND ANIMAL LABOUR   133

model. On the contrary, he is emphasizing the great variety of forms that it may take. Its results need not be the creation of a material product, it may also be intended to conserve an object, to change the character of animals or people, to transform social relations, etc.   (Sayers 2011: 35)

The strident tone of the Hegelian–Marxist language can easily paint acts of appropriation as Promethean efforts to bend the external world to our will, labour as conquest, with little regard for nature, our dependency on and relationship with others, or the demands of relationality, sociality, and intersubjectivity, but this fundamentally misconstrues both the aim and the content of the appropriative model, even in Hegelian terms. The model is concerned with the ability of animals and humans to experience themselves as effective in the world and to make themselves at home in the world. Hegel often characterizes this relationship in two helpful ways: (i) a form of 'doubling' or duplicating oneself in the world and (ii) a mediation between subject and object.

According to the appropriative model, both humans and animals *duplicate* themselves in the world: 'Things in nature are only *immediate* and *single*, while man . . . *duplicates* himself, in that (i) he *is* as things in nature are, but (ii) he is just as much *for* himself' (Hegel 1975: 31). In rejecting the human/animal distinction, the appropriative model opens the door for further explorations of this process of animal 'doubling'. Given the model's account of the externalization and objectification of essential powers and capacities in the world, this process is less mysterious than it first appears.

However, it is the second characterization of acts of appropriation as levels of mediation between subject and object that is especially illuminating for a theory of alienation. The first thing to note is that the charge of Prometheanism, in its first formulation, presupposes a fixed subject confronting an external world (the object)—but this is precisely what Hegel rejects. As Sayers notes,

One of Hegel's most fruitful and suggestive ideas is that the subject and object change and develop in relation to each other. He thus questions the enlightenment idea that a fixed and given subject faces a separate and distinct external world. As the activity of the subject develops, so the object to which the subject relates develops and changes too. This is the organizing principle of Hegel's account of labour.   (Sayers 2011: 35)

More importantly, according to Sayers, Hegel 'conceives of different kinds of labour as different forms of relation of subject to object (nature) . . . the different forms of labour are arranged on an ascending scale according to the degree of mediation they establish between subject and object' (Sayers 2011: 35–6). It follows from this that the appropriative model is not only able to account for a wide

134 ANIMAL LABOUR

spectrum of animal work from alienated labour on one side of the continuum to free creative praxis on the other, but the more mediation that labour establishes between subject and object, the less alienated the subject.

A second charge of Prometheanism acknowledges that the appropriative model can accommodate a wide range of work done by animals, but claims that the model is still biased towards activities that effect a change in the world and is, as a result, hostile to sub-intentional forms of labour. Is Marx's ideal of unalienated labour ultimately one that cannot detach itself from the spectre of production?

In his study of modernity, Marshall Berman reminds us that

> There is something to this [charge of Prometheanism]—certainly "*luxe, calme et volupté*" is far from the center of Marx's imagination—but less than there may at first seem to be. If Marx is fetishistic about anything, it is not work and production but rather the far more complex and comprehensive ideal of development.
>
> (Berman 1982: 127)

In other words, the Marxian ideal of unalienated labour animating the appropriative model is not one of unleashing the productive or Promethean powers of humans and animals, but one which is concerned with the conditions for their development. Moreover, as we saw in our discussion of labour as a form of mediation between subject and object, the appropriative model aims not at establishing a mastery over nature, but an ideal harmony between animals and nature. Nevertheless, Berman goes on to conclude, rightly, that 'it is equally important for us to realize that whatever the concrete content of this balance and harmony might be...it would take an immense amount of Promethean activity and striving to create it' (Berman 1982: 127). In short, what the appropriative model calls for is not a 'radical *revaluation* of nature', but the 'regulation of the metabolism of nature...by associated producers' (Foster and Burkett 2018: 15), which must include animal workers. Hence the central question, according to the appropriative model, is how the aspirations, desires, and needs of human and animal workers can radically transform the labour process in such way that the conditions for unalienated labour and flourishing obtain.

For instance, in their analysis of alienation in the dairy sector, Stuart et al. assess alternative 'grazing-robotic systems' and conclude that, while better than industrial dairy farms, these systems do not eliminate farm animal alienation. Questions about the ownership of the products of labour, the labour process, species-being, and the relationship to fellow creatures persist (Stuart et al. 2012: 212–16). Let us assume, for the sake of argument, that all the four aspects of alienation can be adequately addressed under the humanist model. Have we arrived at an emancipatory conception of unalienated animal labour in which dairy cows can lead flourishing lives?

Under the imported humanist model, the individual cow's own aspirations, desires, needs, and wishes play only a secondary role, if they play any role at all.

Setting aside the differences between domesticated and wild animals, one only needs to look to animal sanctuaries in order to find animals who befriend, act like, and choose to spend their time with members of other species. According to the appropriative model, what such cases demonstrate is that attempts to measure the four aspects of alienation against species-specific 'natural' behaviours will frustrate rather than promote the individual animal's capacity to flourish. By contrast, the appropriative model is directly responsive to the animal's aspirations and wishes, and the conditions necessary for their realization.

Moreover, in the sphere of production, despite alternative systems resulting in more voluntary (albeit still coerced) labour, Stuart et al. note that 'the body of the cow [is still] specialised for the production process. She is still bred for yield and longevity and her existence revolves around milk production' (Stuart et al. 2012: 215). Rather than focus on the four distinct forms of alienation, the appropriative model is concerned with the cow's ability to experience herself as an effective agent in the world, to act and make herself at home in her environment. Hampering this possibility is the transformation of her body into a 'milking machine', incorporated fully into the rhythm of capitalist production. In other words, an analysis of the labour process, alone, will not furnish us with the necessary conditions for her flourishing since it leaves the primacy of production intact and forecloses successful acts of creative appropriation.

We are now in a position to acknowledge the final advantage of the appropriative model. Another difficulty that attaches to the humanist model is its inability to detach itself from the spectre of production. While it subjects the labour process to critical assessment, it nevertheless accepts the value of production, seeking only to ameliorate its conditions. Production remains at the centre of all activity: where the traditional socialist paradigm was concerned with liberating production from capitalist exploitation, the humanist paradigm seeks to liberate work from its alienating nature but leaves the *value* of production unexamined.

Thus Kathi Weeks is not wrong to conclude that 'the [humanist] affirmation of unalienated labour is not an adequate strategy by which to contest contemporary modes of capitalist control; it is too readily co-opted in a context in which the metaphysics of labor and the moralization of work carry so much cultural authority' (Weeks 2011: 107). But if the appropriative model is not satisfied with the democratization of capitalist property relations (the traditional socialist paradigm), nor by the work society qualitatively perfected (the humanist paradigm)—what prescription does it issue in?

In a well-known passage from the third volume of *Capital*, Marx contrasts the 'realm of freedom' with the 'realm of necessity':

> [T]he realm of freedom actually begins only where labour which is determined by necessity and mundane considerations ceases; thus in the very nature of things it lies beyond the sphere of material production...Beyond it begins the

136 ANIMAL LABOUR

development of human energy which is an end in itself, the true realm of freedom...The shortening of the working day is its basic prerequisite.

(Marx 1978b: 441)

Given the ability of the appropriative model to accommodate broad, multifarious conceptions of labour, as well as its indifference to the content of appropriation, the call for less work is not a rejection of unalienated animal labour as free creative praxis, in which unimpeded acts of appropriation abound, but its very condition. Even in instances, should they ever come about, where our direct and brutal exploitation of animals has ceased, and the capitalist relations of production have been democratized, but the primacy of production is preserved, the conditions of the appropriative model are not yet met.[6]

References

Benton, Ted. 1993. *Natural Relations: Ecology, Animal Rights and Social Justice.* New York: Verso.

Berman, Marshall. 1982. *All That Is Solid Melts Into Air.* New York: Verso.

Cochrane, Alasdair. 2016. 'Labour Rights for Animals'. In *The Political Turn in Animal Ethics,* edited by Robert Garner and Siobhan O'Sullivan, 15–31. New York: Rowman & Littlefield.

Chomsky, Noam, and Michel Foucault. 2006. *The Chomsky-Foucault Debate: On Human Nature.* New York: New Press.

Coulter, Kendra. 2016. *Animals, Work, and the Promise of Interspecies Solidarity.* London: Palgrave.

Dickens, Peter. 1996. *Reconstructing Nature: Alienation, Emancipation and the Division of Labour.* Abingdon: Routledge.

Elster, Jon. 1985. *Making Sense of Marx.* Cambridge: Cambridge University Press.

Foster, John Bellamy, and Paul Burkett. 2018. 'Value Isn't Everything'. *Monthly Review* 70(6): 1–15.

Gunderson, Ryan. 2011. 'From Cattle to Capital: Exchange Value, Animal Commodification and Barbarism'. *Critical Sociology* 39(2): 259–75.

Gunderson, Ryan. 2011. 'Marx's Comments on Animal Welfare'. *Rethinking Marxism* 23(4): 543–8.

Hegel, Georg Wilhelm Friedrich. 1975. *Aesthetics: Lectures on Fine Art, Volume 1.* Oxford: Oxford University Press.

---

[6] I am grateful to the participants of the Animal Labour Conference at Queen's University for their feedback on an early draft of this chapter, and especially to Will Kymlicka and Charlotte Blattner for their helpful comments.

Hikmet, Nazim. 2002. *Poems of Nazim Hikmet*. Trans. Randy Blasing and Mutlu Konuk. New York: Persea Books.

Hribal, Jason. 2003. '"Animals Are Part of the Working Class": A Challenge to Labor History'. *Labor History* 44(4): 435–53.

Hribal, Jason. 2010. *Fear of the Animal Planet: The Hidden History of Animal Resistance*. Oakland: CounterPunch and AK Press.

Ingold, Tim. 1983. 'The Architect and the Bee: Reflections on the Work of Animals and Men'. *Man* 18(1): 1–20.

Jaeggi, Rahel. 2014. *Alienation*. New York: Columbia University Press.

Kymlicka, Will. 2002. *Contemporary Political Philosophy: An Introduction*, 2nd ed. Oxford: Oxford University Press.

Kymlicka, Will, and Sue Donaldson. 2016. 'Locating Animals in Political Philosophy'. *Philosophy Compass*, 11(11): 692–701.

Leopold, David. 2009. *The Young Karl Marx: German Philosophy, Modern Politics, and Human Flourishing*. Cambridge: Cambridge University Press.

Marx, Karl. 1973. *Grundrisse: Critique of Political Economy*. New York: Penguin.

Marx, Karl. 1978a. 'Capital, Volume One'. In *The Marx-Engels Reader*, edited by Robert C. Tucker, 294–438. 2nd ed. New York: Norton.

Marx, Karl. 1978b. 'Capital, Volume Three'. In *The Marx-Engels Reader*, edited by Robert C. Tucker, 439–442. 2nd ed. New York: Norton.

Marx, Karl. 1978c. 'The German Ideology: Part I'. In *The Marx-Engels Reader*, edited by Robert C. Tucker, 146–200. 2nd ed. New York: Norton.

Marx, Karl. 1988. *Economic and Philosophic Manuscripts of 1844* and the *Communist Manifesto*. New York: Prometheus.

Marx, Karl. 1994a. 'Excerpt-Notes of 1844'. In *Selected Writings*, edited by Lawrence H. Simon, 40–53. Indianapolis: Hackett.

Marx, Karl. 1994b. 'Alienated Labour'. In *Selected Writings*, edited by Lawrence H. Simon, 58–68. Indianapolis: Hackett.

Mulhall, Stephen. 1998. 'Species-Being, Teleology and Individuality, Part I: Marx on Species-Being'. *Angelaki* 3: 9–27.

Murray, Mary. 2011. 'The Underdog in History'. In *Theorizing Animals: Rethinking Humanimal Relations*, edited by Nik Taylor and Tania Signal, 87–106. Leiden: Brill.

Nibert, David (ed.). 2017. *Animal Oppression and Capitalism*. Santa Barbara: Praeger.

Noske, Barbara. 1997. *Beyond Boundaries: Humans and Animals*. Montréal: Black Rose.

Ollman, Bertell. 1976. *Alienation: Marx's Concept of Man in Capitalist Society*. Cambridge: Cambridge University Press.

Rinehart, James W. 2006. *The Tyranny of Work: Alienation and the Labour Process*, 5th ed. Toronto: Thomson Nelson.

Sayers, Sean. 2011. *Marx and Alienation*. London: Palgrave.

138   ANIMAL LABOUR

Schacht, Richard. 1970. *Alienation*. New York: Psychology Press.

Seeman, Melvin. 1959. 'On the Meaning of Alienation'. *American Sociological Review* 24(6): 783–91.

Seeman, Melvin. 1972. 'Alienation and Engagement'. In *The Human Meaning of Social Change*, edited by Angus Campbell and Philip E. Converse, 467–527. New York: Russell Sage.

Singer, Peter. 1975. *Animal Liberation*. New York: HarperCollins.

Stuart, Diane, and Rebecca L. Schewe, and Ryan Gunderson. 2012. 'Extending Social Theory to Farm Animals: Addressing Alienation in the Dairy Sector'. *Sociologia Ruralis* 53(2): 201–22.

TenHouten, Warren. 2017. *Alienation and Affect*. London: Routledge.

Torres, Bob. 2007. *Making a Killing*. Oakland: AK Press.

Wilde, Lawrence. 2000. '"The Creatures, Too, Must Become Free": Marx and the Human/Animal Distinction'. *Capital & Class* 72: 37–53.

Weeks, Kathi. 2011. *The Problem with Work: Feminism, Marxism, Antiwork Politics and Postwork Imaginaries*. Durham: Duke University Press.

7

Down on the Farm

Status, Exploitation, and Agricultural Exceptionalism

Jessica Eisen

Introduction

The field of human–animal labour studies includes a range of projects, from descriptive catalogues of the work animals perform to the adoption of labour studies analyses developed in the human context to animal exploitation. In this chapter, I focus on a particular analytic move that emerges in some of this literature, which I will call the 'labour-recognition-transformation' thesis. The thesis, in essence, is that animal advocates ought to rely on the fact of animal 'work' (especially for human beings) as a mode of identifying animals with the social category of 'workers', in the hopes that this identification will improve animals' social, legal, and political status.

My primary concern with this analytic move relates to its application to the agricultural context, and my main focus in this chapter will be the application of the labour-recognition-transformation argument to farmed animals. In particular, I propose that a labour-recognition-transformation argument respecting farmed animals risks overlooking the broader context of agricultural exceptionalism that characterizes this sphere of social life. Agricultural exceptionalism has consistently insulated agricultural producers from regulation advancing a range of social priorities—not only in the field of animal protection, but also in the fields of trade, environmental protection, and, of particular importance to this study, labour and employment law.

The use of the labour-recognition-transformation argument in the agricultural context gives rise to two interrelated political concerns. The first concern is that the labelling of farmed animals as 'workers' risks whitewashing conditions of routine confinement, forced reproduction, and death—a risk that is not hypothetical but is instead already realized by agricultural industries seeking to present these practices as normalized and continuous with accepted aspects of our shared social life. The second concern is that the claim that farmed animals might enjoy an elevation in status as a result of recognition as 'workers' risks whitewashing the circumstances of agricultural workers whose sociolegal status is in fact characterized

---

Jessica Eisen, *Down on the Farm: Status, Exploitation, and Agricultural Exceptionalism* In: *Animal Labour: A New Frontier of Interspecies Justice?*. Edited by: Charlotte Blattner, Kendra Coulter, and Will Kymlicka, Oxford University Press (2020). © Oxford University Press. DOI: 10.1093/oso/9780198846192.003.0007

140 ANIMAL LABOUR

by discrimination and precarious and dangerous employment conditions. Having set out this critique of the labour-recognition-transformation argument to farmed animals, this chapter will conclude with some more tentative reflections on the application of this argument outside the farming context.

Animal Labour, Recognition, and Social Transformation

A number of scholars have called for the recognition of animals as 'workers' or 'labourers' as a mode of elevating the social, legal, and political status of animals. This scholarship is variously motivated by 'a labor studies commitment to taking work and workers seriously' (Coulter 2016a: 14), an acknowledgement of the centrality of work to 'the construction of social relations' (Porcher 2014: 4), and the view that political communities ought to recognize labour rights as a means of taking the interests of animals seriously (Cochrane 2016: 17). A distinct but related concern is the imperative to recognize animals as *agents* in an effort to combat the prevailing view of animals as inert or unthinking objects (Blattner, chapter 5 of this volume; Fraser 2017; Hribal 2012; cf. Coulter 2016a: 68). In some cases, the argument in favour of recognizing animal labour is aligned with feminist and critical analyses calling for recognition and valuation of the traditionally overlooked work of women and other marginalized human social groups (Coulter 2016a: 65, 77, 93, 147). The aim is not merely one of 'identifying' or 'understanding', as an ontological fact, that animals work, but to pursue a political project of recognition and associated transformation (Clark 2014: 157; Coulter 2016a: 94–5, 146–7; Haraway 2008: 73; Porcher 2012: 56–7; Porcher 2014: 2 and 7–8; Porcher 2017a: 303).

Although the power of labour recognition to generate positive sociomaterial transformation is not necessarily cast as certain, this literature generally adopts an explicit or implicit stance that recognizing animals as workers will prompt greater respect and social standing: that '[b]ecoming "useful" can change how individuals and/or species are seen and treated' (Coulter 2016a: 146). It is proposed that some of the material benefits that might flow from such recognition include a decent retirement, a greater respect for animals' consent or enthusiasm for (or resistance to) particular kinds of work, and broad consideration or incorporation of their interests in industrial decision-making (Porcher 2017a: 314–15; Blattner, chapter 5 of this volume; Cochrane 2016: 27–30). Kendra Coulter takes as a 'contradiction' the acceptance of animal 'work' and 'agency' without a concomitant acceptance that broader social 'analyses or politics' ought to extend to animals (Coulter 2016a: 68), and offers 'interspecies solidarity' as a form of politics and analysis that might flow from recognition of animals as workers. To this end, Coulter cites Jonathan Clark's summary of the view that recognizing animals as labourers might 'challenge the paradigm of human exceptionalism that justifies so much violence against animals', and Donna Haraway's query as to whether '[t]aking animals seriously as workers…might help stem the killing machines' (Coulter 2016a: 93; Clark 2014: 157; Haraway 2008: 78). Joceylne Porcher posits a similar dynamic of recognition producing material benefits, reflecting in respect of service animals that '[a]n improvement in the care of retired animals comes about through a recognition of their involvement in work and the attribution of a specific status' (Porcher 2017a: 314–15). While there are differences in the nature and scope of these various authors' transformative aspirations (see, e.g., Coulter 2016b: 201, distinguishing her own approach to recognition from that of Porcher), a common thread is the argument or implication that acknowledgement of animals as workers would provoke some positive material changes for those animals.

Scholars advancing a labour-recognition-transformation approach differ as to whether and how they view farmed animals as part of this political project. In some cases, agricultural animals are cast as core examples of animal workers that therefore deserve recognition and transformed circumstances; in some cases, agricultural animals are not seen as 'doing' enough work to fit this paradigm; and in other cases agricultural animals are perceived to be 'doing' work, but in circumstances so oppressive that the labour model is inappropriate (leaving open the possibility that these animals might be usefully considered workers if agricultural practices were improved). The first approach is exemplified by Porcher, who proposes that agricultural animals should be understood to be workers, including those being raised for slaughter—although she recognizes this as a significant point of divergence from labour relations in the human sphere since 'slaughter and euthanasia are management options that do not exist between humans' (Porcher 2017a: 315; see also Porcher 2012: 41). For Porcher, thinking of animals as workers serves both to require more humane agricultural practices, and to justify the underlying practice of raising and killing animals (as refuted by Nicolas Delon in chapter 8 of this volume). An example of the labour-recognition-transformation approach as limited by a 'doing' requirement can be found in the work of Coulter, who questions whether animals whose 'sole "task" is to eat and fatten in order to physically become meat or fur' are even doing 'work' at all (Coulter 2016a: 90).

The labour-recognition-transformation approach as limited by the harmful realities of contemporary animal use is evident in the work of both Coulter and Cochrane. Both agree that killing animals always falls outside the scope of permissible labour practices (Cochrane 2016: 25; Coulter 2016a). But both authors imply that some animal farming practices, such as dairying and egg production, might be productively brought within the labour model if circumstances were sufficiently transformed. Coulter, for example, believes that producing 'babies, eggs, or milk' constitutes 'a kind of work', albeit 'alienated' under contemporary conditions (Coulter 2016a: 90, citing Noske 1989). Despite these animals' fulfilment of the 'doing' requirement, Coulter goes on to question whether it is

142 ANIMAL LABOUR

'conceptually, ethically, and politically useful' to frame animals as workers in the context of industries 'within which most animals lives are almost exclusively about suffering, extreme instrumentalism, and indignity in the pursuit of profit' (Coulter 2016a: 90). For his part, Cochrane suggests that it is 'possible to imagine radically different forms of harmless milk production, where non-productive animals are not killed and the calf is given suitable time to feed from the mother' (Cochrane 2016: 25). The killing, on this account, is severable from reproductive control, and we might legitimately make 'work' of the latter as long as we forbid the former. It is admitted that this would require substantial social and economic transformation, with the resulting agricultural system involving 'few animals and few farmers', and an attendant increase in the price of products (Cochrane 2016: 25).

These approaches universally call for substantial reorganization of contemporary agricultural practices. For Porcher, this is expressed as an endorsement of a 'collaborative utopia' in which the trend toward profit-driven agricultural intensification is tempered by a view of animals as respected co-labourers (Porcher 2017b). On Coulter's account, conditions of extreme alienation, suffering, instrumentalism, and indignity must be overcome as a preliminary matter before the labour recognition model can be usefully applied to agricultural animals. And in Cochrane's view, labour recognition helps us to understand the necessity of a broad reorganization of agricultural industries in favour of small-scale, ethical production methods, likely requiring an increase in the price of animal products. Whether transformation of animal agriculture is seen as a prerequisite to the usefulness of the labour-recognition-transformation argument in this sphere, or whether the labour-recognition-transformation model is seen as an engine for such transformation, the durability of industrial agricultural systems poses serious challenges. As the following section will elaborate, the persistence of animal agriculture as a particularly extreme sphere of legalized animal exploitation is reflective of a broader trend of insulating agriculture from the demands of a range of social justice imperatives—including, significantly for our purposes, labour rights. And, as the section thereafter will demonstrate, the abject status of both animals and human workers within this exceptionalist policy paradigm limits the political appeal of the labour-recognition-transformation argument in this context.

Agricultural Exceptionalism

Dinesh Wadiwel observes that in 'factory farming' animal lives are 'always caught in an exceptionary space' (Wadiwel 2002: para. 11). Many legal regimes around the world are characterized by animal protection laws that either explicitly or implicitly exempt farmed animals from their purview. In Canada, the federal Criminal Code prohibits cruelty toward animals, but this prohibition has been interpreted to exclude otherwise illegal conduct that occurs in the normal course of agriculture (Bisgould 2011: 74; cf. Sykes 2015). Provincial laws also prohibit cruelty, but again include explicit or implied exemptions for agricultural animals (Bisgould 2011: 190–2). In the United States, the primary piece of legislation governing the commercial use of animals, the Animal Welfare Act, actually excludes farmed animals from its definition of 'animal', and by extension from all of its protections.[1] At the state level, even as punishments for animal cruelty have intensified, so too has the exclusion of farmed animals from the scope of these laws, with a growing number of states adopting explicit statutory exemptions for farmed animals (Wolfson and Sullivan 2004; Marceau 2019). The result in each jurisdiction is a legal regime that demonstrates some concern for animal well-being, but which also creates an increasingly firm delineation of the farm as a 'private sphere' within which legal interventions on behalf of animals have no place (Cohen 2017: 152 n.238; Eisen 2017: 239–40; Eisen 2019).

This treatment of farms as 'exceptionary spaces' is not unique to the context of animal protection. The term 'agricultural exceptionalism' is often invoked to describe the special sociolegal place of agriculture within regimes governing such diverse policy fields as international trade, environmental protection, and workers' rights. I could find no examples of the term 'agricultural exceptionalism' being employed to describe the exceptional legal treatment of farmed animals, though the law's failure to protect farmed animals is consistent with a broader phenomenon of special legal treatment for farms. Carsten Daugbjerg and Peter Feindt's description of the components and mechanics of agricultural policy exceptionalism seems to capture well the complaints of animal advocates describing the legal failure to protect farm animals: 'a set of exceptionalist *ideas*' that serve to define and support 'compartmental *institutions*' that enable a defined '*policy community*' to 'adopt and implement *policy instruments and programs* that serve their interests and comply with their ideas' (Daugbjerg and Feindt 2017: 1567, emphasis in the original). In the context of animal agriculture, exceptionalist ideas range from tradition to species hierarchy; compartmental institutions include ministries of agriculture; policy communities include marketing boards and voluntary associations; and policy instruments and programmes include the network of legal exceptions that shield the farm from state interventions on behalf of animals.

The exceptional treatment of farmed animals as beyond the scope of legal protection, and the farm as a space outside the scope of the usual rules of social and legal conduct respecting animals, is continuous with the treatment of farms in other contexts. Scholars of international trade law, for example, have identified agriculture as an economic sphere that has been uniquely resistant to international legal regimes mandating the free flow of goods across international borders (Smart and Smart 2017: 112). In most Western democratic states, agricultural exceptionalism (in this context referencing protectionism) was 'fully established as part of

---

[1] 9 C.F.R. §1.1 (2017).

144   ANIMAL LABOUR

the post-war welfare consensus' and has since been largely successful in resisting the global legal trend toward neoliberalism from the 1980s onward (Daugbjerg and Feindt 2017: 1570; Trebilcock 2014: 81; Trebilcock and Pue 2015). Michael Trebilcock, a critic of agricultural exceptionalism in this context, observes that 'farm groups' that stand to lose out if agricultural products were treated like other commodities find their own 'strong financial incentives' to be bolstered by 'concentrated interest group advantage, public sympathy for farmers, concerns about food security and foreign dependence, ignorance among consumers or taxpayers, and financial features of local political systems, such as the disproportionate weight accorded to rural electorates' (Trebilcock 2014: 82; *see also* Daugbjerg and Swinbank 2009: 3, 5–6). Whether or not one shares Trebilcock's orientation toward free trade, it is remarkable for our purposes that agriculture stands out in this field of law as a distinct and exceptional policy field—one in which a general trend toward more open markets has been effectively resisted by interested parties who benefit from prevailing social attitudes toward farmers. In a similar vein, Daugbjerg and Swinbank conclude that even despite a growing ideological shift within trade policy in favour of 'agricultural normalism' as opposed to 'agricultural exceptionalism', protectionist policy frameworks have resisted substantial transformation—a tension that the authors identify as a disconnection between the regime's 'ideational and operational levels' (Daugbjerg and Swinbank 2009: 12–14).

So too in the environmental sphere have agricultural operations enjoyed special treatment, with most OECD countries explicitly exempting agricultural facilities from the operation of 'general environmental protection laws', despite their significant environmental impact (Montpetit 2002: 2). Although Canada has no entrenched constitutional right to private property, cultural and common law reverence for rural property rights in particular have played a major role in defining the limits of environmental protection legislation in Canada (Bowden 2006: 69–70; Boyd 2003: 112). The Species at Risk Act, for example, was the subject of intense lobbying efforts by farmers concerned to avoid any definition of protected habitats that might encroach on private lands (Bowden 2006: 69; Jones and Fredricksen 1999: 22). The resulting legislative compromise is a legal regime that primarily targets federally owned lands, which represent only 5 per cent of the land in Canadian provinces (Bowden 2006: 70; Smallwood 2003: 5). In another instance of agricultural exceptionalism, as it emerges in the field of environmental law, Marie-Ann Bowden explains that the 'polluter pays principle' is widely accepted in Canadian law, but is almost never applied in the agricultural context (Bowden 2006: 63–5). In some Canadian jurisdictions, environmental protection legislation is subordinate to specialized agricultural legislation that places authority to police and discipline pollution in the hands of agricultural rather than environmental ministries (Bowden 2006: 65–6). Often, agricultural activities are exempt from broadly applicable environmental protections, including respecting the use of pesticides (Bowden 2006: 66; Boyd 2003: 123). In Ontario, the

STATUS, EXPLOITATION, AND AGRICULTURAL EXCEPTIONALISM   145

Environmental Protection Act expressly exempts the disposal of animal waste 'in accordance with normal farming practices' from otherwise applicable laws respecting discharge, notifications, and spilling of contaminants, with supplementary agriculture-specific rules instituted following the Walkerton Commission Inquiry (Bowden 2006: 71). Agricultural operations are often subject only to voluntary guidelines and policies, even where primary legislation has conferred the authority to create binding regulations governing the environmental impact of agricultural operations (Bowden 2006: 69–70; Boyd 2003: 112). The United States similarly carves out various 'active and passive safe harbors' for farms in its environmental laws, amounting to an '"anti-law" of farms and the environment' (Ruhl 2000: 263; Schneider 2010: 936). The Clean Water Act, for example, specifically exempts agricultural water contamination from its requirements, leaving utilities providers to bear the cost and effort of water treatment necessitated by agricultural pollution (Pollans 2016). This exceptional treatment of agriculture across a number of environmental regimes has been bolstered in both Canada and the United States by 'right to farm' legislation that insulates farms from common law nuisance suits arising from common agricultural practices—a standard that is effectively defined by the industry itself, and for which the burden of proof is most commonly placed on plaintiffs claiming to have been harmed by farming practices (Bowden 2006: 76–7; McCormally 2007; Hamilton 1998; Dowell 2011).

Again, the term 'agricultural exceptionalism' emerges in the sphere of labour law, here denoting the tendency of legal regimes to exclude agricultural labourers from legal protections enjoyed by other workers. There are at least three prongs to this exceptionalism as it appears in Canada and the United States: 1) limits on the application of basic employment standards to farm workers, 2) exclusion of farm workers from statutory schemes designed to enhance the ability of workers to bargain collectively with their employers, and 3) adoption of special immigration rules for agricultural workers. First, general health and safety regulations, minimum wage, and overtime requirements are all subject to exceptions for agricultural workers.[2] Second, agricultural workers are often excluded from legislative schemes designed to structure and support collective bargaining and unionization. The National Labor Relations Act, the United States' primary legislation governing the rights of workers to bargain collectively, excludes 'agricultural laborers' from its definition of 'employee' and its attendant protections.[3] Guadalupe Luna juxtaposes the legal frustration of efforts by workers to engage in 'mutual aid activity' in the agricultural context with the fact that producers receive specific

---

[2] See, for example, 29 U.S.C. §213(a)(6) (2006), and the discussion in Schneider 2010: 936 n.4; Schell 2002; Tucker 2012: 34.
[3] 29 U.S.C. §213(b)(12) (2006); Schneider 2010: 936 n.4; Schell 2002: 150–1.

146   ANIMAL LABOUR

statutory support to 'join cooperative organizations to protect their marketing and bargaining positions' (Luna 1998: 491–2). In several Canadian provinces, farm workers are statutorily excluded from standard labour relations regimes, leaving them with a more limited set of associational rights.[4] Third, legal and pseudo-legal immigration and guest worker programmes have been developed in both Canada and the United States to produce a dedicated agricultural workforce comprising labourers from impoverished countries, whose immigration status strictly limits their employment mobility and ties them to particular employers (Linder 1987: 1336; Smith 2013).

Farmed Animals as Workers: Limits and Challenges

To the extent that theorists apply the labour-recognition-transformation argument to farmed animals (as Porcher, in particular, does), this context of legal exceptionalism presents two interrelated challenges. The first is the risk of painting animal farming as an essentially salutary relationship that needs simply to be tweaked in favour of greater recognition of animals' contributions—and in so doing supports sanitizing tropes of animal use already deployed by defenders of status quo agricultural practices. The second is the risk of painting agricultural labour with a similarly sanguine brush, treating some of the most marginalized and exploited of human workers as exemplars of a complete and successful justice movement in which adequate recognition and rights have already been achieved.

Whitewashing Animal Use

The suggestion that animals are workers, and should be recognized as such, risks normalizing the extreme conditions of animal agriculture by positioning current forms of animal use as continuous with intra-human relational structures that are broadly accepted as healthy and productive, if occasionally imperfect. (Of course, as we will see below, this image of intra-human labour relations is contestable and contested, especially in the field of agriculture.) For this reason, animal industries already occasionally invoke images of animals as workers in advertising campaigns designed to obscure the realities of animal use in general, and dairy production in particular. The female cattle in these accounts of dairying are cast as having struck a good deal—as workers in cushy jobs, often described in terms that echo the minimization and denigration of women's work more broadly.

---

[4] *Ontario (Attorney General) v. Fraser*, 2011 SCC 20, and the discussion in Tucker 2012.

STATUS, EXPLOITATION, AND AGRICULTURAL EXCEPTIONALISM   147

Carol Adams, for example, recounts a grocery store flyer from the United States that sets out the following 'benefit package' enjoyed by dairy cows, 'tongue in cheek':

> To start with, the cows receive full-time pay for part-time work. The work (of being milked) takes about 20–30 minutes per day. The employer provides paid medical coverage, with a doctor (veterinarian) on call 24/7, 365 days per year. Meals are prepared by a nutritionist, with room service and clean up every time. There is a full-time housekeeper who even cleans the bathrooms. A paid team of experts is always available for these bovine beauties; hair dresser, pedicurist and spa facilities are provided. There is 24-hour surveillance. No need for online dating... there is mate selection provided through a directory of selective traits, and could be a different mate each year. All transportation is provided free of charge for a lifetime.   (quoted in Adams 2017: 25)

This image of dairy cows as carefree working girls, interested in beauty treatments and dating, relies on tropes of female frivolity and leisurely service to cast a sheen of normalcy over an industry that relies on routine artificial insemination, separation of calves from their grieving mothers, intensive zero-graze confinement of lactating cows in 'tie stall' barns, and slaughter (Eisen 2019; Gillespie 2014; Adams 2017: 26).

These public-facing images of dairying as normalized 'work' is sharpened within intra-industry publications that expressly include pregnancy as an aspect of this feminized labour. Kathryn Gillespie, for example, describes an advertisement for Bovi-Shield Gold cattle vaccine that asks 'If she can't stay pregnant, what else will she do? Keep your cows pregnant and on the job' (quoted in Gillespie 2014: 1329). Another ad in the same series, described by Adams, asks the same question, this time depicting a cow in the traditionally male occupation of driving a firetruck—in Adams' assessment, offering '[t]he unstated answer: she may be taking your job' (Adams 2017: 34). These depictions of a dairy cows' labour as traditionally female, and to be policed as such, intersect with another set of common images and metaphors used to normalize dairying, namely the casting of the farm as family (Eisen 2017; Eisen 2019). Together, these themes of work and family operate in concert with legal treatment of the farm as a 'private sphere' of social life, characterized by ostensibly apolitical roles, with background legal supports for hierarchical relations rendered invisible by narratives of government non-intervention (Eisen 2017; Eisen 2019; cf. Cohen 2017; but see Kymlicka 2017: n.55 and n.73). Insofar as agricultural exceptionalism operates to subsidize and support farmed animals' treatment as production units, while also insulating the farm from interventions in support of competing social goals, this exceptionalism might be understood as a component of the social and legal casting of the farm as 'private sphere'.

The challenges of whitewashing extend beyond these more explicitly gendered representations, emerging also in the dairy industry's use of labour metaphors to

148   ANIMAL LABOUR

conceal or distract from the necessity of death and physical coercion in dairying. Greta Gaard, for example, notes the industry use of the term 'herd retirement' to describe the slaughter of a half-million young American cows as part of a scheme to influence the price of milk (Gaard 2013: 602). Responding specifically to Porcher's and Haraway's respective casting of dairy cattle and experimental animals as workers, Gaard criticizes the implication that 'the animal whose body is confined within the structures of industrial animal production' enjoys 'a sustainable "job" that animals might willingly choose, or resign from' (Gaard 2013: 598; see also Clark 2014 and Weisberg 2009: 37, offering similar critiques specific to Haraway's treatment of laboratory animals). The extent to which, given the right circumstances, animals might be capable of entering into formal contract-like relations is open to debate (Enman-Beech, forthcoming). But, without a doubt, the circumstances of controlled breeding, physical confinement, and death that characterize contemporary agricultural practices make labour language, and associated images of choice and free exchange, inappropriate and misleading.

Whitewashing Farm Labour

A second related challenge arises from the suggestion that casting farmed animals as workers might serve as a route to inclusion and improved status: that this framing risks minimizing or ignoring the dire circumstances and incomplete justice struggles of human farm workers. As described above, agricultural workers are *de jure* and *de facto* exempt from many of the legal protections that aim to ensure decent working conditions and democratized workplaces. The result is a sphere of social life in which the status of 'worker' is associated with exclusion and abuse rather than inclusion and respect.

Farm labour is among the most physically hazardous forms of employment (Otero and Preibisch 2010: 24), with workers most commonly suffering from lacerations, eye injuries, musculoskeletal problems, hearing loss, and respiratory illness (Arcury and Quandt 2011). One report on occupational hazards of agricultural labour in North Carolina reported that '[f]ew years pass without a death from heat stress' in that state, with all farmworkers exposed to dangerous pesticide exposures and a quarter of farmworkers suffering from acute nicotine poisoning, characterized by dizziness, nausea, vomiting, insomnia, and anorexia' (Arcury and Quandt 2011). Housing conditions are overcrowded and characterized by environmental hazards, rodent infestations, and spread of communicable diseases like tuberculosis (Arcury and Quandt 2011; Otero and Preibisch 2010: 5). Sexual violence and harassment, especially targeting female farm workers, is pervasive, including reprisals for workers who reject the sexual advances of supervisors and employers (Otero and Preibisch 2010; Castañeda and Zavella 2003; Ontiveros 2003; Preibisch and Encalada Grez 2010). In the United States, some of these

STATUS, EXPLOITATION, AND AGRICULTURAL EXCEPTIONALISM   149

workers are children as young as the legal cut-off age of twelve years old (Arcury and Quandt 2011), with investigations finding children as young as five years old working in the fields (Patel, Hill, Elslocker, and Ross 2010). The average life expectancy of a migrant or seasonal farmworker in the United States is only forty-nine years (Hansen and Donohue 2003). Collectively, these working and living conditions, combined with experiences of racial discrimination and humili-ation in the workplace, provoke high rates of anxiety, depression, and other mental health challenges among farm labourers (Arcury and Quandt 2011; Otero and Preibisch 2010: 29; Hovey and Magaña 2002).

Agricultural exceptionalism in the labour context is deeply interlaced with social processes of racialization and colonial hierarchy (Satzewich 1991). Eric Linder has traced the legislative history of the American Fair Labor Standards Act, arguing that the exclusion of farm workers from maximum hour and overtime provisions was directly motivated by racial animus—in particular by the desire to preserve the racialized labour structure of the southern plantation system. Juan Perea has persuasively demonstrated similar racial motivations behind the exclusion of agricultural workers from the National Labor Relations Act (Perea 2011). In Canada, the Seasonal Agricultural Workers Program works to combine 'precarious migratory status and the threat of repatriation' to create an 'impenetrable obstacle to the wide dispersal of industrial unionism in agri-culture' (Smith 2013: 32). In the United States, the overwhelming majority of farm workers are foreign-born. The Bracero Program, operative until the 1960s, was characterized by harsh conditions and threats of deportation—a basic structure that persists under the current regime which relies largely on undocu-mented farm workers (Luna 1998: 493, 505–6; Massey and Brown 2011). Because of the relative rightlessness and precarious immigration statuses of agricultural workers in both countries, agricultural employment has been termed a sphere of 'unfree labour' (Tucker 2012: 39; Smith 2013: 17). Adrian Smith catalogues efforts by agricultural workers to improve their social and legal status, challen-ging the assumption that these workers 'acquiesce to the conditions of subor-dination', and observing that 'worker resistance tends to be covert or difficult to unearth and complicated by racism' (Smith 2013: 28). Agricultural 'labour unfreedom' is understood to be distinct from the 'dull economic compulsion' Marx attributed to all capitalist labour schemes, instead drawing on racialized migration regimes to generate a system of 'super or hyper-exploitation' (Smith 2013: 29–30).

In considering arguments that animals' social inclusion would be improved by treatment as workers, it is worth noting that the primary context of animal oppression—the farm—represents a space where agricultural exceptionalism con-sistently 'fails to reflect democratic conceptions of the workplace and thwarts widespread participation of workers' (Luna 1998: 509). Holding out the status of 'workers' as an emblem of inclusion and respect in this context not only risks

150   ANIMAL LABOUR

minimizing the extent to which the broader currents of agricultural exceptionalism works to frustrate social justice struggles of all kinds, but also risks eliding the specific struggles of human agricultural workers. In this respect, the invocation of workers' rights as an emblem of progress towards which animal advocates might aspire mirrors a similar invocation of the civil rights movement within some strands of animal advocacy. As Angela P. Harris has explained:

> [One] objection to the use of [civil rights struggles] as anchors for the Animal Liberation Movement is that civil rights struggle is not the orderly procession toward moral perfection that these dreaded comparisons suggest.... [N]ew rights claims are routinely analogized to African American rights claims, and it is invariably suggested that if the treatment being protested were being visited upon black people, it would never be tolerated. What's wrong with such arguments is their implicit assumption that the African American struggle for rights is over, and that it was successful. The use of analogy misrepresents history— strategically, it must be admitted—as the unfolding of a natural, organic process.
>
> (Harris 2009: 25)

In other words, the suggestion that animals would be treated appropriately if they were socially categorized together with marginalized people casts ongoing human justice struggles as complete in a way that is both inaccurate and potentially harmful to those struggles. These harms are magnified in circumstances where analogies between animals and marginalized human groups echo the ongoing denigration of those groups in the language of animality (Harris 2009). The suggestion that agricultural animals would be treated appropriately if they were recognized as being 'workers' risks overlooking the severity of human agricultural workers' exclusion and oppression. Moreover, farm workers are overrepresented among those undocumented immigrants whom the US president has identified as 'animals' in justifying their physical and political exclusion—making the analogy doubly harmful (Davis 2018).

Of course, this is not to say that advocates of the labour-recognition-transformation model are unconcerned with the conditions of human labourers. Porcher certainly attends to the harsh labour conditions facing workers in industrial animal agriculture and slaughter (Porcher 2011). And Coulter (whose treatment of farmed animals as potential workers is more cautious than Porcher's as noted above), advocates for animal labour recognition in the context of a broader 'humane jobs' agenda that specifically embraces the transformation of human workplaces (Coulter 2017a, 2017b). Nonetheless, to the extent that Porcher, in particular, emphasizes labour recognition for farmed animals as a route to transformed relations, this analytic move carries the problematic implication that agricultural industries are models of worker inclusion. (As in the North American context discussed above, France, where Porcher's research is largely conducted,

STATUS, EXPLOITATION, AND AGRICULTURAL EXCEPTIONALISM 151

relies on seasonal immigrant labourers 'whose living and health conditions are increasingly catastrophic' (Verhaeren 1986; Potot 2016).)

Nor does this caution against the labour-recognition-transformation argument preclude the use of labour analyses in understanding the structures and experiences of exploitation that characterize human–animal relations. Dinesh Wadiwel's contribution to this volume (chapter 9), for example, explores Marx's accounts of 'the working day' and 'labour time' as a useful entry point to understanding the structures of exploitation that characterize industrial animal use. His analysis does not, however, make the labour-recognition-transformation argument of suggesting that animals deserve or earn transformed conditions on the basis of the recognition of their work as such. So too does Barbara Noske deploy Marxist concepts like alienation to illuminate the workings of industrial agriculture, but without employing a labour-recognition-transformation argument to explain how or why animal lives might become objects of moral concern (Noske 1989; 1997). As Maneesha Deckha has explained, there is a difference between 'drawing parallels between oppressions' and 'comparing animals to humans so that we care about them' (Deckha 2018: 227). The former approach can offer productive insights into shared root causes and structures of exploitation; the latter, especially when animals' status is claimed to be elevated through comparison to marginalized and disadvantaged peoples, raises the concerns flagged here (Deckha 2018; Harris 2009; Ko 2017).

Conclusion: The Broader Case for Labour Recognition

But what of those advocates of recognizing animal labour who more or less exclude animal agriculture from their vision of animal labour-recognition-transformation? My tentative reaction is that there is reason to be concerned about a vision of animal inclusion that excludes this critical constituency. As farmed animals represent 98 per cent of domesticated and captive animals, David Wolfson and Mariann Sullivan note that '[f]rom a statistician's point of view, . . . all animals are farmed animals' (Wolfson and Sullivan 2004: 206). Farmed animals, moreover, are subject to some of the grimmest and most gruesome forms of exclusion and exploitation of any domesticated animals. The harsh conditions in which farmed animals live are particularly salient when we consider some of the claims to which the labour-recognition-transformation argument might give rise: entitlements to retirement (which we might think of as a right not to be killed), to choose whether and how to submit to human exploitation, to social respect, to protection from violence, and to the opportunity to develop their own familial and community relations. These strike me as goods that are not well understood as 'earned' through work, but rather as springing from more fundamental relational goals. (For similar reasons, the moralization of work has been criticized as underwriting the social exclusions of some of the most vulnerable members of human society, as Donaldson and Kymlicka explore in chapter 10 of this volume.) An argument for social inclusion that seeks these goods for police dogs and carriage horses through a lens that hives off the problems of animal agriculture strikes me as materially under-inclusive. Of course, attention to a relevant category of social life (e.g. the lives of police dogs and carriage horses) as warranting ideological transformation does not necessarily require that all aspects of every related social problem be captured by a proposed transformative lens. But since we know that farmed animals are a particularly, and perhaps paradigmatically, debased constituency, we should be cautious of theories of animal inclusion that seem not to embrace this category. This is especially so where the proposed mechanism for inclusion is already recognized—as labour is—as having exclusionary or marginalizing effects on those left out. In short, whether farmed animals are 'in' the labour-transformation-recognition argument, or left out, farmed animals pose a problem for this analysis.

In fact, those advocates of the labour-recognition-transformation thesis who do limit or reject the argument's application to farmed animals are not satisfied to just leave farmed animals out of the picture, instead invoking concerns about killing and suffering as defining the wrongs of agriculture (Cochrane 2016; 2016a). But, of course, deontological and utilitarian arguments that animal rights and suffering should constrain human behaviour are not new. If animal life, freedom, and well-being are captured by such background commitments, it is unclear what the recognition of animal 'work' adds to this picture, or why (or what) additional goods should flow only to animals recognized as workers.

Advocates of the labour-recognition-transformation argument might suggest that their approach adds something important even when cast as overlaying background commitments to rights or welfare. In particular, the labour-recognition-transformation model builds on Donaldson and Kymlicka's insight that a positive programme of membership and inclusion is necessary to transform human–animal relations (Donaldson and Kymlicka 2011). While I agree that a more relational approach to animals' social and legal status is necessary to the project of transformation (Eisen 2018), I think that, given the shortcomings I have identified with labour as a model in the agricultural sphere, other categories of relationship might be more fruitful. In particular, my intuition is that the best starting point for identifying categories of animal experience that warrant social and legal recognition is an exploration of what animals themselves seem to value most.

While there is certainly evidence that many dogs, in particular, enjoy aspects of their work for people, I am sceptical that work for people is a *core priority* for dogs—and even more sceptical that this would be so absent the systems of reproductive control and intra-species isolation that characterize contemporary human uses of dogs. It is certainly the case that coercion and limited opportunities also characterize human labour relationships to greater or lesser degrees. This reality has provoked debates over whether, at the extreme ends of exploitation, 'work' ceases to serve as a useful lens for describing the underlying relationship. Roiling disagreements as to whether and when 'sex work' or 'trafficking' are more appropriate descriptors for pay-for-sex relationships are perhaps the clearest examples, with the factual and ideological terms on which opposing camps debate generally defined by questions of consent and contract, including in relation to age, use of force, and the possibility of meaningful consent under circumstances of inequality (see, e.g., MacKinnon 2011: 272; Sutherland 2004: 3–7; Rubin 1984). In the context of farmed animals—where conditions of inequality are so severe, where no veneer of consent is expected or required, and where physical domination and killing are formal and integral elements of the relationships—I see little room for such debate. Of course, it might be argued, that extreme material transformations could alter this landscape in ways that might make 'work' a more appropriate lens: that animals and species whose lives are now characterized by agricultural confinement might instead be invited, and have opportunities to meaningfully consent, to other kinds of relationships that better align with a positive vision of 'work'. The critique I pose here certainly does not foreclose the possibility that a 'work' lens might take on a different valence in radically transformed circumstances. Instead, my aim has been to question whether a labour-recognition-transformation approach is a useful heuristic in the context of prevailing realities, including agricultural exceptionalism and its associated legal, political, and material distributions. And under prevailing conditions, I don't see reason to believe, or to base a theory of social transformation, on the prospect that animals deeply value work for human beings, much less that they would do so if and when they might be empowered to live and act under less coercive terms.

For this reason, I would be inclined to seek models of inclusion and recognition that are not predicated on animals' interest and willingness to do things *for us* in circumstances of unequal power. Instead, I would propose approaches to relational transformation grounded in an exploration of what animals seem to value most, and what priorities of theirs are most frustrated under current conditions. But what can we know about what animals value, and how can we build theories of transformation grounded in those priorities? In my own work on dairy cows, I have suggested that recognition and inclusion might be predicated on understanding cows as *parents* and as *friends*. There is ample evidence that cows care deeply about their friends and offspring, and that the harms of social dislocation and frustration of familial bonds are both devastating and pervasive (Eisen 2019). Rather than thinking about how to convince people to see dairy cows as workers not getting their due—a lens that seems at best speculatively related to how cows might themselves value their own lives—we might build models of empathy and inclusion around recognition of animals as parents and friends whose most valued bonds are severed and denied. Of course, identifying *recognition of kinship* as a vehicle for inclusion represents only a direction of

154 ANIMAL LABOUR

inquiry, not a conclusion—particularly if the aim is legal, political, and material transformation. Among human communities, kinship is a source of social categories for which legal recognition has always required fiercely contested inquiries into individual and collective accounts of value and connection (Eisen 2019; see also Bryant 2010; Coulter 2016b). The aim, in the context of animals, farmed or otherwise, is expressly *not* to demonstrate that animal parenthood and friendship ought to be recognized as relevantly *like* human affective connections, but rather that these bonds represents their own sources of relational value grounded in the lives and experiences of animals themselves.

It might be argued that this kind of recognition—predicated on what animals value most rather than on how animals fit into schemes of human use and activity—disregards the 'link' between humans and animals (a theme discussed at length in Delon's contribution to this volume, chapter 8). It is possible that a focus on what diverse animals value might lead to dogs, and certainly farmed animals, performing much less, or less consistent, activities that enrich or add direct value to our human communities. If the link is only seen to be satisfied where we breed and cage and instruct animals, I am sceptical of its value. But I suspect that there is another, richer version of the link that might be served by an attention to social categories that focus on the social relationships that animals value themselves. In my view, a link between humans and animals would be strengthened and preserved if we understood ourselves to be in a broad interspecies community of, for example, parents and friends, pursuing individual and collective ends that attract recognition across difference, and where commonalities and identification are resources for understanding, not bases for inclusion (Harris 2009: 31). It is this version of the link that I think is most promising, and I am not convinced that the labour-recognition-transformation model points us in this direction.

References

Adams, Carol J. 2017. 'Feminized Protein: Meaning, Representations, and Implications'. In *Making Milk: The Past, Present, and Future of our Primary Food*, edited by Mathilde Cohen and Yoriko Otomo, 19–40. London: Bloomsbury.

Arcury, Thomas A., and Sara A. Quandt. 2011. 'Living and Working Safely: Challenges for Migrant and Seasonal Farmworkers'. *North Carolina Medical Journal* 72(6): 466–70.

Bisgould, Lesli. 2011. *Animals and the Law*. Toronto: Irwin Law.

Bowden, Marie-Anne. 2006. 'The Polluter Pays Principle in Canadian Agriculture'. *Oklahoma Law Review* 59(1): 53–88.

Boyd, David. 2003. *Unnatural Law: Rethinking Canadian Environmental Law Policy*. Vancouver: UBC Press.

Bryant, Taimie. 2010. 'Denying Animals Childhood and its Implications for Animal-Protective Law Reform'. *Law, Culture and the Humanities* 61(1): 56–74.

Castañeda, Xóchitl, and Patricia Zavella. 2003. 'Changing Constructions of Sexuality and Risk: Migrant Mexican Women Farmworkers in California'. *Journal of Latin American Anthropology* 8: 126–51.

Clark, Jonathan. 2014. 'Labourers or Lab Tools? Rethinking the Role of Lab Animals in Clinical Trials'. In *The Rise of Critical Animal Studies: From the Margins to the Centre*, edited by Nik Taylor and Richard Twine, 139–64. London: Routledge.

Cochrane, Alasdair. 2016. 'Labour Rights for Animals'. In *The Political Turn in Animal Ethics*, edited by Robert Garner and Siobhan O'Sullivan, 15–32. New York: Rowman & Littlefield.

Cohen, Mathilde. 2017. 'Of Milk and the Constitution'. *Harvard Journal of Law and Gender* 40: 115–82.

Coulter, Kendra. 2016a. *Animals, Work, and the Promise of Interspecies Solidarity*. New York: Palgrave Macmillan.

Coulter, Kendra. 2016b. 'Beyond Human to Humane: A Multispecies Analysis of Care Work, Its Repression, and Its Potential'. *Studies in Social Justice* 10(2): 199–219.

Coulter, Kendra. 2017a. 'Humane Jobs: A Political Economic Vision for Interspecies Solidarity and Human-Animal Wellbeing'. *Politics and Animals* 3: 31–41.

Coulter, Kendra. 2017b. 'Towards Humane Jobs: Recognizing Gendered and Multi-species Intersections and Possibilities'. In *Gender, Work, and Climate Change in the Global North: Work, Public Policy and Action*, edited by Marjorie Griffin Cohen, 167–82. Milton Park: Routledge.

Daugbjerg, Carsten, and Alan Swinbank. 2009. *Ideas, Institutions, and Trade: The WTO and the Curious Role of EU Farm Policy in Trade Liberalization*. Oxford: Oxford University Press.

Daugbjerg, Carsten, and Peter Feindt. 2017. 'Post-exceptionalism in Public Policy: Transforming Food and Agricultural Policy'. *Journal of European Public Policy* 24(11): 1565–84.

Davis, Julie Hirschfeld. 2018. 'Trump Calls Some Unauthorized Immigrants "Animals" in Rant'. *The New York Times*, 16 May 2018. https://www.nytimes.com/2018/05/16/us/politics/trump-undocumented-immigrants-animals.html

Deckha, Maneesha. 2018. 'Humanizing the Non-Human: A Legitimate Way for Animals to Escape Juridical Property Status?'. In *Critical Animal Studies: Towards Trans-species Social Justice*, edited by Atsuko Karin Matsuoka and John Sorenson, 209–33. London: Rowman & Littlefield.

Donaldson, Sue, and Will Kymlicka. 2011. *Zoopolis: A Political Theory of Animal Rights*. Oxford: Oxford University Press.

Dowell, Tiffany. 2011. 'Understanding and Interpreting Right to Farm Laws'. *Natural Resources and Environment* 26: 39–43.

Eisen, Jessica. 2017. 'Milk and Meaning: Puzzles in Posthumanist Method'. In *Making Milk: The Past, Present and Future of our Primary Food*, edited Mathilde Cohen and Yoriko Otomo, 237–46. New York: Bloomsbury.

Eisen, Jessica. 2018. 'Beyond Rights and Welfare: Democracy, Dialogue, and the Animal Welfare Act'. *University of Michigan Journal of Law Reform* 51(3): 469–547.

Eisen, Jessica. 2019. 'Milked: Nature, Necessity, and American Law'. *Berkeley Journal of Gender Law and Justice* 34: 71–115.

Enman-Beech, John. forthcoming. 'Can Animals Contract?' (manuscript on file with the author).

Fraser, Rachel Elizabeth. 2017. 'Animal Citizens, Animal Workers'. *The New Inquiry*, 14 November 2017. https://thenewinquiry.com/animal-citizens-animal-workers/.

Gaard, Greta. 2013. 'Toward a Feminist Postcolonial Milk Studies'. *American Quarterly* 65(3): 595–618.

Gillespie, Kathryn. 2014. 'Sexualized Violence and the Gendered Commodification of the Animal Body in Pacific Northwest US Dairy Production'. *Gender, Place & Culture: A Journal of Feminist Geography* 21(10): 1321–37.

Hamilton, Neil. 1998. 'Right-to-Farm Laws Reconsidered: Ten Reasons Why Legislative Efforts to Resolve Agricultural Nuisances May Be Ineffective'. *Drake Journal of Agricultural Law* 3(1): 103–18.

Hansen, Eric, and Martin Donohue. 2003. 'Health Issues of Migrant and Seasonal Farmworkers'. *Journal of Health Care for the Poor and Underserved* 14: 153–64.

Haraway, Donna. 2008. *When Species Meet*. Minneapolis: University of Minnesota Press.

Harris, Angela P. 2009. 'Should People of Color Support Animal Rights?'. *Journal of Animal Law* 5: 15–32.

Hovey, Joseph D., and Christina G. Magaña. 2002. 'Psychosocial Predictors of Anxiety Among Immigrant Mexican Migrant Farmworkers: Implications for Prevention and Treatment'. *Cultural Diversity and Ethnic Minority Psychology* 8: 274–89.

Hribal, Jason. 2012. 'Animals Are Part of the Working Class Reviewed'. *Borderlands* 11: 1–37.

Jones, Laura, with Liv Fredricksen. 1999. *Crying Wolf? Public Policy on Endangered Species in Canada*. Vancouver: Fraser Institute.

Ko, Syl. 2017. 'Emphasizing Similarities Does Nothing for the Oppressed'. In *Aphroism: Essays on Pop Culture, Feminism, and Black Veganism from Two Sisters*, edited by Aph Ko and Syl Ko, 37–43. New York: Lantern Books.

Kymlicka, Will. 2017. 'Social Membership: Animal Law Beyond the Property/Personhood Impasse'. *Dalhousie Law Journal* 40(1): 123–55.

Linder, Marc. 1987. 'Farm Workers and the Fair Labor Standards Act: Racial Discrimination in the New Deal'. *Texas Law Review* 65(7): 1335–93.

STATUS, EXPLOITATION, AND AGRICULTURAL EXCEPTIONALISM   157

Luna, Guadalupe. 1998. 'An Infinite Distance?: Agricultural Exceptionalism and Agricultural Labor'. *University of Pennsylvania Journal of Labor and Employment Law* 1(2): 487–510.

MacKinnon, Catharine. 2011. 'Trafficking, Prostitution, and Inequality'. *Harvard Civil Rights-Civil Liberties Law Review* 46: 271–309.

Marceau, Justin. 2019. *Beyond Cages: Animal Law and Criminal Punishment.* Cambridge: Cambridge University Press.

Massey, Douglas, and Amelia Brown. 2011. 'Movement between Mexico and Canada: Analysis of a New Migration Stream'. *International Migration* 6(1): 119–44.

McCormally, Patrick. 2007. *Right to Farm Legislation in Canada.* Toronto: Probe International. http://www.probeinternational.org/envirowaterarticles/righttofarmcanada. pdf.

Montpetit, Éric. 2002. 'Policy Networks, Federal Arrangements, and the Development of Environmental Regulations: A Comparison of the Canadian and American Agricultural Sectors'. *Governance: An International Journal of Policy, Administration, and Institutions* 15(1): 1–20.

Noske, Barbara. 1989. *Humans and Other Animals.* London: Pluto Press.

Noske, Barbara. 1997. *Beyond Boundaries: Humans and Animals.* Montréal: Black Rose.

Ontiveros, Maria. 2003. 'Lessons from the Fields: Female Farmworkers and the Law'. *Maine Law Review* 55: 157–90.

Otero, Gerardo, and Kerry Preibisch. 2010. *Farmworker Health and Safety: Challenges for British Columbia.* Vancouver: WorkSafe BC.

Patel, Avni, Angela Hill, Asa Eslocker, and Brian Ross. 2009. 'The Blueberry Children'. *ABC News*, 30 October 2009. http://abcnews.go.com/Blotter/young-children-working-blueberry-fields-walmart-severs-ties/story?id=8951044

Perea, Juan. 2011. 'The Echoes of Slavery: Recognizing the Racist Origins of the Agricultural and Domestic Worker Exclusion from the National Labor Relations Act'. *Ohio State Law Journal* 72(1): 95–138.

Pollans, Margot. 2016. 'Drinking Water Protection and Agricultural Exceptionalism'. *Ohio State Law Journal* 77(6): 1195–260.

Porcher, Jocelyne. 2011. 'The Relationship Between Workers and Animals in the Pork Industry: A Shared Suffering'. *Journal of Agricultural and Environmental Ethics* 24(1): 3–17.

Porcher, Jocelyne. 2012. 'Dairy Cows: Workers in the Shadows?'. *Society and Animals* 20: 39–60.

Porcher, Jocelyne. 2014. 'The Work of Animals: A Challenge for Social Sciences'. *HUMaNIMALIA* 6(1): 1–9.

Porcher, Jocelyne. 2017a. 'Animal Work'. In *The Oxford Handbook of Animal Studies*, edited by Linda Kalof, 302–16. Oxford: Oxford University Press.

Porcher, Jocelyne. 2017b. *The Ethics of Animal Labor: A Collaborative Utopia*. Basingstoke: Palgrave Macmillan.

Potot, Swanie. 2016. 'Sans Papier: Self-Censored Social Identities of Farm Workers in Southern France'. In *Seasonal Workers in Mediterranean Agriculture: The Social Costs of Eating Fresh*, edited by Jörg Gertel and Sarah Ruth Sippel. London: Routledge.

Preibisch, Kerry, and Evelyn Encalada Grez. 2010. 'The Other Side of 'El Otro Lado'': Mexican Migrant Women and Labor Flexibility in Canadian Agriculture'. *Signs: Journal of Women in Culture and Society* 35: 289–316.

Rubin, Gayle. 1984. 'Thinking Sex: Notes for a Radical Theory of the Politics of Sexuality'. In *Pleasure and Danger: Exploring Female Sexuality*, edited by Carol Vance, 267–319. Boston: Routledge & Kegan Paul.

Ruhl, J.B. 2000. 'Farms, Their Environmental Harms, and Environmental Law'. *Ecology Law Quarterly* 27: 263–349.

Satzewich, Vic. 1991. *Racism and the Incorporation of Foreign Labour: Farm Labour Migration to Canada since 1945*. London: Routledge.

Schell, Greg. 2002. 'Farmworker Exceptionalism under the Law: How the Legal System Contributes to Farmworker Poverty and Powerlessness'. In *The Human Cost of Food: Farmworkers' Lives, Labor and Advocacy*, edited by Charles Thompson and Melinda Wiggins, 139–66. Austin: University of Texas Press.

Schneider, Susan. 2010. 'A Reconsideration of Agricultural Law: A Call for the Law of Food, Farming, and Sustainability'. *William and Mary Environmental Law and Policy Review* 34(3): 935–63.

Smallwood, Kate. 2003. *A Guide to Canada's Species at Risk Act*. Vancouver: Sierra Legal Defence Fund. http://www.sfu.ca/~amooers/scientists4species/SARA_Guide_May2003.pdf.

Smart, Alan, and Josephine Smart. 2017. 'Agricultural Exceptionalism: A Potential TPP Roadblock'. In *The Changing Currents of Transpacific Integration: China, the TPP, and Beyond*, edited by Adrian Hearn and Margaret Myers, 99–113. Boulder: Lynne Rienner.

Smith, Adrian. 2013. 'Racialized in Justice: The Legal and Extra-Legal Struggles of Migrant Agricultural Workers in Canada'. *Windsor Year Book of Access to Justice* 31: 15–38.

Sutherland, Kate. 2004. 'Work, Sex, and Sex-Work: Competing Feminist Discourses on the International Sex Trade'. *Osgoode Hall Law Journal* 42(1): 139–67.

Sykes, Katie. 2015. 'Rethinking the Application of Canadian Criminal Law to Factory Farming'. In *Canadian Perspectives on Animals and the Law*, edited by Peter Sankoff, Vaughan Black, and Katie Sykes. Toronto: Irwin Law.

Trebilcock, Michael. 2014. *Dealing with Losers: The Political Economy of Policy Transitions*. Oxford: Oxford University Press.

Trebilcock, Michael, and Kristen Pue. 2015. 'The Puzzle of Agricultural Exceptionalism in Trade Policy'. *Journal of International Economic Law* 18: 233–60.

Tucker, Eric. 2012. 'Farm Worker Exceptionalism: Past, Present, and the post-*Fraser* Future'. In *Constitutional Labour Rights in Canada: Farm Workers and the* Fraser *Case*, edited by Fay Faraday, Judy Fudge, and Eric Tucker, 30–56. Toronto: Irwin Law.

Verhaeren, R. 1986. 'The Role of Foreign Workers in the Seasonal Fluctuations of the French Economy'. *International Immigration Review* 20(4): 856–74.

Wadiwel, Dinesh. 2002. 'Cows and Sovereignty: Biopower and Animal Life'. *Borderlands E-Journal* 1(2).

Weisberg, Zipporah. 2009. 'The Broken Promises of Monsters: Haraway, Animals and the Humanist Legacy'. *Journal for Critical Animal Studies* 7(2): 21–61.

Wolfson, David, and Mariann Sullivan. 2004. 'Foxes in the Henhouse: Animals, Agribusiness, and the Law: A Modern American Fable'. In *Animal Rights: Current Debates and New Directions*, edited by Cass Sunstein and Martha Nussbaum, 205–33. Oxford: Oxford University Press.

8

The Meaning of Animal Labour

Nicolas Delon

Introduction

The critique of factory farming generates some of the starkest disagreements among those whose concerns include animal welfare, food justice, labour rights, global warming, and pollution. On the one hand, many animal rights advocates argue for the abolition of animal agriculture, not just factory farming. On the other hand, advocates of humane husbandry argue that the ills of factory farming call for more traditional, small-scale, sustainable practices and a shift in consumption. The contrast overlooks some intermediate positions but should suffice for preliminary purposes. The bone of contention is this: It does not follow from critiquing factory farming that domesticated animals have a claim not to be used in agriculture. Both sides claim to be advocates, even friends, of animals. Yet, despite their common target, they appear to make incompatible claims—about what a good life for animals entails; whether we may kill them for food; and whether their use in any agricultural system is exploitation. In other words, what are domesticated animals' interests? And what is a relationship between humans and other animals? One instance of this disagreement is the claim that domesticated animals have an interest in the continuation of certain relationships with human beings, and that work is one such valuable relationship. The abolition of animal agriculture, the reasoning goes, would eliminate work, which is the sole valuable relationship animals can have with human beings. Farm animals, on this view, are workers performing a valuable activity that is necessary for their existence, flourishing, and our mutually rewarding relations.

This chapter addresses the strategy of using the value of work as a justification for raising and killing animals for food (RKA for short), and in particular the assumption that animal agriculture, insofar as it entails slaughter, is an irreplaceable form of human–animal relationship. I will question this and other assumptions of what I call the labour-based defence of humane agriculture (LDHA) and consider alternative opportunities to sustain meaningful relationships with domesticated animals that do not entail raising and killing them for food. RKA makes husbandry (breeding and raising) conditional on slaughter. My thesis is that LDHA fails to support RKA and leaves unscathed a number of criticisms. I focus on an influential critic of veganism, representative of the humane

Nicolas Delon, *The Meaning of Animal Labour* In: *Animal Labour: A New Frontier of Interspecies Justice?*.
Edited by: Charlotte Blattner, Kendra Coulter, and Will Kymlicka, Oxford University Press (2020).
© Oxford University Press. DOI: 10.1093/oso/9780198846192.003.0008

THE MEANING OF ANIMAL LABOUR   161

husbandry movement. French sociologist and former farmer Jocelyne Porcher offers a distinctly labour-based version of the so-called compassionate or conscientious omnivore position. In doing so, Porcher also offers a husbandry-based version of the case for animal labour. Both arguments go hand in hand. Work is valuable for its own sake, and husbandry is one, though not the only, way to promote it. Happy meat without work is not truly happy. More broadly, Porcher envisions a 'reinvented' (but in some way ancestral) way of living together with animals, a 'collaborative utopia' for the twenty-first century (Porcher 2011a; 2017). My central question is whether Porcher succeeds in vindicating RKA, merely LDHA, or neither. I believe that she only succeeds in championing the value of work. But LDHA or RKA do not follow. I will thus push against the idea that we need to kill and eat animals in order to preserve valuable relationships with them. Porcher stands out insofar as she sees killing as a constitutive part (if a necessary evil) of husbandry. Porcher's strategy is therefore a unique illustration of LDHA in that she ties together justifications for work *and* justifications for RKA. Mirroring Porcher's utopia, the abolitionist ideal is sometimes perceived as 'dystopian', severing meaningful connections between vegan urbanites and nature and animals (Weele and Driessen 2013: 656). In this chapter I explain why I believe Porcher tackles, not a strawman, but a crude, non-representative critique of RKA. Valuing interspecies relationships, including work, need not entail LDHA, much less RKA.

In the first section, I introduce Porcher's terminological, conceptual, and evaluative distinction between 'animal productions' (livestock industry) and 'animal husbandry', and how it fits into the debate about humane RKA.[1] In the second section, I discuss Porcher's appeal to 'the link', as instantiated in work, as a justification for RKA. In the third section, I look more closely at the idea of animal co-worker, and I consider alternatives. In the fourth section, I rely on Purves and Delon (2018) to argue that RKA deprives animals of meaning in their life.

Industry vs. Husbandry

Here's the central problem raised by the intensification of agricultural production. The growth of farm operations—absolute size, number of animals, output, and profitability—allows for economies of scale which appear to benefit farmers. On the other hand, farmers increasingly lose direct control over their operations, in particular the ability to oversee closely the day-to-day operation of their farm and the individual behaviours and needs of their animals. Traditional farmers, as praised in agrarian thought, used to know their animals on a personal basis,

---

[1] For a recent comprehensive statement of Porcher's views in English, see Porcher 2017.

162 ANIMAL LABOUR

were in the best position to care for them and speak on their behalf, and doing so preserved land, communities, and practices (Bruxvoort Lipscomb 2016). But they have been supplanted or increasingly assisted by a range of technology and technicians over which they have at best limited control. The good shepherd's identity and role are fading, as public opinion increasingly blames farmers—often indiscriminately and sometimes unfairly—for a range of ills from pollution to animal cruelty. A large factor in this change is the exponential growth of demand for animal products over the second half of the twentieth century in Western countries and, lately, in the emerging, so-called BRIC, countries (Brazil, Russia, India, and China). These global trends outweigh the slight rise of vegetarianism, and the growing demand for products that comply with stricter welfare standards, in North America and Europe. In the United States, concentrated animal feeding operations (CAFOs) are the epitome of industrial systems, and their model is gaining traction in countries like China.

Let us begin by considering Porcher's distinction between 'animal husbandry' (*élevage*) and 'animal productions'. Husbandry is a relationship between farmers (*éleveurs*) and animals, 'meaningful labor with multiple rationalities—economic, but also relational and identity-based' (Porcher 2009: 162). Industrial (e.g. pig, chicken, rabbit) and intensified (e.g. dairy, veal) productions are the outgrowth of an industrialization process that began in the mid-nineteenth century with emerging 'zootechnics', or science-based breeding and husbandry, which she calls the 'science of the exploitation of animal machines'. Animal husbandry is 'part of our culture and...*is* a culture the value and fragility of which we fail to appreciate' (Porcher 2009: 162). In contrast, animal productions lack culture or history. The distinction yields two distinct triads: animal-farmer-husbandry *vs.* product-production-producer. The latter generates a tension between livestock animals being individuals (incidentally presented as such for advertising purposes) and their treatment and perception as products (Porcher 2009: 163).

Much of Porcher's sociological fieldwork is about the 'lived subjective experience of labor' of human workers, in particular their suffering, which results from the suffering that the industry expects them to inflict on animals for the sake of efficiency, the necessity of inflicting or tolerating death (whether in slaughterhouses or on farms), and their public image (critics of animal productions end up blaming animal farming as a whole). For instance, Pascale Molinier and Porcher emphasize the suffering stemming from 'lack of recognition' for workers on an industrial pig farm, from 'their boss, the farmers' assisting team (veterinarians and technicians), consumers and, broadly, co-citizens who seemingly perceive the job of pig farmer as dirty work' (Molinier and Porcher 2006: 6). Pigs and farmers experience 'shared suffering' (Porcher 2011b).

Domestication, thinks Porcher, has been misconstrued. A single term applies to plants and animals. This translates into practice: 'today we can treat farm animals

THE MEANING OF ANIMAL LABOUR   163

as "raw material" and use it like we use plant matter' (Porcher 2009: 165).[2] Indeed, in the industry, common phrases include 'animal matter' (for edible animal products), 'destruction' (for the slaughter of animals for economic or safety reasons), and *valorisation* (in French, i.e. 'exploitation' of 'matter' and 'waste' as sources of fuel or compost) (Porcher 2009: 163–4). Porcher argues that both animal liberationists and the livestock industry misconstrue farming as the exploitation of matter. But, she argues, husbandry does not inherently use animals as resources. Accordingly, the husbandry/production distinction makes space for *relations* (not use) that can be emancipatory for human and non-human co-workers.[3] Instead, animal productions make it impossible for workers, such as female employees on industrial pig farms, to work *well* and act on this possibility. The high turnover in the industry owes a lot to a double bind:

> Because of the intersubjective nature of relations between human beings and animals, the link inevitably persists even in industrial systems...but it is distorted because the organizational structure of work denies the existence of this link *qua* link.... [W]orkers can be subject to the double order of being 'their sows' friend' and of being disposed to knock their head with a sledgehammer
> (Porcher 2009: 167–8; also see Porcher 2008)

In other words, workers are prevented from treating animals as society expects them because it also expects them to provide a cheap food supply. Farmers and farm workers do their job with the sense of accomplishing a mission, 'the most important part of which is "feeding people"' (Porcher 2009: 169; also see Mouret 2012). But it's 'overshadowed' by the critique of industrial systems, whose workers are 'accused of polluting, mistreating animals and producing a suspicious food'. Ultimately, the breakdown of relations jeopardizes the recognition of workers by animals themselves, who would otherwise 'collaborate intentionally'. In industrial systems, '[a]nimals do not say thank you; they can even sabotage the work' (Porcher 2009: 169).[4] Porcher's explanation of workers' suffering suggests that

---

[2] Larrère (2010) illuminates the Cartesian model of living things as machines as primarily a representation of life. The model evolved from mechanism (the clock or automaton analogy) to thermodynamic to biotechnological models. The representation of the organism then enables its use as a machine.

[3] Porcher (2014) writes: 'In farming...this centrality of work is defeated by the livestock production industry, which reduces man and beast to their behaviors and standardized means of functioning. It is equally defeated by theories of animal liberation, which reject the question of work.... Why do animal liberators, many of whom claim to be political, even revolutionary in their doctrines, ignore the question of work, which is the political question par excellence? I believe it is because a political analysis of work with animals evidences the extreme closeness of man to beast, and the objective of animal "liberation" is in fact to separate them. Work recognition is a recognition of ties. It is thus effectively revolutionary.'

[4] On animal resistance in labour, see e.g. Hribal (2007). On the resistance of animals through the slaughter process, see Rémy's (2009) ethnography.

164 ANIMAL LABOUR

animal abuse is a *symptom* of the system, which inflicts suffering on animals by proxy so to speak.

We can now restate our problem following Porcher. We do not appreciate the possible value of RKA because we conflate husbandry and unconscionable farming practices. By the same token, animal liberation *or* exploitation is a false dichotomy. LDHA can purportedly evade the exploitation of animals as raw material if we appreciate the history of human–animal entanglement and work as its irreplaceable embodiment. With Porcher's diagnosis and pivotal distinctions laid out, I spell out her conception of animal labour in the next section. I argue that Porcher replaces a false dichotomy with another one (abolitionism *or* RKA). Indeed, I argue that taking the view that animals can be co-workers seriously undermines the case for RKA.

Porcher's Conception of Animal Labour

We have a diagnosis of what can go wrong with RKA. Can traditional husbandry provide a cure? Porcher's conception of animal labour purports to. Labour, on this view, implies a dyadic or collective relation between human and non-human co-workers. Its value is inherently relational. Indeed, it's 'the link' that Porcher considers worth preserving for its own sake. So, what is genuine labour on this conception?

Before delving further into her case for LHDA, let us consider a non-genuine type of work. Recently, the livestock industry has invested in new techniques attempting to remedy the ills of factory farming while preserving large-scale production. It knows that treating livestock as individuals with particular needs and preferences, as opposed to interchangeable production units, can serve optimized production. 'Precision Livestock Farming' (PLF) involves standardized, certified methods, supported by the European Union, which seek to improve agricultural sustainability (environmental impact, efficiency, food safety, welfare) while meeting both a steady or growing demand for animal products (indeed, food for a forecasted 9 billion human population by 2050) and stricter welfare standards (Berckmans 2004; Lehr 2014; Werkheiser 2018). PLF prolongs the livestock industry through novel means—information technology and innovative techniques such as 'automatic milking systems, micro-chipping, remote electronic surveillance, precision feeding, building atmosphere surveillance, virtual fences, artificial insemination technologies and robotization'. In a way, PLF replicates on a large scale the agrarian ideal of the good shepherd. Ironically, because it is focused on animals' individual characteristics, this system, which purports to be the most effective and attuned to particular needs, makes farmers replaceable. PLF seeks to minimize negative impacts on animals. But since, because they are so numerous, factory farmed animals are not accustomed to human interaction, PLF does that by minimizing interaction. Advocates of the good shepherd like Porcher see these trends as an outgrowth of alienating production systems—destroying workers, jobs, and relations. Instead of promoting farmers who familiarize themselves with animals early on, which only small farms allow for, the welcome attention to individuals has fostered a kind of contactless exploitation. PLF makes 'intensive ecological livestock farming' possible (Porcher 2017: 36).

How does Porcher's husbandry differ from PLF? CEMA (European Agricultural Machinery), the European association representing the agricultural machinery industry in Europe, is a major promoter of 'smart farming'. Among its many virtues, says CEMA, are that automatic solutions dispense with the constraints of human labour and thus offer more opportunities for animals to choose and engage in natural behaviours, in addition to improved productivity, real-time digital information, and big data.[5] On the other hand, PLF restricts the expression of animals' preferences, hence participation, in structuring signal reception and interpretation by imposing a system designed by engineers, biologists, and economists for optimization, in consultation with only poorly informed farmers (Lehr 2014; Werkheiser 2018). Traditional husbandry purports to foster direct attention to particular animals so that they can communicate their needs and preferences effectively to farmers, which PLF seeks to replicate at scale. Unlike both PLF and standard intensive agriculture, though, husbandry promotes active animal participation. For instance, on some farms, cows can participate in the milking process by choosing whether or not to interact with the milking robots, and who goes first, sometimes even declining the expected reward in exchange for some quiet time (Driessen 2014; Driessen and Heutinck 2015; Porcher and Schmitt 2010; 2012; Stuart, Schewe, and Gunderson 2013). While larger operations could allow for some degree of choice, PLF tends to discourage participation. PLF techniques undermine animals' autonomy and expression, thereby undermining their status as co-workers and active community members. PLF, in sum, does not fit the bill of Porcher's LDHA.

How plausible, in contrast, is Porcher's account of the value of work? We need to ask why we should live with animals in the first place, and why living together would entail labour. Porcher's main argument starts from an empirical premise blending history and anthropology—in a nutshell: we are happier together and have always lived together: 'Farmers and domesticated animals have lived and worked together for thousands of years, perhaps simply because it's much more interesting and a much greater source of joy to live together than separately' (Porcher 2009: 166). The empirical premise implies an axiological one: work uniquely embodies the intrinsic value of living together. To the extent that husbandry has been a central type of valuable work throughout history, it seems

---

[5] See 'Smart Farming' at http://www.CEMA-agri.org [Accessed 15 January 2019].

166   ANIMAL LABOUR

to follow that we should promote husbandry. And since husbandry entails killing (in order to feed people and for various practical reasons), the intrinsic value of living together seems to entail that we should promote RKA. Why does it merely seem so? Because the inference is fallacious. Let me explain.

For one thing, as I will continue asking: Why assume that, if joy motivates the existence and continuation of relationships, these have to be *work*, especially killing-based productive work? Porcher is suspicious that the detached, commercial way most pet owners currently relate to their pets involves the relevant type of relationship. Both pets and farm animals can be true companions, but only if we conceive of companionship as work (Porcher 2017: 1–22). But even so, why think that the value of work requires husbandry, much less RKA?

Furthermore, Porcher's argument is one from history. She rests her case on mutually rewarding relations. So, she is rightly concerned with individual welfare interests. But while she praises relations between particular individuals over particular lifetimes, the historical argument appears to turn on relations between our species and others over time. Let us grant that domestication has been beneficial for a range of species and breeds, including for human beings, in terms of evolutionary fitness. Many domesticated species and breeds are part of ecological symbiotic associations.[6] But, even so, it's only a descriptive point. History per se provides no justification for domestication, let alone current practices. Justifying present relations and inferring their best possible form on the basis of their origins are instances of the *genetic fallacy*. In particular, domestication can hardly justify the practices it gave rise to. By exploiting created dependency, modern farming turned what *might* have been a symbiotic relation into one of asymmetrical vulnerability. Granted, current farming practices may be unjust but leave the core value of domestication unscathed. My objections to Porcher do not concern domestication per se. I simply point out how little we can infer about the value of current practices from their history.

One final point concerning history. LDHA arguments typically involve the so-called *replaceability argument* to justify humane RKA. In a nutshell, we create happy individuals who would otherwise not exist and kill them for food (relatively young), and as long as we replace them with equally happy animals, the practice generates overall net benefits for animals, farmers, consumers, and the environment and society at large. Even if death were a harm to animals, the argument goes, it would be offset by the benefit of a pleasant life. A short happy life is worth more than no life at all. Examining the argument closely is beyond the scope of this chapter,[7] so let me simply note, first, that Porcher often appears to endorse, if implicitly, a version of the replaceability argument, where farmers give animals a

---

[6] The empirical story is sometimes deployed in support of the idea of a social 'domestic' compact (Budiansky 1999; Larrère and Larrère 2000). For a critique, see Palmer 2010: 57–62.

[7] See Delon (2016) for an overview, and Utria (2014) for a critique.

THE MEANING OF ANIMAL LABOUR   167

good life cut short by a good death as late as possible (which is still prematurely and for food);[8] second, that the argument assumes that someone, presumably animals, would be worse off if they did not exist (or at least someone better off existing). But that it is good for them to exist does not entail that it better for them to exist than never to have been. If we were to motivate the argument by appealing to the existence of breeds and species, the alleged benefits would be even more abstract. Existing individuals do not enjoy them. If they do, relative to what baseline are they better off? The farming relation persisted because it was mutually adaptive, but this tells us nothing about *welfare* benefits to individuals. That some species have thrived evolutionarily speaking (think dogs vs. wolves) tells us little if anything about how to treat individuals. The unit of selection, the gene, is morally irrelevant. The standpoint that matters is that of animals themselves.

Porcher's argument, then, is incomplete unless she can show both that husbandry is necessary to preserve the intrinsic value of living together and that individual animals enjoy benefits that they could not other otherwise enjoy and which outweigh the harm of a premature death. To Porcher's credit, not just any life will be good enough:

A good life ... means a life that is in accord with the animal world and its relational, cognitive and affective potentialities. It also means a habitat that is co-constructed with animals, a place where they can go or not go, and an individual or a collective space. It means diversified food that not only accords with the needs of animals, but equally with their tastes. It means an organization of work which respects the animals' rhythms, which takes into account relations animals have between themselves: the ties of friendship, the ties between mothers and their young but also ties of conflict. It means an organization of work which ... gives animals a chance to live their lives, and allows them a life expectancy that is congruent with this project, both inside and outside the field of production, so that for domestic animals, there is a life outside of work, and after the working years.   (Porcher 2017: 119)

Is it worth it? The farmer, coming back from the nursing of calves by their mothers, calls himself 'the happiest man' (Porcher 2009: 166), experiencing a joy based on 'harmony', 'a shared well-being'. Setting aside replaceability, we can

---

[8] In her work, the argument draws on the Maussian idea of '*don/contre-don*' (gift/counter-gift) (Mouret 2012; Porcher 2002; 2017: 73–83). For instance: 'Because the farmer gave them life, he is committed to his animals and they should be able to rely on him ... This gift of life that animals received and which puts them under the farmer's responsibility, as well as his daily protection and care, commits them to giving back' (Porcher 2002: 27). Farmers' gift is repeated, sustained throughout the animal's life, in particular when they postpone or try to avoid culling. 'Farmers commonly appear to think that this repeated gift of life ... which is against their economic interests ... implies an increased counter-gift on the animal's part' (31). Porcher presupposes that RKA is a gift of comparable significance to animals' giving their own life.

168 ANIMAL LABOUR

at least imagine that farming truly involves mutual flourishing. But Porcher conflates two things. On the one hand, there is the loss that actual animals would incur if they could not work as farm animals. On the other hand, there is the loss that non-existent animals would incur if we were to phase them out, as would likely be the case for breeds, if not species, that we would cease to breed for food. But non-existent beings never experience any loss. As for actual animals, they might be harmed by poorly managed retirement, neglect, or euthanasia. But we should neither assume that these are the only alternatives nor that species or breeds themselves can be harmed.

Interestingly, one example of Porcher's does not involve farming. Mahout elephants used for logging in Asia, or donkeys and horses in France, are deprived of work by the mechanization of labour. As a result, in order to preserve the link, '[b]reeders are now seeking employment for elephants and donkeys, such as carrying tourists...so that these animals don't disappear from the human world' (Porcher 2009: 167). Plausibly, elephant labour is one way to preserve a form of interspecies collaboration, including for conservation purposes. Nicolas Lainé (2017) has described the seasonal working routine of elephants with people from remote villages in Laos, the elephants helping the villagers transport goods and clean out the forests and weed. If Porcher and Lainé are right that these constitute valuable embodiments of 'the link', then it need not involve domestication or captivity. Let's assume their working conditions are compatible with their flourishing. The mahout–elephant relation is ancestral (potentially 5,000 years old), embedded in familial traditions (Hart and Sundar 2000), and considered a form of work partnership (Hart 1994). For these relationships to be truly flourishing, though, we would need to ensure that elephants are only held captive temporarily. For, despite our ancestral shared history, elephants' highly complex mental and social lives make them unfit for captivity (Poole and Moss 2008; Vanitha et al. 2011). Finally, these elephants are not bred in order to be killed for food—an altogether distinct type of relation than husbandry. The lesson to be drawn from this example is that mutually rewarding work is highly demanding and likely to be species- and context-sensitive. It tells us little about farming.

The argument from work, then, is of limited scope. If elephants, donkeys, and horses are at least as well off as workers as farm animals can be, then preserving 'the link' does not require RKA. Further, if these animals are better off as workers than they would be without work, the benefits are only conferred to *these* particular animals. Again, non-existent animals would not be worse off. Porcher's argument, in sum, proves too much or too little. The comparison between two possible lives for existing beings would only justify creating new ones with either of these lives if we could show that we *must* create new beings. But we're considering possible, not necessary beings, whose very existence depends on the choices we make. Porcher owes us an argument that we have decisive reasons to bring to existence beings with lives worth living. If it were the case, we would likely

THE MEANING OF ANIMAL LABOUR   169

have a duty to preserve an immense range of practices as long as the animals' lives would be sufficiently worth living. Even Porcher is not making that claim.

Hers is a more demanding case for giving animals good lives, not just lives worth living. Porcher, as we saw, appeals to affects, joy in particular. I wonder if, taken seriously, this does not create a more stringent standard than she suspects. For one thing, many current practices involving animals would no longer be permissible by this standard—if anything, the balance of joy over misery in the lives of most currently farmed animals is dramatically negative. A more intriguing question is what sort of work, including husbandry, can meet the standard of joy. Animal labour is typically hard work, structured by rigid external constraints (e.g., the labour of carriage horses, tourism elephants, dogs used for police, security, search, among others, draft animals, etc.) (DeMello 2012: 194–214). Surely, many of these interactions involve shared positive affects—police and military work can involve meaningful personal bonds (DeMello 2012: 194–214, 234–5). Despite the inherent risks and constraints of a strenuous job, these very well may be joyful, mutually rewarding interactions. And the standpoint of human workers matters too. Like traditional farmers, animal handlers, trainers, and other people working with animals acquire valuable insights into animals' wants and needs. Their testimony is a valuable source of 'folk expertise' (Andrews 2009) and provides a counterpoint to the industrial perception of animals. Yet work may also obscure some signals. Specific aims, values and needs, inherent biases can distort the perception and interpretation of signals. Humans are not just guardians or trustees; they breed and raise, buy and sell, train and confine livestock and other animals for specific purposes that shape what signals to pay attention to. Hence, what kind of jobs can provide for good lives remains an empirical question. We can't simply assume that anecdotal evidence collected among workers accurately captures the experiences of animals themselves over a wide range of jobs and working conditions.

So, we can agree with Porcher that the flourishing of many domesticated animals requires interactions, perhaps even partnership or friendship, with human beings, possibly fostered by work, 'guaranteeing [humans'] income and [animals'] daily bread' (Porcher 2009: 167). But why restrict meaningful forms of association to labour? Even Porcher's conception of friendship is strained. Typically, work and friendship are distinct spheres, even when they overlap. It's often a bad idea to have friends working for you. I'm sure there are plenty of exceptions, but friendship thrives in non-hierarchical relationships and work often requires constraints inimical to friendship. If the analogy with friendship is to carry any weight anyway, the onus is on Porcher to show that friendship allows, let alone requires, breeding, fattening, and slaughtering you, or confining and coercing you to work hard, in order for me to make a living. Now, companionship (as between companion animals and their persons) may be preferable to labour from the perspective of friendship, but one might reply that labour is preferable to

170 ANIMAL LABOUR

companionship from the perspective of agency. Indeed, Porcher sometimes reproaches current pet-keeping practices for not involving genuine meaningful interactions. Pets have to fulfil *some* form of (pet-specific) work: 'Without work, however discrete it may be, as with the work of pets, there are no ties' (Porcher 2017: 120). Being a companion *is* a form of work. Moreover, companion animals also provide care work, emotional support, assisted therapy, among other services they fulfil. Porcher is right that many existing forms of pet-keeping thwart animals' agency. Just because, say, dogs can only be captive does not mean we can't enhance their dog-like agency (Horowitz 2014). The question then becomes: why can't companionship be sufficient for preserving the link if we can foster agency therein. In companionship, including with trained dogs, horses, and birds, we find models of meaningful human–animal bonds whereby companions, albeit not equal in abilities, stand in genuinely reciprocal affective relations. Gary Varner (2002), for instance, has described a type of relationship with companion animals, such as dogs and horses, dubbed 'domesticated partnerships', which foster the respectful development and exercise of their faculties.

Porcher has described symptoms, a diagnosis, and a possible cure. I have argued that, as it stands, Porcher's LDHA fails to establish that we have decisive reasons to preserve strenuous work, much less husbandry, much less RKA. The next section adduces further reasons to reject LDHA and to consider alternatives.

Husbandry or What?

In this section, I review two respects in which Porcher's account of labour fails to support husbandry: her failure to consider alternatives and her failure to draw the full implications of the idea of animal co-workers.

1. Porcher lays out a trilemma (husbandry, liberation, or industrial agriculture). She argues that the last two horns entail breaking 'the link'. Even synthetic or cultured meat and animal products, she has repeatedly alleged in press and in public lectures, rests on the biotechnological industrial exploitation of matter and constitutes a strategic alliance with animal rights activists and industrial conglomerates with a view to producing 'living death' on a massive scale while dispensing with real life (Porcher 2017: 99–100; 2007; 2014). For the sake of argument, I have granted that we have reasons to preserve the link. Indeed, in the last section I argue we have reasons to do so for the sake of animals themselves. I don't think most animal advocates would recognize themselves in Porcher's depiction— many, if not most, of them want to preserve meaningful human–animal interactions (more on this below). What I reject is the trilemma. In her reply to my previous article (Delon 2017), Porcher (2018) lays bare the tragic toll of attempts to preserve the link without husbandry. If we want to live with, say, cows, she

THE MEANING OF ANIMAL LABOUR   171

notes, health requires genetic diversity, which requires that we have large enough populations. But this itself requires managing them through culling, i.e. RKA-based husbandry. As she wrote elsewhere: 'Animal reproduction and the sale of the young are a means of making relations durable' (Porcher 2017: 113). In other words, if we reject RKA, according to Porcher, we are committed to sterilization (ultimately having to phase out the animals we wanted to preserve), euthanasia, or letting them starve. That is, animal ethicists who, like me, value relationships really 'promote husbandry without knowing it' (like Molière's Monsieur Jourdain speaking prose) (Porcher 2018: 120–1).

Porcher thus suggests that rejecting both husbandry (assuming it entails RKA, which it does by her own lights) and factory farming entails abolitionism. But many advocates, like her, agree that domestication could be a form of 'emancipation' rather than exploitation (Porcher 2009: 164)—just on very different terms. The abolition–exploitation dichotomy is a false one and not one most animal ethicists now put forth. If, like Porcher, we assume that any acceptable form of the link entails a tragic cost—killing really, not merely death—then we are begging the question.[9] Many animal rights theorists and activists are not abolitionists regarding 'the link' even though most are regarding RKA (e.g. Donaldson and Kymlicka 2011; Cochrane 2012).[10] Porcher conflates the critique of RKA with the critique of human–animal relationships, but one need not imply the other, and defending the potential value of animal labour fails to motivate LDHA.

Suppose the social identities and occupations embedded in husbandry are morally significant and give people a sense of meaning (which they certainly do for many small-scale farmers). Still, as old practices disappear, new ones emerge, along with new identities and occupations. The point is well put by Josh Milburn in a recent paper on 'clean milk':

> It is true that large-scale adoption of clean milk may mean that certain *modes* of relating to cows—specifically, certain careers—would no longer be open to people, but this is the standard consequence of moral, social and technological

---

[9] Porcher repeatedly emphasizes in her fieldwork the suffering that the necessity of death causes to farmers and slaughterhouse workers, who allegedly wish it were not necessary and seek to postpone it as much as is economically feasible. 'For animals do not want to die and we know that. The question remains, particularly because of the changing sensibility of farmers with regard to animals.... [T]here are now vegetarian farmers. There are also farmers who would really be content with only 20 cows, even with 2 or 3' (Porcher 2017: 113). RKA implies premature death, but husbandry only reluctantly accepts it. Mouret (2012) describes the relation between (pig) farmers and death as 'grieving' (see also Porcher 2002; Mouret and Porcher 2007). On Mouret's account, this attitude is a complex of relational affects and recognition of the badness of death, whether through euthanasia, culling, or slaughter, against a background of cyclical 'gift-counter-gift' (Mouret 2012: 77–80). Mouret acknowledges that gift is snatched from animals rather than consented.

[10] Even abolitionist critics of Porcher (e.g. Utria 2014) do not condone phasing out domesticated animals.

172 ANIMAL LABOUR

> advancement. Indeed, it is not normally presented as a cause for concern. It is
> hard to imagine that many people lacking financial interests worry about the loss
> of jobs in the tobacco industry as smoking becomes less socially acceptable.
> Similarly, people are no longer employed as pin-setters, ice-cutters, or telegram
> operators due to technological advancement, while work as a cockfighter, resur-
> rectionist, or hangman is hard to find due to changing ethical/legal norms. In the
> future, the professions of dairy farmer and slaughterhouse worker may face a
> similar fate ... At the same time, new—more humane—jobs should be created,
> including those tied to a new dairy industry, and those grounded in new (or
> expanded) modes of peaceful human/animal coexistence.   (Milburn 2018: 270)

For sure, the automobile, fossil fuel, and tobacco industries do not involve the sort
of link that Porcher finds valuable. Yet the existence of a career per se has little
normative weight.

2. Yet another ground for scepticism vis-à-vis Porcher's cure lies in what
legitimate work entails. Recently, she has suggested

> putting some sort of "labour law" in place for domestic animals ... which would
> form the basis of our duties to animals depending on the work that we expect
> from them, and on what they expect from the work. We could imagine that in
> our utopia the gift of a good life for animals would be a prerequisite.
>
> (Porcher 2017: 119)

As we saw, the 'good life' 'gives animals a chance to live their lives, and allows
them a life expectancy that is congruent with this project, both inside and
outside the field of production, so that for domestic animals, there is a life
outside of work, and after the working years' (Porcher 2017:119). Indeed, if we
really think animals can be workers (Porcher and Schmitt 2010; 2012;
Cochrane 2016; Coulter 2016), labour entails a certain status. Animal workers
are not simply domesticated animals with whom we share a spatial, social, and
potentially political community; nor are they reducible to either pets, livestock,
or sanctuary animals. It's a distinct category with implications of its own.
Co-workers share a *workplace*—e.g. farm, field, or street—and have certain
rights. For instance, Cochrane (2016) considers the rights to unionize, to fair
wage, a safe and healthy environment, rest days, retirement, and benefits. In
this volume, Cochrane argues that 'good work' for animals has a three-fold
basis: it provides pleasure through affording opportunities to use and develop
skills; which allows for the exercise of animals' agency; and which provides a
context in which animals can be esteemed as valuable workers recognized as
members of the communities in which they labour. But we should also note
that if animals are entitled to meaningful retirement, it is prima facie unjust to

THE MEANING OF ANIMAL LABOUR   173

cull them once their productive life is over. Porcher has recently considered the upshot in more detail:

> we can imagine other rules governing the retirement of animals, or of slaughter. First of all, this should concern the choice of breeds, as they determine the life expectancy of animals. Rather than slaughtering industrial pigs at five and a half months, it would be better to breed Limousin pigs up to the age of 18 months.... Is providing us with meat all that it can do? In my opinion, it is not. Pigs can have many other jobs, particularly in the forest...It is the same for calves and lambs. If the gift and counter gift between animals and us is expressed by a good life for the animals, they must have more time to live their lives. If, for example,...animals have an active place in work, the question of when to retire them must be asked. Many farmers, particularly of goats, do not send their old animals to the abattoir, but construct a sub-herd, retired from production but not from the collective.   (Porcher 2017: 113–14)

In this remarkable passage, Porcher comes close to defending ('without knowing it'!) a no-kill form of husbandry—as far as harvesting milk, eggs, or wool at least—many animal ethicists might welcome (Cochrane 2012: 86-89; Donaldson and Kymlicka 2011: 139; Milburn 2018).[11] Still, according to Porcher, farm animals typically won't be retired, unlike, say, police dogs: breeding them entails killing them (Porcher 2018). If, on the other hand, retirement is not among their rights, are they meaningfully workers? Porcher (implicitly) dissociates the status of worker from the right to *choose one's employment*, unlike Donaldson and Kymlicka or Blattner (chapters 10 and 5 of this volume). Porcher's conception appears tailored to rationalize the continuation of what many would plausibly count as exploitation.

Retirement is thus an issue. So is consent, or lack thereof. Despite the Industrial Revolution, some types of work continued or even intensified animal use in the nineteenth century, mainly of horses, cattle, and dogs, for dairy production, mining, transportation, draft, and war. As French historian Eric Baratay (2008) has argued, such work typically turned animals into *proletarians* more than co-workers (also see Hribal 2007), much less friends. Further, a worker, at least in

---

[11] On the model of intentional communities, Donaldson and Kymlicka (2015) argue that radically novel forms of human–animal coexistence are possible in farmed animal sanctuaries, which do not require harms characteristic of RKA, while offering space, protection, companionship, and presumptive non-interference with fundamental interests (e.g. life, reproduction, within- and between-species socialization). Porcher (2018) tackles *Zoopolis* (more than she engages with Delon 2017, in fact). The authors of a recent paper (critical of anti-speciecism) state: 'Donaldson and Kymlicka's project is to reinvent a type of relation, husbandry, that has existed for thousands of years, but by removing killing from the equation. Whereas husbandry is a situation in which, when animals are born, others must die, *Zoopolis* offers a project of cohabitation, with no killing' (Gardin et al. 2018: 8; edited translation).

174 ANIMAL LABOUR

contexts where work is praised, is supposed to *consent* to work and written or tacit contractual terms. Even when animals cannot express consent, they can *assent*, at the very least *dissent* (see Blattner, chapter 5 of this volume). While dissent clearly indicates refusal to work, we should also attempt to secure the animal's assent, expressed non-verbally, to providing services in exchange for life, food, housing, and care. Even then, work animals typically have a very limited range of options which cast doubt on the import of their choice. Because they are bred and sold for particular purposes, they may have no choice at all. Whatever freedom they have within the bounds of work, they often lack freedom to enter or exit.

In sum, Porcher's trilemma only concerns abolitionists like Gary Francione (2008), who consider any use of sentient beings as inherently wrong regardless of its effects on welfare.[12] Domestication, on this view, entails inherent dependency, which is bad, and exploitation, which is unjust. This is not my view or that of other theorists mentioned earlier. The extinctionist approach holds that, ultimately, we should painlessly phase out domesticated animals and abolish our mutual relations. On Francione's account, it is wrong to use sheep to graze a field, even if everyone is thereby made better off. Donaldson and Kymlicka, in contrast, allow for using animals in ways that foster mutually respectful relations as co-citizens (e.g. donkeys or dogs for herding or, under stringent conditions, farm animals for wool, eggs, or milk). However, use is only just if it guarantees flourishing and genuine freedom of choice (whether or not and when to work) and does not presuppose premature killing (Donaldson and Kymlicka 2011: 134–40). In fact, reconstructing our relations to domesticated animals on a just basis can partly repair the historical injustices of domestication, unlike extinction. *Pace* Porcher, criticisms of domestication need not be extinctionist.

Such possibilities are no less plausible than Porcher's fancied husbandry. Porcher's LDHA fails. I have, however, suggested that she and animal ethicists converge more than she recognizes on the value of 'the link'. They disagree about what types of communities they want to promote. In the last section, I rely on recent work with Duncan Purves to suggest what meaningful work could look like for domesticated animals.

Meaningful Work and Life

Purves and Delon (2018) argues that an individual's life is meaningful if and to the extent that the individual contributes through intentional agency to some finally valuable state of affairs. In other words, by actively doing good, whether or not one

---

[12] Unless one reads Francione's view as stating that dependency and being used as a resource are contrary to welfare. But Francione uses 'welfare' to refer to welfarism (as opposed to abolitionism and rights) (Francione and Garner 2010).

intends to do so (qua good), one confers meaning on one's life (more locally, on one's actions). Meaning can but need not supervene on a life as a whole, construed as a coherent narrative. It applies to life chapters, moments, or discrete actions. Because a narrative sense of one's life as a whole, or a concept of meaning, is not required, and because many animals are agents of a sufficient sort, many animals can act and live meaningfully.

Animals can act intentionally and do good. Anecdotes abound: a dog risking his own life to remove from the road a canine companion hit by a car on a busy Chilean highway; a female elephant distressed and trying to help the dying matriarch of another family; and a gorilla rescuing a small boy, who has fallen into her enclosure, handing him over to zookeepers (Rowlands 2012). Meaningful action need not be morally grandiose or involve some grand purpose. Infant-rearing is a way of contributing intentionally to well-being, something that matters for its own sake. Non-human parents or caretakers (predominantly though not exclusively mothers) engage in intentional nursing, play, and protection in ways appropriately connected to value. A meaningful interaction of which we routinely deprive farm animals.

Here, I contend that our view accounts for meaningful work insofar as it fosters good-contributing agency. Contributing to value is intentionally left open—human and/or animal interests count. Animals could meaningfully sacrifice their own good for the good of humans or other animals (we mention, for example, rescue animals, animals in war, and seeing-eye dogs). In fact, our account itself does not preclude work as construed by Porcher from conferring meaning onto human and animal actions. Work on the farm, tourism, security, and search and rescue work all contribute to some good, and they all rely to some extent on animals' agency. Porcher and I agree that work should be meaningful and that, when it is, it can be valuable.

Yet severe constraints exerted to make animals work compromise their agency, hence the meaning of their actions. The account of meaning I introduced, to the extent that it involves agency, thus leaves little room for exploitative work. Moreover, if we supplement it with an account of justice, the requirements of just work (see the previous section) preclude the type of work that would thwart animals' flourishing in the service of human interests. In our article, we considered novel research practices to better promote meaning in the lives of animal subjects (Purves and Delon 2018: 336). In contrast with standard biomedical practice, Marino and Frohoff have described nascent 'interspecies collaborative research' (ICR) for working with cetaceans: 'possibilities for studying free-ranging cetaceans who initiate close proximity and even sociable interactions with humans...providing unique scientific opportunities for an era of less-invasive cetacean research' (2011: 4). Whether or not research qualifies as work, 'ICR holds the potential to yield valuable results for researchers (and cetaceans) while accommodating the complex psychological and social needs and preferences of animals' (Purves and Delon 2018: 336).

176 ANIMAL LABOUR

Varner's 'domesticated partnerships' and Donaldson and Kymlicka's intentional-community sanctuaries could generate meaning in similar ways.

In contrast, exploitative work undermines opportunities for meaning by preventing animals from doing things that matter to them by themselves. Unjust labour can curtail the sort of basic agency that matters for meaning, thereby undermining the material conditions constitutive of a good life—if meaning is part of a good life. When control is pervasive, as it is in work driven by economic considerations, such that animals depend on their captors for their basic needs, whatever agency they have left may be insufficient for meaning. Animals on farms, industrial and sometimes 'humane' and 'organic' alike, do not merely suffer, physically and psychologically, from pain, stress, boredom, and anxiety; they're deprived of opportunities to exercise agency. Again, Porcher is not defending this kind of unjust labour. But we need to take the question seriously: What are acceptable constraints on animal agency from the standpoint of meaning?

For meaning is something that matters to an animal's well-being beyond the bare satisfaction of needs. Indeed, recent research in motivation psychology argues for a richer model of the 'good life' (the Effective Organization of Motives or Effectiveness Theory of Motivation) as requiring *truth*, *control*, and *value* motives to work together effectively (Franks and Higgins 2012). Animals are motivated to act 'beyond a motivation for adequate nutrition and safety (value motivation)'. They are 'also motivated to manage their environment (control motivation) and to learn about it (truth motivation)' (Franks and Higgins 2012: 165) These features contribute to meaning in their lives and, the authors argue, are relevant to questions of human and animal well-being.

The connection between well-being and agency gives ammunition to a defence of animal labour. But as noted, it does not support LDHA, let alone RKA, especially relative to alternatives. Constraints fall along a spectrum, of course. Likewise, the material conditions of a meaningful life vary according to the relevant range of possible options. To the extent that labour curtails agency, by preventing one from engaging in the exploratory and social behaviours that contribute to value, it curtails opportunities for meaning. By contrast, by raising challenges and inducing adaptations, agency-enhancing work (but also play or activities not directly involving human beings, production, or service—see Donaldson and Kymlicka, chapter 10 of this volume) may create opportunities for meaning. In sum, a concern for animal agency and well-being within human–animal relationships need not commit us to RKA.

Conclusion

I have argued that Porcher's defence of animal husbandry fails. Insofar as her work is representative of LDHA, the onus remains on advocates of husbandry to explain how work can justify RKA. Porcher, a prominent advocate of husbandry, delivers a conception of labour that perpetuates unjust work and obscures alternatives to RKA. Insofar as other relations can meet the desiderata of a commitment to human–animal relationships LDHA fails. Killing in the context of work undermines the alleged dimension of joy and mutual respect meant to justify it. Finally, while meaningful work for animals is possible, it rules out RKA.[13]

References

Andrews, Kristin. 2009. 'Politics or Metaphysics? On Attributing Mental Properties to Animals'. *Biology and Philosophy* 24(1): 51–63.

Baratay, Eric. 2008. *Bêtes de Somme: Des Animaux au Service des Hommes*. Paris: La Martinière/Seuil.

Berckmans, Daniel. 2004. 'Automatic On-Line Monitoring of Animals by Precision Livestock Farming'. *International Society for Animal Hygiène*—Saint-Malo: 27–30.

Bruxvoort Lipscomb, Benjamin. 2016. '"Eat Responsibly": Agrarianism and Meat'. In *Philosophy Comes to Dinner: Arguments about the Ethics of Eating*, edited by Matthew Halteman, Terence Cuneo, and Andrew Chignell, 56–72. London: Routledge.

Budiansky, Stephen. 1999. *The Covenant of the Wild: Why Animals Chose Domestication*. New Haven, CT: Yale University Press.

Cochrane, Alasdair. 2012. *Animal Rights Without Liberation*. New York: Columbia University Press.

Cochrane, Alasdair. 2016. 'Labour Rights for Animals'. In *The Political Turn in Animal Ethics*, edited by Robert Garner and Siobhan O'Sullivan, 15–32. London: Rowman & Littlefield.

Coulter, Kendra. 2016. *Animals, Work and the Promise of Interspecies Solidarity*. New York: Palgrave Macmillan.

Delon, Nicolas. 2016. 'The Replaceability Argument in the Ethics of Animal Husbandry'. In *Encyclopedia of Food and Agricultural Ethics*, edited by Paul B. Thompson and David Kaplan. Dordrecht: Springer.

Delon, Nicolas. 2017. 'L'Animal d' Élevage Compagnon de Travail : L'Éthique des Fables Alimentaires'. *Revue française d'éthique appliquée* 4(2): 61–75.

DeMello, Margo. 2012. *Animals and Society: An Introduction to Human-Animal Studies*. New York: Columbia University Press.

---

[13] I'm indebted to Charlotte Blattner, Frédéric Côté-Boudreau, Kendra Coulter, Valéry Giroux, Will Kymlicka, referees for the *Revue française d'éthique appliquée* (where a previous iteration of this discussion appeared; Delon 2017), and participants at the 2018 Animal Labour workshop at Queen's University in Kingston.

178 ANIMAL LABOUR

Donaldson, Sue, and Will Kymlicka. 2011. *Zoopolis: A Political Theory of Animal Rights*. Oxford: Oxford University Press.

Donaldson, Sue, and Will Kymlicka. 2015. 'Farmed Animal Sanctuaries: The Heart of the Movement?'. *Politics & Animals* 1(1): 50–74.

Driessen, Clemens. 2014. 'Animal Deliberation'. In *Political Animals and Animal Politics*, edited by Marcel Wissenburg and David Schlosberg, 90–104. Basingstoke: Palgrave Macmillan.

Driessen, Clemens, and Leonie Heutinck. 2015. 'Cows Desiring to be Milked? Milking Robots and the Co-Evolution of Ethics and Technology on Dutch Dairy Farms'. *Agriculture and Human Values* 32(1): 3–20.

Francione, Gary. 2008. *Animals as Persons*. New York: Columbia University Press.

Francione, Gary, and Robert Garner. 2010. *The Animal Rights Debate: Abolition or Regulation?* New York: Columbia University Press.

Franks, Becca, and E. Tory Higgins. 2012. 'Effectiveness in Humans and Other Animals: A Common Basis for Well-being and Welfare'. *Advances in Experimental Social Psychology* 46: 285–346.

Gardin, Jean, Jean Estebanez, and Sophie Moreau. 2018. 'Comme la Biche Tétanisée Dans les Phares de la Bagnole: La Justice Spatiale et les Animaux'. *Justice Spatiale/ Spatial Justice* 12(7): 1–20. https://www.jssj.org/article/comme-la-biche-tetanisee-dans-les-phares-de-la-bagnole-la-justice-spatiale-et-les-animaux/

Hart, Lynette. 1994. 'The Asian Elephants-Driver Partnership—The Drivers Perspective'. *Applied Animal Behaviour Science* 40(3/4): 297–312.

Hart, Lynette, and Sundar. 2000. 'Family Traditions for Mahouts of Asian Elephants'. *Anthrozoös*, 13(1): 34–42.

Horowitz, Alexandra. 2014. 'Canis familiaris: Companion and Captive'. In *The Ethics of Captivity*, edited by Lori Gruen, 7–21. Oxford: Oxford University Press.

Hribal, Jason. 2007. 'Animals, Agency, and Class: Writing the History of Animals from Below'. *Human Ecology Forum* 14(1): 101–12.

Lainé, Nicolas. 2017. 'Travail Interespèces et Conservation: Le Cas des Éléphants d'Asie'. *Ecologie et Politique* 54(1): 45–64.

Larrère, Catherine. 2010. 'Des Animaux-Machines aux Machines Animales'. In *Qui Sont Les Animaux?*, edited by Jean Birnbaum, 88–109. Paris: Gallimard.

Larrère, Catherine, and Raphaël Larrère. 2000. 'Animal Rearing as a Contract?'. *Journal of Agricultural and Environmental Ethics* 12(1): 51–8.

Lehr, Heiner. 2014. 'Recent Advances in Precision Livestock Farming'. *International Animal Health Journal* (2)1: 44–9.

Marino, Lori, and Toni Frohoff. 2011. 'Towards a New Paradigm of Non-Captive Research on Cetacean Cognition'. *PLoS ONE* 6(9): e24121.

Milburn, Josh. 2018. 'Death-Free Dairy? The Ethics of Clean Milk'. *Journal of Agricultural and Environmental Ethics* 31(2): 261–79.

Molinier, Pascale, and Jocelyne Porcher. 2006. 'À l'Envers du Bien-Être Animal: Enquête de Psychodynamique du Travail Auprès de Salariés d' Élevages Industriels Porcins'. *Nouvelle revue de psychosociologie* 1(1): 55–71.

Mouret, Sébastien. 2012. *Élever et Tuer des Animaux*. Paris: PUF.

Mouret, Sébastien, and Jocelyne Porcher. 2007. 'Les Systèmes Industriels Porcins: La Mort Comme Travail Ordinaire'. *Natures, sciences, sociétés* 15(3): 245–52.

Palmer, Clare. 2010. *Animal Ethics in Context*. New York: Columbia University Press.

Poole, Joyce, and Cynthia Moss. 2008. 'Elephant Sociality and Complexity: The Scientific Evidence'. In *Elephants and Ethics: Toward a Morality of Coexistence*, edited by Christen Wemmer and Catherine Christen, 69–98. Baltimore: Johns Hopkins University Press.

Porcher, Jocelyne. 2002. 'L'Esprit du don, Archaïsme ou Modernité de l'Élevage: Éléments pour une Réflexion sur la Place des Animaux d'Élevage dans le Lien Social'. *Revue du MAUSS* 20: 245–62.

Porcher, Jocelyne. 2007. 'Ne Libérez pas les Animaux ! Plaidoyer Contre un Conformisme « analphabête »'. *Revue du MAUSS* 29(2): 352–62.

Porcher, Jocelyne. 2008. 'Ouvrière en Production Porcine Industrielle: Le Prix de la Reconnaissance'. *Ethnographiques.org* 15. http://www.ethnographiques.org/2008/ Porcher [Accessed 15 January 2019].

Porcher, Jocelyne. 2009. 'Culture de l'Élevage et Barbarie des Productions Animales'. In *Homme et animal: la question des frontières*, edited by Valérie Camos, Frank Cézilly, Pierre Guenancia, and Jean-Pierre Sylvestre, 161–74. Versailles: Quae.

Porcher, Jocelyne. 2011a. *Vivre avec les Animaux: Une Utopie pour le XXIe Siècle*. Paris: La Découverte.

Porcher, Jocelyne. 2011b. 'The Relationship Between Workers and Animals in the Pork Industry: A Shared Suffering'. *Journal of Environmental and Agricultural Ethics* 24(1): 3–17.

Porcher, Jocelyn. 2014. 'The Work of Animals: A Challenge for Social Sciences'. *Humanimalia* 6(1): 1–9.

Porcher, Jocelyne. 2017. *The Ethics of Animal Labor: A Collaborative Utopia*. London: Palgrave Macmillan.

Porcher, Jocelyne. 2018. 'Défendre l'Élevage Sans le Savoir: Commentaire Critique à Propos de l'Article de Nicolas Delon 'L'Animal d'Élevage Compagnon de Travail. L'Éthique des Fables Alimentaires'. *Revue française d'éthique appliquée* 6(2): 119–24.

Porcher, Jocelyne, and Tiphaine Schmitt. 2010. 'Les Vaches Collaborent-elles au Travail? Une Question de Sociologie'. *Revue du MAUSS* 35(1): 235–61.

Porcher Jocelyne, and Tiphaine Schmitt. 2012. 'Dairy Cows: Workers in the Shadows?'. *Society & Animals* 20: 39–60.

Purves, Duncan, and Nicolas Delon. 2018. 'Meaning in the Lives of Humans and Other Animals'. *Philosophical Studies* 175(2): 317–38.

180   ANIMAL LABOUR

Rémy, Catherine. 2009. *La Fin des Bêtes. Une Ethnographie de la Mise à Mort des Animaux*. Paris: Economica.

Rowlands, Mark. 2012. *Can Animals be Moral?* Oxford: Oxford University Press.

Stuart, Diana, Rebecca Schewe and Ryan Gunderson. 2013. 'Extending Social Theory to Farm Animals: Addressing Alienation in the Dairy Sector'. *Sociologica Ruralis* 53(2): 201–22.

Utria, Enrique. 2014. 'La Viande Heureuse et les Cervelles Miséricordieuses'. In *Souffrances animales et traditions humaines*, edited by Lucille Desblaches, 37–52. Éditions Universitaires de Dijon.

Vanitha, Varadharajan, Krishnamoorthy Thiyagesan, and Nagarajan Baskaran. 2011. 'Social Life of Captive Asian Elephants (*Elephas maximus*) in Southern India: Implications for Elephant Welfare'. *Journal of Applied Animal Welfare Science* 14(1): 42–58.

Varner, Gary. 2002. 'Pets, Companion Animals, and Domesticated Partners'. In *Ethics for Everyday*, edited by David Benatar, 450–75. New York: McGraw-Hill.

Weele, Cor van der, and Clemens Driessen. 2013. 'Emerging Profiles for Cultured Meat: Ethics Through and as Design'. *Animals* 3(3): 647–62.

Werkheiser, Ian. 2018. 'Precision Livestock Farming and Farmers' Duties to Livestock'. *Journal of Agricultural and Environmental Ethics* 31(2): 181–5.

9
The Working Day
Animals, Capitalism, and Surplus Time

Dinesh J. Wadiwel

Chapter 10 of *Capital*—'The Working Day'—is a truly remarkable example of how Karl Marx's value theory is materialized in the bodies and lives of labourers. In this text, Marx effectively situates the body of the human worker—this worker's physicality, sustenance, capacities, biological life—as a biopolitical battleground for the extraction of surplus. It is also in this chapter that Marx reveals the texture of one of the trajectories of his analysis of capitalism as a social, economic, and political relation: namely, *labour time* as a source of conflict. In a remarkable section of the text, Marx lays bare the contestation that shapes working time:

'What is a working-day? What is the length of time during which capital may consume the labour-power whose daily value it buys? How far may the working-day be extended beyond the working-time necessary for the reproduction of labour-power itself?' We have seen capital's reply to these questions is this: the working-day contains the full 24 hours, with the deduction of the few hours of rest without which labour-power absolutely incapable of renewing its services. Hence it is self-evident that the worker is nothing other than labour power for the duration of his whole life, and that therefore all his disposable time is by nature and by right labour-time, to be devoted to the self-valorization of capital. Time for education, for intellectual development, for the fulfilling of social functions, for social intercourse, for the free-play of the vital forces of his body and mind, even the rest time of Sunday (and that in a country of Sabbatarians!)—what foolishness! But in its blind and measureless drive, its insatiable appetite for surplus-labour,[1] capital oversteps not only the moral, but even the merely physical maximum bounds of the working-day. It usurps the time for growth, development, and healthy maintenance of the body. It steals the time required for the consumption of fresh air and sunlight. It haggles over a meal-times, where possible incorporating then into the production process itself, so that food is added to the worker as to a mere means of production, as coal is supplied to the boiler, and grease and oil to the machinery. It reduces the sound sleep needed for the

---

[1] Note that Ben Folkes chooses to translate this section as 'insatiable appetite for surplus-labour'. The German text reads 'Wehrwolfs-Heisshunger nach Mehrarbeit': a 'werewolf's voracious hunger for surplus labour'.

Dinesh J. Wadiwel, *The Working Day: Animals, Capitalism, and Surplus Time* In: *Animal Labour: A New Frontier of Interspecies Justice?*. Edited by: Charlotte Blattner, Kendra Coulter, and Will Kymlicka, Oxford University Press (2020). © Oxford University Press. DOI: 10.1093/oso/9780198846192.003.0009

182 ANIMAL LABOUR

restoration, renewal and refreshment of the vital forces to the exact amount of torpor essential to the revival of an absolutely exhausted organism. It is not the normal maintenance of the labour-power which determines the limits of the working-day here, but rather the greatest possible daily expenditure of labour-power, no matter how diseased, compulsory, and painful it may be, which determines the limits of the workers' period of rest. Capital asks no questions about the length of life of labour-power. What interests it is purely and simply the maximum labour power that can be set in motion in a working day. It attains this objective by shortening the life of labour-power, in the same way as a greedy farmer snatches more produce from the soil by robbing it of its fertility.   (Marx 1986: 375–6)

While it may be tempting to read *Capital* as a description of the logic and process of wage exploitation—that is the unequal extraction of surplus through the wage relation—'The Working Day' reveals instead a different site of antagonism that sits at the centre of capitalism. As the section of text above reveals, the dynamics of the continuing theft of free time and the drive for all living time to be subsumed into the rhythms of capital forms the defining rationality of capitalism as a social, economic, and political relation.

I would argue that Marx's chapter 'The Working Day' is a potent tool for animal advocates. This is not because Marx directly considers animal labour in the text: indeed far from it. We know that Marx was largely antagonistic towards the idea that animals labour in ways that are fundamentally comparable to humans (Marx 1978: 70–81; see also Johnson 2017: 278–83). And Chapter 10 of *Capital*, while mentioning animals and the animal protection movement, fails to offer any theorization of animals as workers.[2] However, this chapter of *Capital* is

---

[2] There are in this chapter, as in other parts of *Capital*, numerous references to animals. I will discuss below an example of Marx comparing limits on the working day between humans and horses, but there are others. For example, Marx compares the objectification of children as labour commodities to the use of animals as commodities:

The Act of 1844 certainly 'robbed' them of the 'liberty' of employing children under 11 longer than 6½ hours a day. But it secured to them, on the other hand, the privilege of working children between 11 and 13, 10 hours a day, and of annulling in their case the education made compulsory for all other factory children. This time the pretext was 'the delicate texture of the fabric in which they were employed, requiring a lightness of touch, only to be acquired by their early introduction to these factories.' The children were slaughtered out-and-out for the sake of their delicate fingers, as in Southern Russia the horned cattle for the sake of their hide and tallow.   (Marx 1986: 406)

Note Chapter 10 of *Capital Vol. 1* also provides an example of Marx's view that animal protection was a bourgeois fixation. Imagining himself as a worker and addressing the capitalist, Marx exclaims:

I therefore demand a working day of normal length, and I demand it without any appeal to your heart, for in money matters sentiment is out of place. You may be a model citizen, perhaps a member of the R.S.P.C.A., and you may be in the odour of sanctity as well; but the thing you represent when you come face to face with me has no heart in its breast. What seems to throb there is my own heartbeat. I demand a normal working day because, like every seller, I demand the value of my commodity.   (Marx 1986: 343; see also Gunderson 2011)

THE WORKING DAY: ANIMALS, CAPITALISM, AND SURPLUS TIME 183

useful for animal advocates because it reveals at least one central concern within Marx's project: namely the relationship between labour time and free time as a site of antagonism under capitalism. This way of reading *Capital* is highly product- ive for animal advocates. On one hand, it removes focus from the wage relation as central to capitalism; revealing instead capitalism as an organism (a 'were- wolf' or a 'vampire') which seeks to 'absorb' or 'suck' all spare energies and labour. Here the *human* worker need not be a focus; instead all life, human or otherwise, might be understood as a target of accumulation strategies (Moore 2015; Cooper 2008; Barua 2018). Secondly, Marx's analysis in 'The Working Day' offers a political narrative for change which resonates around the politics of labour time. In *Capital* Marx makes clear that 'the creation of a normal working-day is...the product of a protracted civil war, more or less dissembled, between the capitalist class and the working-class' (Marx 1986: 412–13). Time here is the site of antagonism. And, hence political action aimed at reducing labour time becomes a goal for social and political change. As I will argue, this insight opens the way to consider progressive political action that aims to reduce animal labour time within production systems.

This chapter seeks to use *time* as a productive focus for thinking about animal labour, and developing strategies for change. As I shall argue, a focus on labour time allows us to offer a unique narration for the position of animals, particularly animals used for food, under conditions of intensifying industrial animal agriculture: here, we shall see that 'the working day' for animals is never ending; indeed, intensive production systems aim to turn all time into labour time for animal workers. The second part of this chapter moves to thinking about the implications of this analysis for social and political change for animals.

Is Labour Good? Or Is It Domination?

As the chapters in this book highlight, there has been a fascinating growth in interest in 'labour' as a category of analysis within animal studies (in addition to this volume, see for example Painter 2016; Stuart et al. 2013; Beldo 2017; Haraway 2007; Barua 2017; 2019; Hribal 2003; Porcher 2014; Perlo 2002; Coulter 2016; Cochrane 2016). Labour as a category of analysis is in part useful because it moves beyond the language of rights and welfare that has largely dominated animal ethics. 'Labour' has additional potential in situating centrally the 'agency' of animals within productive processes. While rights approaches, for example, have made strong contributions to illustrating the intrinsic value of non-human animals and their rights to non-interference, a labour approach offers the

184 ANIMAL LABOUR

opportunity to understand the specific roles of animals as active forces within various productive circuits, and as forms of value creation.

A portion of the scholarship within this emerging set of perspectives on animal labour assesses the normative value of animals as labourers and argues for improvements in how animals as labourers are valued and understood. This scholarship offers the twin perspective that suggests that much animal labour today is exploitative and lacks necessity, but *at the same time*, there are grounds to imagine work as something tied to potential flourishing for animals (in this volume see for example Cochrane, chapter 3; D'Souza, Hovorka, and Niel, chapter 4; and Coulter, chapter 2) For example, Kendra Coulter summarizes:

> certain practices and some whole kinds of animal work cannot be rationalized or sustained. We simply cannot justify requiring a number of species—and individual animals—to work, even if people garner material and/or symbolic gain. In other cases, animals' work may be appropriate, and mutually beneficial, provided that both protections and positive entitlements are afforded.
>
> (Coulter 2016: 155)

While Coulter acknowledges that there are cases in which animal labour should be eliminated, or that animals should be allocated free time and the 'right not to work at all' (Coulter 2016: 160), there is here also a commitment to a progressive political project towards supporting work that contributes towards animal flourishing. In this context, Coulter expresses a demand for 'humane jobs' which aims to 'prioritize both material and experiential well-being and that are about helping rather than harming' (Coulter 2016: 163). Work here is positioned as potential libratory, for both humans and animals.

A similar approach is put forward by Jocelyne Porcher on the possibility of work that is fulfilling for animals. Re-narrating domestication as 'above all the cooperative process of inserting animals into human society through work' Porcher suggests that the co-relationality between farmer and animal produces a space for potential 'emancipation' (Porcher 2014). Work is situated as central to animal being and flourishing. Here, Porcher weighs the value of work for animals against the harm of death, suggesting that the meaningful fulfilled life is the most important ethical consideration:

> What possible economic, emotional, and social life expectations are there for a dairy cow? How does the death of a dairy cow matter? What kind of society must we construct to enable cows, pigs, and chickens to have a worthwhile life? What society can we construct so that we can have, alongside them, a life that reaches our highest expectations?   (Porcher 2014)

THE WORKING DAY: ANIMALS, CAPITALISM, AND SURPLUS TIME   185

In a sense Porcher is consciously distancing this perspective on animal labour from animal rights conceptions of ethics;[3] instead, work is described as a way to enable a flourishing for animals that exceeds the harms associated with their instrumental utilization within animal agriculture (in this volume, see chapter 8 by Delon for a comprehensive discussion of Porcher's approach).

But is 'work' a grounds for flourishing?[4] In part, this view of labour as integral to the flourishing of beings owes something to the account of alienation offered by the 'early' Marx in the *1844 Economic and Philosophic Manuscripts*[5] (see Bachour, chapter 6 of this volume). In this text Marx famously outlined the nature of labour under capitalism as forcing a rupture in the human worker, one that removed human activity from its essentially creative role within a human 'species being' (Marx 1978: 70–81). This labour under capitalism created work as something that the human could no longer associate or affiliate with; it became 'estranged', detached:

> The fact that labour is *external* to the worker, i.e., it does not belong to his intrinsic nature; that in his work, therefore, he does not affirm himself but denies himself, does not feel content but unhappy, does not develop freely his physical and mental energy but mortifies his body and ruins his mind. The worker therefore only feels himself outside his work, and in his work feels outside himself. He feels at home when he is not working, and when he is working he does not feel at home. His labour is therefore not voluntary, but coerced; it is forced labour. It is therefore not the satisfaction of a need; it is merely a *means* to satisfy needs external to it.   (Marx 1978: 74, italics in original)

The structural elements of the wage relation under capitalism produce this rupture. The fact that the worker must surrender their labour to sustain

---

[3] Indeed, Porcher is openly antagonistic towards animal rights/liberation approaches. She states:

> In farming, however, this centrality of work is defeated by the livestock production industry, which reduces man and beast to their behaviors and standardized means of functioning. It is equally defeated by theories of animal liberation, which reject the question of work. I stress this because this seems to me to be important. Why do animal liberators, many of whom claim to be political, even revolutionary in their doctrines, ignore the question of work, which is the political question par excellence? I believe it is because a political analysis of work with animals evidences the extreme closeness of man to beast, and the objective of animal 'liberation' is in fact to separate them. Work recognition is a recognition of ties. It is thus effectively revolutionary; too revolutionary without doubt for the followers of animal liberation, amongst whom some are more sensitive to the sirens of the bio-technical industry than to communal emancipation.   (Porcher 2014)

[4] Note that I use 'flourishing' here deliberately to signal a relationship to both virtue ethic and capability approaches, which in a sense both potentially have capacity to highlight the value of labour in contributing to well-being in an ethical and political sense. I leave aside here capabilities approaches and what they may have to offer thinking on the place of animal labour. I do note however that while Martha Nussbaum lists work as part of human capabilities (see particularly '10. Control over one's Environment') animal work appears missing from the list of animal capabilities, at least as a direct reference (Nussbaum 2004).

[5] Porcher, discussed above, directly references Marx's view on alienation from the *1844 Economic and Philosophic Manuscripts* (Porcher 2014).

186 ANIMAL LABOUR

themselves, and that the products of this labour do not belong to the worker, removes any self-investment in the creative activity of labour, producing the empty productivity that characterizes work under capitalism. In this reading, labour in itself is not problematic; rather, labour is in essence a central aspect of human being. However, the way labour is deployed within the exploitative context of capitalism mobilizes this central aspect of human life against that life: 'in the conditions dealt with by political economy this realization of labour appears as a *loss of reality* for the workers; objectification *as loss of the object* and *object-bondage*; appropriation as *estrangement*, as *alienation*' (Marx 1978: 72, italics in original).

It is well known that in this text, Marx is at pains to point out that the labour of humans differs from the activity of animals. In Marx's account animals cannot distinguish themselves from their life activity; humans on the other hand labour consciously and can produce regardless of necessity (Marx 1978). A number of animal studies scholars have offered correctives to this point of view (see for example Benton 1993; Noske 1997: 12–21; Painter 2016; Stuart et al. 2013; Foster 2018). Noske in particular lays out a sophisticated reading of Marx on alienation, both rejecting the view than only humans can creatively labour, and simultaneously offering perspectives on how animals are perhaps uniquely alienated within capitalist agriculture (Noske 1997: 12–21). In a sense these views seek to extend labour as a category to the non-human, by offering a perspective which illustrates the distinct ways animals are alienated in a fashion that resonates with human worker alienation, simultaneously pointing to the potential for labour under non-exploitative conditions to be a valuable sphere of flourishing. Labour in this reading is essentially good. Capitalism and exploitative processes *corrupt* the capacity of labour to contribute to a being's flourishing; this corruption creates a progressive political project which aims to liberate labour from exploitation, and return or correct it to an ideal role as integral to a being's creativity.

However, labour need not be merely read as a positive activity that contributes to flourishing. A different reading of Marx would treat labour as something that stands in the way of our capacity to flourish. In this view, labour time imposed by capital stands in the way of free time for 'growth, development, and healthy maintenance of the body' (Marx 1986: 375–6). This view of labour treats work as a mode of domination.[6] Here, work is imposed on the labouring subject, and the dream of productive processes is to amplify labour time, reducing free time, so that it would seem that all time is subsumed by production for capital. Here I am

---

[6] I am leaving 'domination' undefined here, although of course the question of whether work represents a mode of subordination is ideological. The definition provided by Iris Marion Young is however informative: 'institutional conditions which inhibit or prevent people from participating in determining their actions or the conditions of their actions. Persons live within structures of domination if other persons or groups can determine without reciprocation the conditions of their action, either directly or by virtue of the structural consequences of their actions' (Young 1990: 38). In a sense this is the permanent political situation for almost all animals in relation with human societies: that is, violent domination characterizes most human–animal relations (Wadiwel 2015).

THE WORKING DAY: ANIMALS, CAPITALISM, AND SURPLUS TIME   187

deliberately pointing to a reading of later Marx that problematizes work as a social relation. This reading is certainly apparent in the pages of *Capital*, where the struggle over the working day is a site of intense antagonism, highlighting the role of capitalism as a system that seeks to dominate and extract labour (on forced labour, see Blattner, chapter 5 of this volume), and against this the interest of the worker in minimizing labour:

> There is here therefore an antinomy, of right against right, both equally bearing the seal of the law of exchange. Between equal rights, force decides. Hence in the history of capitalist production, the establishment of a norm for the working day presents itself as a struggle over the limits of that day, a struggle between collective capital, i.e., the class of capitalists, and collective labour, i.e., the working-class. (Marx 1986: 344)

Antonio Negri in particular draws attention to this conflict over work described by Marx, and points to the continuing antagonism generated between *Capital*'s drive to turn all time into labour time, and the worker's desire to escape this toil: 'What does it mean to struggle against capital when capital has subjugated all of lived time, not only that of the working day, but all of it. Reproduction is like production, life is like work. At this level, to break with capital is to make a prison break' (Negri 1991: xvi).[7] The point here is to highlight that work emerges as a relation under capitalism that is at odds with flourishing. It is imposed on beings, and drains time away from other activities that contribute to well-being. This reading of labour time, as William James Booth reminds us, draws from a different tradition of ancient political philosophy which valued free time as the ground upon which individuals developed themselves: 'Free time was the precondition of friendship, of citizenship in the better polities and of the pursuit of the good life, and it was one of the philosophical boundary lines separating the free from the unfree' (Booth 1991: 7–8). As Booth points out here, the division of labour produces states of relative freedom and unfreedom, and the complete loss of free time—the placing of one being at the total service of another—was the mark of slavery.[8] Here labour is a source of domination and stands in the way of flourishing. As I shall discuss, the view that labour time is a mode of domination

---

[7] Negri is here reading Marx's 'middle period' notebook, *Grundrisse*, which arguably contained more depth on the political struggle of workers against capitalist subsumption. While Negri and others would highlight that Marx never completed a planned volume of *Capital* that would expand on this political struggle (Negri 1991: 4–19; Lebowitz 2003), arguably there are strong traces of this struggle against work within the pages of *Capital Vol. 1*. Chapter 10 on the 'Working Day' would be one example.

[8] Indeed, Booth notes that the aim of the ancient slave economy was to produce free time for the master: 'time free from necessary labour and the ranked activities that were to fill those hours were seen as among the most important goods to be secured by the slave economy' (Booth 1991: 7). How this perspective on time and its relation to forced labour might relate to modern forms of slavery, including racial slavery, is not discussed by Booth here, and beckons deeper analysis.

188   ANIMAL LABOUR

resonates with the experience for animals, particularly animals used for food within the production systems of animal agriculture.

The Working Day

There are a two perspectives advanced by Marx in the Chapter on 'The Working Day' that remain highly useful for understanding the structural position of animal labour, particularly animals used for food, within contemporary production systems.

The first perspective is that the labour time necessary for the reproduction of life differs from labour time that is imposed upon the worker within a productive system. This highlights the core of the Marxist perspective; namely that exploitative economic systems, such as capitalism, seek to extract some sort of surplus from labour beyond the reproduction costs of that labour to the productive system. While we might on one level understand this surplus in relation to value measured in monetary terms (i.e. wages, costs, etc.), it is not clear from reading Marx that this is the only way to measure surplus. Indeed, the analysis laid out in *Capital* moves between different metrics of surplus, including surplus measured in relation to *labour time*. The reason I stress the latter trajectory in reading Marx is that labour time is a more useful measure of animal labour than the wage. While it is nonsensical to think about extraction of surplus from animals using the *strict* parameters set by the wage—animals are not paid a monetary wage, have little use for a monetary wage, and therefore cannot experience theft of value in money terms—we can, on the other hand, very easily conceptualize the unique exploitation of animals in relation to the difference between the time required to reproduce their own life and the time required by animals to produce for *us* (i.e. for humans, capitalism, productive systems). And Marx gives us a very clear way to think about this:

> The working day is thus not a constant, but a variable quantity. One of its parts, certainly is determined by the labour-time required for the reproduction of the labour-power of the worker himself. But its total amount varies with the duration of the surplus labour. The working day is therefore capable of being determined, but in and for itself indeterminate.   (Marx 1986: 341)

Here labour time is divided into components: the time required within a system to sustain the maintenance costs of labour within it, and the time devoted to extracting a surplus (that is the time required of labour beyond its reproduction costs).

Let us set aside for the moment the fact that Marx was only thinking of the human worker in this paragraph, as Marx's treatment of labour time might work as well for thinking about animals. Here, if we imagine that either a human or a non-human may provide labour, the results are informative. On one hand, any

THE WORKING DAY: ANIMALS, CAPITALISM, AND SURPLUS TIME   189

productive system will need to meet the maintenance costs associated with inputs to that system. For the worker to be able to sustain their labour beyond any one working day—to not be used up and destroyed by this labour—then a portion of labour time over any given period must contribute to the maintenance costs of that labour: food, water, rest, housing, etc. (Marx 1986: 274–7). For a human worker, these costs are managed through payment of the wage; it is with a money income that the worker purchases the means of subsistence that allow them to reproduce their labour. However, the wage for animals differs, and is certainly not in a money form (Coulter 2016: 76).[9] For animal agriculture to generate a surplus, there must be a difference between the subsistence costs associated with keeping animals alive and facilitating their growth prior to slaughter, and the additional value that is extracted beyond these maintenance costs (Beldo 2017). Animal agriculture will see these as input costs associated with production processes: for example, the cost of grain, antibiotics, heating, lighting, infrastructure etc. Costs measure a monetary value of an input. But all costs are resolvable into labour time.[10] The advantage of foregrounding time as a calculation is that it measures the imposition of productive systems upon the subjective being of the living labouring subject. Time matters because life is time limited: as organic subjects our time as living subjects has a definite end, and this means the question of how much time we labour, versus how much time we spend doing other things, is important for us, for our flourishing.[11]

---

[9] Marx is highly antagonistic to the idea that animals may earn a wage; indeed, in *Capital Vol. 2*, Marx mocks Adam's Smith's suggestion that the grain fed to a draught animal might constitute something equivalent to a 'wage' (Marx 1992: 449 n.6; see also Smith 1981: 68). However, Marx forgets his own understanding of surplus value as something that may be measured in both terms dictated by money values and in terms dictated by labour time, or at least only can imagine conversion of money values into *human* labour time. See n.10.

[10] Indeed, Marx notes this in relation to inputs into animal agriculture in *Capital Vol. 2*. However the implication of Marx's analysis is that human labour time is the favoured measurement (Marx 1992: 458).

[11] To forget that labour time matters also for animals (that is, not all costs are resolvable into simply *human* labour time) is of course an indication of our own anthropocentrism, an anthropocentricism that is made patently clear when we note that the balance sheets of animal agriculture continually treat animals as static resource inputs, rather than measure their inputs to production in terms of labour time that includes the time devoted by animals to production (including the temporal imposition of capital on the lives of animals). Treating animals as mere costs forgets that our production systems take away the lives of animals as lives experienced as time lost. Note further that there are deeper philosophical underpinnings for this forgetting of animal time. Consider for example Martin Heidegger's contention that boredom is an experience that reveals a human capacity to disconnect and reflect on experience, rather than be consumed by life activity in an animalistic way (Agamben 2004: 70). The fact that our epistemic systems reveal that we cannot imagine that animals are bored (that is, can experience, reflect on, and despair at the passing of time) is revealed by countless material systems of incarceration and production—Concentrated Animal Feeding Operations (CAFOs), experimental labs, sea pens, zoos—which treat animals as if they have no interest in the passing of time. Indeed, perhaps a more insidious aspect of this epistemic rendering of animals as uninterested in their own time is the belief that because animals used in agriculture are stripped of meaningful activity, a life where all of their needs have been taken care of, that they therefore enjoy a life of minimal labour and endless free time (Adams 2017: 25).

190   ANIMAL LABOUR

On the other hand, Marx points out that productive systems under capitalism will always determine labour time as a combination of the necessary labour time required to maintain the life of the labouring subject and the additional or surplus time extracted for the productive system. In other words, the working day is a tussle between the time involved in maintaining life and the exploitation time involved in giving up labour for capital. This exploitation is potentially as meaningful for animals as it is for human workers, something that is apparent when we consider the intensification of animal agriculture. Consider the global move towards aquaculture systems of fish production. Over the last forty years there has been a dramatic shift away from mechanized forms of wild fish capture towards aquaculture systems or 'fish farms': 'a milestone was reached in 2014 when the aquaculture sector's contribution to the supply of fish for human consumption overtook that of wild-caught fish for the first time' (FAO 2016: 2). The subsumption of fish into intensive aquaculture production systems requires a massive reorientation of approach in relation to human domination of animals.[12] Where mechanized industrial-scale wild fish capture seeks to *episodically* predate on animals who live within environments that are 'wild', fish farms instead seek to apply *continuous* controls over animals within contained, highly monitored, and highly managed environments. This of course illustrates a difference in techniques

---

[12] I use the term 'subsumption' here in a technical sense and deliberately to substitute for 'domestication' in that it alerts us to the immersion of animals in not merely increasingly intensive modes of domination that take control of reproduction, nutrition, movement, sociality, etc., but an immersion of all of life into the rhythms of capital, such that life itself, all of life, becomes inseparable from production. Life for domesticated animals has become inseparable from the systems that dominate them. This is strongly resonant with the process of 'real subsumption' described by Marx, which involved the transformation of labour through collective processes, technologies, machinery, and the evolution of production techniques such that labour no longer could be understood in isolation or on an individual basis:

> The *social* productive powers of labour, or the productive powers of directly *social, socialised* (common) labour, are developed through cooperation, through the division of labour within the workshop, the employment of *machinery*, and in general through the transformation of the production process into a conscious *application* of the natural sciences, mechanics, chemistry, etc., for particular purposes, *technology*, etc., as well as by working on a *large scale*, which corresponds to all these advances, etc. [This socialised labour alone is capable of applying the *general* products of human development, such as mathematics, etc., to the *direct* production process, just as, conversely, the development of the sciences presupposes that the material production process has attained a certain level.] This development of the productive power of *socialised labour*, as opposed to the more or less isolated labour of the individual, etc., and, alongside it, the *application of science,* that *general* product of social development, to the *direct production process,* has the appearance of a *productive power of capital*, not of labour, or it only appears as a productive power of labour in so far as the latter is identical with capital, and in any case it does not appear as the productive power either of the individual worker or of the workers combined together in the production process. The mystification which lies in the capital-relation in general is now much more developed than it was, or could be, in the case of the merely formal subsumption of labour under capital. On the other hand, the historical significance of capitalist production first emerges here in striking fashion (and specifically), precisely through the transformation of the direct production process itself, and the development of the social productive powers of labour.   (Marx 1864; see also Shukin 2009)

THE WORKING DAY: ANIMALS, CAPITALISM, AND SURPLUS TIME   191

that exactly conforms to the template offered by Michel Foucault for the emergence of biopower: namely, the replacement of episodic mechanisms of violence and control for continuous methods of discipline and regulation which aim at intensively managing the lives of biological populations (Foucault 1998: 135–8; see also Wadiwel 2018a). But this is also a movement that represents the transformation of labour into labour time for capital, which alters the temporal experience for animals who are subject to this transition in systems of violence. 'Wild fish' experience a world of labour directed towards self-sustenance, perhaps even a difficult life-and-death-stakes world involved in the endless search for food and endless escape from predation. Human fishing cuts short this life. As such, wild fish capture exposes animal life to the episodic intrusions of human violence within lives that are otherwise lived outside of direct human intervention. The fish farm, on the other hand, instead exposes animals to a continuous domination, where it would seem all time has been bent towards the needs of production. Time for fish in aquaculture is time spent in the monotony of crowded sea pens, nourished with only the purpose of attaining value as commodities after slaughter. Aquaculture fish experience time, their whole life time, structured by production systems that extend all living temporality towards achieving a difference between the costs of sustaining life and the value that can be attained in addition to this through the production process. It might be true that in the context of aquaculture systems, fish do not need to labour as long or as hard to maintain themselves; however this only highlights that the working day is extended well beyond necessity, since the whole of life has been structured toward the labour of producing themselves as commodities, and almost all other aspects of living is treated as a distraction to this goal. These animals experience a time of waiting within an environment which lack stimulus (Evans et al. 2015; Makino, Masuda, and Tanaka 2015; Näslund and Johnsson 2016); where every moment, every decision is structured by the economic necessity to stretch labour time in order to attain surplus.

I have above selected an example of fish labour to highlight the way in which the intensification of time accompanies a process of industrial domestication. However, time is operative in different modalities of animal labour, such as that performed by service animals or animals used in law enforcement. Such labour obviously operates under completely different conditions, and is not necessarily accompanied by the overt forms of coercion and control that are commonplace in industrial animal agriculture (Coulter 2016: 60–2). Also, importantly, this labour does not occur within the direct coordinates of capitalist production: where for example, animals are bred, contained, and killed as a process for generating surplus within food production, a police dog, for example, is not directly deployed within the capitalist production process to generate capital. However, distributions of time still shape the lives of these animals. For example, service animals are typically assigned to human individuals for around the clock support, producing a situation where potentially animals lack time away from their duties:

192 ANIMAL LABOUR

Animals assigned to individuals full-time are tasked with year-round work, but generally given short breaks on a daily basis to act in ways of their choosing and relinquish their service responsibility. The dogs are given specific commands and or held in particular ways (e.g., on a leash in contrast to a harness) to identify this 'break' time. Yet there are few protections in place to monitor the lives and conditions of service dogs once they are in someone's private home, and the measures that do exist certainly cannot monitor treatment 24 hours a day and 365 days a year. Most people who employ service dogs do not harm the animals. Yet cruel treatment is possible and occasionally evident, even in public.

(Coulter 2016: 81; see also DeMello 2012: 201–4)

The issue of how we understand service animals, particularly in the context of disability support, is complex and beyond the scope of this chapter, which is focused primarily on animals within industrial production.[13] However, it is notable that time remains a vector by which we can understand domination, at least in so far as there is a discrepancy between time bound to expected (and perhaps imposed) labour, and free time away from this labour.

This highlights the way in which social norms might shape the duration of animal labour time within productive circuits. The second perspective we might draw from Marx's on the working day is that this time period is structured by maximum *limits* that are both 'physical and social':

the working day does have a maximum limit. It cannot be prolonged beyond a certain point. This maximum limit is conditioned by two things. First by the physical limits to labour-power. Within the 24 hours of the natural day a man can only expend a certain quantity of his vital force. Similarly a horse can work regularly for only 8 hours a day. During part of the day the vital force must rest, sleep; during another part of the man has to satisfy other physical needs, to feed wash and clothe himself. Besides these purely physical limitations, the extension of the working day encounters moral obstacles. The worker needs time in which to satisfy his intellectual and social requirements, and the extent of these requirements is conditioned by the general level of civilization. The length of the working day therefore fluctuates within boundaries both physical and social.

(Marx 1986: 341)

Notice that Marx in this section momentarily lets go of a structuring anthropocentricism: in this account *even a horse has limits on their working day*. Indeed all life has 'natural' limits on labour in this way; the capacity for any continuous activity will be tempered by the biological parameters of that organism, including

---

[13] In addition to Coulter's work, see Kelly Oliver's careful analysis of the politics of service animals (Oliver 2016).

THE WORKING DAY: ANIMALS, CAPITALISM, AND SURPLUS TIME   193

their length of life, their needs for sustenance, and their needs for recuperation before continued exertion. Marx's description of the social or moral limits on the working day appears to return to the early Marx of the *1844 Economic and Philosophic Manuscripts* in so far as it seeks to describe the flourishing needs of humans as a species-being. However we can note two caveats. Firstly, labour is separated from other needs ('time in which to satisfy his intellectual and social requirements') and is potentially an obstacle to achievement of these forms of flourishing. This appears to work against the view associated with the earlier Marx that labour is intimately connected to flourishing. Secondly, and importantly for thinking about animals, labour time is determined by the limits on labour that are deemed socially acceptable. In other words, these limits are not self-evident or guided by a detached philosophical or empirical analysis of the characteristics of organisms; instead norms around work arrive through social relations.

Human social relations of course today support the mass domination of animals. The labour time of animals is determined by these human relations. We deem, as part of our domination of animals, how animals are going to spend their lives within the intensive systems we have created for them. Indeed, this perspective tells us something of the temporal politics of our biopolitical violence towards animals. The intensive confinement systems of the feedlot or the sea pen or the shoe box cages of experimental animals reveal that humans regard the value of time for animals themselves as inconsequential;[14] we assume that animals have no needs to flourish outside of the production time we impose on them, and thus we turn all time into production time. It is as if humans regard animals as lacking interest in free time, in time outside of the time we require from them as part of their utilization. Indeed, in this context, one may assert that the nature of our anthropocentric violence is marked by the fact that it is almost without limits or regulation when it comes to time: there is no apparent social limit on the time we demand from animals.[15]

---

[14] See n.11 above.

[15] As I have previously argued, our 'war against animals' represents relations of hostility that appear almost unlimited in scope and constitute an overarching context of utter domination, where we subject trillions of animals to ongoing control, violence, suffering, and death almost unchecked by law, regulation, or norm (Wadiwel 2015). We permit this hyperbolic violent relationality because our social relations allow this: despite knowledge that animals have a capacity to suffer, possess cognitive abilities, and have a will to thrive and flourish in ways that are comparable to humans, we nevertheless persist in relations with animals that epistemically construct animals as if they do not have these qualities. In *The War Against Animals* I argued that in the case of human relations with animals, sovereignty precedes ethics. Ethical engagement does not inform our relations with animals; instead, the force of our sovereign domination of animals sets in place our relations, and establishes the limited bases for any ethical consideration which follows (Wadiwel 2015: 36–55). Welfarist approaches to animal ethics are an example of this, since the right to use or kill animals are not questioned in these viewpoints; instead the field of ethics is constrained to whether we can offer animals minimized suffering after we have established our sovereign right to use them and kill them for our own purposes. Thus it would appear that sovereignty informs ethics, and not the other way around.

194   ANIMAL LABOUR

The reason I raise this here is that we glimpse another example of how a lack of socially imposed limits on our violence towards animals shapes the working day for animals, particularly those in food production. As animals are almost completely open to unfettered violence within our production systems, this means that all social limits appear absent in relation to how we treat animals, and instead the main calculus for the working day is the bare biopolitical problem of the 'physical' limits that animals impose on the production process. Thus the overt character of management of these animals will circulate around questions of life; with deep controls over nutrition, movement, space, relationality with other animals, sexuality and reproduction, and of course perfect temporal control over when the animal lives and when the animal dies in order to maximize value within the value chain (Wadiwel 2015: 65–96; 2018a). Freed of any social limits, the violence of animal agriculture takes on the absolute parameters of naked biopolitical violence: hence its peculiar horror.

Further, the strategies used to intensify and extract ever more surplus from animal labourers will obey the exact logic Marx sets out in relation to the battle over the working day, which wrestles between strategies aimed at increasing 'absolute surplus value' and 'relative surplus value'.[16] The latter strategy—that is, the attempt to increase relative surplus value—relies on reducing the costs to production associated with the reproduction of labour power. For animal labourers, we see this reality play out in successive attempts to reduce the costs associated with inputs to production, such as by the remanufacture of slaughterhouse by-products to be used as feed for intensively farmed land and sea animals (Jayathilakan et al. 2012); or alternatively, increasing massification of production in order to achieve the delicate balance of efficiencies of scale (Duffy 2009). Note here, against Marx's view, alterations to relative surplus value are not merely related to human labour efficiencies: on the contrary, reduction in the cost of feed is a reduction in the costs (for animal agriculture) associated with the labour of animals in metabolizing feed in the form of bodily growth and development. That is, these transitions are aimed at reducing animal labour costs.[17]

---

[16] Marx's (1986: 432) definition in *Capital Vol. 1* is instructive: 'I call surplus-value which is produced by the lengthening of the working day, absolute surplus-value. In contrast to this, I call that surplus-value which arises from the curtailment of the necessary labour time, and from the corresponding alteration in the respective lengths of the two components of the working day, relative surplus-value.' Note here, and relevant to my discussion, that necessary labour time in Marx's formulation refers explicitly to human labour time.

[17] Note that even contemporary theorists continue to treat labour efficiencies with a focus on human labour time. For example, Jason Moore in his influential *Capitalism in the Web of Life* appears to treat animals as an example of 'cheap nature' which is appropriated in order to alter the dynamics of human labour exploitation (Moore 2015; see also Patel and Moore 2018). This misses the crucial interplay between human labour efficiencies and animal labour efficiencies in animal agriculture: reductions in the human labour through labour efficiencies depend on transformations in animal labour (Wadiwel 2018b).

THE WORKING DAY: ANIMALS, CAPITALISM, AND SURPLUS TIME   195

However, expansions in *absolute surplus value* are perhaps the most diabolical under conditions of animal agriculture. Firstly, intensive farming systems will aim to increasingly dominate all time, such that the working day has no actual limits, physical or otherwise. How is this possible?[18] This reflects the reality that animals used in various productive processes, particularly animal agriculture, have a unique position as *a hybrid of both constant and variable capital* (Wadiwel 2018b). Food animals are deployed in the scene of production as a raw material to be produced or worked upon and transformed into a commodity with a new use value. But perhaps what makes the food animal different from an inanimate, non-sentient, object is the collaboration of the animal in the process of production. The animal is required to work on their own body through their metabolic processes to produce the final commodity. If the animal were not alive, then this commodity production would not be possible; instead the fact of living enables a labour on the self. Intensive farming systems mobilize all resources towards facilitating this labour so that every moment of production aims at efficient creation of a commodity for sale (i.e., the flesh of the animal). The more these production systems intensify, the more they control movement, nutrition, sexuality, reproduction, sleep, and socialization, so that every moment of the food animal's life will be optimized towards this final product. As such, freed of any normative limits, the factory farm might be said to have perfected the capitalist dream of the expansion of the working day, since all time for these animals is time geared toward production. There is no limit on the working day; the whole day becomes a day of labour. Even sleep time, in so far as it is configured and located in such a way as to not threaten the final product but enhance it, becomes a productive labour by animals towards meat as a valued commodity (see for example Alvino et al. 2009). Here we might note that the expansions of the working day in animal agriculture surpass the limits that Marx himself imagined might be possible to impose on the organic body of the labourer. Since the goal of production is the creation of the animal body itself as a finished commodity, and every moment of production is geared ruthlessly towards this aim, night and day, then all moments of the animal's life are directed towards this labour.

Secondly, since the whole of the working day has already been subsumed by animal agriculture, the whole of life becomes the time of production. Production becomes equivalent to the time taken to grow the animal: not a minute before or a minute late. This brute economics produces a perverse biopolitics that seeks to speed growth and shorten the lives of animals in order to reduce production time.

---

[18] Marx notes: 'To appropriate labour during all the 24 hours of the day is, therefore, the inherent tendency of capitalist production. But as it is physically impossible to exploit the same individual labour-power constantly during the night as well as the day...' (Marx 1986, Beginning of Section 4). However, we can see that animal agriculture realizes this dream.

196   ANIMAL LABOUR

Thus, for example, over the past fifty years, broiler chickens have been genetically selected to effectively halve 'growing' time (Petracci et al. 2015: 364; Tallentire, Leinonen, and Kyriazakis 2016; Moore 2015: 232), speeding production and increasing profitability.[19] Similar techniques are emerging in relation to feed and technology to facilitate improved efficiencies in fish production (Muir 2005: 196–9). Here surplus value is attained, not by reducing the length of the working day (which has already been extended to its limit in an absolute sense), but by speeding up the labour of life and simultaneously reducing the time the animal has to live (the number of working days) in order to shorten the production cycle. In a sense, animals used for food in intensive animal agriculture realize a particular fantasy of capital; on one hand the whole of the life time has been captured by production so that all time is labour time; however, simultaneously, since animals represent the whole production phase, the shortening of lives becomes a useful strategy to expand surplus. The absence of almost any normative limits on how we treat animals—inherent to a dominant anthropocentrism—provides the licence to pursue this fantasy.

Beyond Necessary Labour, Beyond Work

Understanding labour through the frame of labour time offers some distinct avenues for change. Below I provide some provisional speculations on how we might move forward. Indeed the vectors I have outlined above—labour as labour time, the shortening of lives inherent to animal agriculture, the struggle for the working day and freedom from the domination of production, and the collective demand for the reduction of necessary labour time and freedom from work—will help structure the speculations I have proposed below.

Reduce Unnecessary Labour, not Just Unnecessary Suffering

Extending Alasdair Cochrane's impulse that an animal labour rights approach offers a 'third way' in between animal rights and animal welfare (Cochrane 2016), a focus on animal labour time provides a very useful alternative to the

---

[19] Note Marx was aware of this biopolitical capacity to shorten animal lives:

> It is impossible, of course, to deliver a five-year old animal before the end of five years. But what is possible within certain limits is to prepare animals for their fate more quickly by new modes of treatment. This was precisely what Bakewell managed to do ... In Bakewell's system, one year old sheep can already be fattened, and in case they are fully grown before the second year has elapsed. By careful selective breeding, Bakewell ... reduced the bone structure of his sheep to the minimum necessary for existence.   (Marx 1992: 315)

THE WORKING DAY: ANIMALS, CAPITALISM, AND SURPLUS TIME   197

limits of animal welfare approaches, including consideration of collective representation of animal interests in labour time reduction. Welfarist approaches primarily aim towards reduction in 'unnecessary' suffering for animals used in production systems, but do not aim to fundamentally challenge the existence of those systems in themselves. By necessity this means that animal welfare lacks capacity to challenge human utilization of animals; indeed, 'animal welfare legislation is often used not just to protect animals but also regulate, indeed facilitate, the ongoing use of animals' (Bourke 2009: 133). Even more radical welfare visions, such as John Webster's 'Five Freedoms', read more like a list of bare biopolitical norms for living organisms than something that might be understood as informing political demands for animals (Webster 2001: 233).[20] Labour offers a different set of framings. And these framing are already in effect. As Cochrane notes, campaigns to offer retirement packages to police dogs, or re-home racehorses after their working lives are complete, reflect an awareness of the need to remunerate animals for their labour (Cochrane 2016; see also DeMello 2012: 202). However, I want to stress that this politics is not so much about the value of labour as a good thing that must be recognized, but about the battle over *labour time*; it reflects the demand for animals to enjoy time during their lives that is not dominated by the processes we thrust them into. Indeed this politics of labour time can be pushed further. Labour time is not merely about the time that might be owed to animals at the end of their lives after they have been put to toil for us, but might also be an opportunity to open a conversation about the necessary daily interruptions to productive processes that may be required to free animals from this domination. This after all was the point of the battle for the eight-hour day in labour history: it acknowledged that each day represents a potential for flourishing that was impeded by exploitative labour which was forced upon the worker.[21]

When should the working day for animals start and end? Certainly, for food animals this is a pressing question. If, as I have described above, all time has been dominated by production systems, then the challenge of claiming the working day is daunting, since all time is labour time: there is no working day for most animals. However I would argue that time offers a very useful framing which might shift us away from the dead end of the politics of welfare. This is because it forces a move from a politics that is informed by an imperative merely to reduce unnecessary suffering to a politics that aims to reduce labour time (both

---

[20] These freedoms include: 'freedom from thirst, hunger and malnutrition'; 'freedom from discomfort'; 'freedom from pain, injury and disease'; 'freedom to express normal behaviour'; 'freedom from fear and distress'.

[21] As such Marx saw this struggle over the working day as a more grounded basis for politics than liberal rights: 'In place of the pompous catalogue of the "inalienable rights of man" there steps the modest Magna Carta of the legally limited working day, which at least makes clear 'when the time when the worker sells is ended, and when his own begins' (Marx 1986: 416).

'necessary' and 'unnecessary'[22]). If animals are to be pushed into the living hell of intensive farming systems, should they not be granted regular breaks from this labour where these animals might be able to flourish in ways that intensive systems prevent?

Naturally, any campaign for a working day for animals would be highly fraught. It seems highly implausible that global animal agriculture will surrender this time to the animals they incarcerate and force into labour. However, in some respects, existing campaigning around welfare reforms are already dealing with these questions of time. Consider global moves towards 'free range' systems for the production of chicken eggs. At least part of the political framing of these campaigns has been structured by a logic of *space*. For example, in Australia, advocates have successfully used the image of an 'A4 Piece of Paper' to highlight the limited space available to laying hens within intensive caged egg production systems (RSPCA 2018).[23] This has helped alter public perceptions and drive down demand for 'cage eggs'. However, animal producers have responded in an attempt to safeguard the profitability of the industry. Recent changes to Australian legislation, driven by a strong industry lobby, have successfully watered down the definition of 'free range' to: 'meaningful and regular access to an outdoor range during daylight hours during the laying cycle; (b) . . . able to roam and forage on the outdoor range; and (c) . . . subject to a stocking density of 10,000 hens or less'.[24] The legislation is notable in its lack of detail over what 'meaningful and regular access to an outdoor range' constitutes. But there is here an interesting opportunity. While space is at issue in the legislation, in so far as 'free range' implies a spatial freedom from intensive barn laying systems, it is curious that this reorientation of the legislation creates a political opportunity in relation to *time*. Indeed, the battle ground for advocates within the context of this legislation, is *how much time animals will have outside of the intensive confinement of the barn*: that is, to paraphrase Marx, when the time the worker finishes selling their labour ends, and when their own begins.[25] And although the question of what animals do when they are not being dominated by our production systems is fraught (an assessment of the quality of free time for animals

---

[22] 'Necessary' and 'unnecessary' labour is noted here with deliberate reference to Marx's concept of 'socially necessary labour time', that is, average labour time required to produce a use value. This concept remains vague in Marx (Marx 1986: 129–31; Marx 1991: 287–9) and is open to scholarly debate (Tombazos 2014: 33–41). However, we might broadly consider necessary labour time as reflective of the average social exertion associated with production to meet social needs. This necessary labour is of interest to capitalist production in different ways, including in determining the necessary labour time required by the worker to reproduce their own labour, which in turn will determine the expected level of surplus within a production process: 'it is the tendency of capital to appropriate all time, that is, to transform the free time which it makes possible into surplus time (i.e., into time for the production of expanded surplus value)' (Booth 1991: 17).

[23] These reasonable suggestions from advocates have promoted perverse responses from industries. Some sections of the industry have responded by arguing that increased space does not necessarily reduce mortality or improve health outcomes for laying hens (Locke 2018); other parts of the industry are taking advantage of inconsistent regulation over stocking densities in different jurisdictions (Han 2015).

[24] *Australian Consumer Law [Free Range Egg Labelling] Information Standard 2017.*

[25] See n.21 above.

beyond work is beyond the scope of this chapter), I note that advocates have already begun the work of imagining this life: 'Roosting, building a nest and laying in private, foraging and dust-bathing: these are the simple and essential pleasures that the cage egg industry denies hens' (Animals Australia 2018). In these cases, space is not necessarily the key battle ground for advocacy; rather time, and the difference between labour time and time not spent labouring, is key.

Slow Down Production; Challenge the Shortening of Lives

I note here that perhaps what is interesting about the movement from space to time as a focus of advocacy is that it potentially offers a challenge to the accelerative logic of contemporary animal agriculture which has sped up production as part of the intensification process. There are here some curious resonances between the work of animal advocates and that of other social movements. On one hand, intensification of animal production, including increasing speed and automation, do no favours to human workers, particularly in relation to work-related safety and stress (Erwin 2017). Indeed there is, at least prima facie, a strong case for slowing production that both labour rights activists and animal advocates might share commitments around. On the other hand, there are a curious set of resonances here with the strong demands being made by other social movements—such as environmental justice movements—to 'slow down capitalism' through reduced work, reduced production, and reduced consumption (see for example D'Alisa, Demaria and Kallis 2014). As I shall discuss below, this offers a useful shared structural critique of capitalism, and with it, the possibility of developing shared social movements to realize a different vision for future post-capitalist societies.

The battle for the working day has one more potential tangent, and this relates to a different problem: namely, how much life animal labourers should have. Under the totalizing conditions of animal agriculture, the length of life lived by the animals we dominate is determined solely by the economics of production. Animals will live exactly as long as is required to extract maximal value within any given production system. As I have described above, in many food animal production systems (such as poultry and fish) industries have sought to produce relative efficiencies in surplus value extraction by reducing the length of time animals live: reducing life reduces necessary animal labour and this minimizes the costs of the means of subsistence, expanding the surplus value that can be attained. Perhaps due to a focus on unnecessary suffering, and a lack of interest in the problem of animal death as a harm, welfarist politics has largely been ineffective in countering this manipulation of the length of life. Not only have we seen lives shortened for profit, but simultaneously an absence of public discussion over what constitutes a reasonable length of life for an animal used in food production, and a lack of consideration of the justice or ethics of abrupt shortenings of life aimed to

200   ANIMAL LABOUR

meet arbitrary human desires,[26] such as the routinized slaughter of juvenile animals because of a market for meats such as lamb. We might speculate that the advantage of a discussion around labour time, and by extension the time animals have to live, might open a conversation about what a reasonable life might look like; perhaps undoing the epistemic violence that silences any contemplation over whether animal agriculture has the right to shorten lives, and what the social or normative limits on this violence should be. With this question, as I have suggested above, lurks the deeper philosophical problem of whether time matters to animals; and asking this question forces us to challenge our anthropocentric assumption that time is somehow less meaningfully lived by animals.[27]

A World Without Work?

I want to stress that perhaps the most promising aspect of a focus on labour time is that it connects with a broader political discussion on the role of necessary labour within society. While some political visions imagine socialism as a political movement aimed at redistribution of property and resources, whereas others frame socialism with respect to the project of democratic control over surplus labour (Spivak 2012: 192), there is at least *one more vision* which relates to a systematic project which aims at reducing necessary labour: enabling flourishing by diminishing work. This latter reading stresses that capitalism continues a history of class differentiation where the characteristic of domination is the erasure of free time: 'all major servile classes have been characterized, according to Marx, by the fact that their bound time yielded surplus or free time, whether for their leisured masters or for the creation of surplus value' (Booth 1991: 23). In stressing a vision of social change that seeks to minimize labour, I am highlighting the need for a project that continually challenges the necessity of work, and its existence as an obstacle to flourishing in the societies we might want to build. This returns us to a reading of work as a mode of domination in societies, and the project of reducing and perhaps eliminating work in order to attain flourishing (see Donaldson and Kymlicka's extensive discussion of 'the work society' in chapter 10 of this volume). Negri is at pains to point out in *Marx Beyond Marx* that contemporary capitalism is shaped by the subsumption of all time into capital's time, in such a way that life becomes a social factory:

> Society appears to us as capital's society. It is through this passage that all social conditions are subsumed by capital, that is, they become part of its 'organic composition.' And besides the social conditions—which present themselves in

---

[26] Although curiously, some of these conversations have arisen in the context of 'ethical meat' discourse (Fox 2015).

[27] See n.11 above.

THE WORKING DAY: ANIMALS, CAPITALISM, AND SURPLUS TIME   201

their immediacy—capital progressively subsumes all the elements and materials
of the process of circulation (money and exchange in the first place, as functions
of mediation) and, thereafter, all those pertaining to the process of production, so
that herein lies the foundation for the passage from manufacture to big industry
to social factory.   (Negri 1991: 114)

It does not take much imagination to notice that the social factory Negri describes
follows closely the coordinates of the factory farm, since all time for animals becomes
captured into capital's flows (Wadiwel 2018b). Indeed, the situation for animals
globally within the context of animal agriculture (and to an extent animal used in
experimentation) is that capital's dream has been ruthlessly realized: the whole of the
social world of animals has been subsumed into production, so that free time for
animals has become nonsensical, instead, all time is the time of production.

As I have described above, there are now numerous competing visions for post-
capitalist solutions emerging from left and green politics, some of which have, for
example, attempted to imagine no growth or negative growth economies. At the same
time, there has been discussion of the politics of work and its place within progressive
politics (Weeks 2011: 20), and a growing interest in automation, and the promise this
holds for a 'post-work' society (Mason 2016). However, none of these visions of postcapitalism have been post-anthropocentric. Indeed, in so far as they may be premised
on maintaining the mass utilization of animals as labourers, they are simply proposals
to alter the technical composition of capitalism, shifting human labourers away from
production while still maintaining a non-human labour force.[28]

But what does a post-anthropocentric project aimed at reducing necessary
labour time (and increasing free time) look like?[29] What attracts me to this latter

---

[28] I have elsewhere pointed out (Wadiwel 2018b) that acknowledging animal labour as a value alters
a Marxist analysis of animal agriculture. Although the increased intensification of production has
reduced the presence of human labour in production while also increasing the use of machines,
enclosures etc. (hence a rising 'technical composition'), the reality of this production is that the mass
of animal labour perversely rises. This is because animals are also the object of production, and thus
their labour cannot be dispensed with, only made more efficient.

[29] To be clear, 'free time' for animals is not something imagined here as an individual proprietary
right. Collective processes enable successive reductions in the socially necessary labour time required to
nurture life and allow it to flourish. As discussed in n.22, 'socially necessary labour time' is a potentially
contested idea (Tombazos 2013: 33–41); however, at its most expansive it includes all labour and
energies that are required to enable an instance of production. In this context, labour can only be
understood within the context of its social character; as Bachour (chapter 6 in this volume) states 'the
wealth of resources available to, and produced by, individuals is always social in nature: the process of
individual production (re)produces society as a whole.' Thus a social conception of labour time not
only includes formal paid labour or work within the immediate sphere of production, but also material
and immaterial labour that enables this production, including unpaid care work, reproductive labour,
social reproduction, 'nature', etc. This means free time is a product of collective processes, and how
time is spent by individuals towards flourishing is structured itself by social processes and norms.
Perhaps it is true that some labour will always be necessary and important, and should be recognized
and valued—such as time spent caring for other individuals. But even here there is scope to imagine
how labour time may be saved in order to increase free time: for example, the use of collective labour
processes and technologies to reduce the time associated with care labour.

202 ANIMAL LABOUR

project is that it opens a set of questions that applies equally between humans and non-humans: namely, how much labour is required within our social and economic organizations to sustain life and allow it to flourish? How much more labour is required to meet our future needs as a society? *And do we actually need to labour?* The latter question remains unanswered within the contemporary world of continuing mass accumulation. On one hand, this is a technical question which relates to whether our use of technologies and modes of organization have created a world where a minimal amount of labour might be required to reproduce life and allow it to flourish. On the other hand, there are deeper questions about how life might be spent if it is not devoted to labour (see Donaldson and Kymlicka's chapter 10 of this volume). But these questions are impossible to disentangle from the normative question: what exactly is the value of work? Does it contribute or degrade the flourishing of beings? And what would it mean to be rid of work, either human or non-human, from the societies we are imagining?[30]

References

Adams, Carol J. 2017. 'Feminized Protein: Meaning, Representations, and Implications'. In *Making Milk: The Past, Present and Future of Our Primary Food*, edited by Mathilde Cohen and Yoriko Otomo. London: Bloomsbury.

Agamben, Giorgio. 2004. *The Open: Man and Animal*. Stanford: Stanford University Press.

Alvino, G.M., R.A. Blatchford, G.S. Archer, and J.A. Mench. 2009. 'Light Intensity During Rearing Affects the Behavioural Synchrony and Resting Patterns of Broiler Chickens'. *British Poultry Science* 50(3): 275–83.

Animals Australia. '8 epic failures of current Poultry Laws (and how you can help Aussie hens!)' Animals Australia, 12 January 2018. https://www.animalsaustralia.org/features/australian-poultry-laws-epic-fail.php

Barua, Maan. 2017. 'Nonhuman Labour, Encounter Value, Spectacular Accumulation: The Geographies of a Lively Commodity'. *Transactions of the Institute of British Geographers* 42(2): 274–88.

Barua, Maan. 2019. 'Animating Capital: Work, Commodities, Circulation'. *Progress in Human Geography*. https://doi.org/10.1177/0309132518819057

Beldo, Les. 2017. 'Metabolic Labor: Broiler Chickens and the Exploitation of Vitality'. *Environmental Humanities* 9(1): 108–28.

---

[30] My sincere thanks to Will Kymlicka, Charlotte Blattner, Kendra Coulter, and all the participants in the 'Animal Labour: Ethical, Legal and Political Perspectives on Recognizing Animals' Work' workshop, for all the advice and suggestions provided, which have informed the development of this chapter.

Benton, Ted. 1993. *Natural Relations: Ecology, Animal Rights and Social Justice*. London: Verso.

Booth, William James. 1991. 'Economies of Time: On the Idea of Time in Marx's Political Economy'. *Political Theory* 19(1): 7–27.

Bourke, Deirdre. 2009. 'The Use and Misuse of "Rights Talk" by the Animal Rights Movement'. In *Animal Law in Australasia: A New Dialogue*, edited by Peter Sankoff and Steven White. Sydney: Federation Press.

Cochrane, Alasdair. 2016. 'Labour Rights for Animals'. In *The Political Turn in Animal Ethics*, edited by Robert Garner and Siobhan O'Sullivan, 15–32. London: Rowman & Littlefield.

Cooper, Melinda. 2008. *Life as Surplus: Biotechnology and Capitalism in the Neoliberal Era*. Seattle: University of Washington Press.

Coulter, Kendra. 2016. *Animals, Work, and the Promise of Interspecies Solidarity*. New York: Palgrave Macmillan.

D'Alisa, Giacomo, Federico Demaria, and Giorgos Kallis (eds.). 2014. *Degrowth: A Vocabulary for a New Era*. London: Routledge.

DeMello, Margo. 2012. *Animals and Society: An Introduction to Human-Animal Studies*. Columbia University Press.

Duffy, Michael. 2009. 'Economies of Size in Production Agriculture'. *Journal of Hunger & Environmental Nutrition* 4(3–4): 375–92.

Erwin, Nicole. 2017. 'Too Fast For Safety? Poultry Industry Wants To Speed Up The Slaughter Line'. *The Salt*, 27 October 2017. https://www.npr.org/sections/thesalt/2017/10/27/559572147/too-fast-for-safety-poultry-industry-wants-to-speed-up-the-slaughter-line

Evans, Melissa, Tiago Hori, Matthew Rise, and Ian Fleming. 2015. 'Transcriptomic Responses of Atlantic Salmon (Salmo salar) to Environmental Enrichment During Juvenile Rearing. *PLoS One* 10(3).

Food and Agriculture Organization of the United Nations. 2016. *State of the World Fisheries and Aquaculture: Contributing to Food Security and Nutrition for All*. Rome: Food and Agriculture Organization of the United Nations.

Foster, John Bellamy. 2018. 'Marx and Alienated Speciesism'. *Monthly Review: An Independent Socialist Magazine*, 1 December 2018. https://monthlyreview.org/2018/12/01/marx-and-alienated-speciesism/

Foucault, Michel. 1998. *The Will to Knowledge. The History of Sexuality: 1*. London: Penguin Books.

Fox, Eva. 2015. 'The Case For Eating Older Animals'. *Modern Farmer*, 20 January 2015. https://modernfarmer.com/2015/01/case-eating-older-animals/

Gunderson, Ryan. 2011. 'Marx's Comments on Animal Welfare'. *Rethinking Marxism* 23(4): 543–8.

Han, Esther. 2015. 'Free Range Eggs: Ministers Urged to Get Cracking on an Enforceable Standard'. *The Sydney Morning Herald*, 9 June 2015. https://www.smh.com.au/

business/companies/free-range-eggs-ministers-urged-to-get-cracking-on-an-enforceable-standard-20150608-ghivmo.html

Haraway, Donna. 2007. *When Species Meet*. Minneapolis: University of Minnesota Press.

Hribal, Jason. 2003. '"Animals are Part of the Working Class": A Challenge to Labor History'. *Labor History* 44(4): 435–53.

Jayathilakan, Kizhekkedath, Khudsia Sultana, K. Radhakrishna, and Amarinder Singh Bawa. 2012. 'Utilization of Byproducts and Waste Materials From Meat, Poultry and Fish processing Industries: A Review'. *Journal of Food Science and Technology* 49(3): 278–93.

Johnson, Elizabeth. 2017. 'At the Limits of Species Being: Sensing the Anthropocene'. *South Atlantic Quarterly* 116(2): 275–92.

Kidd, Charles. 1992. 'The Evolution of Sustainability'. *Journal of Agricultural and Environmental Ethics* 5(1): 1–26.

Lebowitz, Michael. 2003. *Beyond Capital: Marx's Political Economy of the Working Class*. Houndsmills: Palgrave Macmillan.

Locke, Sarina 2018. 'Cages are Better for Chickens than Intensive Free-Range, Farmers say, as Calls for a Ban Get Louder'. ABC News, 27 February 2018. http://www.abc.net.au/news/rural/2018-02-20/protests-over-caged-eggs-have-farmers-worried/9461064

Makino, Hirona, Reiji Masuda, and Masuru Tanaka. 2015. 'Environmental Stimuli Improve Learning Capability in Striped Knifejaw Juveniles: The Stage-Specific Effect of Environmental Enrichment and the Comparison Between Wild and Hatchery-Reared Fish'. *Fisheries Science* 81(6): 1035–42.

Marx, Karl. 1864. 'Results of the Direct Production Process'. Trans. Ben Fawkes. https://www.marxists.org/archive/marx/works/1864/economic/index.htm

Marx, Karl. 1978. 'Economic and Philosophic Manuscripts of 1844'. In *The Marx-Engels Reader: Second Edition*, edited by Robert Tucker, 66–125. New York: W.W. Norton.

Marx, Karl. 1986. *Capital Vol. 1*. London: Penguin.

Marx, Karl. 1991. *Capital Vol. 3*. London: Penguin.

Marx, Karl. 1992. *Capital Vol. 2*. London: Penguin.

Mason, Paul. 2016. *PostCapitalism: A Guide to Our Future*. London: Penguin.

Moore, Jason. 2015. *Capitalism in the Web of Life: Ecology and the Accumulation of Capital*. London: Verso.

Muir, James. 2005. 'Managing to Harvest? Perspectives on the Potential of Aquaculture'. *Philosophical Transactions of the Royal Society B: Biological Sciences* 360(1453): 191–218.

Näslund, Joacim, and Jörgen Johnsson. 2016. 'Environmental Enrichment for Fish in Captive Environments: Effects of Physical Structures and Substrates'. *Fish & Fisheries* 17(1):1–30.

Negri, Antonio. 1991. *Marx Beyond Marx: Lessons on the Grundrisse*. Brooklyn, NY: Autonomedia.

Noske, Barbara. 1997. *Beyond Boundaries: Humans and Animals*. Montreal: Black Rose.

Nussbaum, Martha. 2004. 'Beyond "Compassion and Humanity"'. In *Animal Rights: Current Debates and New Directions*, edited by Cass Sunstein and Martha Nussbaum, 299–320. Oxford: Oxford University Press.

Oliver, Kelly. 2016. 'Service Dogs: Between Animal Studies and Disability Studies'. *philoSOPHIA* 6(2): 241–58.

Painter, Corinne. 2016. 'Non-human Animals within Contemporary Capitalism: A Marxist Account of Non-human Animal Liberation'. *Capital and Class* 40(2): 1–19.

Patel, Raj, and Jason Moore. 2018. 'How the Chicken Nugget Became the True Symbol of Our Era'. *The Guardian*, 8 May 2018. https://www.theguardian.com/news/2018/may/08/how-the-chicken-nugget-became-the-true-symbol-of-our-era

Perlo, Katherine. 2002. 'Marxism and the Underdog'. *Society & Animals* 10: 303–18.

Petracci, M., Samar Mudalal, Francesca Soglia, and Cavani Claudio. 2015. 'Meat Quality in Fast-Growing Broiler Chickens'. *World's Poultry Science Journal* 71(2): 363–74.

Porcher, Jocelyne. 2014. 'The Work of Animals: A Challenge for Social Sciences'. *Humanimalia* 6(1).

RSPCA. 2018. 'Layer Hen FAQ'. RSPCA: For All Creatures Great and Small. https://www.rspca.org.au/layer-hen-faq

Shukin, Nicole. 2009. *Animal Capital*. Minneapolis: University of Minnesota Press.

Smith, Adam. 1981. *An Inquiry into the Nature and Causes of the Wealth of Nations*. Indianapolis: Liberty Press.

Spivak, Gayatri Chakravorty. 2012. *An Aesthetic Education in the Era of Globalization*. Cambridge, MA: Harvard University Press.

Stuart, Diana, Rebecca Schewe, and Ryan Gunderson. 2013. 'Extending Social Theory to Farm Animals: Addressing Alienation in the Dairy Sector'. *Sociologia Ruralis* 53(2): 201–29.

Tallentire, Craig W., Ilkka Leinonen, and Ilias Kyriazakis. 2016. 'Breeding for efficiency in the broiler chicken: A review'. *Agronomy for Sustainable Development* 36: 66. https://doi.org/10.1007/s13593-016-0398-2

Tombazos, Stavros. 2014. *Time in Marx: The Categories of Time in Marx's Capital*. Leiden: Brill.

Wadiwel, Dinesh Joseph. 2015. *The War Against Animals*. Leiden: Brill.

Wadiwel, Dinesh Joseph. 2018a. 'Biopolitics'. In *Critical Terms for Animal Studies*, edited by Lori Gruen. Chicago: University of Chicago Press.

Wadiwel, Dinesh Joseph. 2018b. 'Chicken Harvesting Machine: Animal Labour, Resistance and The Time of Production'. *South Atlantic Quarterly* 117(3): 525–48.

Webster, John. 2001. "Farm Animal Welfare: The Five Freedoms and the Free Market." *Veterinary Journal*. 161(3): 229–37.

Weeks, Kathi. 2011. *The Problem with Work: Feminism, Marxism, Antiwork Politics and Post-Work Imaginaries*. Durham: Duke University Press.

Young, Iris Marion. 1990 *Justice and the Politics of Difference*. Princeton: Princeton University Press.

10

Animal Labour in a Post-Work Society

Sue Donaldson and Will Kymlicka

When we first started thinking about animals and work, it seemed clear to us that being shut out of the category of worker might be a major problem for animals, especially for domesticated animals who, at least for the foreseeable future, will be part of a shared society with us. Insofar as work bestows recognition and social status, defines citizenship, grounds opportunities for self-development through chosen purposeful activity and social cooperation, and provides income so that basic material needs are secured, the exclusion of animals from the public discourse and legal category of 'work' is problematic. It reflects and perpetuates their abject status in society. To remedy this, we thought, it was important to recognize the work that animals already do, and to create opportunities for animals to explore new forms of 'good work' that are chosen, safe, and non-exploitative.

However, as we investigated the role of work in contemporary society, it became clear that the overwhelming centrality of paid employment in securing citizenship, meeting basic needs, and coordinating cooperative social life is deeply problematic, leading many thinkers to consider alternatives under the rubric of the 'post-work society'.[1] Theorists of the post-work society argue that endorsing productivism and the work ethic as the lynchpin of society inevitably generates a series of political, economic, social, and environmental harms and injustices. A post-work society would denaturalize and de-sanctify work—in part through a universal basic income—in order to disincentivize work for work's sake, distribute necessary work more fairly, reduce environmentally damaging patterns of production and consumption, and open up alternative pathways to self-development and social belonging.[2]

Our goal in this chapter is to locate animal workers within the emerging debate about the post-work society. To date, defenders of the post-work society have said little about the place of animals in their post-work vision. Indeed, they tend to view society in the same human-exclusive terms as defenders of the work society,

---

[1] The term 'post-work society' should be parsed as post-'work society', rather than a society that is 'post-work'. In other words, people would still work, and many would engage in paid employment, but as we explain below, paid employment would no longer serve as the lynchpin of belonging, security, and meaning.

[2] For recent defences of this post-work perspective, see Fitzpatrick 2004; Weeks 2011; Hunnicutt 2013; Frayne 2015; Livingston 2016; Srnicek and Williams 2016; Chamberlain 2018.

Sue Donaldson and Will Kymlicka, *Animal Labour in a Post-Work Society* In: *Animal Labour: A New Frontier of Interspecies Justice?*. Edited by: Charlotte Blattner, Kendra Coulter, and Will Kymlicka, Oxford University Press (2020). © Oxford University Press. DOI: 10.1093/oso/9780198846192.003.0010

208 ANIMAL LABOUR

and to adopt the same human-supremacist tropes.[3] Nonetheless, we will argue that the post-work perspective offers important advantages for theorizing inter-species justice. While there are benefits in recognizing that animals engage in 'work' or 'labour', this promise can best be realized in a post-work society that has de-sanctified work. Indeed, we will argue that focusing on the case of animals helps to illuminate important benefits of the post-work society.

We begin by exploring some of the defining features of the 'work society', in particular its naturalization and moralization of work (section 1). We then turn to some of the most serious drawbacks of the work society (section 2), how a post-work society would address these (section 3), and how these changes would benefit animal labourers and citizens (section 4).

What is the Work Society?

One of the defining features of modern Western societies is the *normalization* of work: that is, the idea that full-time, life-long labour is normal or natural. And since this is seen as normal and natural, socializing, educating, and training people for such a life also becomes normal and natural. Education becomes first and foremost preparation for a life of full-time labour. Work dominates our life, not only in the workplace during work hours, but in all of the spaces and time devoted to making us 'employable' and 'work-ready'.[4]

This normalization of work is now so deeply embedded that we have trouble imagining alternatives. But it is far from inevitable. As both Marx and Weber noted, modernizing states and capitalist employers needed to pressure, even coerce, people to comply with the discipline of a full-time work day. And while the rise of the work society certainly helped increase the production of goods and services, the rise of technology and automation means that it is no longer economically necessary for everyone to work full-time in order to produce the material basis for a decent standard of living. Already in the 1920s economists were noting that the rise of technology allowed for a dramatic reduction in the number of working hours, and the most recent phase of automation has just amplified this point. Commentators have argued that it would be entirely feasible to shift to a twenty-one-hour work week, for example (Coote, Franklin, and Simms 2010), or to give everyone (not just academics!) a 'sabbatical account' which would allow them to take a year off work on a regular basis (Offe 1997), or to adopt an unconditional basic income (Van Parijs and Vanderborght 2017).

---

[3] Just as defenders of the work ethic often say that work is what distinguishes humans from the animals; so too defenders of the post-work society often say that freeing people from work will allow us to mark our difference from and superiority to animals.

[4] On how work, and the need to be employable, colonizes an increasing percentage of our lives, see Weeks 2011; Frayne 2015: 73–4.

ANIMAL LABOUR IN A POST-WORK SOCIETY   209

Why then are we still locked into a work society? A large part of the answer is that work is not only normalized, but also *moralized*. Society privileges work, not only for its economic output, but also as the basis of self-respect, social membership, and citizenship. We establish our identities, and our worth, through earning.[5] Work is how we show to others, and to ourselves, that we are responsible adults and contributing members of society, and as such are entitled to political voice and to social benefits.[6] In short, the work society is built on an *ethic* of work, and not just on an economics of work.

It is important to note that this work ethic initially was a major 'democratizing force' (Weeks 2011: 44). In the ancient Greek and Roman world, and in medieval Europe, political power and social status were tied to the avoidance of work, inherently limited to an aristocratic or priestly elite. Work was seen as degrading, contrary to a civilized life, and incompatible with the virtues and requirements of political rule. The rise of a work ethic—which rejected aristocratic idleness, while valorizing the dignity of work—was an enormous and progressive cultural shift. It empowered the masses against the elites, putting the keys to social standing and political power in the hands of everyday people.

As a result, a commitment to the work ethic remains a powerful part of the political imaginary on both the right and the left (Livingston 2016). Indeed, far from weakening in the face of automation and structural unemployment, we have seen 'the aggressive return of the work ethic in the context of neoliberalism' (Frayne 2015: 99). On the right, this has taken the nasty form of a 'revamped ideological focus on the virtues of "hardworking people" versus society's so-called scroungers and skivers' (Frayne 2015: 16). In the words of George Osborne, the Conservative Chancellor of the Exchequer in the UK:

Where is the fairness, we ask, for the shift-worker, leaving home in the dark hours of the early morning, who looks up at the closed blinds of their next door neighbour sleeping off a life on benefits? When we say that we're all in this together, we speak for that worker. We speak for all those who want to work hard and get on.[7]

---

[5] 'Work is the primary means by which individuals are integrated not only into the economic system, but also into social, political, and familial modes of cooperation. That individuals should work is fundamental to the basic social contract: indeed, working is part of what is supposed to transform subjects into the independent individuals of the liberal imaginary, and for that reason is treated as a basic obligation of citizenship... Dreams of individual accomplishment and desires to contribute to the common good become firmly attached to waged work... the wage relation generates not just income and capital, but disciplined individuals, governable subjects, worthy citizens, and responsible family members' (Weeks 2011: 8).

[6] On the centrality of earning as the basis for claims to citizenship in the US, see the classic discussion in Shklar 1991.

[7] Quoted in Coote and Lyall 2013: 1. And in the words of Conservative leader David Cameron: 'we are building a country for those who work and want to get on. And we are saying to each and every

210　ANIMAL LABOUR

And while less likely to blame the unemployed for their fate, the centre and left, too, share the goal of turning us all into 'hard-working people'. It was under New Labour (and Clinton Democrats) that social policies were revamped to put greater pressure on single parents and people with disabilities to get a job, and more generally, to 'rebuild the welfare state around work' (Frayne 2015: 103–4).[8] Across the political spectrum we see the same chorus: work is reaffirmed as the core of citizenship.[9]

There have always been voices challenging the work society, arguing instead for prioritizing the freedom of individuals to voluntarily exit from the labour market (to work fewer hours; to retire earlier; to have basic needs guaranteed regardless of employment). And we live in an era which could in fact provide this freedom to a much wider range of people, and in a more equitable way, than ever before. However, neoliberalism has pushed us in the opposite direction, not only by forcing the poor to work (workfare) and advocating for delayed retirement, but also at a more general ideological level, by delegitimizing the very idea that the freedom to voluntarily exit the labour market is a value to be promoted. On the contrary, in our neoliberal era, claims of justice must increasingly be framed or filtered as ways of enhancing labour market participation.

Against this background, it is not surprising that animal advocates have started to press for recognition of animals as workers. Several recent theorists have argued that domesticated animals should be seen as members of our society, with the rights and responsibilities of social membership.[10] But in a work society, these rights and responsibilities are mediated through work, and so domesticated animals' claim to social membership will be precarious at best if they are unable to be seen as workers. Put crudely, if the members of society are divided into 'strivers' and 'skivers' (as the neoliberal work ethic implies), and if the government is unambiguous that it stands for the strivers not the skivers, then the prospects of justice for domesticated animals may depend on showing that they too are workers.

And so we see various efforts to show that domesticated animals can indeed meet the standards of work-based justice claims (e.g., Valentini 2014; Cochrane

---

hard-working person in our country: we are on your side.... This is a government for hard-working people, and that's the way it will stay' (quoted in Frayne: 2015: 99).

[8] In the words of Liam Byrne, the Labour Shadow Secretary for Work and Pensions, 'tough times expose your values, and Labour is clear: we are on the side of people who work hard and do the right thing' (quoted in Coote and Lyall 2013: 2).

[9] While the work ethic is sometimes seen as an idiosyncratic feature of 'liberal' Anglo-American states, Azmanova (2010; 2012) shows the consistency of this ethic across the different 'varieties of capitalism' (including 'continental' corporatist welfare states and 'Scandinavian' social democratic welfare states). See also Lødemel and Moreira (2014) for the salience of these ideas across the Western democracies.

[10] For our version of this argument, see Donaldson and Kymlicka 2011. See also Smith 2012; Cochrane 2016.

ANIMAL LABOUR IN A POST-WORK SOCIETY   211

2016; Shaw 2018; Boettcher 2018). This is an important and valuable task. The fact that our society currently excludes animals from work-based claims is the result of human supremacist ideologies, and it is right and proper that animal advocates contest these ideologies and struggle for the unbiased recognition of animal work. Just as the denial or denigration of women's work has been central to systems of patriarchy, so too the denial or denigration of animals' work has been central to human supremacism, and justice requires tackling these biases head on.

However, at the same time as we challenge biases in the way animal labour is (mis)recognized and uncompensated, it is equally important that we question the underlying assumptions of a work society. While the normalization and moralization of work may once have served a democratic and emancipatory function, it almost certainly is having the opposite effect today, to the detriment of both humans and animals.

The Limits of the Work Society

There are several reasons why the work society can no longer provide the framework for a just society. First, there simply are not enough jobs to go around, and as a result, an increasing number of people are being relegated to lives of precarious employment, resulting in precarious access to social membership.[11] The fact that technology has reduced the number of hours of work needed to produce cars or computers could have led to a reduced workweek for all workers—a kind of leisure dividend for everyone. Due to the work ethic, however, increased productivity has led instead to a dual labour market in which some workers can still fulfil the socially sanctioned model of full-time life-long employment, while others are relegated to socially stigmatized unemployment or precarious employment,[12] with pernicious effects both on their social status and their individual well-being.[13]

---

[11] 'Never has the "irreplaceable", "indispensable", function of labour as the sources of "social ties", "social cohesion", "integration", "socialization", "personalization", "personal identity" and meaning been invoked so obsessively as it has since the day it became unable to fulfil any of these functions' (Gorz 1999: 57).

[12] As Bertrand Russell noted, this perverse reaction to increased productivity has ensured that 'unavoidable leisure shall cause misery all around instead of being a universal source of happiness. Can anything more insane be imagined?' (quoted in Frayne: 2015: 38).

[13] The association between unemployment and negative health outcomes is well known, but as Sage (2019) shows, this correlation is mediated by the work ethic: that is, it is not the lack of work per se that causes the drop in well-being, but the perceived failure to comply with the social norm of moralized labour. When this norm no longer applies—for example, when the long-term unemployed shift into the 'retired' category, and so are no longer expected to work—their well-being goes up, even if their actual life activities do not change (Hetschko et al. 2014). Conversely, the positive health benefits of labour come not from the intrinsic rewards of work, which most people find unpleasurable, but from the high social status that comes with having a job (Bryson and MacKerron 2017). Sage concludes that the best way to enhance well-being is to weaken the grip of the work ethic.

212   ANIMAL LABOUR

Moreover, these lines of inclusion and exclusion are not random, but are deeply tied to race, gender, and species. The moralization of work may once have challenged aristocratic privilege in the name of the people, but it now operates to create insidious hierarchies within 'the people', by privileging certain forms of work and certain types of workplaces. The work ethic has operated, for example, to privilege men's productive work over women's reproductive labour, to privilege able-bodied workers over people with disabilities, and to privilege the work ethic of white Euro-Americans over that of Blacks and immigrants. Indeed, prejudiced beliefs concerning commitment to the work ethic are the main factor explaining white opposition to social benefits for Blacks in the US (Gilens 1999).[14] The white male working class upholds the work ethic not only or primarily to push aristocratic elites off their pedestal, but also to assert their own superior deservingness over women and Blacks. In the words of James Livingston, 'gender and race overdetermine our inability to think past work' (2016: 87). Or as Kathi Weeks puts it, 'the work ethic traveled down the class ladder in part on the energies of racism, ethnicity, and nationalism' (Weeks 2011: 62). And we can certainly add speciesism to her list. Accounts of the work ethic typically insist that human 'work' is categorically different from, and superior to, animal 'instinct', and so operates to justify sanctifying human work while instrumentalizing animal labour.[15]

Of course, all of these biases in what counts as work, and in who counts as a worker, can and should be challenged. But the idea that we could articulate a truly inclusive conception of the work ethic—across lines of gender, ability, race, ethnicity, and species—is optimistic, to say the least. The reality is that the work ethic is not only prone to unjust exclusions, but is upheld in part precisely to justify those exclusions. Many people cling to the work ethic, not because they love their work (far from it),[16] but because they believe it justifies putting social distance between them and various despised or denigrated others.[17]

Moreover, even if we could solve these first two problems—that is, even if we could grow the economy to create more jobs, and articulate a more inclusive conception of work—the reality is that productivism is environmentally

---

[14] 'Politics is often viewed, by élites at least, as a process centered on the question "who gets what." For ordinary Americans, however, politics is more often about "who *deserves* what" and the welfare state is no exception' (Gilens 1999: 1–2). These perceptions of deservingness are rooted in racialized assessments of the work ethic.

[15] For an important early critique of this distinction, see Ingold 1983.

[16] For the evidence that most people do not find their work intrinsically rewarding, see Bryson and MacKerron (2017), and the series of Gallup polls: http://news.gallup.com/poll/165269/worldwide-employees-engaged-work.aspx

[17] As reflected in 'ongoing debates regarding the supposed inadequacies of the work orientations of "inner city residents", "the underclass", "welfare mothers", or "illegal aliens", the work ethic is a deep discursive reservoir on which to draw to obscure and legitimate processes and logics of racial, gender, and nationalist formations past and present ... the work ethic continues to serve as a respectable vehicle for what would otherwise be exposed as publicly unacceptable claims about racial difference' (Weeks 2011: 62–3).

unsustainable. Our overriding task must be to shrink our ecological footprint, not ramp up production and consumption. The work ethic has locked us into a lifestyle that rewards intensive work with commodity-intensive consumption. In return for working hard, we get to consume intensively, and 'society's conventions, temporal rhythms and built environments' are increasingly being reshaped 'in ways which construct commodity-intensive lifestyles as the norm' (Frayne 2015: 91). We all know the result: runaway environmental degradation, global warming, habitat destruction, and species extinction. Any remotely plausible account of how we deal with the ecological challenges will require shifting to a 'post-productivist' ethic for a post-work society.[18]

Finally, from a more speculative perspective, we might ask what forms of freedom and flourishing are being occluded by our stubborn clinging to the work ethic. At the moment, our lives are comprehensively shaped to fit the work society, including 'the cultivation of habits, the internalization of routines, the incitement of desires, and the adjustment of hopes, all to guarantee a subject's adequacy to the lifetime demands of work' (Weeks 2011: 54). What is lost in this process? All forms of social organization involve the internalizing of routines and adjustment of hopes, but as Weeks notes, the work ethic is part of a long tradition of 'political asceticism', originally rooted in religious doctrines about the inevitability of suffering in this life, with pleasure deferred for the next life (Weeks 2011: 46). Few citizens still believe in this theology, but it continues to shape our political imaginaries, including on the left.[19] What desires are we suppressing, or failing to cultivate, in order to fit into the ascetic strictures of the work society?

In short, the work society is unrealistic (there aren't enough jobs), unfair (it underpins social hierarchy), ecologically unsustainable, and an ascetic renunciation of other possible forms of freedom, meaning, and pleasure. For all of these reasons, the work society does not provide a viable basis for a just society, including interspecies justice. And so even as animal advocates seek recognition of animals as workers, we need simultaneously to pursue the shift to a post-work society, and to ask how animals fit into it.

The Post-Work Society

What then is the post-work society? Insofar as the work society is defined as the normalization and moralization of work, then a post-work society is, in the first

---

[18] On the ecological case for shifting to a post-work society, see Fitzpatrick 2004; Van Parijs 2013. We should note that it is productivism in combination with population growth that produces unsustainability. If we reduced our population, the environmental consequences of productivism might be less urgent.

[19] Within left asceticism, 'workers' demands should echo, not contest, the discourses of poverty, sacrifice, hard work, and self-restraint that are part of the system's rationalization' (Weeks 2011: 103).

214   ANIMAL LABOUR

instance, the de-normalization and de-sanctification of paid employment.[20] There will continue to be forms of paid work available, and indeed this work might continue to play a fundamental life-shaping role for many people, but fulfilling the role of worker would no longer be the only route to citizenship, and those who refuse this role will not be subject to punishment, stigmatization, surveillance, invisibility, or social isolation. Put more positively, a post-work society seeks to support and legitimize alternatives to full-time, life-long work; and seeks to de-centre the ethic of work as the basis for citizenship or the social contract.

There are different theories of the post-work society, and of how to achieve it, but there is wide consensus that a good first step is to adopt a universal basic income (UBI)—that is, a basic monthly income granted to all individuals that is not conditional on work (or on proving willingness to work).[21] Such a UBI would enable individuals to choose to work less, or not to work at all for periods of time, and would also instantiate the idea that citizenship rights do not depend on or derive from work. According to advocates, a UBI would facilitate the emergence of a rich and innovative array of practices beyond work, and would help develop a new conception of social solidarity that does not measure someone's standing as a citizen through their labour market participation.

What would such a post-work society look like in practice? Advocates are hesitant to draw detailed blueprints, in part because they believe we are not yet in a position to imagine what these new social practices and new forms of social solidarity will look like. It is only after we are liberated from the tyranny of the work ethic—it is only once work no longer colonizes our lives—that we can begin to discover and cultivate the desires and relationships that will underpin a post-work society. As Weeks puts it, to try to specify the details of a post-work society would be to claim 'to know too much too soon'.[22]

However, advocates are keen to challenge two recurring anxieties about such a society. One anxiety is that the alternative to work is idleness or laziness, or that the alternative to a life of work is an empty life (Frayne 2015: 191). Much of the grip of the work ethic comes from the false dichotomy between work and idleness:

---

[20] In talking about the de-sanctification or demoralization of work, we mean in the specific sense of challenging the equation of the work ethic with 'deservingness', and displacing the work ethic as the compulsory route to citizenship, social inclusion, and self-development. We do not mean that individuals would not find moral significance in the activities, including paid employment, they choose to undertake in a post-work society.

[21] While advocates of a post-work society generally agree on the UBI, not all defenders of the UBI are advocates of a post-work society. On the contrary, the UBI also has many productivist supporters on the left (as a means to reduce poverty, unemployment, and exploitative work conditions) and on the right (as a means to reduce state bureaucracy and to encourage entrepreneurship and labour mobility). For a recent discussion of the diversity of ideological grounds for the UBI, see Raventos and Wark 2018. Our focus in this chapter is on the post-work interpretation of the UBI.

[22] A phrase she takes from Carl Freedman's discussion of some of the pitfalls of utopian thinking (quoted on Weeks 2011: 213). We hasten to add that we recognize that transitioning to a post-work society (or to a specific policy such as UBI) is at best one dimension of the broader struggle for a more just society.

ANIMAL LABOUR IN A POST-WORK SOCIETY 215

> Productivist ethics assume that productivity is what defines and refines us, so that when human capacities for speech, intellect, thought and fabrication are not directed to productive ends, they are reduced to mere idle talk, idle curiosity, idle thoughts, and idle hands, their noninstrumentality a shameful corruption of these human qualities. (Weeks 2011: 170)

Studies of those who 'refuse work' suggest that they often do so, not in order to do less with their lives, but rather from 'a strongly felt desire to do *more*' (Frayne 2015: 141): to devote themselves to issues and relationships and projects that they see as more worthwhile than their previous paid employment. For many people, the objection to work is not that it involves strenuous effort or dedication or self-discipline, but that these are all put to the service of mindless, and perhaps even socially and environmentally damaging, forms of production and consumption. Many people wish to dedicate their efforts to more worthwhile goals, such as caring for loved ones, protecting ecosystems, enriching the cultural environment, engaging in political advocacy, or serving God. (Frayne has therefore suggested a post-work society replaces a 'work ethic' with a 'worthwhile ethic'). These activities may not produce goods or services that can be sold profitably in the marketplace, and hence are not the jobs made available within the labour market, but they are certainly not idle or lazy. In many respects, they are indeed forms of work or labour—just not the sort of productivist work that is privileged by the work ethic.[23] The choice is not between a life of effort and a life of idleness, but a choice about whether the labour market is the sole determinant of what sorts of effort are worthwhile.

A related but distinct anxiety is that abandoning the work ethic entails abandoning any idea of civic responsibility or social obligation. We typically think of society as a scheme of social cooperation that generates both benefits and burdens, and that in return for accessing the benefits of social cooperation, each person should also do their bit in taking on the burdens of social cooperation. This idea of a 'duty of fair play', and its corollary opposition to 'free-riding', is a powerful dimension of everyday morality, and evolutionary psychologists argue that it has deep evolutionary roots (Bowles and Gintis 1998). A universal basic income, however, seems to contradict this duty of fair play: it allows some to benefit from the work of others without expecting or requiring any work in return.

---

[23] As Howard notes, much of the literature operates with a simplistic dichotomy between paid employment and 'leisure' understood as 'free time' (Howard 2015: 294). In fact, as we discuss below, much of what people do outside paid employment is socially necessary, and so can be considered forms of work or labour. The explanation for why particular forms of work fall inside or outside the labour market is tied up with histories of capitalism and its relationship to patriarchy, imperialism, and racism, and there is no reason why we should let these facts predetermine what we wish to recognize as work. However, since our focus in this chapter is on the contrast between the work society and the post-work society, and since this debate hinges on the normalization and moralization of paid employment, we will generally follow this narrower terminology.

216 ANIMAL LABOUR

Commentators have argued that this is indeed the single greatest source of opposition to the UBI. For example, when a version of the UBI was proposed in the US in the 1970s, with the support of administration economists, the decisive objection was not its cost, but its ethics. It was seen, by both right and left, as violating a basic duty of fair play, 'enabling recipients to reap the benefits of citizenship without contributing to the common good' (Steensland 2008: 229; cf. Livingston 2016).

This objection goes to the heart of conceptions of solidarity and social justice. On the one hand, the UBI instantiates a strong ethic of solidarity. It says that we care about our co-citizens in a non-instrumental way: we do not first ask whether someone will 'pay their way' before recognizing their rights and status as a member of society. On the other hand, the UBI could be seen as allowing the *beneficiaries* of the UBI to adopt an instrumental attitude to the rest of society. At first glance, there is nothing in the UBI that expects or encourages the beneficiary to adopt a non-instrumental attitude towards her co-citizens. On the contrary, it seems to allow individuals to opt out of social cooperation whenever it does not serve their own instrumental good. This seems inconsistent with a key feature of solidarity, which is mutual concern (unlike unilateral charity or altruism). For many left theorists, this is a serious, even fatal, objection to UBI: it extends the hand of solidarity, but does not ask for any gesture of solidarity in return.[24]

Advocates typically respond that their objection is not to the idea of civic responsibility as such, but rather to 'any ideal of social reciprocity that is reduced to a series of individual contracts' (Weeks 2011: 145), or to any conception of social solidarity that operates through 'commodity relations' (Frayne 2015: 237). Engaging in paid labour should not be the only or privileged way of showing concern for others, or of contributing to a shared society. The challenge remains, however, to clarify how the UBI—and a post-work society more generally—relates to ideas of civic responsibility, reciprocity, or mutual concern.[25]

Advocates have taken a range of positions in response to this objection. Some agree that it is appropriate to require some form of contribution in return for the UBI, but insist that this need not take the form of paid work but rather some looser requirement of participation, including care for family members or civic volunteering,[26] although the implementation challenges of any such requirement

---

[24] For criticisms of UBI from the perspective of 'left reciprocity', see White 2003; Anderson 2004; Miller 2003.

[25] Van Parijs' view is that the UBI is not in fact grounded in 'cooperative justice'—that is, the distribution of benefits and burdens of social cooperation—but rather is best understood as a principle of gift distribution. Both natural resources and the inherited wealth of previous generations are all in effect gifts bestowed on the current members of society, and the UBI can be funded out of these inherited gifts, without drawing upon the benefits of ongoing social cooperation (Van Parijs and Vanderborght 2017).

[26] See Atkinson's (1996) proposal for a 'participation income', Pérez-Muñoz 2016b.

ANIMAL LABOUR IN A POST-WORK SOCIETY   217

are forbidding.[27] Yet others argue that while there should not be any formal requirements for either work or participation, the state can foster an *ethos* of mutuality, publicly endorsing and inculcating the idea that citizens are expected to find ways to participate and contribute to the public good.[28] In a society with such an ethos, we would expect and trust our co-citizens to adopt a non-instrumental attitude towards their co-citizens and to do their bit to uphold the scheme of social cooperation.

Yet others argue that this preoccupation with free-riding rests on a mistaken conception of what is involved in upholding social cooperation. It implies that we contribute to the public good when we consciously decide to engage in some specific and scheduled goal-oriented task, paid or unpaid—say, when we agree to do six hours of X or Y task. In reality, social reproduction depends upon a broader and more diffuse set of dispositions and activities, including the ongoing willing-ness of members to exercise self-restraint in public spaces, to comply with social norms of civility, to uphold a public culture of tolerance and the rule of law, to respond to signals of distress or discomfort amongst friends and neighbours, and so on. Much of this is not particularly conscious—it is often habitual and unreflective—and is not necessarily tied to discrete scheduled tasks. But it is central to social reproduction, and social life would be impossible if we did not 'do our bit' to maintain and repair the social fabric in this way.[29] Someone who spontaneously spends an hour listening to a neighbour in distress contributes much more to society than someone whose hour of paid labour is to produce sugary drinks for children.

Thinking about social contribution in this way—as maintaining and repairing the social fabric that underpins any scheme of social cooperation—suggests a different citizenship ethic for a post-work society. Rather than material produc-tion, the focus of a post-work citizenship ethic would be social reproduction (Fitzpatrick 2004: 216). As Weeks puts it, basic income should be defended 'as income not for the common production of value but for the common

---

[27] Critics have argued that even if such a participation requirement is defensible in principle, it could not be implemented in an even-handed way, and would inevitably end up penalizing the poor while allowing the rich to free-ride (De Wispelaere and Stirton 2007; Noguera 2007). Segall argues that even if a duty of participation is both defensible and implementable, it should still not be tied to the UBI. For example, there may be a legal obligation to engage in jury duty, but failure to perform this duty does not deprive one of one's unconditional right to healthcare. One can have both unconditional citizenship rights and legal duties (Segall 2005).

[28] As Birnbaum notes, 'most people, including supporters of basic income, would find it absurd to propose that our educational institutions and shared public norms not express *any* duty-based expectations to contribute' (Birnbaum 2011: 414). In some early discussions of the UBI, the proposed ethos was distinctly productivist, inculcating a feeling of obligation to engage in paid employment (Carens 1981; Van Parijs 1995). But in more recent accounts, the proposed ethos tends to focus on a broader conception of contribution beyond paid labour. For a discussion of this 'ethos' strategy, see Midtgaard 2008; Birnbaum 2011; Pérez-Muñoz 2016a.

[29] Widerquist 2006 and Howard 2015 cite what they call 'passive contributions' as a basis for answering the reciprocity objection, but we think this category is much larger than they suggest.

218   ANIMAL LABOUR

reproduction of life' (Weeks 2011: 230). Similarly, Michael Bauwens and Rogier De Langhe argue that 'even though it is unconditional, a basic income is not "money for nothing", but rather a lump sum compensation for participation in the commons'.[30]

In our view, these post-work ideas about an ethic of citizenship tied to 'the common reproduction of life' and 'participation in the commons' are evocative and powerful. Moreover, they have the potential to address the limits of the work society we identified earlier. Citizenship tied to social reproduction is accessible to all (unlike scarce paid employment), inclusionary (unlike racialized, ableist, and gendered notions of the work ethic), ecologically sustainable,[31] and opens up rather than forecloses space for the cultivation of new desires and relationships.

However, as we noted earlier, articulations of the post-work society to date have said little about the place of animals. (And conversely, the emerging literature on animal labour has said little or nothing about the post-work society). In the final section of the chapter, we explore how the post-work society might facilitate inclusion of animals in society, and recognition of their forms of participation and belonging.

Animals in the Post-Work Society

While animals have been ignored to date in the post-work literature, they are in fact exemplary of the issues and challenges raised by this debate. Attending to the question of animal work illustrates both the gravitational pull of the work society, and also the need to resist and refuse this gravitational pull.

The new literature on animal work starts from two premises:

(a) the history of incorporating animals into the workplace as commodities and 'beasts of burden' has been oppressive and exploitative, instrumentalizing them for human purposes;

(b) the remedy for this injustice is not to abolish all forms of animal labour, or to exclude animals from the workplace, since work—freely chosen, and suitably designed and regulated—may be desirable for many domesticated animals.[32]

---

[30] Quoted in Van Parijs and Vanderborght 2017: 280 n.17.

[31] Note that by social reproduction we do not make any implication about biological reproduction. Social reproduction is consistent with a concern for reducing population growth in light of environmental limitations, and just relations with other species.

[32] See, e.g., Young and Baker 2018; Porcher 2017; Coulter 2016a; Cochrane 2016; Weisberg 2017; Fraser 2017.

For advocates of this view, work at its best can be an effective route to important goods: not only material goods, but also the chance to be part of socially cooperative activity; to develop new relationships; to explore and cultivate new skills and interests, to have a sense of purpose and accomplishment; and to achieve social standing and recognition. Indeed, insofar as our work society ties these goods primarily if not exclusively to work, exclusion from the workplace is potentially a serious injustice.

This argument is not unique to animals: we see versions of it in relation to women, people with disabilities, children, and other groups marginalized by the structure of employment under capitalism. All of these groups at various times and places have been excluded from the workplace, often in the name of 'protecting' them, yet advocates for these groups insist that access to the labour market can be beneficial, not only in terms of economic security, but also in terms of social status and personal development.[33] Moreover, as with animals, advocates argue that exclusion from formal employment does not in fact protect these groups from exploitation: it simply renders invisible all the informal work they do—for example, all of the unpaid work children do in caring for sick or dependent family members (Becker 2007).[34] This basic line of argument naturally extends across the human–animal line. Domesticated animals are excluded from good jobs, while the work they do perform goes unrecognized and uncompensated. We do not wish to challenge this argument (and indeed we have made versions of it ourselves).[35] However, it is increasingly clear that—for all these groups—the emancipatory promise of work is being undercut by core features of the work society. We would highlight three such limits.

First, in the work society, *some work is more equal than others*. As we noted earlier, there are steep hierarchies in the extent to which different kinds of work and workers are seen as fulfilling the work ethic. The work that women have performed as mothers, keepers of the household, or in the service industry is an obvious case. It is dismissed or denigrated as being private not public; or as being 'natural' behaviour and hence not real work; or as reproductive rather than truly productive work. As a result, no matter how hard women work—even working the well-known 'second shift' (Hochschild and Machung 1990)—their work doesn't translate into full citizenship except insofar as it fits the reigning productivist

---

[33] The case of children is interesting in this regard. While the international community is formally committed to abolishing all forms of child labour, the evidence is that children themselves value the opportunity to engage in (regulated) forms of labour, and indeed can benefit from doing so (Bourdillon et al. 2009; Aufseeser et al. 2018).

[34] Studies estimate that hundreds of thousands of children in the UK are involved in providing care work for family members (and there are similar statistics for other countries). Most do not wish to be absolved from this work—indeed they cannot imagine not providing this care—but they do want material support and social recognition for their work.

[35] Donaldson and Kymlicka 2011; 2015.

220   ANIMAL LABOUR

model. It seems likely that the work of animals will be subject to the same discounting. It will be discounted as mere play or instinct, not real work.

Second, in the work society, *the moralization of work is tied to a 'pay your way' ethic of self-sufficiency and reciprocity*. As a result, anyone who is perceived as dependent or burdensome is stigmatized, no matter how hard they might work, or how richly they might contribute. It is not enough to work, but one should 'stand on one's own two feet' while working, and not ask for or expect costly or burdensome accommodations. As Simplican notes, the perception that people with disability are 'burdens' who do not pay their way has underpinned their relegation to second-class citizenship (Simplican 2015). Of course, the drive to increase employment opportunities amongst people with disabilities is intended in part to challenge this perception of burdensomeness. But as many commentators have noted, the net effect of normalizing and moralizing paid labour for people with disabilities has simply been to reinforce the very ideologies of self-sufficient ableism that underpinned the stigmatization of disability in the first place.[36] This illustrates the built-in limitations of 'efforts to claim the title of work when that also involves making use of the legitimacy conferred by its dominant ethic' (Weeks 2011: 67).

Here again, it seems likely that the work of animals will be subject to the same dilemma. While there may be some examples of animals who are perceived as living up to the model of a self-sufficient worker who pays their way (e.g. police horses or service dogs), the reality is that most domesticated animals are perceived as dependent and burdensome.[37] And while integrating animals into the workplace may help contest such perceptions, it simultaneously reinforces the idea that independence and self-sufficiency are the metric of citizenship.

Third, in the work society, work is tied to a *productivist ethos that privileges material production and commodity consumption*. As we saw earlier, the work society is built on the idea that in return for fast-paced, intensive, and productive work, we get to consume intensively, and society's 'conventions, temporal rhythms, and built environments' are built around this norm (Frayne 2015: 91). This trade-off is dubious for all of us, as well as being environmentally unsustainable—but it is a particularly bad deal for domesticated animals. For them (as for children) the quality of their social relationships and access to a flourishing environment and a welcoming commons is more important than the

---

[36] Mitchell and Snyder 2015 argue that neoliberal work reform for people with disabilities has reinforced what they call 'ablenationalism'.

[37] Consider the widespread perception that the end of animal agriculture—exploiting domesticated animals for their meat, milk, skins, and pelts—would remove animals' utility, and thus spell their doom. After all, if they aren't meeting a human need for food and clothing, what is their purpose? How would they pay their way? Obviously, this kind of thinking is firmly rooted in conceptions of citizenship as mutual advantage: on this view, humans would only want, or tolerate, domesticated animals if we can benefit or profit from them. (It also reflects the general invisibility of animals' labour and their contributions to our shared society.)

accumulation of private wealth or the private consumption of commodities.[38] Animals who are integrated into the work society suffer the costs of a productivist orientation to work without being able to enjoy the (alleged) consumerist benefits.

In other words, animals are not an easy 'fit' for the work society. Access to work can indeed be a source of social goods, and exclusion from work can indeed be a form of injustice, but unless productivist values are challenged, animals (and other groups marginalized by the productivist model) will only have a precarious claim to these social goods, and the very ideologies that have underpinned animals' subordination will simply be further entrenched. We shouldn't try to shoehorn everyone into a model of the work society which is often a poor match for the ways they inhabit and participate in our social world.

What then is a post-work alternative for animals? Since this question has not (to our knowledge) been explicitly addressed before, our suggestions here will be tentative and schematic. But we can start with the focus of a post-work citizenship ethic, variously described as 'social reproduction' (Fitzpatrick), the 'common reproduction of life' (Weeks), or 'participation in the commons' (Bauwens and De Langhe). For all these authors, the aim of a post-work society—and the justification for UBI as a citizenship right—is our participation, not in any particular scheme of economic production, but in the reproduction of our shared social world and natural environment.

Citizenship, on this view, is not about paying one's way, but about sociality, the desire to be together. In the post-work society, citizenship would centre on a conception of belonging, not bargaining for mutual advantage—it would be, in other words, a society of those who wish to be together and to remain together in a shared society.[39] Domesticated animals participate, join together, cooperate, and desire to be part of a society with each other, and often with us. In the post-work society they would be entitled to a basic income just like everyone else.[40] And as their forebears played a major role in creating the modern world, they have the same birthright as the rest of us to benefit from the inherited fruits of civilization, and the technological developments which have reduced the need for 'horse power'.[41]

In the post-work society there would be no issue of compelling animals to work—no forced contribution. Since basic needs are met as a condition of

---

[38] On the importance of the commons for children and animals, see Donaldson 2018.

[39] And what if some domesticated animals do not want to be part of a shared society with us? We should make available opportunities for them to safely and gradually explore the option of exit—see Donaldson and Kymlicka 2014.

[40] How would such a UBI be administered in a way that is responsive to the preferences of the animal? For reflections on this, see Donaldson 2018, but it's worth noting that similar issues arise already in relation to children, people with cognitive disabilities, or those with dementia, all of whom are assumed to be beneficiaries of the UBI on most post-work accounts.

[41] Recall that on Van Parijs' account, the UBI is justified as a principle of gift distribution: both natural resources and the inherited wealth and technology of previous generations are all in effect gifts bestowed on the current members of society, and the UBI is funded out of these inherited gifts. If so, domesticated animals have as much claim to these gifts as human members.

citizenship, animals would be free, like everyone else, to choose how they participate in society (which may or may not involve earning additional income). Would domesticated animals choose to work under these circumstances? It seems unlikely they would be motivated as many humans might by the desire to earn additional income or status by participating in paid employment—let alone a desire to amass surplus out of sheer greed. But they might be motivated by the inherent interest of particular activities, or the satisfactions of learning, or the pleasure of joint endeavour and cooperation, or the esteem of others. Indeed, we can only start to explore these motivations with animals once we expunge the idea that they are obliged to work either to support themselves or to contribute their fair share.[42] A post-work vision of animal labour would promote exploration of the ways in which work can indeed promote social goods of friendship, participation, learning, and accomplishment for animals, as an exploration of freedom, rather than as a doomed attempt to show that animals can comply with the strictures of a productivist work ethic.

The fact that animals wouldn't be compelled to work to 'pay their way' is not, by itself, sufficient protection that their work is freely chosen and non-exploitative. In addition, we will need to guard against manipulation, adaptive preferences, and misinterpretation and misrepresentation of what animals indicate to us about what they wish to do. And they will still need full protection as workers regarding workplace safety, time off, etc., as well as assurances that work supports the norms and practices of equal membership.[43] But the post-work ethos is a good start in reconceiving work as an activity that is self-chosen and meaningful to the individual, rather than a compulsory form of contribution for survival and citizenship.

The post-work society also reshapes the chasm between paid and unpaid forms of labour. The question of whether or not work is financially compensated no longer determines the social recognition of its value. A UBI premised on the idea of the 'common reproduction of life' and 'participation in the commons' recognizes that countless types of activities and practices, inside and outside the labour market, are both valuable and essential. As a result, those kinds of work—like volunteer work, or domestic labour, or going to school—which have been uncompensated and therefore undervalued (or undervalued and therefore uncompensated) can more readily be recognized as social contribution on a par with traditional waged jobs and entrepreneurial activity.

---

[42] Some readers might wonder whether our societies can afford to support domesticated animals in this sense. This is a complicated question, but it's important to note that the forced breeding of domesticated animals for agricultural and other purposes would be prohibited on our co-citizenship model, and so there would be a dramatic reduction in their numbers. For a discussion of reproduction/population control under conditions of animal citizenship see Donaldson & Kymlicka 2011: 144–9.

[43] For reflections on some of these safeguards, see Cochrane 2016; Delon 2019; Blattner (chapter 5, this volume).

This is particularly relevant to domesticated animals, since the kinds of work they perform—especially the kinds of work that might continue in a just post-work society—often fall into the categories of care, emotional, and communicative work which have been marginalized by mainstream theories of the economy, markets, and compensation (Coulter 2016b).[44] Consider the work that animals do to care for their offspring, to communicate with us and each other to negotiate a shared world, and to provide us with companionship. Forms of therapy, support work, and education assistance provided by animals is burgeoning (Weisberg 2017).

A post-work society ethic, by diminishing the hierarchy between paid versus unpaid jobs (or productive versus socially reproductive), obviates any need for sharp distinctions between animals working in the public or corporate sector, in what look like more traditional occupations (e.g., police horses, rescue dogs, conservation goats), and animals working in our homes or in caring or service roles. We would not have one privileged class of animal workers—like the rescue dogs—who would earn wages and benefits, and then another class of animal dependents (e.g. animal companions) without entitlement to recognition and protection. Rather, all would be recognized as members of society entitled to a UBI and similar protections regardless of the kinds of activity they participate in. Put another way, much of the work currently performed by animals (especially in Western countries) looks more like the work performed by women and children in the private sphere and service industries than it does the 'productivist' work in traditional wage-earning jobs. And these are precisely the kind of workers that UBI offers some recognition and protection to.

But perhaps the most important dimension of thinking about animals in the post-work society is their role in maintaining and repairing the social fabric that is a precondition of cooperative society. Citizenship is as much—and perhaps more—about building relations of social trust and conviviality as it is about producing commodities or even reproducing society. In particular, it is about building trust and connection across divides of age, gender, ability, race, and, we would add, species. In his study of work opportunities for people with intellectual disabilities, Hans Reinders found that formal inclusion in the workplace is of little or no benefit if individuals are not welcomed and befriended (Reinders 2002; see also Simplican 2015). And this in turn requires that we view social cooperation, not only through narrow conceptions of contribution focused on the production of marketable goods and services, but also through key dimensions of sociality and social cohesion such as our willingness to befriend, to participate, and to belong.

We now have extensive evidence about how humans benefit from contact with non-human animals—hence the explosion of animal therapy programs in multiple contexts. In the presence of animals we feel less anxious and judged, allowing

---

[44] In many non-Western countries, domesticated animals are still widely visible as workers in agriculture, transport, and other sectors.

224   ANIMAL LABOUR

us to relax, to heal, to learn, to find our voice (Suen 2015). We become more willing to engage with and trust our fellow citizens (Wood et al. 2007). Many domesticated animals display readiness to engage, to play, to take part, to share affection, to trust, to forgive.[45] In the context of families and sanctuary life, domesticated animals readily befriend across the species divide, learning to communicate and to play with members of other species, even those considered their natural 'enemies' (Feuerstein and Terkel 2008). Of course this is not always the case, but given the severe injustices meted out to them, domesticated animals' commitment to maintaining and repairing the social fabric is extraordinary. We take these qualities for granted, when what we should do is recognize the crucial role they can play in the post-work—or indeed any just society.

Conclusion

Along multiple dimensions, then, the post-work society seems a good fit for domesticated animals. Rather than trying to shoehorn animals into a productivist ethic that is inherently biased against many animals (and many humans), a post-work perspective redirects us towards ideas of social reproduction that are expansive, humane, egalitarian, and sustainable.

Is this vision of animals in a post-work society feasible? No doubt many readers will see it as utopian, perhaps because of pervasive tendencies to view domesticated animals as an unproductive burden. We cannot fully address that anxiety here, except to note that disability theory has already embarked on the task of rethinking citizenship beyond the ableist assumptions of the work society. While it is undoubtedly true that society requires workers—individuals engaged in purposeful activity to make products, provide services, etc.—society also requires many additional forms of relationship amongst its members. We do not meet each other solely in the role of contributors exchanging goods and services. We meet each other as members of a society, committed to creating and perpetuating a cooperative community together. The fundamental question is not, 'how can we benefit from one another?', but 'do we want to be part of a community together?' From this perspective, when meeting a fellow citizen our first questions are 'Does she want to be with me?' 'Does she see us as part of a shared community?' 'Is she willing to trust me, to befriend me, to cooperate with me?' 'Does she wish me well?' All of these questions come prior to the question of economic exchange.

Disability theorists have written about ideas of trust and friendship and conviviality as being central to the ethics of citizenship (Silvers and Francis 2005; Reinders 2002). As noted, the idea is not that this ethic replaces the willingness to

---

[45] These tendencies are, unfortunately, pathologized by many commentators—including some animal rights theorists—as servile and needy.

ANIMAL LABOUR IN A POST-WORK SOCIETY 225

work with, for, and alongside others, but it does de-centre the work ethic, and in so doing helps us to recognize a greater diversity of ways of being a member of society and a good citizen. And when we look at domesticated animals with this broader lens of the ethics of citizenship, we can see that many of them are citizens par excellence—extraordinarily inclined to trust us, to want to befriend us, to wish us well, to want to engage with us, and to cooperate with us. Their desires and inclinations have not been wildly distorted by markets and the work ethic, nor are they driven by greed. Many humans who spend time with animals find this time intrinsically well spent, as well as a source of renewal, pleasure, and joy. These are not superficial extras, or side benefits, of living with domesticated animals. They are a fundamental glue of society, upon which complex relations of cooperation, negotiation, and reciprocity depend.

The idea of the post-work society de-centres the work ethic, and brings to the fore an alternate ethos of citizenship—one which helps us to see precisely the virtues that many domesticated animals exemplify. Animals would benefit from the shift to a post-work society that recognizes these virtues, and we would all benefit from their example as we look beyond the work ethic to a richer and more inclusive conception of the bonds of citizenship.

References

Anderson, Elizabeth. 2004. 'Welfare, Work Requirements, and Dependant-Care'. *Journal of Applied Philosophy* 21(3): 243–56.

Atkinson, Anthony. 1996. 'The Case for a Participation Income'. *Political Quarterly* 67(1): 67–70.

Aufseeser, Dena, Michael Bourdillon, Richard Carothers, and Olivia Lecoufle. 2018. 'Children's Work and Children's Well-Being: Implications for Policy'. *Development Policy Review* 36(2): 241–61.

Azmanova, Albena. 2010. 'Capitalism Reorganized: Social Justice after Neo-Liberalism'. *Constellations* 17(3): 390–406.

Azmanova, Albena. 2012. 'Social Justice and Varieties of Capitalism: An Immanent Critique'. *New Political Economy* 17(4): 445–63.

Becker, Saul. 2007. 'Global Perspectives on Children's Unpaid Caregiving in the Family'. *Global Social Policy* 7(1): 23–50.

Birnbaum, Simon. 2011. 'Should Surfers be Ostracized? Basic Income, Liberal Neutrality, and the Work Ethos'. *Politics, Philosophy & Economics* 10(4): 396–419.

Boettcher, Oliver. 2018. *An Interest-Based Account of Police Service Dog Labour Rights*. Dalhousie University, MA Dissertation.

Bourdillon, Michael, Ben White and William Myers. 2009. 'Re-Assessing Minimum-Age Standards for Children's Work'. *International Journal of Sociology and Social Policy* 29(3): 106–17.

226 ANIMAL LABOUR

Bowles, Samuel, and Herbert Gintis. 1998. 'Is Egalitarianism Passé? Homo Reciprocans and the Future of Egalitarian Politics'. *Boston Review* 23: 4–10.

Bryson, Alex and George MacKerron. 2017. 'Are You Happy While You Work?'. *The Economic Journal* 127(599): 106–25.

Carens, Joseph. 1981. *Equality, Moral Incentives, and the Market*. Chicago: University of Chicago Press.

Chamberlain, James. 2018. *Undoing Work, Rethinking Community: A Critique of the Social Function of Work*. Ithaca: Cornell University Press.

Cochrane, Alasdair. 2016. 'Labour Rights for Animals'. In *The Political Turn in Animal Ethics*, edited by Robert Garner and Siobhan O'Sullivan, 15–32. London: Rowman & Littlefield.

Coote, Anna, Jane Franklin, and Andrew Simms. 2010. *21 Hours: Why a Shorter Working Week Can Help Us All to Flourish in the 21st Century*. London: New Economics Foundation.

Coote, Anna, and Sarah Lyall. 2013. *Strivers v. Skivers: The Workless are Worthless*. London: New Economics Foundation.

Coulter, Kendra. 2016a. *Animals, Work, and the Promise of Interspecies Solidarity*. London: Palgrave.

Coulter, Kendra. 2016b. 'Beyond Human to Humane: A Multispecies Analysis of Care Work, its Repression, and its Potential'. *Studies in Social Justice* 10(2): 199–219.

Delon, Nicolas. 2019. 'Commentary: Setting the Bar Higher'. *Cambridge Quarterly of Healthcare Ethics* 28(1): 40–5.

De Wispelaere, Jurgen, and Lindsay Stirton. 2007. 'The Public Administration Case Against Participation Income'. *Social Service Review* 81(3): 523–49.

Donaldson, Sue. 2018. 'Animal Agora: Animals Citizens and the Democratic Challenge' (paper presented at CRE workshop on animal politics).

Donaldson, Sue, and Will Kymlicka. 2011. *Zoopolis: A Political Theory of Animal Rights*. Oxford: Oxford University Press.

Donaldson, Sue, and Will Kymlicka. 2014. 'Animals and the Frontiers of Citizenship'. *Oxford Journal of Legal Studies* 34(2): 201–19.

Donaldson, Sue, and Will Kymlicka. 2015. 'Farmed Animal Sanctuaries: The Heart of the Movement'. *Politics and Animals* 1(1): 50–74.

Feuerstein, N. and Joseph Terkel. 2008. 'Interrelations of Dogs (*canis familiaris*) and Cats (*felix catus L.*) Living under the Same Roof'. *Applied Animal Behaviour Science* 113(1): 150–65.

Fitzpatrick, Tony. 2004. 'A Post-Productivist Future for Social Democracy?'. *Social Policy and Society* 3(3): 213–22.

Fraser, Rachel Elizabeth. 2017. 'Animal Citizens, Animal Workers'. *The New Inquiry*, 14 November 2017. https://thenewinquiry.com/animal-citizens-animal-workers/

Frayne, David. 2015. *The Refusal of Work*. London: Zed.

Gilens, Martin. 1999. *Why Americans Hate Welfare*. Chicago: University of Chicago Press.

Gorz, Andre. 1999. *Reclaiming Work: Beyond the Wage-Based Society*. Cambridge: Polity.

Hetschko, Clemens, Andreas Knabe, and Ronnie Schöb. 2014. 'Changing Identity: Retiring from Unemployment'. *Economic Journal* 124(575): 149–66.

Hochschild, Arlie, and Anne Machung. 1990. *The Second Shift*. New York: Avon.

Howard, Michael. 2015. 'Exploitation, Labor, and Basic Income'. *Analyse & Kritik* 37(1): 281–304.

Hunnicutt, Benjamin. 2013. *Free Time: The Forgotten American Dream*. Philadelphia: Temple University Press.

Ingold, Tim. 1983. 'The Architect and the Bee: Reflections on the Work of Animals and Men'. *Man* 18(1): 1–20.

Livingston, James. 2016. *No More Work: Why Full Employment Is a Bad Idea*. Chapel Hill: University of North Carolina Press.

Lødemel, Ivar, and Amilcar Moreira. 2014. *Activation or Workfare? Governance and the Neo-Liberal Convergence*. Oxford: Oxford University Press.

Midtgaard, Søren. 2008. 'Rawlsian Stability and Basic Income'. *Basic income studies* 3(2): 1–17.

Miller, David. 2003. 'What's Left of the Welfare State'. *Social Philosophy and Policy* 20(1): 92–112.

Mitchell, David, and Sharon Snyder. 2015. *The Biopolitics of Disability: Neoliberalism, Ablenationalism, and Peripheral Embodiment*. Ann Arbor: University of Michigan Press.

Noguera, José. 2007. 'Why Left Reciprocity Theories Are Inconsistent'. *Basic Income Studies* 2(1): 1–22.

Offe, Claus. 1997. 'Towards a New Equilibrium of Citizens' Rights and Economic Resources?'. In *Societal Cohesion and the Globalising Economy*, 81–108. Paris: OECD.

Pérez-Muñoz, Cristian. 2016a. 'The Problem of Stability and the Ethos-Based Solution'. *Critical Review of International Social and Political Philosophy* 19(2): 163–83.

Pérez-Muñoz, Cristian. 2016b. 'A Defence of Participation Income'. *Journal of Public Policy* 36(2): 169–93.

Porcher, Jocelyne. 2017. 'Animal Work'. In *The Oxford Handbook of Animal Studies*, edited by Linda Kalof. Oxford: Oxford University Press.

Raventos, Daniel, and Julie Wark. 2018. 'Universal Basic Income: Left or Right?'. *Counterpunch*, 6 April 2018. https://www.counterpunch.org/2018/04/06/universal-basic-income-left-or-right/

Reinders, J.S. 2002. 'The Good Life for Citizens with Intellectual Disability'. *Journal of Intellectual Disability Research* 46(1): 1–5.

Segall, Shlomi. 2005. 'Unconditional Welfare Benefits and the Principle of Reciprocity'. *Politics, Philosophy & Economics* 4(3): 331–54.

Sage, Daniel. 2019. 'Unemployment, Wellbeing and the Power of the Work Ethic: Implications for Social Policy'. *Critical Social Policy*, 39(2): 205–28.

Shklar, Judith. 1991. *American Citizenship: The Quest for Inclusion*. Harvard University Press.

Shaw, Rosemary. 2018. 'A Case for Recognizing the Rights of Animals as Workers'. *Journal of Animal Ethics* 8(2): 182–98.

Silvers, Anita, and Leslie Pickering Francis. 2005. 'Justice Through Trust: Disability and the 'Outlier Problem' in Social Contract Theory'. *Ethics* 116(1): 40–76.

Simplican, Stacy Clifford. 2015. *The Capacity Contract: Intellectual Disability and the Question of Citizenship*. Minneapolis: University of Minnesota Press.

Smith, Kim. 2012. *Governing Animals: Animal Welfare and the Liberal State*. Oxford: Oxford University Press.

Srnicek, Nick, and Alex Williams. 2016. *Inventing the Future: Postcapitalism and a World Without Work*. London: Verso.

Steensland, Brian. 2008. *The Failed Welfare Revolution: America's Struggle over Guaranteed Income Policy*. Princeton: Princeton University Press.

Suen, Alison. 2015. *The Speaking Animal: Ethics, Language and the Human-Animal Divide*. London: Rowman & Littlefield.

Valentini, Laura. 2014. 'Canine Justice: An Associative Account'. *Political Studies* 62(1): 37–52.

Van Parijs, Philippe. 1995. *Real Freedom for All: What (If Anything) Can Justify Capitalism?* Oxford: Oxford University Press.

Van Parijs, Philippe. 2013. 'A Green Case for Basic Income?'. In *Basic Income: An Anthology of Contemporary Research*, edited by Karl Wilderquist, José Noguera, Yannick Vanderborght, and Jurgen De Wispelaere, 269–74. Hoboken: Wiley.

Van Parijs, Philippe, and Yannick Vanderborght. 2017. *Basic Income: A Radical Proposal for a Free Society and a Sane Economy*. Cambridge, MA: Harvard University Press.

Weeks, Kathi. 2011. *The Problem with Work: Feminism, Marxism, Antiwork Politics, and Postwork Imaginaries*. Durham: Duke University Press.

Weisberg, Zipporah. 2017. 'Animal Assisted Intervention and Citizenship Theory'. In *Pets and People*, edited by Christine Overall. Oxford: Oxford University Press.

White, Stuart. 2003. *The Civic Minimum*. Oxford: Oxford University Press.

Widerquist, Karl. 2006. 'Who Exploits Who?'. *Political Studies* 54(3): 444–64.

Wood, Lisa, Max Bulsara, Billie Giles-Corti, and Darcy Bosch. 2007. 'More Than a Furry Companion: The Ripple Effect of Companion Animals on Neighborhood Interactions and Sense of Community'. *Society and Animals* 15: 43–65.

Young, Janette, and Amy Baker. 2018. 'From Labour to Leisure: The Relocation of Animals in Modern Western Society'. In *Domestic Animals, Humans, and Leisure*, edited by Janette Young and Neil Carr, 128–45. London: Routledge.

Index of Authors/People

Adams, Carol J. 8, 10 and n.15, 147
Andrews, Kristen 8n.14
Aquinas, Thomas 97n.9
Aristotle 97n.9
Augustine 97n.9
Azmanova, Albena 210n.9

Bachour, Omar 15, 201n.29
Balcombe, Jonathan 108
Baratay, Eric 173
Bauwens, Michael 218, 221
Bekoff, Marc 6
Benton, Ted 116–17, 126, 128–9
Berman, Marshall 134
Birke, Linda 37
Birnbaum 217n.28
Blattner, Charlotte 14–15, 38, 173, 187
Booth, William James 187 and n.8
Bowden, Marie-Ann 144
Broom, Donald 53
Byrne, Liam 210n.8

Cameron, David 209n.7
Clark, Jonathan 140
Clark, Samuel 49, 52–3, 93
Clinton, Bill 210
Cochrane, Alasdair 13, 30, 42–3, 93 and n.4,
    94–7, 130, 141–2, 172, 196–7
Coulter, Kendra 8, 12–13, 30, 49, 60, 65, 80–1,
    127, 140–1, 150, 184, 192n.13

Daugbjerg, Carsten 143–4
Deckha, Maneesha 151
De Langhe, Rogier 218, 221
Delon, Nicolas 16, 141, 154, 161, 174, 185
Descartes, René 163n.2
Despret, Vinciane 100
Dickens, Peter 129
Dobson, Andrew 58
Donaldson, Sue 3n.9, 17–19, 38, 104n.14, 105,
    152, 173 and n.11, 176
Donovan, Josephine 8
D'Souza, Renée 13–14, 42, 68, 107, 108n.16

Eisen, Jessica 15–16
Elster, Jon 50, 52–3, 59, 123
Eshete, Andreas 56

Fedigan, Linda 6n.11
Feindt, Peter 143
Fitzpatrick, Tony 221
Folkes, Ben 181n.1
Foucault, Michel 116, 191
Francione, Gary 174 and n.12
Fraser, Nancy 33 and n.3
Frayne, David 215
Freedman, Carl 214n.22
Frohoff, Toni 175

Gaard, Greta 8, 148
Gillespie, Kathryn 147
Greenhough, Beth 103
Gunderson, Ryan 121, 128

Hagen, Kristen 53
Hamilton, Carrie 109
Haraway, Donna 141, 148
Harris, Angela P. 150
Hegel, Georg Wilhelm Friedrich 97n.9, 117n.3,
    130–3
Heidegger, Martin 189n.11
Hikmet, Nazim 127n.5
Hovorka, Alice 13–14, 42, 68, 107
Howard, Michael 215n.23, 217n.29
Hribal, Jason 91–2, 99, 100
Hume, David 97n.9

Jaeggi, Rahel 15, 126, 131
Jamieson, Dale 7n.13
Johnson, Kij 91, 110

Kant, Immanuel 97n.9
Kheel, Marti 8
Kymlicka, Will 3n.9, 17–19, 30, 38,
    104n.14, 105, 123, 152, 173 and
    n.11, 176

Lainé, Nicolas 168
Larrère, Catherine 163n.2
Libet, Benjamin 97n.8
Locke, John 1 and n.2
Lødemel, Ivar 210n.9
Leopold, David 126
Linder, Eric 149
Luna, Guadalupe 145

230 INDEX OF AUTHORS/PEOPLE

Maier, Steven 95
Marino, Lori 175
Marx, Karl 1 and nn.1–2, 15, 17, 32–3, 50,
  116, 117 and nn.2–3, 118–19, 121–8,
  130–6, 149, 151, 181, 182 and n.2, 183,
  185 and n.5, 186, 187 and n.7, 188, 189
  and nn.9–11, 190 and n.12, 192–3, 194
  and n.16, 195 and n.18, 196n.19, 197n.21,
  198 and n.22, 200, 201n.28, 208 *see also*
  marxism *in General Index*
Mauss, Marcel 167n.8
McAlevey, Jane 41
Milburn, Josh 171–2
Molinier, Pascale 162
Moore, Jason 194n.17
Moreira, Amilcar 210n.9
Morris, William 53
Mouret, Sébastien 171n.9
Mulhall, Stephen 125

Negri, Antonio 187 and n.7, 200–1
Niel, Lee 13–14, 42, 107
Nietzsche, Friedrich 97n.9
Noske, Barbara 5, 119, 186
Nussbaum, Martha 43, 185n.4

Oliver, Kelly 192n.13
Ollman, Bertell 125
Osborne, George 209

Parsons, Sarah 101
Perea, Juan 149
Plumwood, Val 8
Porcher, Jocelyne 16–17, 58, 93, 141–2, 148, 150,
  161–2, 163 and n.3, 164–6, 167 and n.8,
  168–70, 171 and nn.9–10, 172, 173 and n.11,
  174–7, 184 and n.3, 185 and n.6
Purves, Duncan 161, 174

Regan, Tom 3n.8

Reinders, Hans 223
Rinehart, James 121, 123
Roe, Emma 103
Russell, Bertrand 211n.12

Sage, Daniel 211n.13
Sayers, Sean 133
Schmidt, Andreas 93
Schopenhauer, Arthur 97n.9
Schwartz, Adina 56
Segall, Shlomi 217n.27
Seligman, Martin 95
Simplican, Stacey Clifford 220
Smith, Adam 189n.9
Smith, Adrian 149
Smuts, Barbara 6n.11
Stuart, Diana 119–20, 129, 134–5
Sullivan, Mariann 151
Swinbank, Alan 144

Thompson, Kirrilly 37
Tipping, Paddy 2n.6
Tombazos, Stavros 198n.22
Torres, Bob 92
Trebilcock, Michael 144

Van Parjis, Philippe 216n.25, 221n.41
Varner, Gary 176

de Waal, Frans 30n.1
Wadiwel, Dinesh 17, 151, 193n15
Weber, Max 208
Webster, John 197
Weeks, Kathi 135, 214–15, 217, 221
Wegner, Daniel 97n.8
Weisberg, Zipporah 91
Widerquist, Karl 217n.29
Wolfson, David 151

Young, Iris Marion 186n.6

General Index

'ablenationalism' 220n.36

agency 7, 7n.13, 8–9, 56–7, 61, 97nn.8–9, 109, 170, 174, 176
  of animals *see* animals, agency of

agricultural exceptionalism 16, 139, 142–5, 147, 149–50, 153, 198

'agricultural normalism' 144, 146–7

agriculture 16, 35, 139–54, 164–9, 189 *see also* agricultural exceptionalism *and* aquaculture *and* farmers *and* workers, agricultural
  animal 160–2, 163 and n.3, 164–9, 176, 185, 188, 189 and nn.9–11, 190–1, 193–4, 195 and n.18, 196, 198–200, 201 and n.28, 222n.42, 223n.44 *see also* 'Precision Livestock Farming' (PLF)
  abolition of 160, 171 and n.10, 174, 220n.37
  'free range' 198
  husbandry-based version of 161, 163–71, 173–4, 176–7 *see also* animal husbandry
  labour-based defence of humane (LDHA) 160–1, 164–6, 170–1, 173–4, 176–7
  labour-based version of 161
  dairy 10, 35n.4, 109, 119–20, 129, 134–5, 146–8, 153, 165, 171, 173 *see also* 'clean milk'
  fish farming 17, 190–1, 196, 199
  industrial 10, 16, 32, 100, 142, 151, 160–2, 163 and n.3, 164, 170–1, 173, 191–2, 196, 198 and n.23, 201 *see also* factory farms
  intensive 17, 165, 195–6, 198
  poultry 35n.4, 199
  'smart' 165

alienation 15, 116, 117 and nn.2–3, 118–25, 127–30, 134–5, 151, 185 and n.6, 186 *see also* labour, alienation and
  of animals *see* animals, alienation of *and* animals, labour of, alienated
  community 120
  labour-process 119–20, 127, 186
  product 119
  from 'species-life' 120–1

androcentrism 32–3, 41

animal advocates 6, 9, 11n.17, 17–18, 91, 160, 163n.3, 199, 210

animal ethics 3 and n.7, 5–6, 8, 171–2, 184, 193n.15
  'abolitionist' 3 and n.8, 4, 10, 36, 218
  'abolitionist/extinctionist' 3n.9
  intersectional 19
  'welfarist' 3–4 *see also* 'human use approach', the
  'welfarist-abolitionist' dichotomy 8

animal handlers 68, 70–3, 75–81, 101, 108, 169
  see also guardians/guardianship

animal husbandry 162–71, 173, 176–7

animal production 120–3, 127–8, 147, 161, 163 and n.3, 166, 195
  de-intensification of 17

animal productions 162

animal sanctuaries 35, 104n.14, 135

animal studies 19
  'political turn' in 4, 9

'animal turn', the 2 and n.5

animal welfare *see* animal welfare science *and* animals, welfare of
  five freedoms of 80–1, 197 and n.20

animal welfare science 7n.12, 14, 65–6

animality 121, 128, 150
  negation of 126

animals 17, 94, 96, 105, 124, 151, 154, 161, 168, 186n.6, 219, 221n.38
  abilities/skills of 36, 51, 53–4, 61, 66, 129, 172 *see also* animals, traits of
  abuse/mistreatment of 13, 37, 60, 95, 139, 146, 150–3, 162, 164, 193n.15, 194 *see also* animals, violence against
    intergenerational 29, 52, 160
  adoption of 70
  agency of 6, 7 and nn.12–13, 8, 13, 31, 37–9, 55–8, 61, 81, 91–3, 96, 106–7, 109, 116, 170, 172, 174–6 *see also* animals, choice of *and* animals, freedom of *and* animals, unfreedom of
  alienation of 116, 119–21, 125, 128–9, 134–5, 141, 151 *see also* animals, labour of, alienated

232 GENERAL INDEX

animals *(cont.)*
  autonomy of 55–7, 92n.2, 93 and n.4,
    94–7, 101
  awareness possessed by 2, 7n.12, 59, 96,
    123, 175
  'bad work' for 13
  behaviour/action of 66–8, 70–2, 75–7, 79–80,
    95–6, 108, 128, 135, 175–6
    assessments of 68, 70–1, 75–6, 80
    'natural' 81–2, 135
    species-type 96
  benefits accorded to 42, 82, 166–7, 225
  breeding of 14, 52, 74, 107, 129, 160, 168–9,
    171, 191
  captive 35
  caring for 169
  choice of 7, 10, 14, 36, 56–7, 93, 95–7, 99–100,
    102, 107–9, 148, 173–4, 218 *see also*
    rights, of animals, regarding the refusal
    of work
    freedom of 81–2, 92–3, 108–9, 174
    lack of 148
  as co-citizens 174, 222, 224–5
  co-determination of 109–10
  collective bargaining of 92, 109
  commodification of 92, 118, 144, 147, 169,
    191, 195, 200–1, 218
  as companions/friends 223–5
  conceptualization of 11
  and consent 65, 99, 102–3, 104 and n.13,
    105–9, 174 *see also* consent
  cultures of 5 *see also* cultures, multispecies
  decisions of 93, 95–6, 101–2, 104 and
    nn.13–14, 105–8, 140
  definition of 30n.1
  demands placed upon 36
  domesticated 3, 16–18, 35–6, 49, 51–2, 135,
    160, 162, 165–6, 169–70, 171 and n.10,
    172, 174, 176, 184, 191, 207, 210,
    218–19, 220n.37, 221 and n.39,
    222n.42, 223 and n.44, 224–5
  domination/control of 7, 190 and n.12, 191–2,
    193 and n.15, 194 and n.17, 195–7,
    200–1, 221
  denigration of 211
  emancipation of 163 and n.3, 170–1,
    184n.3, 219
  emotions of 5, 39, 70, 79, 169, 223
  as enjoying work 48, 61, 65, 73, 78–9, 82 *see also*
    animals, experience of, enjoyment *and*
    animals, 'good work' for *and* work, as
    being good for animals
  entitlements of 30 *see also* rights, of animals
  esteem of/respect for 60–2, 107

experience of 6–7, 18–19, 31–2, 39–41, 54,
    62, 70–3, 76, 79–80, 104, 133, 154,
    168–9, 191, 222 *see also* animals,
    awareness possessed by *and* animals,
    happiness/pleasure of *and* animals,
    subjectivities of
  engagement with work 32, 34, 40, 55, 58
  enjoyment 4, 39–40, 48, 53–5, 58, 61, 65,
    70, 78–9, 82, 169, 184, 190n.11, 222,
    225 *see also* animals, as enjoying work
  interrogating 32
  stress 70–2, 75–7, 79
    mitigation of 72, 77
  suffering 39, 48, 65, 79, 82, 95, 108, 152,
    162, 194n.15, 196
exploitation of 3n.8, 10–11, 48, 52, 91–2, 102,
    109–10, 128, 136, 142, 146–9, 151, 153,
    163–4, 170–1, 173, 184–5, 188, 190,
    195, 201, 218–19, 221–2
  ending/precluding 17, 220n.37, 222
  'human use' model of 10, 142
  legitimization of 10, 16
exposed to danger 95, 101
flourishing of 116, 129, 135, 168–9, 174–5,
    184, 185 and n.4, 198, 222
freedom of 65, 93–6, 106–7, 128, 163, 170,
    174–5, 222 *see also* animals, choice
    of, freedom of *and* animal,
    emancipation of
  lack of 93–5, 175 *see also* animals,
    unfreedom of
functions of 125, 132
'good lives' for 70, 73, 78, 80, 92, 96, 109, 167,
    169, 172, 176, 190n.11, 200, 222
  see also animals, meaningful lives for
'good work' for 13–16, 41, 48–55, 57–8, 60–2,
    65, 78, 80, 172, 184, 207, 219 *see also*
    animals, jobs for, humane *and* work, as
    being good for animals
happiness/pleasure of 13, 52–5, 58, 61, 70, 73,
    75, 78, 82, 169, 172, 177, 225 *see also*
    animals, experience of, enjoyment
'home lives' of *see* non-work lives of
housing/confinement of 70, 75, 95, 106, 139,
    153, 169, 191, 193, 198
and humans 8, 11, 72, 79, 122–9, 160–1, 163,
    165, 167 and n.8, 169–70, 174–6,
    186n.6, 193, 197, 201–2, 218–19,
    221n.39, 223, 225 *see also*
    relationships, between animals and
    human beings
  friendship between *see* friendship
  idea of continuity between 7n.13,
    8n.14, 224

idea of discontinuity between 116, 123–8,
132–3 see also *differentia specifica*
challenges to 5, 132
instincts of 106–7
intentionality of 175–6
interests of 93–4, 96–7, 99–101, 105, 109–10,
140, 160, 166, 173n.11, 175, 193
isolation of 55
jobs for 36, 41, 219, 223 see also animals,
labour of
harmless 49, 57, 60–1
humane 19, 29–31, 33–6, 39, 41–2, 44, 49,
65–6, 79–80, 82, 141, 184, 224 see also
animals, 'good work' for
as satisfying 13, 59, 61
as containing variety 54, 58
juvenile 200
killing and eating of (RKA) 16, 35, 60,
139, 141–2, 148, 152–3, 160–1,
163n.4, 164, 166, 167n.8, 168,
170, 171 and n.9, 173 and n.11,
176–7, 191, 196, 199–200 see also
slaughterhouses
labour of 91–2, 94, 119–20, 127–8, 136,
140–1, 152, 163n.3, 164, 166, 169, 176–
7, 182, 184, 186, 192–3, 194 and n.17,
195 and n.18, 196–7, 201 and nn.28–9,
208, 219–20 see also agriculture,
animal, labour-based defence of
humane (LDHA) *and* animals, jobs of
abolition of 218
alienated 116–17, 119–21, 125, 128, 130,
134, 141
'appropriative' model of 117, 130–6
'humanist' model of 117, 120–1, 125,
127–8, 130–2, 134
compensation for 211, 222–3
context of 39, 61, 82
deprivation of 168
elimination of 184
emotional 36
formal 41, 49, 61
instrumentalization of 4, 9, 212, 220n.37, 221
as a 'lively commodity' 2n.5
meaning of 160
as meaningful 12–13, 17, 19, 41, 49,
56, 92, 170, 174–5, 177, 185,
189n.11, 200
nature of 12–13, 17, 30–31, 33, 54, 60, 62,
94, 122, 127, 160, 169–72, 183–6,
188–9, 192–3, 194 and n.17, 195 and
nn.17–18, 196, 198–9, 223
quality of 17, 41–3, 62, 185

recognition of 8, 15, 19, 91–2, 109,
140–2, 146, 151–4, 162, 210–11,
219–20, 222–4 see also
labour-recognition-transformation
thesis, the
reduction of 17, 198
social practices of 18, 222
studies of 38
unalienated 117, 128, 136
lack of respect for 60
legal status of 3, 36, 140
meaningful lives for 174–6, 189n.11
medical care for 92
as members of the communities in which they
labour 13, 60–2, 65, 82, 110, 151, 169,
223–5 see also animals, social
membership of
memorials to 60
minds of 5–7, 8n.14, 18, 39, 54, 59, 96 see also
animals, awareness possessed by
motivation of 70, 176, 222
needs of 81, 167
non-work lives of 13, 40, 73, 80, 97, 151,
154, 161
as not 'fixed in their life activity' 15
objectification of 92, 134, 201
opportunities for 54–5, 58, 61–2, 207,
221n.39
oppression of 116, 149, 151–2, 218, 221
participation of 9, 104n.14, 221–2
personality of 39, 57, 71, 74, 76
portrayal of 147, 163n.2
and a post-'work society' 18, 207, 213, 218,
221–5
preferences/desires/will of 8, 18, 39–40, 56,
81, 96, 101–5, 107–8, 110, 132, 134–5,
153–4, 165
interpretation of 104 and n.14, 105–6, 108,
153–4, 174
as property 75, 108n.16
protection of 3, 30, 42–4, 65, 92, 101–2,
104–5, 108, 142–3, 173n.11, 182n.2,
219, 222–3 see also laws, animal
protection
psychology of 66, 102
punishment of 71, 76
as 'raw material' 1n.2
representation of 9
resistance/defiance of 7, 30, 36–8, 93,
99–100, 108n.15, 163n.4 see also assent
and consent *and* dissent *and* animals,
rights of, regarding the refusal of work
responsibility towards 38–9, 108, 167n.8

animals (*cont.*)
retirement of 13, 70, 92, 109, 172–3, 197
  see also rights, of animals, regarding
  retirement
rights of *see* rights, of animals
self-determination of 94–9, 101, 107, 109–10
  see also animals, agency of *and*
  animals, autonomy of *and*
  animals, choice of, freedom of
  and rights, of animals, regarding,
  self-determination
self-realization of 51
sentience of 37, 56
social membership of 30, 60–2, 65, 82, 91,
  149, 221, 223–5
social relations of 5–6, 18, 39–41, 55, 62,
  55, 65, 80, 96, 128, 140, 146, 151,
  153, 160, 163, 166–7, 169–71,
  175, 177
subjectivities of 9, 31, 93, 101, 104–6
temperament of 36
training of 13–14, 57, 61, 67, 70, 108
  and n.15, 169
traits of 52, 66, 74, 107–8
treatment of 60, 62, 81, 106, 144, 150–3, 160,
  162–4, 167, 169, 173, 189n.11, 190–2,
  193 and n.15, 194–5, 196n.19,
  198–201, 211–12, 221–2, 224–5
  guidelines for 81
  humane 13, 79–80, 160, 224 *see also*
  agriculture, animal, labour-based
  defence of humane (LDHA) *and*
  animals, jobs of, humane
types of 39
  cats 48
  cattle/cows 1n.2, 10, 109, 119–20, 129, 134–
  5, 146–8, 153, 165, 170, 173
  cetaceans 175
  chickens 35n.4, 198 and n.23, 199
  chimpanzees 96
  dogs 36–8, 48, 53–5, 57, 65–6, 74, 81, 95,
  107, 108 and n.15, 152, 154, 167, 170,
  173, 175, 220, 223
    conservation 14, 65–82, 107, 108
    and n.16
    military and police 2 and n.6, 60–1,
    67, 220
    rothounds 48, 51, 61
  donkeys 168
  elephants 99, 168, 175
  fish 17, 190–1, 196, 199
  geese 48, 51
  giant pandas 96
  goats 96, 223

gorillas 96, 175
horses 37, 40, 43n.10, 48, 168, 173, 193,
  220, 223
marmosets 95
pigs 162–3, 173
  Beltsville 52
polar bears 96
rats 35n.5, 48
rhesus monkeys 100
sheep 48, 96, 196n.19, 200
by type of work 39, 49, 51, 54, 58, 65
  agriculture 9, 17, 35, 139, 141–54, 161–70,
    175, 185, 188, 189 and nn.9–11,
    190–1, 193–4, 195 and n.18, 196, 198
    and n.23, 199–200, 201n.28, 222n.42,
    223n.44 *see also under* agriculture
  ambassadorial 81
  assistance 55, 57
  circus 9, 35
  conservation 13–14, 42, 48, 51, 65–82,
    107–8, 223
  facility 36
  guarding 48, 51
  guide 38
  'interspecies collaborative research'
    (ICR) 175
  laboratory 9, 11n.16, 148
  landmine detection 35n.5
  logging 168
  service 13, 36–8, 60, 78–9, 191, 192
    and n.13, 220, 223 *see also* animals,
    types of, dogs, military and police
  subsistence 13
  therapy/caring 8, 13, 19, 36–8, 42, 43n.10,
    48, 223
understanding/perception of 5–6, 32, 40,
  76, 81, 92–6, 108, 130, 132, 163n.2,
  173, 184, 190, 193, 194n.17, 211,
  219, 221–4 *see also* animals,
  commodification of *and* animals,
  objectification of *and* animals,
  portrayal of
unfreedom of 10 and n.15, 91, 95
value of 7n.12, 92, 135, 172, 183–4,
  222–3, 225
views/perspective of 37, 110, 153–4
violence against 17, 141, 186n.6, 191, 193n.15,
  194 *see also* animals, abuse/
  mistreatment of
  institutionalized 29, 104n.14
voice of 7–9, 91–3, 101–4, 106, 110
welfare of 67, 72, 76, 81–2, 152, 160, 166–7,
  174 and n.12, 196, 198 and n.23, 199
  see also animal welfare

GENERAL INDEX   235

well-being of 2, 13, 39, 42, 49, 51, 61, 70, 76, 81, 94–6, 104n.14, 109, 130, 167–9, 176, 184
wild 3, 6, 18–19, 33, 35 and n.5, 67, 135, 190–1
as willing to work 36–7, 93, 99–100, 102, 107, 109, 153 *see also* assent *and* consent *and* rights, of animals, regarding the refusal of work
at work 32, 39, 48, 51, 54, 58, 60, 79–80, 93, 97, 108–9, 140, 154, 166, 168, 170, 177, 198
as workers/co-workers 2–3, 11, 16, 37, 39, 61, 82, 91–2, 110, 139–42, 146, 149–54, 160, 163, 165–6, 168, 170, 172, 177, 183–6, 192, 194, 196, 198, 207–8, 210, 218–21, 223–4
 euphemistically portrayed as 9–11, 142, 146–50, 160
  for purposes of whitewashing 139, 142, 146–50, 160
 highly valued as 37–8, 60–1, 73, 78–9, 82, 142, 146, 165, 172, 210, 222–3
 not valued as 60, 110, 196, 211–12, 218–21
working conditions of 29, 33, 41, 49, 54–5, 58, 62, 70, 92, 99, 109, 136, 140, 151, 169, 172, 198–9
working environment of 55, 58, 95, 97, 109
working hours of 13, 36, 70, 80–1, 184, 197–9, 201n.29
working schedules of 75, 80–1
work-lives of 13–14, 31, 39–42, 44, 49, 65, 80–2
anthropocentrism 5, 32–3, 41, 43, 131, 193, 196, 200–1
anthropology 132, 165
appropriation 131–2 *see also* animals, labour of, alienation of, 'appropriative' model of
aquaculture 100
Arizona State University 102
asceticism 213 and n.19
Asia 168
assent 38, 99–102, 104–8, 174 *see also* consent, informed
 mediated 108
Australia 198
automation 109, 165, 199, 208
autonomy 4, 55–7, 59, 92n.2, 93 and n.4, 94–6, 97 and n.9, 101
 of animals *see* animals, autonomy of

behaviour
 of animals *see* animals, behaviour of
belonging 207n.1

biopower/biopolitics 191, 194, 196 and n.19
bourgeoisie, the 182n.2
Bovi-Shield Gold cattle vaccine 147
Bracero Program, the 149
Brazil 162
BRIC countries 162

Cambridge Declaration on Animal Consciousness 5–6
Canada 14, 65–7, 143–6
 laws of
  Criminal Code of 142
  Environmental Protection Act 145
  Seasonal Agricultural Workers Program 149
  Species at Risk Act 144
 provinces of
  Alberta 13, 66–75, 79–82, 107–8
   Aquatic Invasive Species Unit 69
   Environment and Parks Ministry 69
   Fisheries Act 70
  British Columbia 67
  Manitoba 67
  New Brunswick 67
  Ontario 13, 66–8, 74–82, 107–8, 144–5
   Ministry of Natural Resources and Forestry 74
  Quebec 67
  Saskatchewan 67
'capability theory' 43
capitalism 2 and n.5, 17, 92, 116–20, 129, 135–6, 182–3, 186–8, 190–1, 195 and n.18, 196, 198n.22, 199–201, 210n.9, 215n.23, 219
care work 8, 37–8, 42, 202n.29, 216, 219 and n.34, 223 *see also* animals, by type of work/use, therapy/caring
CEMA (European Agricultural Machinery) 165
children 94, 99, 149, 182n.2, 219 and nn.33–4, 221nn.38 and 40
China 162
choice 7, 56, 58, 93–7, 102, 107, 148
 of animals *see* animals, choices of
 freedom of 14 *see also* rights, freedom of choice
 lack of 148
circuses 9
citizenship 18, 44, 207, 209n.6, 214, 217–18, 220 and n.37, 221–5
 post-work 217–18, 221–5
'clean milk' 171
coercion 148, 191 *see also* animals, freedom of, lack of
colonialism 2, 34, 149

236 GENERAL INDEX

commodification 118, 195, 220 *see also* animals, commodification of *and* 'commodity relations' *and* work, commodification of
'commodity relations', 216
'commons', the *see* public good, the
communication 8, 39, 40 and n.9, 80, 101–4, 106, 108, 223 *see also* animals, expressions of *and* language
  embodied 108
  interspecies 8–9, 40n.9
communities 19, 60–1, 151, 154, 217
  interspecies 35n.6, 60, 154
  membership of 60–1
community 120, 224 *see also* animals, as members of the communities in which they labour
  conceptions of 18
  membership of *see also* membership
concentrated animal feeding standards (CAFOs) 162, 189n.11
consent 15, 36, 38, 57, 99, 101–9, 174 *see also* animals, and consent
  embodied 103, 104 and n.13, 105–8
  informed 100, 102–3, 106–7
  manufactured 109
  mediated 101
  ongoing 104n.13, 108
  securing of
    initial 99
    periodic 99
  standards of 102–3
  validity of 105
conservation 42, 107 *see also* animals, by type of work/use, conservation
consumption 17, 35n.4, 199, 202, 207, 213, 215, 220–1
control 82
cooperation/collaboration 5, 10, 123, 127, 175–6, 207, 209n.5, 215, 216 and n.25, 217, 219, 220n.37, 223, 225 *see also* mutuality
  interspecies 168
creativity 186
culture 94, 116, 125, 162
  multispecies 42

data
  collection of 68
de-animalization theory 119
decisions/decision-making 56, 81, 93, 95, 97n.8, 101–2, 104 and nn.13–14, 106–8, 140
  animals and 9, 93 *see also* animals, decisions of

differentia specifica 123–4, 126–7, 129
dissent 99–100, 102, 106–8, 174 *see also* rights, to dissent

ecofeminism 8
ecology 132
economics 32, 94, 167n.8, 189n.9, 191, 196, 201–2, 212
ecosocial reproduction 33 *see also* social reproduction
education/learning 208, 217n.28, 222–3
empathy
  entangled 8
employers 41, 58, 62
employment 207 and n.1, 214, 219, 223 *see also* unemployment
  paid 214, 216, 217 and n.28, 223 *see also* 'participation income' *and* wages
  unpaid 217 *see also* social reproduction
environment, the 34, 67, 78–9, 81–2, 132, 144–5, 160, 164, 166, 199, 213 and n.18, 215, 218 *see also* environmental hazards *and* global warming
  protection of 139, 143–5, 160
environmental hazards 148
essentialism 131
ethics 8, 33, 37, 39, 67, 82, 102–3, 172, 184, 194n.15, 200, 215–16, 218, 220, 223–4
ethograms 66, 68
ethology 132
  cognitive 6, 40
ethnography
  interspecies 19
ethnoprimatology 6n.11
'eureka effect', the 53
Eurocentrism 32–4
Europe 162, 165
European Union (EU), the 93, 164
evolutionary cognition 6
exclusion 212, 214
exploitation 5, 11, 117 and n.3, 151, 184, 186, 190, 214n.21 *see also* animals, exploitation of
externalization 133

factory farms 9, 142, 160, 171, 201 *see also* agriculture
fairness 17, 215–16
farmers 93, 144, 147, 161–2, 164–6, 167 and n.8, 169, 171n.9
farms *see also* agriculture
feminism 12, 33, 41–2, 140 *see also* ecofeminism *and* feminist primatology
feminist primatology 6n.11

GENERAL INDEX 237

flourishing 51, 61, 92, 124, 129–30, 186–7, 189,
        193, 200, 202, 213 *see also* animals,
        flourishing of
food 163, 166, 188, 191, 198, 200, 220n.37
    and justice *see* justice, food
France 150, 168
freedom 4, 17, 38n.8, 56, 93–5, 125, 163, 182n.2,
        187, 196, 210, 213, 222 *see also*
        autonomy
    of animals *see* animals, freedom of
    distributed account of 106
    lack of 149, 187 *see also* animals, freedom of,
        lack of *and* animals, unfreedom of
free-riding 217 and n.27
friendship 169–70, 222, 224

gifts 216n.25, 221n.41
guardians/guardianship 101–2, 104 and n.14,
        105, 108, 169
gender 19, 44, 147, 212 and n.17 *see also* work,
        gendered nature of
global north, the 19, 34, 35 and n.5
global south, the 34, 35n.5
global warming 160
globalization 34
'good life', the 50, 59
'good listening' 58

happiness/pleasure 52–3, 61, 211n.12, 225
        see also animals, happiness/pleasure of
Havasupai Tribe, the 102–3
health and safety 145, 198n.23, 211n.13, 217n.27
hierarchy 149, 212 and n.17, 213, 223
    species 15
historical transcendence 126
history 126–7, 162, 165–6
homelessness 117n.2
human beings 1, 8n.14, 17, 50, 82, 94–5, 97 and
        n.8, 98, 102, 118–19, 122–8, 130–4,
        148, 150–4, 163, 176, 186 and n.6,
        191–2, 194, 225
    and animals 39, 101, 105–6, 108, 130, 134,
        153–3, 169, 191, 202, 208n.4, 219, 221,
        223, 225 *see also* animal handlers *and*
        animals, and human beings *and*
        guardianship
    minds of 97n.8
    nature of *see* human nature
    rights of *see* rights, of humans
    use of animals by 60, 107, 109, 140, 142,
        147, 152, 168–9, 173, 175, 185, 188,
        190–1, 193 and n.15, 194n.17, 195–7,
        200–1, 218, 220n.37, 221 *see also*
        animals,

exploitation of
    for income 37, 169, 191
human exceptionalism 7n.13, 140
'human-mediated conditions' 129
human nature 116, 118, 131
human supremacism 208, 211
'human use approach', the, 3 *see also* animal
        ethics, 'welfarist'
humanism 15, 19, 117, 121, 124–6 *see also*
        animals, labour of, alienated,
        'humanist' model of
humanization 126, 130

identity 44, 58–9, 171
immigrants/migrants 4, 146, 149, 151, 212n.17
inclusion 19, 152–4, 212
India 162
Indigenous people 19
Industrial Revolution, the 173
inequality/inequity 34, 153, 224
instrumentalization 5, 142, 216 *see also* animals,
        labour of, intrumentalization of
intentionality 123
internal heterogeneity 44
International Labour Organization (ILO),
        the 94, 98–9
    Abolition of Forced Labour Convention 98
    A Global Alliance Against Forced Labour 98
intersectionality 44
'intersubjective attunement' 8

judgements 59
justice 11, 62, 148, 150, 160, 176, 200, 210, 219,
        224 *see also* fairness
    for animals 91, 146
    cooperative 216n.25
    environmental 17, 199 *see also* laws,
        environmental
    food 160
    interspecies 4–5, 12, 109–10, 208
    social 4, 142, 214n.22, 216 and n.25, 219, 224
    'wild' 6
    work-based claims to 210–11

kinship 153–4
Kommunal (union) 43

labour 1 and nn.1–3, 17, 32–4, 94, 98, 123, 128,
        133–4, 182, 185, 187–9, 190 and n.12, 191,
        193, 194 and n.17, 196, 202 *see also* work
    alienated 116–19, 121, 130, 132, 134, 185–6
        see also alienation *and* animals, labour
        of, alienation of
    of animals *see* animals, labour of

238 GENERAL INDEX

labour (*cont.*)
  as a category 5
  child 219 and n.33
  concept of 2, 11–12, 17, 19, 32–3, 94, 118
  conceptualizations of/ideas about 37, 43, 50,
        94, 122–3, 130, 132–6, 147–9, 151–3,
        183, 185–9, 190 and n.12, 191, 193, 194
        and n.17, 195–8, 200, 201n.29, 202,
        212, 222–3
  definition of 94, 130
  distortion of 117
  as domination 183, 186 and n.6, 187–8, 190,
        192–3, 195, 200
  efficiencies 194 and n.17, 195n.17, 201n.28
  a good 183
  instrumentalization of 212, 216
  manual 32, 37, 123
  meaning of 12, 17, 31
  minimizing 187, 190n.11
  nature of *see* work, nature of
  'necessary' 17, 196, 198 and n.22, 200,
        202n.29, 207
  process of 118–19, 121, 123, 127, 202n.29
  products of 118–19, 121–3, 128, 130, 132, 135,
        190 and n.12, 191, 195
  productive 52–3, 189
  skill-enhancing 52, 61 *see also* skills
  unalienated 124, 127, 130, 134 *see also*
        animals, labour of, unalienated
  unnecessary 196, 198 and n.22, 200, 207
  value of 12, 17, 33, 135, 183, 189n.9, 202n.29,
        211nn.11–13, 222 *see also* work, value of
  wage 32
labour movement, the 1, 11
labour perspective, the 16
labour process theory, the 32
labour-recognition-transformation thesis,
        the 15, 139–42, 150–4, 195
labour relations 146
labour studies 132, 139
'labour washing' 11
labs 9, 11 *see also* vivisection industry, the
language 102, 106, 123, 133, 150 *see also* social
        interaction, language-based
  interspecies 40n.9, 106
Laos 168
laws 9, 18–19, 101–3, 108n.16, 109, 139,
        143–5, 149, 172, 207
  animal protection 3, 16, 30 and n.2, 44, 142–4
  employment 99, 139
  environmental 16, 144–5 *see also* justice,
        environmental
  labour 3, 16, 94n.5, 139, 145–6, 149
    relating to animals 44
life plans 59

marxism 33, 37, 50, 98, 127n.5, 129
meaning 2, 12, 16–17, 19, 31, 49, 117,
        161, 174–6, 207n.1 *see also*
        animals, labour of, as
        meaningful *and* labour,
        meaning of *and* relationships,
        meaningful
medicine 175
membership 17, 30 *see also* animals, social
        membership of
methodology 19, 66, 68, 82 *see also* data
mutuality 217

'natural-powers' 123–5, 127, 129
naturalism
  nonreductive 128
nature 5, 126, 130–4, 161, 163n.2,
        194n.17, 202n.29 *see also*
        world, the
neoliberalism 34, 144, 209–10, 220n.36
North America 150, 162 *see also* Canada *and*
        United States, the
Nottingham Police 2 and n.6

observational trials 68, 71, 76, 80
objectification 130, 133–4, 186 *see also* animals,
        objectification of
OECD, the 144
opportunities 53, 61–2
  for animals *see* animals, opportunities for
oppression 7, 116, 150–1 *see also* animals,
        oppression of
other, the 59, 106, 117–19, 131, 133, 135, 212
        see also realization-for-others

paleo-anthropology 132
participation 19, 221–2
'participation income' 216
paternalism 101, 105–6, 108
people with disabilities 4, 94, 97, 192, 219, 220
        and n.36, 221n.40
perfectionism 131
play 97, 220
policy 143–4
politics 9, 18–19, 32–3, 94, 139–41, 150,
        163n.3, 192n.13, 194, 196–8, 201,
        210, 212n.14, 213
'polluter pays principle' 144
pollution 144, 160, 162–3
post-'work society' *see* society, post-work
power relations 7, 92, 109, 153
powerlessness 117 and n.2
'Precision Livestock Farming' (PLF) 164–5
private sphere, the 41, 147
privileges 34, 99

GENERAL INDEX 239

production 119–23, 126–8, 132, 134–5, 188, 189
    and n.11, 190 and n.12, 192, 194, 195 and
    n.18, 198n.22, 199, 201 and nn.28–9,
    202n.29, 207, 213, 215, 217, 220
  agricultural 161–2, 191–2, 195, 198–9
  cooperative 123, 127
  process of 118–19, 127, 135, 183, 186, 188,
    195, 199
productivism 132, 213 and n.18, 215, 217n.28,
    219–21, 223–4 see also society,
    'post-productivist'
productivity 18, 53, 211 and n.12
Promethianism 133–4
property 135, 144, 200
protectionism 144
psychology 97 and n.8, 102, 117, 176, 215
    see also animals, psychology of
public good, the 217–19, 221 and n.38, 222–3
public sphere, the 41, 104
purpose 17

Queen's University General Research Ethics
    Board 67

race 44, 97, 149, 212 and n.17
rationality 97nn.8–9, 98, 102–3
realization-for-others 51
recognition 17, 33, 222 see also animals, labour
    of, recognition of and
labour-recognition-transformation thesis, the
    and work, recognition of
relational dynamics 68, 104, 133, 152, 154,
    193n.15, 194
relationlessness 117 see also alienation
relationships 5, 12, 19, 39, 41, 55, 59, 98, 100,
    103–4, 117–18, 124, 131, 133, 135, 151,
    153–4, 163, 166, 171n.9, 218 see also
    relationlessness
  between animals 39, 55
  between animals and human beings 16–17,
    31, 39, 55, 72–4, 76, 79, 101, 103–6,
    108, 119, 128–9, 146, 151–4, 160–1,
    163, 165–6, 167 and n.8, 169–71, 174,
    177, 186n.6, 193–4, 196–7, 201–2,
    208 and n.4, 221n.39, 223–5 see also
    relationships, social, interspecies
  meaningful 16–17, 19
  non-hierarchical 169
  social 163
    of animals see animals, social relations of
    interspecies 4, 6, 8, 11–12, 128–9 see also
      relationships, between animals and
      human beings
  and rights 4, 9, 100

religion 213
reproduction 188, 190n.12, 218 and n.31, 221–2
    see also ecosocial reproduction and
    social reproduction
resistance/defiance see animals, resistance/
    defiance of
respect 60, 107 see also self-respect and esteem
responsibility 104, 108, 167n.8, 210, 215
rights 92n.2, 93–5, 97 and n.9, 98–9, 110, 160,
    210, 221
  of animals 1, 14, 30, 42–3, 49, 91, 93, 95, 98–9,
    109–10, 142, 146, 152, 172, 184 and
    n.3, 196, 200, 201n.29, 221, 224
  protection of 65
  regarding breaks from/time off work 30,
    198, 201n.29 see also animals, working
    hours of
  regarding co-determination 109–10
  regarding collective bargaining 92, 109
    see also animals, collective bargaining of
  regarding conditions at work 14–15, 30, 92,
    109 see also animals, working
    conditions of
  regarding freedom of choice 14, 99, 173–4
    see also animals, choice of, freedom of
  regarding life after work 30
  regarding medical care 14, 92 see also
    animals, medical care for
  regarding the refusal of work 30, 36, 38, 56,
    92–3, 98–100, 107, 173–4 see also
    animals, choice of and animals,
    resistance/defiance of and assent and
    consent
  regarding remuneration 14, 92, 97
  regarding retirement 14, 92, 109, 172–3
    see also animals, retirement of
  regarding self-determination of 93, 95,
    98, 110
  to assent 100
  to choose 14, 38n.8, 94, 98–9, 102
  to consent 102
  to dissent 99 see also rights, of animals,
    regarding the refusal of work
  to freedom 93–4, 98
  of humans 1, 93–4, 98–9, 197n.21
    over animals 1
  labour 43, 49, 98–9, 142, 149, 160, 196
  lack/loss of 99, 149–50
  process-oriented 110
  property 1
  and relationships 4, 9, 98
  of women 97n.9
Royal Canadian Mounted Police 67
Russia 162

240 GENERAL INDEX

San Francisco Zoo 99
security 17, 207n.1
self 131
self-consciousness 123
self-determination 91, 92n.2, 93–5, 97–9, 101, 107, 109, 131
self-development 17, 207
self-estrangement 117 *see also* alienation
self-realization 50–2 *see also* animals, self-realization of *and* realization-for-others
self-respect and esteem 58–61 *see also* animals, esteem of/respect for
self-sacrifice 51
self-sufficiency 17, 220
senses/sensation 124–5
sex/sexuality 44, 97, 153
shared membership 5, 224
skills 52–3, 61, 219
  of animals *see* animals, abilities/skills of
slaughterhouses 60, 160, 163n.4
slavery 187n.8
sociability 8, 133
  interspecies 9
social constructivism 105
social interaction 39, 59, 169 *see also* animals, social relations of
  language-based 5
social movements 17, 19
social norms 6
social reproduction 8, 19, 202n.29, 217, 218 and n.31, 221, 223–4 *see also* ecosocial reproduction
social standing 17, 139, 211
socialism 200
sociality 221, 223–4
society 59–62, 94, 116, 125–7, 129, 140, 152–4, 163–4, 166, 171, 186n.6, 193 and n.15, 200–1, 202 and n.29, 207–8, 211 and n.11, 212 and n.17, 213, 214 and n.22, 215–17, 220–5
  good of *see* public good, the
  membership of 211–12, 217, 223–5
  mixed human-animal 49, 55, 60, 129, 154, 210, 221 and n.39, 223–5
  participation in/contribution to 216, 217 and nn.27–9, 218, 221 and n.38, 222–5
  'post-productivist' 213 and n.18, 217n.28, 224
  post-work 18, 200–2, 207, 208 and n.3, 213 and n.18, 214 and nn.20–1, 215 and n.23, 216–18, 221, 223–5 *see also* universal basic income
  roles within 5, 220n.37, 224
  structures of 126

unalienated 116
'work' 208–14, 219–21, 224
  limits of 211
sociobiology 132
solidarity 60, 82, 214, 216
  interspecies 8, 19, 29, 34, 65, 81–2, 140
  fostering 66
species 212, 224
'species apartheid' 4
'species-being' 116–17, 120, 126, 129–30, 132
'species-life' 118–21, 123–4, 128–9
'species narcissism' 116
'species-powers' 123–5, 127, 129
standards 162, 164, 210
subjectivities 9, 93, 106, 133–4, 162 *see also* animals, subjectivities of
subsumption 190 and n.12, 195
sustainability 35n.4, 224
Sweden 43

tasks 56–7, 80
technology 17, 196, 202n.29, 208
time 17, 181–3, 188–92, 195, 198 and n.22, 200, 202n.29 *see also* working day, the
  free 182–4, 187, 189, 190n.11, 193, 198 and n.22, 199–200, 201 and nn.28–9, 202n.29, 215n.23
  labour 151, 183–3, 187–8, 189 and nn.9 and 11, 190–1, 194n.17, 195, 197, 198 and n.22, 199–200, 202n.29, 208, 215n.23
tools
  making of 123
  use of 123
trade 139, 143–4

unemployment 209, 211 and n.13, 214n.21
unions 43 and n.11, 58, 149
United Kingdom 48, 209 and n.7, 210 and n.8, 219n.34
United Nations, the
  Convention on the Elimination of All Forms of Discrimination against Women 94
  Convention on the Rights of the Child 94
  Convention on the Rights of Persons with Disabilities 94
  International Covenant on Civil and Political Rights 94
  International Covenant on Economic, Social and Cultural Rights 94
United States, the 146–50, 162, 209n.6, 212 and n.14, 216
  laws of
    American Fair Labor Standards Act 149
    Animal Welfare Act, the 143

GENERAL INDEX   241

Clean Water Act 145
National Labor Relations Act 145, 149
states of
Arizona 103
North Carolina 148
universal basic income (UBI) 207–8, 214 and
nn.21–2, 215, 216 and n.25,
217nn.27–8, 218, 221 and nn.40–1,
222–3 *see also* 'participation income'
utilitarianism 152

valorisation 163
value
surplus 194 and n.16, 195, 199
absolute 194–5
relative 194
values 17, 92, 154, 210n.8
veganism 160–1
vivisection industry, the 9 *see also* labs

wages 33, 185, 188–90, 223 *see also* employment,
paid *and* labour, wage *and*
'participation income'
Walkerton Commission Inquiry, the 145
WD4C 70
'welfare ghettoes' 61
welfarism 174 and n.12, 193n.15, 197
well-being 50, 93–5, 176, 187, 211
of animals *see* animals, well-being of
shared 167
Western world, the 143, 162, 208, 210n.9,
223n.44 *see also* global north, the
whitewashing 148 *see also* animals, as workers/
co-workers, euphemistically
portrayed as, for purposes of
whitewashing
women 4, 10, 33, 44, 94, 97n.9, 140, 146–8, 219
work 50, 94, 123, 128, 152–3, 163n.3, 166, 196,
207, 209 and n.5, 210, 219–20
see also labour
as being good for animals 48–51, 61–2 *see also*
animals, 'good work' for
benefits of 49–50, 59
conflict over 187
commodification of 12, 195
conditions at 15, 62, 140, 148, 214n.21
for animals *see* animals, working
conditions of
consent to 99, 102 *see also* consent
decentring of 17
demands of 213
de-sanctification of 207, 213, 214 and n.20,
215, 225
distribution of 207

for work's sake 207–10 *see also* society,
'work'
forced 57, 94, 98–9, 109, 187 and n.8
formal 34, 40–1, 49 *see also* animals, labour of,
formal
freedom from 196, 198, 200, 202, 207, 213
gendered nature of 8, 19
good 4, 13 *see also* animals, 'good work' for
human 50, 58, 182–3, 185–6, 189 and n.9,
190, 193, 194 and n.17, 195n.17,
198–9, 202, 212
as a human activity 1 and nn.1 and 3, 2, 50,
152
ideas about 17–18, 32, 49–50, 52, 58–9, 61, 94,
123, 132, 153, 196, 200, 202, 207–8, 209
and nn.5–7, 210, 211 and
nn.11–13, 212 and nn.16–17, 213–15,
219–20, 222–3, 225 *see also* labour,
conceptualisations of/ideas about *and*
society, post-work
and identity 58–9
informal 34 *see also* animals, labour of,
informal
moralization of 209–12, 214, 220 *see also*
conceptualisation, the
nature of 31–2, 34, 50, 52–3, 58–9, 94, 101,
118, 123, 128, 132, 148, 172, 183,
185–90, 193
non-human 50, 59, 186, 189–90, 193,
194–5n.17, 198, 202, 207, 212, 220,
222–3 *see* animals, labour of
normalization of 208–9, 211, 214
purpose of 59
recognition of 4, 33, 152, 219 *see also* animals,
labour of, recognition of
regulations pertaining to 43, 81, 148 *see also*
laws
and responsibilities 210
and rights 210
types of 13, 222–3
value of 49–52, 58–9, 61, 92, 140, 152, 165,
189n.9, 202, 212n.16, 219–20, 222
see also self-realization
work ethic, the 208 and n.3, 209, 210 and n.9,
211 and n.13, 212 and nn.14 and 17,
213 and n.19, 214–15, 225
workers 5, 94, 99, 118, 130, 139, 146, 148–9, 153,
162–3, 181, 183, 186–90, 198–9, 207,
213n.19, 220, 223
agricultural 139, 145–6, 148–50, 162, 169
unionized 43n.11, 58
working day, the 17, 151, 181–3, 187n.7, 188,
190, 192, 195 and n.18, 196, 197
and n.21, 198, 208

242 GENERAL INDEX

working day, the (*cont.*)
  limits to 192–3
work-life balance 41
work-lives 41
  of animals *see* animals, work lives of
workplace democracy 56, 58,
        108–9, 149

workplaces 31, 60, 100, 172, 219
worthiness 19
'worthwhile ethic', the 215

Zoopolis (film) 173n.11
zoopolitics 30, 99
zootechnics 162